PSYCHOPATHOLOGY

Its Causes and Symptoms

Revised Edition

F. KRÄUPL TAYLOR

M.D., D.P.M., F.R.C.Psych.

*Emeritus Physician, The Bethlem
Royal and Maudsley Hospitals, London
Formerly Lecturer at the Institute of Psychiatry,
the London School of Economics, and
Birkbeck College, London*

QUARTERMAINE HOUSE LTD.
Windmill Road, Sunbury-on-Thames, Middx., England.

1979

First published by Butterworth & Co. (Publishers) Ltd., 1966

Revised Edition published in the United Kingdom, 1979 by
Quartermaine House Ltd., Sunbury-on-Thames, Middlesex,
England

Revised Edition published in the United States of America, 1979 by
The Johns Hopkins University Press, Baltimore, Maryland 21218

ISBN No: 0 905898 03 6, 1979 cloth
ISBN No: 0 905898 04 4, 1979 paper

Printed in Great Britain by
Unwin Brothers Limited, The Gresham Press, Old Woking, Surrey

FOREWORD

Psychiatrists are frequently, and sometimes justly, accused of imprecision in their thinking and of concealing their ignorance behind a screen of ambiguous terminology. It is notorious that even such basic terms as 'hysteria', 'schizophrenia', or 'psychopathic' are used by different psychiatrists to denote rather different concepts.

Dr. Kräupl Taylor, in contrast, is a person who abhors muddle, confusion and all forms of intellectual untidiness. He has made it his aim, in this account of the phenomena of mental disorders, to ensure that every reader will know exactly what he is talking about. In order to do this, he has had to clear the ground with a preliminary re-examination of the concepts implicit in all medical writings about symptoms, diseases, and their aetiology, and to define the nature of psychological phenomena and their relationship to organic processes in the brain and elsewhere in the human body. This enables him to proceed to a systematic account of the observations upon which psychiatrists base their diagnoses of mental illness. Throughout the ensuing descriptive chapters, he is scrupulous to distinguish between data of observation, demonstrably proved explanations of pathological processes (in most cases, based on constitutional or organic malfunction) and explanatory hypotheses which have not yet been objectively verified. From this it will be apparent that he writes in the tradition of that great phenomenologist, Karl Jaspers; but fortunately for the reader he does not follow Jaspers in his sometimes obscure, not to say tortuous, language. Instead, Dr. Kräupl Taylor displays an exemplary simplicity of expression.

In certain schools of thought, psychopathology is held to refer only to the psychodynamics of the unconscious. Dr. Kräupl Taylor recognizes this, and devotes a third of his text to a consideration of 'dynamic psychopathology' in which his appreciation of the consolations of psychotherapy (acquired through many years of teaching and practice in this field) does not prevent him from showing that this richly documented area of psychiatric endeavour is one in which ingenious explanatory hypotheses proliferate much faster than attempts to submit them to rigorous critical examination. Here, many of his readers will be heartened by his refusal to accept any pronouncements, from however authoritative a source, which have not been submitted to objective verification. Some others may not agree with all that he has to say: but at least they will know with what they are disagreeing. Both types of reader will find their thinking at once stimulated and clarified by this book in which we are given an exceptionally lucid account of the subject-matter of psychiatry and the present limits of knowledge in this specialty.

G. M. CARSTAIRS

Department of Psychological Medicine
University of Edinburgh

CONTENTS

Page

Foreword by Professor G. M. Carstairs   v

Introduction   ix

PART I THE SYMPTOMS AND AETIOLOGIES OF DISEASES

Chapter

1. Clinical Symptoms and the Concept of Disease   3

2. Psyche and Brain   11

3. Psychoneural Processes   21

4. Psychological Phenomena   28

5. Psychiatric Nosologies   35

6. The Aetiology of Diseases   40

7. Genetic Aetiologies   47

     Abnormalities of Chromosomes 47; Abnormalities of Genes 52

8. Physiogenic Aetiologies in Psychiatry   64

9. Psychogenic Aetiologies in Psychiatry   77

PART II DESCRIPTIVE PSYCHOPATHOLOGIES

10. The Psychopathology of Perception   93

     Illusions 100; Hallucinations 104

11. The Psychology of Intellect   109

     Collective Beliefs of Social Groups 111

12. The Psychopathology of Intellect   120

     Dementia 120; Delusions 125

13. The Psychopathology of Affect—Functional Psychoses ..   136

     Manic-Depressive Symptoms 137

14. The Psychopathology of Affect—Anxiety-Dominated
     Neuroses   151

     Anxiety Neuroses 155; Obsessive-Compulsive Neuroses 162

15. The Psychopathology of Affect—Emotional Psychopathy   173

16. The Psychopathology of Mobility   191

17. The Psychopathology of Memory   201

CONTENTS

18. The Psychopathology of Consciousness 215
    Sleep 215; Obfuscation 222

PART III DYNAMIC PSYCHOPATHOLOGIES

19. The Psychopathology of Trance States 233
20. The Dynamic Psychopathology of Hysteria 247
21. The Descriptive Psychopathology of Hysterical Symptoms 261

PART IV RECENT DEVELOPMENTS

22. Definition of Disease 279
23. The XYY Syndrome 281
24. The Prevalence of Phenylketonuria (PKU) 283
25. The Genetics of Male Homosexuality 284
26. The Genetics of Schizophrenia 287
27. The Genetics of Manic-Depressive Illnesses 294
28. Pseudo-Hallucinations 301

References to Part IV, Recent Developments 306
References (chapters 1–21) 313
Name Index 335
Subject Index 341

viii

INTRODUCTION

Psychopathology is a word of many meanings. It has had a chequered career in the history of modern psychiatric thought, acquiring new meanings and connotations with the advent of every new theory of mental illness—and there have been many such theories. The inevitable consequence was that psychopathology joined the overlong list of psychiatric terms which owe their popularity to their semantic uncertainty. They seem to make sense, but the sense is not the same in different schools of psychiatric thought. They are thus largely responsible for the semantic confusion that is such a conspicuous feature of the psychiatric scene of today.

In this book, the various meanings of psychopathology have been reviewed, and an attempt has been made to elucidate their implications. To avoid some of the pitfalls of semantic misunderstanding, the opening chapters have been devoted to a consideration of the fundamentals of medical observation and thought. Like most considerations of fundamentals, they run the risk of being thought self-evident or trite. But it is hoped that they have fulfilled their purpose of serving as arbiters of meaning whenever semantic ambiguities are encountered in later chapters.

The nine chapters of Part I try to elucidate the significance of the various observations and concepts which are associated with the term psychopathology. They deal with the meaning of clinical symptoms and diseases, the relationship of psyche and brain, the difference between objective physiological processes and subjective psychological phenomena, the difficulties of nosological classifications, and the various aetiologies of disease (genetic, physiogenic, and psychogenic). The nine chapters of Part II are mainly devoted to an account of descriptive psychopathologies, those of perception, intellect, affect, mobility, memory, and consciousness. The three chapters of Part III try to clarify the essentials of modern dynamic psychopathologies. They are chiefly concerned with the psychopathologies of trance states and hysteria.

Part IV deals with some recent developments, in particular the definition of disease, the XYY syndrome, prevalence of phenylketonuria, the genetics of male homosexuality, the genetics of manic-depressive illnesses and pseudo-hallucinations.

February 1979   F. Kräupl Taylor

To my wife Natalie

PART I

THE SYMPTOMS AND AETIOLOGIES
OF DISEASES

CHAPTER 1

CLINICAL SYMPTOMS AND THE CONCEPT OF DISEASE

When we speak of clinical symptoms, we mean that a person displays certain manifestations which indicate that he is ill. When such manifestations are observed in a person, either by the person himself or his social environment, a physician may be called in who is expected to recognize the particular variety of ill-health from which the patient is suffering. When the physician has thus 'diagnosed' the presence of a particular 'disease', he is also supposed to know its prognosis and the treatment required for curing or alleviating it.

What, then, are clinical symptoms? They may be provisionally defined as morbid abnormalities which can be observed by the patient himself or his lay environment. The adjective 'morbid' is used here to indicate that only those abnormalities are clinical symptoms which, when observed, cause suffering and concern to the patient or his lay environment. 'Abnormality' denotes a deviation from something that is regarded as normal. To understand the meaning of abnormality we therefore have to know first what is meant by normality.

Normality

The concept of normality can be defined in two incompatible ways which may be distinguished as ideal and actuarial normality.

Ideal normality is a state of perfection that can never be attained by anything in this world of imperfection. Nothing that is ideally normal can therefore be observed; it can only be imagined. It may be inferred from this definition that ideal normality is of little value in the practical art of medicine. If no human being can be ideally normal, everybody is bound to be more or less abnormal. In spite of this disadvantage, however, medical men have often been tempted to argue from postulates of ideal normality. Healthy organs, they have reasoned, should function perfectly; those that fall short of this ideal must be regarded as abnormal. Arguments of this kind are normative in that they state what should be the case, but disregard what actually is the case. They do not provide criteria by which to judge whether a person is healthy or not. When the international charter of the World Health Organization laid it down that 'health

3

is a state of *complete* physical, mental and social well-being' (author's italics), it did not say anything of practical usefulness, but merely stated an unattainable ideal.

In contrast, actuarial normality is not derived from high-minded principles, but is an empirically grounded concept. It belongs to the imperfect world in which we live, and therefore lacks the beauty and certainty of an ideal normality. Actuarial standards and norms are never absolutely certain, they are only relative and changeable because they depend on observations; and observations are never quite the same, when we examine different samples of the same items, or even the same samples at different times. Actuarial standards, however, have the great advantage that they can be checked by independent observers who are likely to obtain similar results, when the samples examined are of sufficient size to minimize chance variations in their selection. An actuarial norm indicates what is normal in the sense of usual among the items of a sample. When a sample of human beings is taken, for instance, let us say, a sample of all the people in the British Isles, most people are found to know the English language. Knowledge of the English language is therefore an actuarial norm in this particular sample.

In a clinical context, when a sample consists of different human beings or their attributes, we may speak of a population sample. In statistics, the term population is used in a different sense—namely, to denote the totality of items from which samples are drawn. Actuarial norms in samples of human beings may thus be characterized as 'population norms', or 'population standards'. These vary with the population sample examined. Knowledge of the English language is a population norm in a sample consisting of all the people in the British Isles, but not in a comparable sample of all the people in France.

When a sample is composed of all the different occasions in the life of one individual human being, the actuarial norms in it characterize only this individual, and may therefore be called 'individual norms', or 'individual standards'. When we select a particular person from a population sample, the individual norms of many of his attributes will be within the area of population norms. An adult person selected at random in the British Isles is thus likely to have an individual norm indicating that, on most occasions in his past life, he had a knowledge of the English language.

Clinical Symptoms

When a previously healthy person falls ill, his clinical symptoms are abnormalities by both population and individual standards. For example, the clinical symptom of an adult, resident in the British Isles, may consist in a loss of his command of the English language.

A clinical symptom may, however, be normal by individual standards and only abnormal by population standards. This is the case with an adult person who has never learned to speak English, though he was born and bred in England and has continued to live there. It must, however, be realized that an abnormality by population standards alone is not necessarily morbid. It only becomes morbid when it causes suffering and concern. An unusually high intelligence, for example, or an unusually high athletic achievement, is abnormal by population standards, but not morbid.

An attribute that is only abnormal by individual standards is not necessarily morbid either. As an abnormally successful athlete grows older, his athletic superiority is reduced to proportions which are normal by population standards, though abnormal by his individual standards. Yet neither he nor his environment is likely to feel unduly concerned about the change, or suffer from it.

Clinical symptoms are not the only indications of ill-health; this may also reveal itself by non-clinical manifestations which we shall consider presently. Only those morbid abnormalities are clinical symptoms which can be directly observed by the patient or his lay environment and do not require special tests or investigations for their detection.

We may now amplify our provisional definition of clinical symptoms: they are abnormal deviations from a population and/or individual standard, which are directly observable by the patient or his social environment and cause suffering and concern to them. Clinical symptoms are indicators of disease. The main distinction between symptom and disease is that the former can be observed, whereas the latter has to be be inferred from observations; the former is a percept and the latter a concept.

Clinical Disease Entities

The concept of disease varies with the manifestations from which it is inferred. Disease concepts which are derived from clinical symptoms are clinical disease entities. The relationship between clinical symptoms and clinical disease entities is always to some extent arbitrary. This is particularly true when the symptoms are chronic manifestations which change little in the course of time. In that case, the concept of a particular clinical disease entity is defined as a constellation of symptoms which are regarded as more or less typical, or 'pathognomonic', for it. However, chronic symptoms can generally be grouped together in a variety of different ways, and it

5

depends therefore largely on convention, or personal preferences whether one or the other grouping is considered as constituting a disease entity.

The conceptual construction of clinical disease entities is facilitated when we are dealing with acute and changeable clinical symptoms because the time element and regularities in the change of symptoms provide us with additional diagnostic criteria. A typical clinical disease entity is therefore conceived as composed of typical constellations of concurrent clinical symptoms and an equally typical sequence of consecutive clinical symptoms. A constellation of concurrent clinical symptoms is also called a 'symptom complex' or 'syndrome'. A sequence of consecutive clinical symptoms that is believed to be typical of a disease entity is also referred to as the 'natural history' of that disease.

It sounds odd today to speak of the natural history of a disease, but this usage is a survival from former times, when disease entities were thought to have the same degree of reality as species of animals or plants. It was believed that God had created every species of disease as a separate and distinguishable entity. This was, for instance, the opinion of Sydenham[135], the great English physician of the seventeenth century. He was convinced that every species of disease could be recognized by its clinical symptoms and natural history. He emphasized the importance of accurate and detailed clinical descriptions. With the help of this clinical *nosography* he hoped to distinguish between different diseases and to devise a system of classification, a *nosology*, for the disease entities discovered. His methods were effective with acute diseases. Sydenham, for example, succeeded in differentiating, for the first time, scarlet fever from measles, and in establishing the disease entity of rheumatic chorea which is still called after him.

The difference between a symptom and a disease is often blurred by the habit of labelling a clinical disease entity by its most conspicuous clinical symptom. For example, the disease whose most prominent clinical symptom is a whooping cough is often called a 'whooping cough'; and the disease whose most prominent clinical symptom is a feeling of depression is generally diagnosed as a 'depression'. This linguistic habit has tempted many doctors to assume an identity where none exists, and has sometimes given rise to such diagnostic monstrosities as 'whooping cough' without a whooping cough, or 'depression' without a depression.

It is also necessary to keep in mind that there is a difference between a disease entity and a diseased patient. One of the questions often asked in epidemiology, for instance, is how frequently a particular disease occurs in a certain population. Technically, this is a question about the 'prevalence' of that disease—that is, the number of new and chronic patients suffering from it. 'Incidence' is the term used for the number of new patients only. Normally, the prevalence of a disease is established by counting the number of patients given that diagnosis by doctors. If different populations, or the same population at different times, are thus compared, false answers can be obtained because the sociological and cultural factors in the two populations are not the same. It depends, for example, on the availability of doctors and their diagnostic preferences whether patients with the same disease entity are ever recognized as patients and, if so, correctly diagnosed. An improvement of medical care may have the incidental effect of spuriously increasing the prevalence of diseases. It is certainly true that the more psychiatrists there are in a population, the greater is the apparent prevalence of psychiatric diseases.

As mentioned before, the concept of a disease entity need not necessarily be constructed from clinical symptoms. From the earliest days of medicine, there have been theories that diseases are due to abnormalities in the physical structure and constitution of a patient, to abnormalities in the fluids, tissues and organs of his body. With the revival of the study of human anatomy in the sixteenth century, such theories began to shed much of their speculative ballast. It was at that time that the French physician and polymath, Jean Fernel[454, 455], coined the word 'pathology' for the study of diseased organs. As knowledge of pathological anatomy progressed, and especially since the appearance, in 1761, of Morgagni's monumental work, *De Sedibus et Causis Morborum*, it was realized that it was more profitable to base the concept of disease on the organic changes which could be discovered in the body of a patient than on the clinical symptoms to which they gave rise. These organic pathological symptoms of a disease differed from clinical symptoms in that they could not be directly observed by the patient or his lay environment.

The term 'pathologist' has today still a clear-cut meaning that differentiates it from the term 'clinician'. The main work of the pathologist lies in the laboratory, that of the clinician by the bedside or in the consulting room. Unfortunately, the term 'pathological' has acquired such a wide connotation that it is almost synonymous with 'morbid' in a general sense, and can be applied to everything that is connected with disease. In the present context, we shall use 'pathological' as meaning 'endopathological' changes in the body of a patient.

Endopathological changes produce not only clinical symptoms which the patient and his lay environment can observe, but also *clinical signs* which can only be detected with the help of special investigations, instruments and tests. From the observations of clinical symptoms and signs, doctors diagnose the presence of endopathological abnormalities, and the accuracy of their diagnosis can be checked by the observations of the pathologist in the laboratory or autopsy room.

When the diagnosis of a disease is made dependent on the presence of endopathological changes, clinical disease entities often have to be abandoned and may be replaced by a number of *pathological disease entities* which all share the power of producing similar clinical symptoms. For example, the clinical diagnosis of dropsy had to give way to several pathological diagnoses which vary with the type of abnormality and its location in different organs.

Physiopathology and Psychopathology

The concept of endopathological changes is closely tied up with speculations about the constitution of the human organism. According to age-old beliefs, the human organism consists of two fundamental components: a material body and an immaterial psyche, or soul. These beliefs are still so deeply ingrained in our language that they continue to influence our thinking, even if we no longer accept their validity. In primitive thought, no strict differentiation was made between a material body and an immaterial soul. The body was thought to be the tangible and visible part of the organism, whereas the soul was equated with the intangible and invisible air that entered the body with every breath. Psyche was originally the Greek word for breath, and many of the synonyms of psyche also have their etymological origin in words which refer to breathing and air. Spirit, for instance, is derived from *spirare*, to breathe, and *animus* from a Greek word for wind.

The psyche was originally credited with two important functions: the ability to endow a body with life and animation, and the power to produce in it conscious experiences and thoughts. In the seventeenth century, the French philosopher, Descartes[416, 425] denied that the life-giving function belonged to the psyche. According to him, the life-giving principle was part of the material world; the psyche's only activity was to give rise to conscious thought. The psyche thus ceased to be a soul: it became a mind in the English language and *conscience* (i.e. consciousness) in French. In German, the word *Geist* which was used has retained many of the meanings of psyche. It can denote a disembodied ghost (the English equivalent of *Geist*); an

8

animating spirit; an individual mind; or a collective mind as in *Zeitgeist*, the spirit of an age, and in *Geisteswissenschaft*, the study of the humanities.

According to Descartes' metaphysical speculations, the world consisted of only two ultimate substances. One of them was the 'physical substance', or matter, which was three-dimensional in extension: a *res extensa*. In his metaphysical scheme, all space was filled with matter—a view which was contrary to Newton's later belief that interstellar space was empty, but has a peculiar affinity to the theories of modern physicists about a physical space that is influenced by the vicinity of matter. Descartes' other ultimate substance was a 'mental substance', or mind, which had no extension in any spatial dimension, and was nothing but a thinking substance: a *res cogitans*. It could not exist in space which, after all, was already filled with matter, and it was indivisible. It was not subject to the laws of physics, but had its own laws which revealed themselves in the conscious experiences of human beings.

Interaction between the mental and physical substance occurred, in Descartes' opinion, only in the human body. Animals had no mind and therefore no conscious experiences; they were merely biological machines which acted in accordance with physical laws. In human beings, on the other hand, mind was in contact with matter throughout the whole body, though it was thought to exercise its functions more specifically in certain organs, especially 'the brain because of its relation to the senses [and] the heart because it is there we feel the passions'. The most important contact, however, was thought to occur in the pineal gland. Descartes' reasons for this assertion were as speculative as most of his other views. 'I observe', he said, 'all other parts of the brain to be double. . . . Since of any one thing at any one time we have only one single and simple perception, there must be some place where the two images which come from the two eyes . . . can unite before reaching the mind.' As the only unpaired organ of the brain he knew was the pineal gland, it had to be the place where body and mind were most intimately connected.

Though Descartes' theories were metaphysical conjectures for which there was little or no empirical foundation, they powerfully affected the thinking of later generations, and they are by no means defunct yet. Whenever we talk of body-mind relations, or of psychosomatic interactions, we think in Cartesian terms, even if we deny the existence of two ultimate substances which mutually influence each other.

If the human organism is believed to consist of a body and a

9

mind, endopathological changes may be thought to occur in either of them. If they are in the body, we may speak of *physiopathology*, and, by analogy, if they are thought to be in the mind, of *psychopathology*. However, the practical implications of such concepts of physiopathology and psychopathology are so fundamentally different that they are hardly comparable. Physiopathological, or organic, abnormalities can be directly and objectively observed by pathologists who need not know anything about the patient's clinical symptoms and signs. The diagnosis of the pathologist may therefore differ from that of the clinician. Psychopathological abnormalities, on the other hand, cannot be directly and objectively observed by some independent non-clinical specialist. There are no mental substances, or mental organs, that can be studied in the same way as physical substances, or physical organs. Psychopathological abnormalities are, at most, inferences made from clinical symptoms, and the validity of those inferences cannot be challenged by an independent arbiter.

Psychiatry is sometimes defined as that branch of medicine which deals with psychopathological abnormalities and their clinical manifestations. If this definition is accepted, then psychiatry deals with diseases in which either no physiopathology has yet been detected or no definite connection has yet been established between physiopathological findings and clinical symptoms. In either case, the diagnosis of a psychiatric disease would depend on negative criteria. As medical science advances and a physiopathology is found for what was once regarded as a psychiatric disease, there is a tendency to remove that disease from the psychiatric realm. For example, Graves disease was, at one time, regarded as a psychiatric illness, and psychomotor epilepsy used to be diagnosed as hysteria. Only when an organic illness is associated with severe and prolonged mental disturbances with which a general hospital cannot deal, does it remain a psychiatric disease because it has to be treated in a mental hospital. This is, for instance, the case with the organic illness known as general paralysis of the insane, or G.P.I.

The concept of disease entities may be based, not only on clinical or endopathological symptoms, but also on disease-producing causes. Such aetiological disease entities will be discussed later.

CHAPTER 2

PSYCHE AND BRAIN

Descartes' metaphysical dualism posed an insoluble problem to philosophers. How could two such disparate substances as matter and mind ever manage to interact? There is no need to mention the ingenious, though often abstruse, solutions which were put forward, generally by invoking the intervention of God on every occasion of such an interaction. Many philosophers were prepared to concede that physical manifestations and processes belonged to the province of physicists and physicians, but they considered themselves best qualified to pronounce on mental processes and symptoms. Kant, for instance, suggested that in court cases in which the defence of insanity was raised, philosophers rather than medical men had the expert knowledge to decide on the defendant's mental condition[276].

Physicians rejected such claims. They felt increasingly confident that all biological manifestations, including those of the mind, could be explained without recourse to metaphysical speculations or supernatural agencies. Descartes had already emphasized that the energy of biological processes did not come from the soul, but belonged to the physical realm. A century later, Cullen[65], an Edinburgh physician, suggested that the vitalizing physical energy was generated in the nervous system. He believed that this nervous energy, or *vis nervosa*, ensured the normal vigour and excitability of a healthy person. He also assumed that there were certain diseases which were due to pathological deficiencies in the supply of nervous energy. He coined the name 'neurosis' for such diseases and stated specifically that they did not 'depend upon a topical affection of organs but upon a more general affection of the nervous system'.

Shortly after Cullen's death came Galvani's great discovery of 'animal electricity'[324] and the realization that the application of an electric current to a peripheral nerve stimulated muscular contractions. It certainly was a remarkable spectacle 'to see the mangled limbs of frogs brought to life' again through electricity, as the German physiologist, Du Bois-Reymond[61], once remarked. No wonder that electrotherapy became one of the foremost treatments for 'nervous disorders' in the nineteenth century.

To find a physical basis for the other component of the soul—the mind, or consciousness—has proved to be a challenge to the speculative ingenuity of many generations of physicians. In its simplest form, the problem presented itself as a search for the seat, or organ, of consciousness in the body, and different answers have been suggested from the earliest days of recorded medicine. According to some ancient beliefs, the seat of conscious thoughts and feelings was in the region of the heart and diaphragm. Such words as 'schizophrenia', 'frenzy' or 'frantic' still point to this belief as they are etymologically derived from *phren*, the Greek word for diaphragm.

Hippocrates had opposed this belief. 'I know of no way,' he said, 'in which the diaphragm can think and be conscious, except that a sudden access of pleasure or of pain might make it jump or throb. . . . [It] takes no part in mental operations which are completely undertaken by the brain.' In a remarkable passage, he stated emphatically: 'It ought to be generally known that the source of our pleasure, merriment, laughter, and amusement, as of our grief, pain, anxiety, and tears, is none other than the brain. It is specially the organ which enables us to think, see, and hear, and to distinguish the ugly and the beautiful, the bad and the good, pleasant and unpleasant. . . . It is the brain too which is the seat of madness and delirium, of the fears and frights which assail us, often by night, but sometimes even by day; it is there where lies the cause of insomnia and sleep-walking, of thoughts that will not come, of forgotten duties, and of eccentricities'[236].

In subsequent centuries, there were many attempts to make the localization of mental functions in the brain more definite. Such attempts were, of necessity, entirely speculative. Little was known about the anatomy of the brain for a very long time because it was usually examined in a half decomposed state, when it appeared to have the amorphous consistency of phlegm. It was not until the beginning of the nineteenth century that a theory about the localization of mental functions in different parts of the brain made any impact on medical men and the general public. It was a theory developed by the Viennese physician, Gall (pronounced Gull)[4, 10, 353]. He started with three fundamental postulates, two of which still form the basis of modern views on the functions of the mind and the brain.

The first postulate was that there is only a limited number of basic mental capacities or 'faculties' and that these are completely independent of each other. This assumption is still made by modern factor-analytic psychologists who use elaborate statistical procedures to unearth the relevant capacities, or 'factors' as they are now called. Gall and the factor-analysts also agree in believing that the 'factors' are inherited by different people in individually differing degrees so that a 'profile' of the various factors is uniquely characteristic of a person and distinguishes him from others. The second postulate was that each independent mental capacity is situated in a particular area of the cerebral cortex. This is still believed to be true by many modern neurologists, although they have mental capacities in mind which differ fundamentally from those of Gall. Gall's third postulate is the only one that is completely discredited today and, ironically, he is now chiefly remembered, and ridiculed, because of it. Gall believed that a strongly developed mental capacity revealed itself by an enlargement of the cortical area in which it was situated, and that this enlargement caused a bulging of the part of the skull which covered it. It followed that an examination of a person's skull—a 'cranioscopy' as Gall called it—could disclose the profile of his mental capacities and thus indicate his character and abilities.

Theological circles in Vienna took exception to such 'blasphemous researches' and Gall had to leave the town. He settled in Paris in 1807. His pupil, Spurzheim, accompanied him, but soon began to evolve a moralizing version of Gall's theories which he propagated under the name 'phrenology'. He persuaded a large public in England and the United States, including some well-known writers and psychiatrists, that phrenology was the 'true science of the mind'. Books on phrenology with skull maps, showing the situations of mental 'propensities, sentiments and faculties' could often be found in households, possessing only two other books, the Bible and Pilgrim's Progress. Many phrenological societies and academies sprang up. The treatment of mental patients was thought to require the guidance of phrenological knowledge. Marriage counselling was offered on phrenological lines, and the correct upbringing of children was believed to need a phrenological assessment of their capacities and characters.

Gall had more solid achievements to his credit than these phrenological speculations. As a brain anatomist he had no equal at his time. He introduced a new method of exploring the brain with blunt instruments. He noticed that the white matter was not amorphous, but consisted of fibres originating in the cortex and subcortical ganglia. He compared the brain convolutions of animals and men, and pointed out that there were abnormally few convolutions in the brains of idiots. He discovered post-embryonic myelinization and gave an account of the origins of the third to the seventh cranial nerve; the origin of the eighth was discovered by Freud some 80 years later[146].

When Gall spoke of the 'physiology' of the brain he meant 'psychology'. Other physicians followed this example, and a form of double-talk developed in the medical literature of the nineteenth century which formed a verbal bridge across the mystery separating

13

mind and body. In the academic medical circles of the English-speaking world, the word 'psyche' and its derivatives were taboo; they were only used in quarters of low scientific repute, such as those of charlatans and spiritualists.

There was not quite the same embargo on the use of the word 'soul' or 'psyche' among German professors of medicine. Reil[318, 419], for instance (remembered today mainly as the eponym of the cerebral insula), called the brain a *Seelenorgan*, or 'organ of the soul', and he recommended 'psychic methods of cure' for patients in whom this organ of the soul was assumed to be diseased. In England, similar methods of cure went by the name 'moral' or 'humane' treatment, and there was no mention of anything 'psychic'.

In 1808, Reil[11] coined the name *psychiatry* for his psychic methods of cure. Within a few decades the name took root on the Continent, but its meaning changed and came to denote the branch of medicine concerned with diseases due to a presumed 'nervous' or 'mental' pathology. 'Nervous' diseases, or neuroses, were thought to be mainly characterized by sensory, motor and emotional symptoms; 'mental' diseases (insanities or psychoses), on the other hand, were believed to consist mainly of serious disturbances of perception and thought, and of behaviour that was so gravely disordered that segregation in an 'asylum' and methods of physical or chemical restraint became necessary.

Psychiatric symptoms, whether nervous or mental, were thought to have their origin in a pathology of the brain and nervous system. Kraepelin, for instance, stated in the first edition of his famous textbook of psychiatry in 1883 (then merely called a 'compendium') that psychiatry was 'only a specially developed branch of neuro-pathology'[298]. Other eminent psychiatrists were equally outspoken in expressing this belief.

The Beginnings of Neurology

In 1875, Krafft-Ebing used the term 'psychopathology' for the first time in a book title[299], but he also meant neuropathology. He made this quite clear in a foreword in which he stated that he had chosen the term in order to stress that, when a doctor treated a patient with psychiatric symptoms, it was his duty to look for 'all discoverable signs of a pathological condition of the brain'.

It was unfortunate for the belief in the neuropathological origin of psychiatric disease that the clinical symptoms caused by structural lesions of the brain were generally quite different from the psychiatric symptoms of neurotic or psychotic patients whose brains were, for the most part, without a discoverable structural taint. The art of discovering the clinical signs of structural neuropathological lesions by accurate and refined methods of clinical examination developed into the new medical specialty of neurology.

In the first half of the nineteenth century, only the vaguest theories about the possible connections between brain and mind were entertained by physiologists. The brain-physiological theories of Gall and other phrenologists were completely rejected by them as without foundation. The general view was that the various areas of the cortex were more or less equally involved in the generation of psychological processes of a non-conscious kind. What was called consciousness—and was vaguely understood as wakefulness, vigilance, or alertness—was, at first, thought to be localized in the medulla and, later, in the 'sensory' ganglia and especially the 'optic' thalamus. Sensory impulses from the periphery were believed to remain purely physiological until they reached the sensory ganglia where they were transmuted into conscious sensations. These were somehow capable of arousing unconscious ideas, emotions and motivations in the cortex which, in their turn, became conscious on transmission to the sensory ganglia[521]. All this may sound rather naïve today, but modern theories are hardly more sophisticated, and only appear more acceptable because they happen to be in vogue. There have even been some theories lately which look like those of the last century, if the term 'sensory ganglia' is replaced by 'ascending reticular formation' or 'centrencephalic integrating system' (see page 23).

The views of clinicians about the 'seat of consciousness' began to change after Darwin's book *On the Origin of Species* had appeared in 1859. It began to seem plausible that the highest achievement in the phylogenetic evolution of the nervous system was represented by the forebrain and especially the cortex which was structurally more advanced in man than in the 'lower' mammals. As man also seemed to differ from those mammals in the possession of conscious thought and speech, it seemed justified to assume, as Gall had before, that the seat of conscious thought and of speech was in the cortex. This may explain why, in 1861, Broca's assumption of the existence of a 'motor speech centre' in the cortex of the left frontal lobe was generally accepted, though the lesion he had found in his first patient was rather extensive, involving most of the frontal lobe, the insula, striate body, and even parts of the parietal and temporal lobes[59]. More convincing demonstrations of the existence of such a speech centre, made 36 and 25 years before by Bouillaud and Dax respectively, had been ignored.

In 1870, it was discovered that certain cortical areas could be electrically stimulated, producing motor and, what seemed like sensory, reactions[170]. Clinicians soon jumped to the conclusion that this confirmed the theory that the cortex was the seat of consciousness and that different cortical areas subserved different psychological functions. It seemed that Gall's theories had been vindicated though not exactly in the way formulated by him. The phrenological skull maps of mental faculties were now replaced by cortical maps showing various 'centres' for sensory, motor, linguistic and other psychological functions.

The Viennese psychiatrist, Meynert, from whom Freud acquired his first knowledge of psychiatry, made a thorough histological study of the cortex and became one of the staunchest advocates of the cortex as the seat of consciousness and of the highest psychological processes. Nervous impulses that reached the cortex were supposed by him to lose their 'sensual' character and to become 'images'. All sensory areas in the cortex were therefore called 'psycho'-sensory, and all motor areas in the cortex, 'psycho'-motor. Meynert was convinced that the clinical symptoms of psychiatric patients had their origin in physiopathological changes of the blood supply, or levels of excitation in localized cortical and subcortical regions. His physiopathology was entirely speculative, yet he was so certain of being on the right track that he sub-titled his textbook of psychiatry, which appeared in 1884, 'Clinical Manifestations of the Diseases of the Forebrain'[354]. In 1890, he published another textbook: *Clinical Lectures on Psychiatry from a Scientific Standpoint for Students, Physicians, Lawyers and Psychologists*[355]. Here he elaborated some psychological concepts which have not received sufficient attention, though they are of great topical interest on account of their affinity to some features of the conceptual model of the mind which Freud was developing in the years that followed. In Meynert's opinion, the ego was the psychological counterpart of the totality of cortical processes. He argued, however: 'It will be useful to divide the ego conceptually into two parts according to its development: the *primary* or *infantile* ego, and the *secondary* ego'.

The primary ego is described as bounded in its interests by the surface of the body, or 'narcissistic', as Freud later called it. It is parasitic, devoid of morality and conscience, at the mercy of subcortical excitations, responding reflexly and aiming at satisfaction and pleasure. 'The motivations of the primary or infantile ego derive from bodily sensations: hunger, thirst, creature comfort; and its motor associations are simple.' The secondary ego, on the other hand, derives from interactions of the developing individual with the physical and social world around him. The motivations of the secondary ego derive from so 'numerous, but unknown, earlier experiences that we cannot see, in an individual case, how they are determined, and there *appears* to be a *free will'*. Through social 'mutuality' and co-operation, the secondary ego develops moral principles which inhibit the self-seeking, and delinquent, motivations of the primary ego. 'The secondary ego, the ego of the adult, no longer depends on bodily sensations alone, but on other motivations; we are influenced by the presence of other people, our awareness of the feelings of others, the complex demands of our occupational life and the call of duty.'

Free Will and Determinism

The theory that psychological experiences, like all other biological functions, are due ultimately to the action of physical forces, and nothing but physical forces, had some embarrassing consequences. They threatened to undermine the proud belief of man that, by the power of his mind, he is more than a physical automaton.

Scientists of the nineteenth century firmly believed that all events in the physical universe were governed by the Laws of Universal Determinism. These laws ordained that all physical events were fully determined by inexorable causal links. Therefore, if psychological processes are exclusively dependent on physical events, they are also fully and inexorably predetermined. It follows that our experience of having a free will, of being able to make a deliberate choice, of being responsible for our actions, is mere illusion. In reality, all our thoughts, feelings and actions would be completely predictable, if the information required for this task could be completely known. As Laplace put it in 1812: 'Given for one instant an intelligence which could comprehend all the forces by which nature is animated and the respective situation of the beings who compose it, . . . it would embrace in the same formula the movements of the greatest bodies in the universe and those of the lightest atom; for it nothing would be uncertain, and the future, as the past, would be present in its eyes'[309].

The study of sub-atomic events has forced the physicists of the twentieth century to relinquish their belief in the Laws of Universal Determinism. According to the theories of quantum mechanics, evolved since the middle of the 1920s, individual sub-atomic events are indeterminate. A rigorous analysis of the mathematical foundation of quantum mechanics by von Neumann came to the conclusion that, as long as physics bases itself on the observation of its traditional variables, no theory of a deterministic kind is possible that does not contradict the proved formulae of quantum mechanics[375, 377]. If sub-atomic events are indeterminate, they cannot be predicted—not even by the superhuman intelligence which Laplace hypothesized. However, it is not likely that they affect cortical processes often or to a marked extent. All that can be said is that even the rare and minute influences from sub-atomic sources may set some cortical processes on a new course which, in time, could deviate quite noticeably from the course they might have taken otherwise.[375]

This is all very speculative, but the very existence of indeterminate sub-atomic events has been welcomed as, at least, freeing cortical processes from the strait-jacket of deterministic inevitability. It is, however, still a far cry from the indeterminacy of sub-atomic events to the possibility of free-will and personal responsibility. The bulk of psychological processes must have their origin in large-scale cerebral functions to which the deterministic laws of classical physics apply.

In practice, it makes no difference whether we assume that psychological processes are completely determined by causal laws, or believe in a theoretical loophole of indeterminacy. Even if psychological processes are completely determined, this does not mean that they are therefore predictable. On the contrary, we can be certain that the unpredictability of psychological processes will continue indefinitely because we shall never be able to know, or to master, the multitude and complexity of causal influences which are inevitably involved even in the simplest psychological experience.

Only in very simple mechanical devices can we predict, with a high degree of certainty, what effect will follow upon a particular stimulus—and even then, prediction rests on the implicit assumption that the mechanical device is in good working order. If, for example, the device consists of an electric circuit which can activate a bell, closing the circuit will predictably cause the ringing of the bell, provided there is no mechanical hitch. This is tantamount to saying that the effect is caused by the stimulus, unless it is not.

In a more complex physical system, the situation is obviously more involved. Even if such a system is in good working order, it may be impossible to predict with certainty that a particular stimulus will cause a particular effect. There may be a range of different effects that can be caused by a particular stimulus. In that case, each effect will have a certain probability of occurring, but no effect is certain to occur. When we spin a coin, there are only two possible effects, heads or tails, and each has theoretically the same probability of occurring. The brain is a much more intricate physical system, and every stimulus reaching the brain can cause a wide range of possible effects, each with its own probability of occurring.

Past theories about the brain often assumed excessively simple mechanical conditions. It was, for instance, assumed at one time that each peripheral nerve fibre was connected with a particular cortical cell so that there was a point-to-point projection of the periphery on the cortex. Freud[147] was one of the first to prove that this theory was untenable simply because there were more nerve fibres entering the spinal cord than reached the brain. He also criticized the theory, which was implied in some of the writings of his teacher Meynert, that individual sensations, images or ideas were attached to the function of individual cortical cells. He thought it much more likely that even the most elementary psychological process involved the spread of physiological activities 'over the whole cortex and along certain pathways'. These views of Freud which were unusual when they were first stated in 1891 may appear obvious to modern neurophysiologists. In fact, the views err on the side of being too phrenological still in restricting the physical basis of psychological processes exclusively to the cortex. It is today generally agreed that subcortical cell groups are indispensably involved.

Genesis of Psychological Experiences

The classical neurological view of the genesis of psychological experiences is perhaps best illustrated by an account of the nervous activity presumed to be associated with the perception of an object in the environment. From the object emanate a variety of stimuli, such as pressures, heat or light waves, odorous chemical substances, and the like. Each stimulus excites electric action potentials in specific nerve fibres, and the action potentials are transmitted along definite afferent pathways to higher and higher centres in the nervous system until the highest centres are reached which are presumed to lie in the cortex. There is also an imagined hierarchy of status among these cortical centres. On the lowest rung are 'psychosensory', or 'receptor' areas which are differently localized for every sensory category. The psychosensory area for some somatic sensations from the skin and muscles is localized in the post-central gyrus, though pain and thermal sensations do not seem to reach the cortex at all. Taste sensations seem to have the same post-central receptor area and are localized in the neighbourhood of skin sensations from the face. The olfactory area was at one time assumed to lie in the hippocampus, but this has now been disproved and no other area has been found. The auditory area is believed to lie in the transverse gyrus of Heschl in the superior temporal convolution, but there is much uncertainty about this. The best established psychosensory area is that belonging to visual sensations which is located on the medial surface of the occipital lobe on both sides of the calcarine fissure.

Around these psychosensory areas are supposed to lie higher 'association' centres in which sensations of the same modality are integrated so that they can be recognized as belonging together. In the neighbourhood of the post-central gyrus for instance, skin sensations are allegedly synthesized so that they can be localized and discriminated. In this way the tactile recognition, or 'stereognosis' of objects is made possible. A similar association centre is assumed to exist in the vicinity of the visual psychosensory cortex. Finally there are believed to be still higher and more nebulous areas, 'the highest integrative or ideational centres', in which sensations of different modalities can be united into images and these converted into abstract ideas.

There is very little experimental support for this classical neurological theory of perception. Most laboratory findings are at variance with it, and only the clinical observations of selected cases continue to be quoted as evidence in its favour—an evidence that is very far from reliable, though it has proved influential enough to perpetuate fragments of the classical theory even in modern textbooks on neurophysiology. We know that quite large areas of the cortex can be removed without necessarily affecting perception to a serious degree, though such an interference with higher cortical centres should, according to classical theory, prove disastrous. The whole concept of cortical centres is regarded with suspicion today but all attempts to replace it by a more adequate and less naïve theory have so far failed. The phrenological view that the cortex is the place where psychological experiences are mysteriously generated from physiological processes is still too deeply ingrained. Though there are only two well-established cortical receptor centres, namely the psychosensory areas of the post-central gyrus and the calcarine fissure, and though these areas are not radically distinguished from other relay stations in the nervous system, there is still a widespread desire to regard them as special merely because they are cortical, and to endow them with a mystical nimbus which succeeds only in hiding the depth of our ignorance. It is, however, possible today to discard the phrenological dictum of the exclusive cortical localization of psychological functions. Although the fundamental physical basis of psychological experience remains as obscure as ever, physiological knowledge of neural activity is available nowadays on which more adequate provisional theories of the neural correlates of psychological experience may be built.

CHAPTER 3

PSYCHONEURAL PROCESSES

The Interneural Pool

One of the simplest functional units in the nervous system is the spinal reflex arc, consisting only of two neurones: an afferent neurone transmitting stimuli from the periphery to the spinal cord, and an efferent neurone conveying nerve impulses from the spinal cord to the periphery. Most spinal reflex arcs are, however, more complicated because, between the afferent and efferent peripheral neurones, a network of central neurones exists: the so-called internuncial neurones, or interneurones. The network of inter-neurones can be very elaborate and extend through many regions of the central nervous system.

The interneural networks are not morphologically distinct and have therefore attracted less attention than the 'specific' pathways whose nerve fibres run in close proximity to each other, and connect definite regions of the central nervous system. The topographical vagueness of the pool of interneurones is responsible for the fact that we know comparatively little about them. Physiologically, the pool of interneurones makes its existence felt mainly by the phenomena of spatial and temporal summation, and the consequences which spring from them, such as the gradual 'recruiting' of reflex responses and the 'after-discharges' when the afferent reflex stimuli have ceased.

When an afferent stimulus is too weak to elicit a spinal reflex response, it can still cause subliminal excitement in certain circuits of the interneural pool. When several weak stimuli arrive at the same time or consecutively, there may be a spatial and temporal summation of excitement in certain interneural circuits until it is strong enough to cause a reflex response. Take, for instance, the spinal scratch reflex. A gentle touch of the skin at one spot may not produce scratching, but a crawling insect, touching consecutive spots on the skin, will. Sherrington once suggested that fleas may owe their survival as a species to their hop.

Autoregulation in the Interneural Pool

The network of circuits in the interneural pool is obviously co-ordinated functionally so that an adequate distribution of excitatory and inhibitory impulses to different effector neurones is possible. For example, when the motor neurones of some muscles are reflexly excited, those of the antagonist muscles must be inhibited. This can only be achieved through functional co-ordination in the interneural pool. This co-ordination may have its origin, to a large extent, in processes of *autoregulation*. By this is meant that efferent impulses may give rise to peripheral stimulations which are afferently 'fed back' to the interneural pool in such a way that purposeful co-ordinations in it are improved. For example, a scratch response that is off the mark leads to the stimulation of a skin region outside the target area from which the scratch reflex had originally been provoked. This error is automatically corrected by re-orientations in the interneural pool.

There is nothing mysterious about processes of autoregulation. Mechanical devices with autoregulation have recently attracted much engineering interest. They have been called 'feedback' devices, or 'servo-mechanisms'. One of the earliest mechanical feedback devices formed part of Watt's steam engine. It was called a 'governor' and consisted of two metal balls, swinging on opposite sides of a rotating shaft whose circular velocity varied with the speed of the engine. When the speed increased, the balls were lifted by their centrifugal force and this had the effect of closing valves so that the pressure of steam was reduced and the speed of the engine became slower. This kind of feedback which automatically and quite mechanically corrects deviations from a particular level of speed, or any other variable, is called a 'negative feedback'.

The mathematical theory of such autoregulated systems has been christened 'cybernetics' by Wiener[537]. The term is derived from the Greek word for 'steersman' which is also the root of the word 'governor'. It has become customary to speak generally of cybernetic systems or devices when feedback effects of some kind occur. It is of particular interest that cybernetic systems regulated by negative feedback appear to be goal-directed and purposive. The possibility of goal-direction in mechanical processes has frequently been doubted because it seemed to imply that a future event, the goal, was one of the antecedent causes of a present event. As time was thought of as progressing only in one direction from the past to the future, such a reversal of the time vector seemed impossible. However, the temporal sequence of events in a cybernetic system progresses in a circular fashion so that what is a future goal at one moment becomes an actual effect at the next, and then turns into a cause affecting events which are earlier in the circle of sequences though later in time.

Many cybernetic systems have been demonstrated among physiological functions. In fact, whenever we find a physiological equilibrium, or an apparently purposive co-ordination of activities, it is likely that a negative feedback arrangement is responsible for this autoregulation. Negative feedback certainly seems to play a role in the functional co-ordination of interneurones which control spinal reflexes.

A network of interneurones exists not only in the spinal cord, but also at higher segments of the nervous system. Some parts of this network (situated in the medulla, pons, midbrain, hypothalamus and thalamus) have recently received much attention, and are referred to as the 'reticular formation'[374], a term which is misleading, if it conjures up the concept of a morphological entity. Anatomically, it consists of a large variety of nerve cells which are dispersed over a wide area. Physiologically, it has both excitatory and inhibitory effects on cells in the spinal cord and the cortex. Because of the wide ramification of its influence and its central position, it has been credited with important integrative functions in the central nervous system. In fact, the Canadian neurosurgeon, Penfield, has identified it with that 'highest integrative centre', so confidently assumed by classical neurology, and has named it the 'centrencephalic integrating system'[392]. This view has been criticized because it seems to neglect the contribution of the cortex to psychological experiences. Classical theory over-valued the importance of the cortex; Penfield's theory seems to go to the opposite extreme. It is obvious that the pool of cerebral interneurones comprises more than the reticular formation or the centrencephalic integrating system; it must also contain many interneurones dispersed throughout the cortex.

As in the spinal cord, it is also possible in the brain to distinguish, on the one hand, between specific pathways to and from the cortex which are morphologically distinct and topographically localized and, on the other hand, the non-specific pool of interneurones which does not form a compact morphological structure and cannot be narrowly localized. Specific pathways can thus be interrupted by relatively small lesions. Such a lesion in the occipital cortex, for instance, may interrupt visual pathways, and interfere with the psychological function of seeing; and a lesion in the internal capsule may interrupt the pyramidal tract and interfere with the execution of voluntary movements. The non-specific cerebral pool of interneurones, however, cannot be so easily impaired by a small lesion because diverse interneural circuits in different topographical areas can be functionally equivalent and thus largely interchangeable.

The Psychoneural Pool

It is a plausible assumption that the functions of the interneural cerebral pool are related to the emergence of psychological functions. We therefore feel justified in speaking of a 'psychoneural pool' and of 'psychoneural processes' in it.

Psychoneural processes may manifest themselves in three distinct ways. In the first place, they may reveal themselves through physiological changes in the body. The most immediate changes are due to nerve impulses in the psychoneural pool itself which give rise to minute electric currents that can be picked up from the scalp, in an electroencephalogram (EEG); from the cortex, in an electrocorticogram (ECG); or from electrodes implanted into subcortical layers. The form of these minute electric currents obviously changes with the number, extension and complexity of the psychoneural circuits that are active. In sleep, for instance, when many psychoneural activities are at a resting level slow waves of high voltage appear in the EEG of the neo-cortex and the reticular formation of the midbrain. As the depth of sleep diminishes, the electrical patterns in the neo-cortex and the midbrain reticular formation become faster, more irregular and of lower voltage.

There are, of course, many other physiological changes which may accompany psychoneural processes. Through autonomic nerves and via the hypothalamus the functions of vegetative and endocrine systems are influenced, and through upper motor neurones the functions of somatic muscles are affected. Thus psychoneural processes may reveal themselves through changes in pulse rate, respiration, blushing, perspiration, secretory activities in alimentary or sexual glands, increased muscular tonus, trembling, and so on.

The second mode of manifestation of psychoneural processes is through the behaviour of the organism as a whole, and not merely through physiological part-activities somewhere in the organism. Most behaviour seems purposive and directed towards the attainment of a goal. There is a behaviouristic school of psychology which tries to restrict itself to the study of such overt behavioural patterns.

Conscious Experience

The two modes of psychoneural manifestations so far considered, namely physiological changes and behaviour, are objective events which can be observed directly by outsiders. The third mode of psychoneural manifestation is, however, intrinsically different; it is composed of events which can be directly observed only by the person in whose brain the psychoneural processes occur. He has a specially private and unique awareness of those processes. He is like a person inside a sphere who perceives its concavity, whereas to everybody outside the sphere only its convexity is apparent. This special inside view of psychoneural processes is called a *conscious experience*. It is because of the uniqueness of this experience that it seems to represent a special kind of mental reality which differs essentially from any reality with which the outside world may be credited. The term 'conscious' derives etymologically from *con* (with) and *scire* (to know); its original meaning therefore was 'concomitant knowing'. As Aristotle put it simply: 'In addition to actually seeing and hearing we are also aware that we see and that we hear'[469]. Since then, many other meanings have been given to the term, in particular the meaning of wakefulness and responsiveness to the environment.

Conscious experiences, in the sense of concomitantly known experiences, are traditionally divided into three principal categories: (*a*) cognitive experiences which include all perceiving, imagining, thinking, and remembering; (*b*) affective experiences which comprise all varieties of feeling from prolonged moods to fleeting emotions and intense passions; and (*c*) conative experiences which denote impulses, desires, motivations, and actually initiated movements.

Some conscious experiences relate a person to the world around him, such as perceptions and movements. All others are purely *intrapsychic* experiences which do not refer to the immediate environment, though they may be disclosed to it, without concomitant knowing, through some physiological and behavioural manifestations of the underlying psychoneural processes. The concomitant knowing of intrapsychic experiences can be enhanced by a process of self-reflective perception which we call 'introspection'.

In general, when we speak of conscious experiences, such as thoughts, feelings or desires, we have in mind conceptual categories abstracted from conscious experiences which actually occurred in different people at different times. It is often necessary, however, to indicate the actual conscious experience of a particular person at a particular moment. To avoid misunderstanding we shall refer to such experiences as *existential* experiences, using the term 'existential' in its principal sense as that which exists or emerges in the experience of the moment.

The extent to which existential experiences are concomitantly known varies. The concomitant knowledge of some existential experiences is very clear and detailed, whereas we are hardly aware of others existing at the same moment. This distinction is often expressed by saying that some existential experiences are in the centre of 'consciousness' and others at its fringe. This manner of speaking uses a misleading simile of 'consciousness' as a stage with a centre that is floodlit by 'attention' and with shadowy wings in which little can be discerned. It seems more suitable to think of clearly noticed existential experiences as due to the summation of many equivalent psychoneural circuits, and of poorly noticed existential experiences as due to the summated excitement in relatively few circuits.

Autoregulation in the Psychoneural Pool

We have mentioned that the interneural circuits of the spinal cord seem to show purposiveness through processes of cybernetic autoregulation. Similar cybernetic features are also present in the psychoneural pool of the brain. Sometimes the autoregulation is conscious as, for instance, in the threading of a needle which requires the visual control of an intricate motor performance. More often the autoregulation is not conscious as happens in most motor performances which are controlled automatically by sensory feedback from muscles, tendons and joints. In diseases in which the pathways of this 'deep sensibility' are interrupted, as, for instance, in tabes dorsalis, autoregulation through feedback cannot function properly and poorly controlled, ataxic movements are the result.

Cybernetic engineers have shown that some of the conscious functions of psychoneural processes can be imitated by activities in suitably autoregulated electronic machines. Such 'electronic brains' may even surpass human capacity for logical thought and mathematical calculations by their superiority of speed and, as it were, single-mindedness. Other electronic devices have been constructed in which goal-directed activities through cybernetic autoregulation have been the main feature, such as the 'homing rockets' which adapt their movements to all avoiding actions by their target.

Cybernetic engineers, especially those concerned with the transmission of communications, have realized that the correction of errors can be achieved, not only by autoregulation through feedback, but also by means of redundant information. Ordinary language is redundant in this sense so that we are able to understand a speaker even if many of his syllables and words are drowned by noise. It has been estimated[81, 448] that the information contained in written English is 75 to 80 per cent redundant which helps us in deciphering illegible handwriting and mutilated telegrams. Similar redundancies are likely to occur in the psychoneural information which is existentially experienced. When these redundancies are reduced, as may happen in absent-mindedness, somnolence or through lesions in the psychoneural pool, the number of errors in cognitive and conative experiences is bound to increase.

CHAPTER 4

PSYCHOLOGICAL PHENOMENA

The question whether our mental apparatus is capable of comprehending the reality of processes within and around us has exercised the ingenuity of many philosophers who have returned different answers to this 'epistemological' problem. One of these answers, which has proved specially attractive to medical men, assumes that there is a reality of certain 'given facts', or *data*, which we can never know in their true essence, though our mental apparatus can inform us of the appearances, or *phenomena*, to which such data give rise in our conscious experience.

Yet our conscious experiences consist not only of phenomena that inform us of data, but also of phenomena that correspond to our conscious knowing that we experience something. Phenomena can therefore be divided into two distinct categories: the phenomena of consciously knowing something, the so-called *act-phenomena* or process-phenomena, e.g. seeing, hearing, thinking, feeling, desiring, remembering; and the something that is consciously known, the so-called *object-phenomena* or content-phenomena, e.g. an event seen or heard, an idea thought of, a mood felt, a satisfaction desired, a scene remembered, or even a feedback experience in the form of an act-phenomenon consciously known. Act-phenomena are thus experienced as transitive processes which require for their completion an object-phenomenon.

The object-phenomena of which we can become aware seem to originate in three distinct spheres: the external world around us, the internal world within our bodies, and the conscious world of our mental experiences. The act-phenomena which inform us of object-phenomena in the different spheres can be distinguished as the *exteroception* of external objects, the *interoception* of internal sensations, and the *introspection* of conscious mental phenomena.

External object-phenomena which indicate inanimate physical data are not changed in any way by our acts of exteroception. However, those external object-phenomena which indicate the behavioural data presented by other people can be markedly changed by our exteroception, if the other people are exteroceptively aware of being observed by us. Internal object-phenomena which indicate sensory data arising in our body can be similarly changed by our interoception. An interocepted pain, for example, can become stronger, or a practised habitual movement, such as walking, can disintegrate when it is closely analysed interoceptively.

Conscious act-phenomena which indicate the data of our own psychoneural processes are most seriously changed when we try to introspect them. Because of this introspective difficulty, the French philosopher, Auguste Comte, believed at one time that what he called a 'positivist' approach to psychology, i.e. an empirical science of psychology, is impossible and should be replaced by a positivist study of society, for which he coined the word 'sociology'[87].

The Austrian philosopher, Franz Brentano, however, arrived at a different conclusion. He maintained that mental processes can be introspectively observed in retrospect and also inferred from the behaviour of other people in spite of their awareness of being under observation. In 1874, Brentano published his *Psychology from an Empirical Standpoint*[62], in which he turned against the then customary preoccupation of experimental psychologists (e.g. Fechner, Wundt, Mach) with the introspection of content-phenomena, such as the study of sensations and of the way in which ideas are associated, and emphasized the importance of the introspective investigation of act-phenomena. He expressed himself in terms borrowed from mediaeval scholasticism with which we are no longer familiar today, and he dealt with the problems of psychology by philosophical argument rather than 'from an empirical standpoint'. Yet he had a profound influence, not only on some subsequent philosophical trends, but also on schools of so-called 'act'-psychology. His views had perhaps also some effect on Freud who, as a medical student, attended some of his lectures in Vienna.

Phenomenology

Brentano's pupil, Husserl, continued the philosophical analysis of mental phenomena and established what he called the 'science' of phenomenology[73, 245]. He, at first, concentrated on the detailed description and classification of introspectively ascertained phenomena. Later he tried to evolve a more ambitious 'pure phenomenology' which had as one of its aims the discovery, by means of particular modes of introspection, of the individually different ways of experiencing the 'world of objects'. Pure phenomenology has remained a rather esoteric branch of philosophical speculation, but the descriptive and classificatory form of phenomenology was adopted by some psychologists and psychiatrists who, carefully and circumstantially, collected a large number and variety of psychological phenomena in normal, abnormal, and psychiatrically ill persons.

Descriptive phenomenology keeps strictly to psychological observation and refrains from investigating the relationship between psychological phenomena and physical data. Experimental psychologists, clinical psychiatrists and neurologists, on the other hand, are not similarly restricted, and regard it as part of their task to examine the physical origin of mental phenomena. As far as elementary act-phenomena are concerned, it seems obvious that they belong to the inherited repertoire of the functional capacities of any normal individual. It certainly is normal to have the general ability to see, hear, think, remember, feel, desire, and so on. It therefore has to be assumed that these general abilities have their basis in the inherited structure and physiology of the central nervous system, depending both on specific and localized neural pathways and on unspecific and non-localized psychoneural processes.

The situation is different with content-phenomena. It may be assumed that some primitive and meaningless content-phenomena are inherited stock, but they change with the accumulation of experience into meaningful content-phenomena. Most of the content-phenomena of which an adult becomes conscious are therefore acquired or learned phenomena. Occasionally he again goes through an experience when his content-phenomena change from a senseless jumble to something that has meaning. This happens, for instance, when he listens to a foreign tongue he wishes to learn; at first, his content-phenomena will consist of a babel of undifferentiated noises, but gradually he will distinguish a word or a phrase and understand some of the meaning conveyed. It is plausible to assume that the acquisition of meaningful content-phenomena is accompanied by some physical changes in certain neural processes of the brain. Such neural changes have been given many names such as 'memory traces' or 'engrams'. Among neurologists the term 'schema' is often preferred today.

Heteropsychic Experiences and Intuitive Insight

We know of the existence of mental phenomena not only through introspection. We also perceive the overt manifestations of conscious phenomena in other people and even in animals. The manifestations which disclose such heteropsychic experiences may consist of physiological changes which an outsider can perceive, for example blushing or trembling, or of uncurbed changes in non-verbal behaviour. It has become customary to regard such heteropsychic manifestations as 'objective'.

In human beings, heteropsychic experiences may also be overtly manifested by means of verbal communications or with the help of gesture and mime. A verbal communication allows the most detailed and accurate description of heteropsychic phenomena. The communication itself is, of course, an objective manifestation, but its message refers to a subjective and private experience in another person's mind. It has therefore become customary to disregard the objective aspects of a verbal description of conscious experiences, and to consider the description as a 'subjective' heteropsychic manifestation.

It requires either an emotional act of sympathy or a cognitive act of interpretation on our part to comprehend the heteropsychic phenomena revealed by objective manifestations. When we see another person burst into tears, scream in anguish, concentrate on a puzzle problem or drain a glass of liquid in a few gulps, we may either notice an echoing sympathetic feeling in ourselves or diagnose the heteropsychic processes indicated by our observations in a more detached analytic way.

When we obtain subjective heteropsychic messages from another person who verbally describes his conscious experiences, he himself has already interpreted them, and we are no longer required to carry out this operation. We may, of course, still use our judgment about his truthfulness. We have a peculiarly direct and immediate understanding of most heteropsychic communications, whether they are objective or subjective, because we have had similar experiences ourselves in reality or imagination. This form of understanding has been called 'static intuitive understanding'. We also often have an equally direct and immediate understanding of the psychological origin, or psychogenesis, of heteropsychic communications, and this has been called 'psychogenetic intuitive understanding'.

In general, when the terms 'intuitive understanding' or 'intuitive insight', are used, only the psychogenetic variety is meant. The terms are translations of the German word *verstehen* in the sense in which it is used by the German school of *Verstehende Psychologie*. The German philosopher and psychiatrist, Karl Jaspers, was the first to use the term *Verstehende Psychologie*, and the translators of his book *General Psychopathology* have rendered it variously as 'psychology of meaningful connections', 'meaningful psychology', or 'psychology of meaning'[257]. For example, we have an intuitive understanding that a person who believes he has committed a sin feels guilty, that a person who believes he is unjustly blamed feels annoyed, and that a person who believes that other people want to take advantage of him feels suspicious. In these examples, we intuitively form meaningful connections between two heteropsychic experiences which, in these illustrations, consist of an antecedent belief and a consequent feeling.

Our intuitive understanding of the meaningful connections between psychological experiences has always been relied upon by story-tellers and playwrights who portray the psychological reactions of their fictional characters in a way that provides us with the plausible impression that we can follow what goes on in the minds of the characters and why they react the way they do to their experiences. Intuitive understanding is also constantly employed by us in real life in our dealings with other people. Not only do we have a static intuitive insight into heteropsychic feelings and motivations, but we also search for antecedent heteropsychic experiences which might be meaningfully connected with them. If a person looks depressed, or says he feels depressed, we accept any previous experience as meaningfully connected with the depression, if our intuition supports this as plausible. It does not matter whether it is the death of a near relative, failure in an examination, a frustrated love affair, or a hangover from an unhappy past. If a person looks happy, irritable, suspicious, or emotionally disturbed, our ingenuity and the vicissitudes of life can be similarly relied upon to provide us with the psychogenetic intuitive understanding we desire.

Karl Jaspers, in his *General Psychopathology*, emphasizes that the limitations and pitfalls of intuitive insight must be recognized to avoid error. He says, for example: 'We can perhaps understand how a person who is feeling weak and wretched must feel spiteful, hateful, perhaps envious and revengeful towards people who are better endowed, happy and strong, since psychic poverty is linked with bitterness. But the opposite is just as understandable. The person who feels weak and wretched can be frank about himself, can be unassuming and love what he himself is not.' It follows that 'the most radical mistakes spring from conclusions drawn as to the reality of what has been understood'.

The reality of what has been understood refers only to the conceptual reality of an 'ideally typical mind'. As we never deal with such a mind in practice, intuitive understanding has the further drawback that it can never be proved or disproved by objective investigations. Jaspers, for instance, remarks that we may understand intuitively how the gloom of an autumnal landscape can rouse suicidal thoughts. Yet we may not only be mistaken in applying this understanding to a particular individual, we cannot even demonstrate that our understanding is supported by statistical findings because statistical investigations cannot deal with ideally typical minds either. That the incidence of suicide shows a peak in the spring, and not in the autumn, is therefore irrelevant. Even if the association between autumnal gloom and suicidal thoughts occurred in only one individual, the justification of our intuitive understanding would be established. But if there was not even one individual? Jaspers believes that this would not matter either: 'A poet, for instance, might present convincing connections that we understand immediately though they have never yet occurred. They have not been realized yet but contain their own evidence in the sense of being ideally typical.'

This may seem to be an extreme point of view which denies practical significance to the concept of intuitive understanding in disciplines aspiring to a scientific status. Yet when we look at the disciplines which make use of intuitive understanding, Jaspers' analysis seems confirmed, though his warning is not heeded and the postulated typical minds are assumed to exist in reality. It is too easy and tempting to construct typical minds, endow them with a plausible set of suitable attributes, and the most puzzling problems in sociology, economics, politics, psychology or psychiatry become intuitively intelligible. Among the typical minds thus created we find such phantoms as the 'economic man', 'capitalist', 'communist', 'teenager', 'neurotic', 'psychopath', and the many different 'unconscious minds' of the various schools of 'insight psychology'.

A distinction is often made between intuitive understanding and causal explanation. But the justification for such a distinction is doubtful. In intuitive understanding a meaningful connection between phenomena, and particularly conscious phenomena, is assumed to exist in a specially conceptualized typical mind. In causal explanation a meaningful connection is also assumed to exist, but this time in a specially conceptualized non-mental reality. For example, the good spirits of a person may be meaningfully connected with his being in convivial company because he belongs to the class of typical extraverted minds which have the attribute of enjoying company. This would be intuitive understanding. But his good spirits might also be meaningfully connected with the alcohol he consumed because his brain is conceived as so constructed that it responds to a mild degree of alcohol intoxication with a feeling of carefree enjoyment. This would be a causal explanation. In either case, a meaningful connection is established with the help of concepts that are inferred from a series of observations or a set of assumptions.

Existentialism

Not all insight psychologies rely for their intuitive understanding on the conceptual construction of typical minds. Some have taken their inspiration from the philosophical movement known as existentialism—a movement with many contradictory eddies and a bewildering variety of doctrines whose only common bond seems to be a revolt against the loss of individuality which follows from the adoption of social conventions and customs[49, 89, 277, 305].

The insights of existentialism are not derived from the essential attributes of typical minds, but from the revelations of a typical and subjectively unique experience: the 'existentialist moment', or the 'moment of truth', when the individual, alone and deserted, feels the foreboding of death and nothingness. At that 'moment', he is credited with the freedom of an 'authentic' choice—authentic because it is in accord with his true and unique self. The dread and suffering of a serious disease may plunge the individual into the crisis of an existentialist moment, and it is therefore not surprising that some psychotherapists have adopted, and adapted, the teachings of certain existentialist schools to help their patients to obtain the inner freedom necessary for an 'authentic' choice.

The existentialist movement had its origin in the thoughts of the nineteenth century Danish philosopher Kierkegaard[49, 89, 277, 305], whose writings were translated into German just before the first world war. He believed that, in moments of despair, human beings can become aware of the reality of existence which cannot be rationally grasped and is accessible only to the non-rational, or trans-rational, powers of the human mind. Karl Jaspers has been the first among modern trans-rational philosophers to accept and modify Kierkegaard's thought[256]. He speaks of 'limit situations' causing a 'foundering' in emotional crisis during which man can become vaguely aware of some aspects of the 'encompassing' metaphysical reality which is beyond the limit of rational knowing. Similar doctrines, in more complex language, have been expressed by Heidegger, a pupil of Husserl. Heidegger[229] is fond of etymological subtleties, compound neologisms and un-idiomatic phrases. It is not surprising that he is regarded as a notoriously obscure writer and that he has repeatedly complained of being misunderstood, and even of being wrongly classed among existentialist philosophers.

CHAPTER 5

PSYCHIATRIC NOSOLOGIES

The classification of medical and surgical diseases is today largely based on the localization of endopathological lesions in different organs and tissues, subdivided according to the nature of the lesions and the dysfunctions associated with them. Psychiatric nosologies, however, have not been able to follow the same path. The organ mainly affected in psychiatric diseases is the psychoneural pool of the brain. At present we still know next to nothing about it and its mode of functioning. Many psychiatric diseases therefore have no known endopathology, and their only possible classification is a clinical one, relying on psychological symptoms and their constellations[481].

It is a truism that in organic diseases psychoneural functions are also affected and psychological symptoms produced. The very fact that patients complain and feel ill is a psychological symptom. How then can we differentiate the psychological symptoms occurring in psychiatric and other diseases? There is no definitive answer to this question, but psychological symptoms tend to be regarded as indicating psychiatric diseases in the following circumstances: (1) When the psychological symptoms are so disturbing socially that the segregation of the patient in an institution becomes desirable or necessary. If the patient is blamed for his symptoms because he is thought capable of suppressing them, the institution to which he is likely to be sent is a prison. If the patient arouses sympathy and a more charitable attitude, the institution in which he is segregated is likely to be a mental hospital. (2) When the psychological symptoms are so odd and bizarre that our intuitive understanding of them fails, we are inclined to regard the symptoms as products of a 'diseased mind'. (3) When the psychological symptoms cannot be causally connected with any endopathological lesions, we then tend to assume that, if there are no causes in the physical realm, they may lie in the realm of the mind.

These diagnostic criteria of psychiatric symptoms are not very definite. It is therefore not surprising that the distinction between psychiatric symptoms and the psychological symptoms occurring in the course of other diseases is often a matter of opinion. To avoid futile arguments, hybrid terms are not infrequently used as a compromise, such as 'neuropsychiatric' or 'psychosomatic'[60].

35

It is helpful to distinguish two kinds of psychological or psychiatric symptoms: those which become clinically noticeable because the patient cannot, or does not, inhibit and control them are *objective* symptoms; and those which only become known to others when the patient intentionally communicates them to his social environment are *subjective* symptoms. Examples of objective psychiatric symptoms are: hysterical fainting attacks, stupor, temper outbursts, suicidal attempts, the self-conscious blushing of a shy person, the perspiration and tremor of a patient in the grip of an irrational panic attack, and so on. Examples of subjective psychiatric symptoms are: intentionally adopted attitudes to advertise subjective suffering, and the verbal description or pictorial expression of morbid psychological experiences.

In non-psychiatric patients, there is generally a concordance between subjective and objective psychological symptoms. If a patient subjectively complains of pain, he generally also shows the objective behaviour of a person in pain; and if a person subjectively complains of being blind, he objectively behaves like a blind person. In psychiatric patients, however, there is often a discordance between subjective and objective psychological symptoms. Some psychiatric patients, for instance, complain of subjective pain without displaying the objective symptoms of being in pain; or, conversely, their objective behaviour indicates that they are in pain, yet they deny it when asked. Similarly, patients with the psychiatric symptoms of hysterical blindness complain of not being able to see, but walk about without bumping into objects or falling down stairs. The objective behaviour of other psychiatric patients reveals that they are amblyopic, but they hotly deny that their vision is impaired.

Because psychiatrists have to rely on subjective, as well as objective clinical symptoms, psychiatric nosologies are still reminiscent of the times when all diseases were classified on clinical lines. Such classifications led to the construction of clinical disease entities which were more or less arbitrary, and therefore liable to vary from place to place and time to time.

The most thoroughgoing and systematic attempts to establish clinical nosologies, comprising all possible disease entities, were made in the eighteenth century. The French physician, de Sauvages[437], published several such nosologies which were modelled on classifications that had proved their value in botany. As he regarded diseases as akin to botanic species, such classifications seemed entirely adequate to him. His *Pathologia Methodica* of 1759, for example, divided diseases into ten Classes, the eighth of which dealt with Insanity. It had three Orders which were concerned respectively with what might be called Disturbances of Reason, Affect and Behaviour. Among the Disturbances of Reason, there were six Genera. One of these was labelled 'Melancholia'. It had eight Species, such as 'Melancholia Anglica', or 'Taedium Vitae'; 'Melancholia Mysantropica'; 'Melancholia Attonita', or stuporous melancholy; and 'Aegritudo Imaginaria', or hypochondriasis. In his final classification several years later, de Sauvages distinguished 2400 different species of disease. The Class of Insanity had grown to four Orders, and the Genus 'Melancholia' now contained 14 species with completely new names. Linnaeus, who was then professor of botany in Uppsala, was so impressed by the clinical nosologies of de Sauvages that he published, in 1763, a nosology of his own under the title *Genera Morborum*[327]. Other physicians followed suit and the end result was a perplexing variety of nosologies containing differently named disease entities.

Kraepelin's Nosology

The same perplexing variety is still noticeable in the psychiatric nosologies of our time. They go back to the work of Kraepelin, the German psychiatrist who was most influential in his endeavours to establish definitive psychiatric disease entities and to bring order into psychiatric nosology. In the course of 44 years (1883–1927) he published nine editions, the last one incomplete, of a psychiatric textbook in which he presented his changing nosologies[271]. By studying in detail the symptoms of many psychotic patients, and by comparing the course and outcome of their illnesses, he succeeded in establishing two new categories of 'functional psychoses'—manic-depressive illness and schizophrenia—though he failed in his attempts to subdivide them into clear-cut disease entities.

The general outline of Kraepelin's psychiatric nosologies has stood the test of time, yet the details of diagnosis and nomenclature still vary from country to country, and there is no prospect of achieving uniformity at the present time. The World Health Organization tried to tackle this task in its manuals dealing with the *International Statistical Classification of Diseases* of which Section V referred to psychiatric diseases. Only five countries (Britain among them) have officially adopted this Section—a fact which has not, however, had much influence on the diagnostic habits of the psychiatrists of those countries.

Despite differences of detail, the main features of Kraepelin's nosological scheme are used almost everywhere. Psychiatric diseases are generally divided into the following main categories: organic psychoses (G.P.I., toxic delirium, etc.); functional psychoses (manic-depression, schizophrenia); epilepsies (*grand mal, petit mal,* etc.); neuroses, (hysteria, phobia, etc.); psychopathies (abnormal personalities, drug addicts, etc.); and mental subnormality (subcultural variety, mongolism, etc.).

The distinction between functional psychoses and neuroses does not necessarily imply a fundamental nosological difference, but may have mainly a historical and social origin. Psychotic (mad, insane) patients were treated by 'alienists' in madhouses or asylums, but neurotic (hysterical, nervous) patients were treated by private physicians in consulting rooms. The theory that psychoses were due to a diseased mind, and neuroses due to functional anomalies in the nervous system, was purely speculative. Today it is realized that there is no definite boundary line between psychoses and neuroses. Mild psychotics are now often treated in the community, whereas neurotics are not infrequently admitted to psychiatric hospitals. Diagnostic distinctions may have to put their trust in textbook accounts of typical and fully established clinical pictures. These are, however, of little help in the early and mild stages of a psychosis during which the clinical symptoms presented may be very similar to those in neurotic patients. For this reason, ambiguous hybrid terms are sometimes used which avoid definite diagnostic commitments, e.g. 'neurotic depression' or 'pseudo-neurotic schizophrenia'.

Factor Analysis

To render the differentiation between psychiatric disease categories less arbitrary and less dependent on subjective assessments, academic psychologists have tried to make use of a statistical method known as factor analysis[70, 130, 312, 500, 501]. The assumption underlying this method is briefly this: if some general factors influenced the measurements of several attributes, the measurements would be correlated. Factor analysis provides mathematical procedures designed to extract from a table of correlation coefficients the general factors which had been operative. For example, if a general factor of height affects various measurements of body build, there will be positive correlations between, say, the length of arms and trunks in a random sample of people; this means that in this sample there will be some people in whom arms, legs and trunks are all rather short and other people in whom these three attributes of body build are all rather long. By factor-analysing the correlations found, we can obtain a general factor of height. This merely tells us that a person with, say, long arms tends to be tall, though this tendency is only approximate. The general factor of height can therefore not be as accurate an indicator of a person's height as the direct measurement of this attribute.

If psychologists could measure psychological attributes as directly as we can measure the physical attribute of height, they would not have to resort to the roundabout method of factor analysis. There is, for example, no way of directly measuring a person's intelligence, but from the correlation of the scores obtained by many people on several tests of intelligence, a general factor of intelligence can be established with the help of factor analysis. It is then even possible to assess the 'factor loading' of an individual person and thus to estimate the degree of his intelligence relative to the sample of people from which the general factor of intelligence had been obtained. The measurement of a psychological attribute in an individual person is therefore not only far from accurate, it is also dependent on the sample of people with whom he is compared and the nature of the actual tests used. For these and other reasons, the contribution which factor analysis has been able to make to psychiatric nosology has been rather academic and has not been very helpful in the diagnostic assessment of individual psychiatric patients. However, there is a certain measure of agreement among factor analysts concerning the existence and approximate assessment of some psychological factors. A general factor of *intelligence* was the first to arouse the interests and raise the hopes of psychologists. A factor of *neuroticism* is today assumed to indicate the stability or lability of emotional reactivity. A factor of *introversion–extraversion* divides normal people into thinkers and doers, and neurotic patients into anxious-obsessional and hysterical-psychopathic personalities. Some claims have also been advanced for the existence of a factor of *psychoticism*[132, 134].

Dissatisfaction with the present state of psychiatric nosology has prompted some clinicians to concentrate on a detailed clinical and phenomenological study of the symptoms presented by their psychiatric patients. It has been argued that such studies provide the only observational basis for what has been called 'descriptive' or 'phenomenological' psychopathology. All other kinds of psychopathology and psychiatric nosology are, in contrast, without an observational basis, and therefore mainly speculative or arbitrary.

CHAPTER 6

THE AETIOLOGY OF DISEASES

Aetiological studies of disease are concerned with the discovery of pathogenic, or morbific, causes. In the case of clinical disease entities, the first aetiological step consists in the search for the endopathological changes which cause the clinical symptoms observed. The second, and more specifically aetiological, step consists in the search for events outside the patient's body.

The examination of a causal sequence, which begins with effects already established and looks for their antecedent causes, is a *retrospective* aetiological analysis. It is the kind of aetiological search in which clinicians are commonly engaged. The examination of a causal sequence may, however, also begin by singling out particular pathogenic events and observing the range of pathological changes and clinical symptoms they may cause in different people at different intervals of time. This kind of *prospective* aetiological analysis is used in experimental studies and follow-up investigations.

There are, in every disease, a great number of pathogenic events, though their respective effects vary widely and can be assessed from different aetiological angles. It is possible to divide pathogenic events into several categories. Four main criteria of classification have been found useful: (1) aetiological significance (2) topographical origin (3) morbidity rate and (4) temporal origin.

Aetiological Significance of Pathogenic Events

Pathogenic events can be ranged in an approximate order of assumed aetiological significance. Those which seem to rank highest are specific or salient causes; those of intermediate rank are contributory or adjuvant conditions; and those of lowest rank are fortuitous or chance influences.* For example, one of the specific causes of a disease presented by a patient may be a bronchial infection with tubercle bacilli. Contributory conditions may be an

* Chance influences are conceived as numerous and unidentifiable events of minute effect each. When we talk of a particular, and therefore identifiable, chance event, we mean an unexpected, improbable or incidental event that is best classed with adjuvant conditions. Chance influences are generally regarded as random so that, if several independent effects are possible by chance (e.g. the numbers on a roulette wheel), each has the same probability of occurring. But chance influences often have a bias so that certain effects (e.g. a biassed section of an unbalanced roulette wheel) have a greater probability than others.

inherited or temporarily increased susceptibility to such an infection or the fact that the patient lives in overcrowded conditions. Chance influences may be responsible for determining some of the characteristics, localizations and distribution of the resulting pathological abnormalities.

In retrospective aetiological analyses, chance influences which are, by definition, numerous and unidentifiable are usually disregarded. The same may happen to adjuvant conditions, unless clinical interest is specially directed at them. Generally, a retrospective aetiological study focusses mainly on one or the other specific cause. It is quite possible that such a specific cause—let us say, a bronchial infection with tubercle bacilli—produces merely minor pathological changes which do not become clinically manifest. The clinician is not likely to see such cases as they do not suffer from a clinical disease and therefore have no motive for seeking his help. His analysis of the aetiology of a particular disease thus starts with a restricted group of people in whose past history the same specific pathogenic event has occurred and who have all fallen ill through it. As the clinician may know nothing of the number of people in whom the specific event caused no clinical disease, he is liable to over-estimate the pathogenic power of specific aetiological causes.

The discovery of pathogenic micro-organisms as specific causes of disease by Pasteur and Koch in the second half of the nineteenth century offered the opportunity of a new classification of disease according to aetiological principles. Such an aetiological nosology held out great promise for the treatment and prevention of disease, and this promise has indeed been remarkably fulfilled in the case of many infectious diseases. But for purely diagnostic purposes, a simple aetiological nosology has proved inadequate. It is true that there are certain 'specific fevers', such as malaria or scarlet fever, in which pathogenic micro-organisms produce a typical symptomatology that can be found in most of the patients who fall ill through them. For this very reason, however, these typical symptomatologies had been known for centuries and regarded as disease entities, though it must be admitted that they probably comprised a mixed aetiological bag before they were defined aetiologically and their diagnosis made dependent on the discovery of the specific micro-organisms.

Even in the case of infectious micro-organisms, the range of pathological effects may be so wide and varied that an aetiological diagnosis is quite inadequate to cover the multiformity of pathological and clinical manifestations. An infection with syphilis, for instance, may lead to such apparently diverse clinical diseases as a hard chancre, skin rashes and ulcers, tumours, aortic aneurysms, tabes dorsalis, general paralysis of the insane, and many others. Some of these diseases occur so many years after the original infection that their syphilitic aetiology remained obscure as long as clinicians had to rely on the memory and veracity of patients, and had no laboratory tests at their disposal which have since provided definite answers to this aetiological problem.

Topographical Origin of Pathogenic Events

Pathogenic events may also be classified according to their topographical origin. The most useful classification is a broad division into exogenous and endogenous events. The adjectives 'exogenous' and 'endogenous' require, however, a reference entity to indicate the boundary that decides which of them is applicable. The usual reference entity is the organism of the patient. This divides pathogenic events into those having their origin either outside or inside the patient's organism. The classification of pathogenic events by their topographical origin is independent of the previously considered classification by aetiological significance. The two classifications may be used jointly. It may, for instance, be thought convenient to divide both exogenous and endogenous pathogenic events also into salient causes, adjuvant conditions and chance influences. When salient causes are exogenous, it is often the custom to view endogenous events merely as reactions to them. The ability of the organism to react in a particular way, its *endogenous reactivity*, may then be regarded as an adjuvant condition that contributes to the final pathological outcome. For example, a person's endogenous reactivity may be such that he is immune to an exogenous infection to which the majority of people succumb.

The reference entity deciding the boundary between exogenous and endogenous events is, however, not always the organism as a whole; it may be only a particular organ or tissue in the body. In psychiatry, the essential reference entity is often the psychoneural pool. The endogenous reactivity of the psychoneural pool is normally manifested by the psychological abilities and traits which, in their totality, constitute what is usually called the 'personality' of an individual. The endogenous reactivity of the psychoneural pool is also responsible for the fact that some people respond with psychiatric symptoms to events, exogenous to the psychoneural pool, which are not pathogenic to others.

Pathogenic events which are exogenous to the psychoneural pool, and remain so, are purely physicochemical events. If they are transmitted to the psychoneural pool, they induce endogenous physicochemical events in it which manifest themselves as psychological or psychiatric symptoms. Their transmission to the psychoneural pool can, however, be of two essentially different kinds, and we can accordingly distinguish two kinds of exogenous aetiologies in psychiatric patients.

In the first kind, the pathogenic events are transmitted by other routes than sensory pathways. The events themselves are therefore entirely unperceived by the patient who only becomes aware of the psychological or psychiatric symptoms they cause. Thus a disturbance of blood supply, an abnormally low level of oxygen or glucose, in the blood, the pressence of toxic substances in it, or an increased intracranial pressure are not perceived as such by the patient, though he may, if he remains conscious, notice the morbid effects of the pathogenic causes. Aetiologies of this kind are usually characterized as the *physiogenic* aetiologies of psychiatric symptoms. However, a better word might be *unperceived* aetiologies as their main characteristic is the imperceptiveness of the pathogenic event.

Pathogenic events can also be transmitted to the psychoneural pool by way of afferent pathways. The events are then perceived as such. Their perception, or the meaning attached to it, gives rise to psychological or psychiatric symptoms. The event may, for instance, consist in a dentist preparing to drill a tooth. The patient, perceiving this and recognizing its meaning, may respond with the psychological symptom of feeling anxious or, if his psychoneural reactivity is pathological, with the psychiatric symptom of fainting or even an epileptic fit. The drilling of the tooth is perceived as an event that causes the psychological symptom of pain. Aetiologies of this kind are usually called *psychogenic* aetiologies, though a better name for them might be *perceived* aetiologies, i.e., aetiologies perceived by the patient. Strictly speaking, the pathogenic events of psychogenic aetiology are as physicochemical in nature as those of physiogenic aetiologies.

In many situations there are both perceived and unperceived aetiologies. A person who swallows a drug he believes to be a strong sleeping tablet is aware that his action has the meaning that he will soon be fast asleep. If the drug is a dummy tablet, or 'placebo', but the person being unaware of this, responds with a deep and long sleep, his reaction is entirely due to a psychogenic, or perceived, aetiology. If the drug really is a sleeping tablet, the person's reaction is a mixture of physiogenic and psychogenic aetiologies.

Morbidity Rate of Pathogenic Events

Pathogenic events also differ in the morbidity rate they cause. If the pathogenic event is a fall from a height of several yards on to hard ground, it has a high morbidity rate because it invariably gives rise to endopathological changes and clinical symptoms. It is thus a *generally pathogenic* event. On the other hand, if the pathogenic event is exposure to an invisible cloud of grass pollen, it has a low morbidity rate because it gives rise to endopathological changes and clinical symptoms only in a minority of people who are allergic to grass pollen—that is, they have an idiosyncratic reactivity to it. Exposure to grass pollen is thus only conditionally pathogenic and may be characterized as an *idiosyncratically pathogenic* event.

With physiogenic aetiologies, it is usually easy to make a distinction between generally and idiosyncratically pathogenic events. It is more or less clearly indicated by the frequency with which endopathological changes occur after certain events, though there may be some uncertainty with intermediate morbidity rates. The differentiation between generally and idiosyncratically pathogenic events is more difficult with psychogenic aetiologies. Where endopathological changes are present, we know that we deal with a physical disease. The psychological symptoms associated with such a disease often have a psychogenic aetiology because they are due to sensory stimuli transmitted to the psychoneural pool by afferent pathways where they are interoceptively perceived. This is, for instance, the case in any physical disease in which the psychological symptom of pain occurs. The endopathological changes which form the psychogenic aetiology of such psychological symptoms as pain or discomfort are thus generally pathogenic events.

The situation is entirely different when there are no endopathological changes which can be held responsible for psychological symptoms. If such symptoms have a psychogenic aetiology, this must be due to exteroceptive perception. There are many exteroceptive experiences which produce distressing psychological reactions, for example, such experiences as an unhappy love affair, a failed examination, frustrated ambition, bereavement, overwork, stress, conflict, and so on. The distressing psychological reactions to which they usually give rise are feelings of anxiety, worry, self-blame, pessimism, restlessness, fatigue, apathy, and the like. This array of distressing psychological reactions is, however, not abnormal by population standards. There is no human life without its quota of such distressing reactions. Thus, if psychological reactions to distressing experiences are normal in quality, strength and duration, they are not clinical symptoms because they are not abnormal, when compared with the reactions of most people in the same circumstances. On the other hand, the term psychiatric symptom is only justified, when we deal with clinical manifestations which *are* abnormal by comparison with the reactions of other people. It follows that, if the aetiology of psychiatric symptoms is entirely psychogenic, it is an idiosyncratic aetiology which only affects people with susceptible psychological reactivities.

Temporal Origin of Pathogenic Events

Pathogenic events can also be distinguished according to their temporal origin. Those which precede the onset of a clinical illness by a relatively short interval are known as *precipitating* pathogenic events; those which occurred very much earlier, and perhaps before the inception of an individual, are known as *predisposing* pathogenic events.

When precipitating events are generally pathogenic, there is no need to assume special susceptibilities in the individuals who fall ill. On the other hand, when precipitating events are only idiosyncratically pathogenic, the individuals who fall ill are abnormally susceptible, and this abnormality may be due to predisposing pathogenic events. A predisposing pathogenic event may have merely altered a person's reactivity without causing an overt disease, and the altered reactivity need not become manifest until many years later. When the predisposing pathogenic event, however, originally revealed its presence by overt clinical symptoms and perhaps also endopathological changes, the subsequent existence of an altered reactivity or diminished resistance to stress may be suspected, even when the individual appears clinically healthy. An attack of rheumatic fever, for instance, may give rise to valvular lesions of the heart which are so well compensated that clinical symptoms are entirely absent for many years. When eventually the compensating mechanisms diminish in strength, some unusual physical stress can become the precipitating idiosyncratic cause of a cardiac decompensation which is then regarded as a *reactive illness*. The gradual diminution of the strength of the compensating mechanisms is, however, bound to lead to a cardiac decompensation sooner or later even without the intervention of an unusual physical stress. The clinical symptoms then seem to have arisen as the result of an *endogenous illness*.

Psychiatric patients often reveal their special susceptibilities by a past history of frequent breakdowns of an apparently reactive or endogenous kind. In other patients, psychiatric illnesses occur without previous indications of a pathogenic predisposition. Sometimes psychological shortcomings are well compensated until excessive stress is encountered which overwhelms the compensating mechanisms. This happens, for instance, to students of average intelligence who yet do well at grammar school level, perhaps because of personality traits of studiousness and diligence which compensate for a relative intellectual inadequacy. This compensation is, however, likely to break down, when the students reach the university and have to cope with an increased burden of scholastic demands.

When pathogenic predispositions antedate an individual's conception, we speak of a 'genetic aetiology'. The predisposing events of such a genetic aetiology take place during the formation of germ cells in the sex glands of one or several of his ancestors, and cause enduring abnormalities in chromosomes or genes, the structures and biochemical substances directly concerned with the genetic transmission of reactivities.

CHAPTER 7

GENETIC AETIOLOGIES

ABNORMALITIES OF CHROMOSOMES

A human being begins life as a unicellular organism, a *zygote*, which, if provided with the appropriate environment in the mother's body, starts out on the intricate and complex task of changing into a multicellular human embryo and foetus, containing many millions of cells of different sizes, shapes and functions. When this development has reached a particular stage of maturation, the foetus is expelled from the womb and, in normal circumstances, continues his development through the various stages of infancy, childhood, puberty, adolescence, adulthood, and old age.

This development is, throughout life, regulated by chemical substances and cellular structures which derive from the inherited components of the original zygote. In the nucleus of each somatic cell of a human being, there is a chromatin network which, before every cell division, breaks up into 46 threads of varying lengths, the chromosomes. These are replicas of the 46 chromosomes in the original zygote. In the course of a somatic cell division, or mitosis, each chromosome divides along its length into two halves which separate (disjunction), and become components of one or the other nucleus of the two daughter cells[77, 427]. Along the length of each chromosome, genetic information is stored in a chemical code. Each unit of genetic information is called a gene, and each gene has its own characteristic *locus* on a particular chromosome. Together the genes are responsible for regulating and controlling the development of a maturing organism along the lines typical of a species. Human genes account for the common elements among the propensities, reactivities and attributes of human beings.

Not every cell division in human beings, however, produces daughter cells with a complement of 46 chromosomes. This is only true of the mitoses of somatic cells. When germ cells, or gametes, are formed in the gonads, a special form of cell division takes place which results in halving the number of chromosomes. This cell division is called a 'meiosis', and the gametes resulting from it have only 23 chromosomes—a 'haploid' number as compared with the 'diploid' number in somatic cells.

47

When a male gamete (a sperm cell or spermatozoon) fertilizes a female gamete (an egg cell or ovum), a zygote results which again has a diploid number of chromosomes. Thus half of the 46 chromosomes in the somatic cells of an individual come from his father and half from his mother. Each paternal chromosome lines up with the 'homologous' maternal chromosome in the early phases of a cell division. The 46 chromosomes of somatic cells therefore consist of 23 homologous chromosome pairs.

Sex Chromosomes

The chromosomes in each homologous pair are normally of comparable size and shape, except for one pair in human males which consists of a large chromosome, the so-called 'X chromosome', and a small partner, the so-called 'Y chromosome'. The presence of a Y chromosome in a human zygote indicates male sex. A zygote that contains no Y chromosome develops into a female organism. The somatic cells of normal women have two X chromosomes in their nuclei. The X and Y chromosomes have been distinguished as sex chromosomes from the other 22 pairs of autosomal chromosomes, or 'autosomes'. The latter can be arranged according to size and shape, and have been numbered from 1, the largest pair, to 22, the smallest.

During the formation of gametes by meiotic cell division, the number of chromosomes is halved through a disjunction of undivided homologous chromosomes so that the resulting gametes contain only one member of each homologous chromosome pair. For example, the meiotic disjunction of the XY sex chromosome pair in men gives rise to spermatozoa that have either an X or a Y chromosome.

If faults occur during meiotic cell divisions, gametes may result with an abnormally large or small number of chromosomes, perhaps 24 or 22 instead of the usual 23. This can be brought about when the disjunction of a particular homologous chromosome pair does not take place during meiosis, so that one gamete then contains both members of that pair and therefore has 24 chromosomes altogether, whereas the other gamete is without a member of that pair and has only 22 chromosomes. This *non-disjunction* of a particular chromosome pair during meiosis can be a predisposing and specific pathogenic event, if adjuvant conditions and chance influences are such that gametes with a faulty complement of chromosomes take part in a fertilization process, and engender a zygote that is sufficiently viable to grow into an individual that is born alive. The individual then harbours a pathogenic predisposition that may be clinically manifested at birth, or cause overt clinical symptoms at a later time, perhaps only in the middle life or old age.

If non-disjunction of the sex chromosomes occurs during the formation of ova, egg cells are produced which contain either two X chromosomes or none at all. If the abnormal ovum with two X chromosomes is fertilized by a sperm cell containing an X chromosome, an abnormal zygote with three X chromosomes is the result. The term 'trisomy' is used to denote the presence of three homologous chromosomes in the nuclei of somatic cells. If the abnormal ovum with two X chromosomes is fertilized by a spermatozoon with a Y chromosome in it, the resulting zygote also has a trisomy of sex chromosomes, but the composition is XXY this time.

The abnormal ovum without an X chromosome, if fertilized by an X-carrying sperm cell, produces a zygote with only one X chromosome—a condition that comes under the heading of *monosomy* which denotes the presence of only one of a pair of homologous chromosomes in somatic cells. Somatic cells with only one X and no Y chromosomes are said to have an 'XO chromosome', the O standing for zero. If the X-less ovum is fertilized by a Y carrying sperm cell, the result is a zygote with a monosomic YO chromosome, but such a zygote is apparently not viable and dies because the genes present on the large X chromosome seem to be necessary for survival.

Non-disjunction may also occur during spermatogenesis, yielding spermatozoa which either contain both an X and a Y chromosome, or no sex chromosomes at all. The first kind of spermatazoon leads to a zygote with a trisomic XXY composition, and the second kind of spermatozoon to a zygote with a monosomic XO composition.

Individuals with only 45 chromosomes in their somatic cells, because of a monosomic XO chromosome, are anatomically female[67, 140]. Their pathogenic predisposition is revealed by a Turner syndrome[514] of stunted growth, webbed neck and ovarian dysgenesis which causes failure to mature sexually. They may also have malformations of the heart or suffer from deafness and mental subnormality. The incidence of this syndrome is about one in 3000 female births.

Individuals with 47 chromosomes in their somatic cells because of a trisomic XXY chromosome are clinically male[67, 252]. Among 500 male births, there is likely to be one with this pathogenic predisposition. It leads clinically to a Klinefelter syndrome[290] which emerges at puberty and consists of testicular atrophy, infertility, feminine distribution of subcutaneous fat, and scanty facial and pubic hair. The patients tend to be tall in build and subnormal intellectually.

Among 1000 births of female children, there is at least one with a trisomic X chromosome[67, 251]. Such 'superfemales' or 'triple-X females' may be physically normal and do not necessarily develop any clinical symptoms, though they have a tendency to be infertile, and may be intellectually handicapped[83, 281].

Chromosome 21 and Mongolism

The potentially pathogenic event of non-disjunction during meiosis may also affect an autosomal pair of chromosomes, though the survival of zygotes formed from gametes with such autosomal anomalies seems to be rare. The most frequently encountered zygote of this kind[315] is one with a trisomy of the small chromosome 21. It develops into individuals with the well-known clinical picture of mongolism, or Down's syndrome, characterized by mental subnormality, small round heads, slanting eyes (therefore the misleading name of the illness which suggests a non-existent affinity with the Mongolian race), short fingers and an especially reduced middle phalanx of the little finger, over-stretchable joints, often only a single transverse flexion crease across the palm, and several other potential symptoms[397].

Mongolism occurs with an approximate frequency of one in 700 births in populations of European origin. The frequency, however, varies with the mother's age. In a mother of 20, the risk is about one in 2000, and it remains below one in 1000 until the age of 40 is reached. Then there is a steep rise in incidence, reaching a peak of between 2 and 3 per cent in mothers between 45 and 50. This variation with the age of the mother indicates that the pathogenic non-disjunction occurred during oogenesis. There is some evidence which suggests that a similar non-disjunction during spermato-genesis tends to remain without noticeable ill-effects, perhaps because sperm cells with a chromosomal imbalance are not likely to succeed in fertilizing an ovum.

Mongol women occasionally have children. The ova of these patients are of two equally frequent kinds: ova with two chromosomes 21, and ova with only one chromosome 21. When the first kind of ovum is fertilized, a zygote with a trisomic chromosome 21 results which develops into a mongol child. The other kind of ovum, if fertilized, should produce a normal child. As there are an equal number of normal and abnormal ova, and as fertilization is governed by chance, approximately half the children of mongol mothers should show the symptoms of mongolism. This expectation has indeed been confirmed by investigations.

Because of trisomy, mongols should have a total number of 47 chromosomes in their somatic cells. This is, however, not always the case. Many patients with a normal diploid number of 46 chromosomes have been found. Closer investigation of these patients has revealed that meiotic non-disjunction of chromosome 21 is not the only pathogenic cause of mongolism. Another cause is a meiotic *translocation* of chromosome 21. This leads to a fusion of chromosome 21 with another chromosome, most frequently with the chromosomes 15 or 22. The fused chromosomes are denoted as 15/21 or 21/22[397]. In a 15/21 translocation during meiosis, gametes with four different chromosome constitutions result:

(A) Gametes with one chromosome 15 and one chromosome 21. They are normal and, after fertilization, develop into normal individuals.
(B) Gametes with one chromosome 15 and no chromosome 21. They are not viable because of the deficit of chromosome substance.
(C) Gametes with a fused chromosome 15/21 and one chromosome 21. They give rise to a zygote with this complement of relevant chromosomes: a pair which consists of one normal chromosome 15 and one fused chromosome 15/21, and a pair of normal chromosomes 21. The zygote has a normal diploid number of 46 chromosomes, but is, in effect, trisomic for the substance of chromosome 21. It therefore develops into a mongol child.
(D) Gametes with a fused chromosome 15/21 and no chromosome 21. They give rise to a zygote with this complement of relevant chromosomes: 15, 15/21 and a monosomic 21. It has only 45 chromosomes, but a normal amount of the substance of chromosome 21. It develops into an apparently normal individual that is, however, a potential *carrier of mongolism*. Female individuals with this chromosome constitution have ova of four kinds: (*a*) Those with a chromosome 15 and a chromosome 21: they are normal. (*b*) Those with a chromosome 15 and no chromosome 21: they are not viable. (*c*) Those with a chromosome 15/21 and no chromosome 21; they develop into potential carriers of mongolism again. (*d*) Those with a chromosome 15/21 and a chromosome 21: they develop into a mongol child with a normal diploid number of 46 chromosomes.

Whether there are also potential male carriers of mongolism due to a 15/21 transformation is uncertain. It is possible that spermatozoa with abnormal chromosome constitutions are either not viable or do not succeed in fertilizing an ovum[394].

There is, however, some evidence suggesting that a translocation between the chromosomes 21 and 22 can lead to male carriers of mongolism. Men with a monosomic chromosome 21 and a fused chromosome 21/22 are clinically healthy, but some of their sperm cells contain a chromosome 21 and a fused chromosome 21/22. There is some indication that, with increasing age, such sperm cells are more likely to succeed in fertilizing an ovum. The resulting zygote then develops into a mongol child[396].

ABNORMALITIES OF GENES

When abnormalities occur in the chromosome complement of somatic or germ cells, they exert a pathogenic effect because they are accompanied by a massive change in the number and distribution of genes. Pathogenic effects can also appear when the number and distribution of genes is normal but the chemical constitution of one or the other gene has changed. It should, however, be noted that there is this difference: chromosomal abnormalities can today be made visible so that they can be directly observed; gene abnormalities can only be inferred from their effects.

Great progress has recently been made in establishing the chemical composition of genes so that these substances are no longer quite as mysterious and speculative as before. Chemically, a gene consists of desoxyribonucleic acid which is usually abbreviated to DNA[96, 378, 524]. This is a long asymmetrical molecule, resembling in shape a ladder twisted into a spiral, or double helix. Each rung of the twisted ladder consists of a pair of nucleic bases, and there are no more than four nucleic bases, arranged in long sequences, in DNA. Each sequence of three nucleic bases is a chemical code that is transmitted to certain structures in the cell body, the ribosomes, with the help of a soluble polynucleotide, the messenger ribonucleic acid, or messenger RNA. In the ribosomes, proteins are manufactured in accordance with the chemical codes transmitted from the genes.

When we can identify a particular protein, we obtain fairly direct information about the gene responsible for it. It is convenient to speak of a 'specific', or 'major' gene then. Among the proteins which can be identified chemically, or through their effects, are those produced in large quantities (e.g., haemoglobin, myoglobin), the mucoproteins determining a person's blood groups, enzymes of importance in the general metabolism of the body, or those responsible for colour-sensitive substances in the cones of the retina on which a person's ability to recognize colour depends. Most of the attributes and traits of a person which we can identify, derive from a large number of proteins and therefore from a large number of genes. As each gene then has only a modifying influence on the identifiable characteristic, we speak of 'multifactorial', or 'minor' genes.

It is assumed that, during a cell division, the longitudinal splitting of chromosomes is accompanied by a longitudinal splitting of the long DNA molecule into two halves, each of which grows again into a complete DNA molecule. In this molecular reduplication process, faults may arise, just as they can arise in the reduplication of chromosomes. The result is a variation, or *mutation*, of the normal sequence of nucleic bases in some region of a DNA molecule, and this constitutes a mutated gene, or *allele*. Most mutations seriously interfere with the functions of the cell in which they arise, and perhaps also with the normal activities of the whole multicellular organisms.

Mutations as Predisposing Pathogenic Events

Mutations occurring during meiosis are predisposing pathogenic events, if they lead to germ cells with an abnormal gene constitution. The zygotes produced by such germ cells are usually so pathological that they die after some cell divisions. However, if the zygote survives, it can give rise to an organism which, though viable, is encumbered by a pathogenic predisposition. Symptoms may develop during gestation so that they are clinically noticeable at birth (inborn, or congenital symptoms), or they appear in childhood (developmental symptoms), or later in life, perhaps even only in old age.

The life expectancy of people with pathogenic predispositions due to mutations is usually shortened. If they do not reach the stage of sexual reproductiveness, they cannot pass on their pathogenic alleles to subsequent generations, and their hereditary disease dies with them. The mutational aetiology of such a disease is likely to go unrecognized. If the disease appears later in life, it may be genetically transmitted to some children so that the diagnosis of a hereditary disease is facilitated. Gene mutations are very rarely of a kind which is harmless or even beneficial, but such rare events have been responsible for the creation of new species in biological evolution, and for the existence of innocuous alleles within a species.

Just as there are homologous pairs of chromosomes in somatic cells, there are also homologous pairs of genes, one located on the chromosome inherited from the father, and the other at the corresponding *locus* on the homologous chromosome inherited from the mother. If homologous genes are alleles, the people in whom they occur are said to be *heterozygous* with respect to this particular gene. If the effect of one of the alleles predominates, it is called a *dominant* gene, and its more or less silent partner a *recessive* gene. For example, if a child inherits the innocuous gene for blood group A from one parent and the innocuous gene for blood group O from the other, the former gene is dominant and the child therefore has the muco-protein of blood-group substance A in the membrane of his red blood cells. If the dominant gene is pathogenic, it will cause an illness in the presence of certain adjuvant conditions; and if these adjuvant conditions are usual at certain periods of life, the illness may seem: o appear spontaneously at those times. There may be additional conditions which can expedite or delay the onset of such inherited diseases, or cause them to have a recurrent course.

An inherited disease due to a dominant gene is Huntington's chorea[35, 46, 97, 335, 361, 402], consisting clinically of involuntary movements (motor restlessness, twitching of facial muscles, jerking of the head, shrugging of the shoulders, clumsy hand movements or staggering gait) and a progressive dementia that gives rise to a variety of psychiatric symptoms (poor memory for recent events, defective reasoning and concentration, irresponsible and perhaps delinquent behaviour, irritability, violence, vagrancy, depression or paranoid suspicions). In one family, it was possible to trace the disease through 12 generations. The average duration of the disease in a patient is 13 to 14 years. The average age of onset is 35, but there are wide variations so that some patients fall ill in their teens and others remain well until old age. The majority of patients have children by the time they fall ill, and approximately half these children inherit the chromosome with the pathogenic gene. It has been found that affected individuals tend to have significantly more children than their unaffected siblings, and this obviously contributes to the perpetuation of the illness in a family. In the general population, the gene is rare. The estimated rate of mutation of normal genes into abnormal Huntington alleles is 5 per million per generation[415].

We have as yet no knowledge of the biochemical pathology that is caused by the pathogenic gene of Huntington's chorea. It probably consists in changes in the composition of proteins and enzymes in nerve cells of the brain because these cells show patho-logical damage. Unfortunately we have no means yet of studying adequately the composition of proteins in central neurones. We know, however, from the study of other proteins, such as haemo-globin, which can be easily obtained in relatively large quantities, that pathogenic genes can cause an apparently trivial change in an amino acid sequence that forms part of a protein molecule, and that such a change can have far-reaching pathological effects[488].

For example, it has been found that an exchange of one amino acid among approximately 600 contained in normal adult haemoglobin (haemoglobin A), results in a pathological molecule. The amino acid in question is glutamic acid; if it is exchanged for valine, haemoglobin S is obtained, and if it is exchanged for lysine, the result is haemoglobin C. There is evidence to suggest that both haemoglobin S and C are due to different alleles of the normal gene responsible for that part of the haemoglobin molecule. The normal gene for haemoglobin A is dominant and the alleles for haemoglobin S or C are recessive. Thus, a person who is heterozygous for one of these alleles does not fall ill, though he may have some abnormal haemoglobin in his red blood cells. On the other hand, a person who inherits the recessive gene for haemoglobin S from both his parents, is *homozygous* for it and will fall ill with *sickle cell anaemia* which has been very aptly called a 'molecular disease'[388] as its pathology consists in an abnormally structured haemoglobin molecule.

When pathogenic genes lead to abnormally structured protein molecules, we are generally not able to detect the exact change in molecular composition because most proteins are not as readily available for investigation as haemoglobin. We may, however, obtain some indication that a protein is abnormal, if it functions as an enzyme that is responsible for metabolic changes affecting the whole body. An example of such a disease, due to recessive genes, is *phenylketonuria*[93, 139]. The name refers to its main diagnostic sign, the urinary excretion of phenylpyruvic acid and other derivatives of the amino acid phenylalanine. The most noticeable clinical symptoms of the disease are intellectual subnormality of varying degree, developing soon after birth, and a tendency towards diminished skin and eye pigmentation, especially in early infancy. The pathogenic genes of this disease interfere with the production of a liver enzyme that normally converts phenylalanine into tryosine. As a result, phenylalanine and other by-products of this metabolic disorder accumulate in the blood and have a toxic effect on the brain. The excretion of the toxic substances in the urine makes it possible to diagnose this disease entity and to differentiate it from other forms of mental subnormality. The addition of a 5% solution of ferric chloride to the urine of such children produces an olive-green colouration after a few seconds.

The recessive gene of phenylketonuria is quite frequent in some populations. About two per cent of the people in Northern Europe and North America seem to be heterozygous carriers of the gene. Such carriers are not clinically ill, but may be discovered by their inability to metabolize phenylalanine as much as normal people.

About one child in 10,000 inherits the pathogenic gene from both parents and develops the illness. When such children are diagnosed in good time, they can be put on a diet, containing little phenylalanine, and in this way further intellectual deterioration can be prevented[45, 362, 363, 545]. This illustrates the fallacy of a widely held belief that genetic diseases cannot be prevented or modified through treatment. Pathogenic genes are salient causes of disease, and, like other causes of this kind, are affected and modified by adjuvant conditions and chance influences, originating both inside and outside the body. That is why even dominant genes do not always become overt clinically, a fact which geneticists have taken into account by talking of the 'penetrance' of such genes.

Sex-linked Recessive Genes

If a recessive major gene is located on that part of the X chromosome for which no corresponding *locus* exists on the Y chromosome, it manifests itself in men, but its effect is suppressed if there is a normal and dominant gene on the second X chromosome of women. We call a recessive major gene of this kind sex-linked[77, 427]. Examples of such sex-linked abnormalities are the several varieties of red-green *colour blindness* or weakness. People with this sensory defect find it difficult or impossible to distinguish either red or green colours, and may therefore confuse them. Red blindness and red weakness are due to two abnormal alleles with the same gene-*locus* on the X chromosome. The allele for red weakness is dominant to that for red blindness, but recessive to the normal gene. It seems that the pathogenic alleles interfere with the production of a substance in cone cells of the retina, which specifically responds to red light (erythrolabe). The circumstances are similar in green blindness and green weakness, though a different gene-*locus* on the X chromosome seems to be involved. Another substance is reduced in cone cells of the retina, which specifically responds to green light (chlorolabe). The several varieties of red-green colour blindness and weakness occur in 8 to 9 per cent of men, but in less than $\frac{1}{2}$ per cent of women, because women must be homozygous to be affected.

Colour blindness is not regarded as the symptom of a disease as it does not in itself cause suffering and concern. In fact, it may confer a definite advantage in certain circumstances, such as spotting the outline of animals whose colours blend with the environment, or detecting well camouflaged enemy positions from an aeroplane, which are not perceived by people with normal colour vision.

Another sex-linked abnormality that is much rarer, but definitely a disease, is *haemophilia*. Women who are usually heterozygous for the pathogenic, but recessive, gene of this illness are protected by the normal allele on their other X chromosome. They are, however carriers of the illness so that, on the average, half their sons will be haemophiliac and half their daughters carriers. Queen Victoria, for instance, was a carrier transmitting the pathogenic gene to some of her daughters who then introduced haemophilia into the Russian and Spanish Royal families. King Edward VII did not inherit the disease so that the English Royal family is now free from it. The sons of haemophiliac men will all be healthy as they inherit the normal Y chromosome, but all the daughters of such men will be carriers as they all inherit the X chromosome with the pathogenic gene.

X chromosomes can also contain genes which have a protective or modifying effect on certain genes situated on autosomal chromosomes. There exists, for instance, a dominant autosomal gene which causes premature baldness, but does not manifest itself in women in whom it is counteracted by a pair of homologous genes situated on the X chromosomes. Men lack this protection as they have only one X chromosome. A disease of this kind is called a 'sex-controlled', or 'sex-limited', disease.

Population Variations and Genetically Determined Traits

Attributes and traits which are multifactorially determined by many genes, such as height, weight or emotional stability, are not markedly influenced by the presence of one or the other allelic change in a particular gene. However, the effect of alleles is thought to be additive in multifactorially determined characteristics which therefore manifest themselves as variables with a continuous variation in the general population. Let us consider height as an example of such a continuously varying characteristic. We find that, however closely we measure it, whether to the nearest quarter or sixteenth of an inch or centimetre, there are always people in a large population with heights falling in the interval between two normal measurements.

The height of most people lies more or less close to the average of the natural population to which they belong. The more a particular height deviates from this average, the fewer people belong to it. When we plot the frequency of people belonging to different heights, we obtain the 'normal' curve of the statisticians, and this indicates a multifactorial determination by many small influences. In such a normal curve of height, the most common, or 'modal', frequency is found to coincide with the average population height. 95 per cent of people have heights that lie within two 'standard deviations' on either side of the average, and over 99 per cent of people have heights within three standard deviations of it.

The effect of multifactorial genes on the inheritance of a human variable, such as height, may be investigated by comparing the adult stature of sons and fathers. Systematic studies of this kind were first carried out by Galton in the 1880s and evaluated statistically by means of a 'correlational calculus'[177] that was one of his most significant contributions to science. He could show that there was a marked positive correlation between the stature of fathers and sons because tall fathers tended to have tall sons, and short fathers short sons. The correlation coefficient has since been repeatedly found to be about +0·50. Galton also demonstrated what he called a 'regression towards mediocrity of hereditary stature'[176] because he found that exceptionally tall or short fathers had sons whose average adult height was less exceptional and closer to the population mean. We now know that this 'regression to the mean', as it is called today, does not denote a procreative trend condemning future generations to an increase in mediocrity. It is rather a statistical artefact that owes its origin to selecting a group that is exceptional with regard to a particular variable, and then comparing it with a group, selected by a different principle (e.g. kinship), in which the variable is likely to be less exceptional. One could even use this statistical artefact to prove that sons, far from being more mediocre than their fathers in height, are in fact less so. All that is necessary is to select a group of exceptionally tall or short sons and examine the average height of their fathers. It will be nearer the population mean, as a brief inspection of relevant correlation tables will show. The same result would have been obtained if the exceptional sons had been compared with their mothers or siblings.

What has been said about height applies equally well to other attributes of personality, and specially to most psychological traits, which are multifactorially determined and have a normal frequency distribution in the general population. The trait of intelligence, for instance, as measured by standardized tests and expressed in terms of an intelligence quotient, or I.Q. (i.e. a quotient between the average age indicated by a person's test results and his chronological age, multiplied by 100), has a frequency distribution which approximates that of a normal curve. The mean I.Q. is 100 and signifies that the test-indicated and chronological age are identical. The standard deviation of the I.Q. curve has been found to be about 15. We expect therefore that about 95 per cent of the population will lie between 70 and 130 (i.e. two standard deviations below and above 100), and that more than 99 per cent will lie between 55 and 145.

People with I.Q.s below 70 are usually regarded as intellectually subnormal, though not ill on that account. The number of people with I.Q.s between 45 and 70 corresponds approximately to the number expected by the frequency distribution of the 'normal curve'. It is customary to regard people in this subnormal I.Q. range as a *multifactorial* or *subcultural* group of mental deficiency, i.e. as having an abnormality that is not morbid. The number of people with an I.Q. below 45, although small, is yet greater than expected on the basis of a normal distribution of I.Q.s in the general population[397]. It is generally found that such a severe degree of mental subnormality is due to specific pathogenic causes, such as a pathogenic mutation of a major gene or physical brain injury. It is therefore customary to talk of *specific* or *pathological* mental defects when referring to this group of patients.

If patients with specific mental defects are excluded, an approximate correlation coefficient of +0·50 is found when the intelligence of parents and children, or the intelligence of siblings, is compared. This is apparently a correlation of the same magnitude as that obtained for the personality attribute of height. It is, however, known that correlation coefficients are reduced when variables cannot be accurately measured, and as the measurement of height is certainly more accurate than that of intelligence, the correlation coefficient of +0·50 for intelligence is obviously an underestimate.

It is not surprising that the statistical artefact of a regression to the mean can also be found when a group of normal people with exceptionally high or low intelligence is compared with a group selected by kinship. For example, when Terman and his collaborators re-examined, after an interval of 25 years, a group of exceptionally gifted persons with an average I.Q. of 152, they found that the children of these persons only had an average I.Q. of 128, representing a regression to the mean by nearly one half[496]. A similar regression was found by Fraser Roberts when he selected from a large sample of children the lowest 8 per cent in intelligence, who had an average I.Q. of 77·4, and compared them with their siblings who were found to have a mean I.Q. score of 88·1[426].

Most psychological abilities, skills and temperaments are determined by multifactorial influences of which only some originated in the past while others derive from circumstances that affect the manifestation of psychological traits under test conditions, and from the errors incurred in measuring or ranking the traits. As a result, the measurement of psychological traits is likely to yield scores with a normal frequency distribution in the general population. We may, for instance, choose temperamental traits and range them from, say, timidity to courage, from intrapunitive self-torture to extrapunitive aggression, from indolence to overactivity, from shyness to ostentation, and so on. We may even extract several general factors from such a set of temperamental traits. Both the individual traits and the factors, derived from them, are likely to be normally distributed in the general population. It follows from this that there must always be a minority of people falling at either extreme of the variable's range, and this may mean that the persons concerned have either unusual talents or unusual handicaps. The handicaps may cause suffering and concern, and thus become psychological complaints and symptoms. It has, however, been argued that such symptoms are not due to pathological changes and therefore do not indicate a psychiatric disease. They are then regarded as the symptoms of a 'personality disorder'. According to this argument, neurotic and psychopathic persons, and also the mental defectives of the subcultural group, are merely freak personalities and not patients at all.

Studies on Twins

It is difficult to assess the relative significance of heredity and environment, of 'nature and nurture', in the development of personality attributes or the causation of disease. The most promising results in this field can be obtained by twin studies. This was first realized by Galton who anticipated the later discovery that there can be two kinds of twins: those who develop from two ova, fertilized by different spermatozoa, and those who develop from one fertilized ovum which split into two separate parts after the first mitotic division of the zygote[172]. The first kind of twins we now call *dizygotic*, or fraternal twins; and the second kind, *monozygotic*, or identical twins. Each dizygotic twin inherits different sets of genes from each of his parents. Such twins are therefore no more genetically similar than other siblings and may, for example, be of different sex. Monozygotic twins, on the other hand, are theoretically identical with regard to their genetic endowment and must have the same sex as they are bound to contain the same set of sex chromosomes. Galton reasoned that dizygotic twins who share the same womb antenatally and who, after birth, are brought up together may be thought to encounter approximately the same environmental influences. Any difference between dizygotic twins must therefore be mainly due to differences of heredity. Any difference between monozygotic twins, on the other hand, can only be attributed to differences in the environment.

It is not likely that, in normal circumstances, twins, brought up together, encounter very different environmental events. Monozygotic twins, with their identical heredity, should therefore be much more alike in general than dizygotic twins, with their different heredity. This has, in fact, been borne out by many investigations. Shields[456, 457], for instance, found a correlation coefficient between the heights of monozygotic twins of $+0.94$, which was very near the maximum possible coefficient of $+1.0$—a maximum that is not likely to be obtained in practice because of errors and chance effects. The comparable coefficient in dizygotic twins was only $+0.44$. Personality traits cannot be as accurately measured as height, and this in itself is bound to lower obtainable correlation coefficients. The lower correlations which Shields found for intelligence ($+0.76$ for monozygotic and $+0.51$ for dizygotic twins) might therefore have been partly due to the greater uncertainty of measurement. The even lower correlations obtained for extraversion and neuroticism might similarly have reflected the still greater unreliability of measuring these personality traits by means of self-assessments in answer to brief questionnaires. For extraversion, the respective correlations were $+0.42$ and -0.17; and for neuroticism $+0.38$ and $+0.11$.

The low correlations for these personality traits in monozygotic twins might, however, also have been largely due to environmental differences. Shields' investigation was, in fact, chiefly designed to elucidate the influence of different environments on personality traits by comparing monozygotic twins brought up apart with those brought up together. He succeeded in assembling data on 44 monozygotic twins who had been separated early in life and reared in different homes. The careful analysis of these data, however, revealed that environmental differences had only minor effects on height, intelligence and extraversion, and a slightly more definite effect on self-assessed neuroticism. It must, however, be admitted that the environmental differences encountered by the separated twins were not very large. The twins were all brought up and educated in the same milieu of Western culture. Certainly there were some differences in the respective social environments of the twins brought up apart—in the ages, personalities and psychiatric health of adoptive parents, their social class, urban or rural residence, the presence or absence of other children in the family, and so on. But the effect of such differences on inherited dispositions was relatively trivial. To quote Shields: "By and large, differences in early family structure and upbringing did not, in this investigation, stand out as all-important causes of differences in later personality."

To mention just two examples: A pair of monozygotic female twins remained in the same Children's Home until their separation at 16 months and adoption into different working class families. One of them discovered, at the age of 32, that she was a twin. She succeeded, at the age of 36, in tracing her sister with Shields' help, and met her for the first time. It was found that both were extraverted, talkative, dressed smartly, did not use make-up, and were non-smokers. They had married at the same age, and each had two children. They had taken part in amateur theatricals, preferring comic parts; they had liked taking on jobs as door-to-door saleswomen; and they had kept a variety of animal pets in the house. There was a slight difference in size and weight, and one twin was left-handed.

The other example concerns a pair of monozygotic male twins who were separated at birth, and spent the first five years, respectively, in an orphanage and a few foster homes. After living together for over a year at the age of five, one was subsequently brought up in an Anglo-Chinese working class home, and the other in an English middle class family. They were both of low intelligence, had been enuretic till puberty, had convictions for stealing in their teens, had frightened their environment by a tendency to set fire to things, were heavy smokers, liked to gamble, were fastidious about their appearance, never had girl friends, and developed similar schizophrenic symptoms at the age of 22, from which they had not recovered four years later.

Other twin studies and investigations of family pedigrees have revealed a genetic aetiology in many psychiatric diseases[174, 274, 457]. When heredity plays a major role, both members of a monozygotic twin pair tend to fall ill with the same psychiatric disorder, even if the actual psychiatric manifestations may vary in detail. If this is the case, we speak of a high concordance rate. In the same circumstances, dizygotic twins have a smaller concordance rate because of their different genetic endowment.

Juda[265] examined 189 twins with subcultural (or, as she called it, 'endogenous') mental subnormality and found 100 per cent concordance in monozygotic and only 58 per cent concordance in dizygotic twins. Kallmann[273] found 100 per cent concordance for homosexuality in 37 monozygotic male twins, but some discordant monozygotic pairs have since been discovered[274, 291, 296, 384, 412]. In 26 same-sexed dizygotic male twins the concordance rate for homosexuality was only 12 per cent. In schizophrenia, manic-depressive illness, and idiopathic epilepsy, the concordance rate in monozygotic twins is only between 40 and 50 per cent, but this is still very much higher than the dizygotic concordance rate. In atypical psychotic diseases of a schizophreniform kind, family investigations often detect similar atypical illnesses among the patients' parents and more distance relatives. Shields and Slater found that, in neurotic twins, the monozygotic and dizygotic concordance rate was 53 and 25 per cent, respectively[457].

Hallgren's investigations of specific reading disabilities[210] in children ('specific developmental dyslexia', or 'developmental word-blindness') suggested the existence of a dominant gene because half the children of an affected parent showed the same reading difficulties. A dominant gene has likewise been suspected to be responsible for the inheritance of tune deafness[275]. A recessive gene may be the cause of a harmless taste deficiency for phenylthiocarbamide, a substance in the rind of grapefruits which tastes bitter to 70 per cent of people in our population. The capacity for spatial orientation has also been assumed to have a genetic root.

Little or no evidence for a genetic aetiology has been found with regard to adolescent behaviour disorders and juvenile delinquency. In these disorders, monozygotic and dizygotic concordance rates are almost identical and the concordance may be as much as 70 to 80 per cent.

CHAPTER 8

PHYSIOGENIC AETIOLOGIES IN PSYCHIATRY

In this chapter, we turn to pathogenic events which occur in the course of a patient's life, originate outside the psychoneural pool and are transmitted to it by other routes than preformed sensory pathways so that these physiogenic causes of psychoneural pathology remain unperceived by the patient. The physiogenic aetiology of psychiatric symptoms can be divided into physical and chemical pathogenic events. If the events are precipitating causes and generally pathogenic, they are sometimes called traumas, or traumata.

Physical Trauma

A physical trauma to psychoneural processes can be acute or gradual in onset. An acute trauma, such as a severe blow to the head or an electric shock applied to the brain, causes a sudden stunning through a direct suspension of central nervous functions. On the other hand, a trauma that is gradually increasing in severity allows us to distinguish various stages in the progressive impairment of these functions. We shall therefore begin by considering a gradually increasing physical trauma to the brain, such as a gradually rising intracranial pressure through a brain tumour, cerebral oedema, subdural haematoma, and the like.

Gradually Increasing Physical Trauma

The psychoneural effects of an insidiously rising intracranial pressure change from person to person, partly because the precipitating causes are different and partly because adjuvant conditions vary, such as the rate of increase of the intracranial pressure and differences in the psychoneural reactivities of patients, but there are certain effects which occur typically. The raised intracranial pressure may cause headache. Initially, this subjective symptom often occurs in acute paroxysms, or it starts early in the morning and improves gradually in the course of the day. It is intensified by all procedures which raise the intracranial pressure, such as coughing, straining, or stooping. Another subjective symptom is nausea, and it may be associated with the objective symptoms of retching and vomiting. There is often a discordance between subjective and objective symptoms; some patients vomit without feeling nauseated, and others complain of nausea without showing the objective signs of being nauseated.

A third subjective symptom is the patient's awareness of a dulling of his mental capacities. He notices that he cannot think as clearly as before, that he cannot concentrate as well, and that his actions are not as adequately timed and co-ordinated as they used to be. Objectively, this symptom is revealed in a lowering of the patient's responsiveness. His spontaneous activities are reduced in number, speed and accuracy. As this clouding, or 'obfuscation' of consciousness grows more severe, it becomes obvious that the patient loses contact with his environment and may therefore engage in behaviour that is absurd. He then shows the signs of an organic confusional state.

An early sign of clouded consciousness is the patient's disorientation in time. He may not correctly know what day of the week it is, or be unable to give the correct date, month or even year. As the obfuscation progresses, the patient cannot orient himself adequately in unfamiliar environments, and is thus liable to lose his way and wander about for some time before his plight is recognized. As the patient's appreciation of his environment becomes more blurred, he fails to recognize familiar people and may misidentify them. The first stages of a clouded consciousness are thus characterized by disorientation in time, place and person. He also has difficulties in remembering new experiences so that his memory is paradoxically poor for recent events, but comparatively good for happenings in his earlier life. This memory disturbance is known as the dysmnesic syndrome. Another early symptom is perseveration which causes the patient to continue with a particular response, though a change in the environment has occurred that demands a different reaction from him. Perseveration is often very obvious on clinical examination because the patient, after answering one question, goes on repeating the same reply in response to different questions.

The emotional symptoms patients initially display consist often of a surprising indifference and unconcern in the face of their obvious objective inability to cope adequately with the routine demands of life. It is as though they were not aware of the mental shortcomings they have developed. Some patients go even further and deny having any symptoms, mental or physical. This anosognosia (from the Greek *a*, without; *nosos*, disease; and *gnosis*, knowledge) may be obstinately maintained in defiance of all objective evidence to the contrary[19, 527]. However, when a recognition of his mental and physical inadequacy forces itself on the clouded consciousness of a patient, his indifference can be temporarily replaced by an outburst of irritation and temper—a 'catastrophic reaction' as it has been called by K. Goldstein[191].

An organically confused patient can behave in a way that can have damaging physical or social consequences for him. He may wash his hands in the soup served to him, undress in public, or pass water in the drawing room; he may help himself to other people's property in full view of bystanders; or he may walk across a busy street without paying attention to fast-flowing traffic. As such behaviour does not seem to be controlled by considerations of the environment, it has been regarded as machine-like automatic behaviour, or automatism[196]. The implication of this assumption is that the behaviour is performed in a private, imagined or hallucinated world that is completely divorced from reality. There are, however, all gradations of automatic behaviour, ranging from the absent-minded action of normal people who still respond to many objectively real aspects of the environment, to the erratic actions of confused patients who seem to react to some shadowy impression of the actual environment, and the even more erratic activities of delirious and somnambulistic patients for whom the external world is almost nonexistent.

As the clouding of consciousness deepens, the patient's exteroceptive perceptions are eventually more or less completely replaced by fitfully changing hallucinations similar to those we all know from our dreams. He sees visions, hears sounds, smells odours, or feels bodily sensations which are not objectively justified. At the same time, he is not deprived of sustained motor activity and locomotion as is the case with a sleeping person. He thus often moves restlessly about in response to a hallucinated world he shares with nobody. He may show signs of fear and terror, of pain, anger or curiosity, or of pleasure, joy and even ecstasy. He may mumble to himself, speak to imaginary partners, shout, cry or laugh. Patients with such symptoms are in a state of delirium.

When the clouding of consciousness becomes further intensified, the patient loses contact even with his hallucinated world of delirious experiences. He no longer moves spontaneously, but lies in an unconscious stupor*. In this state, only reflex activities can still be elicited, pain still evokes semipurposive movements, and the muscles still retain their postural tone. When reflexes can no longer be obtained, nor reactions of pain, and when the muscles are flaccid,

---

* There is also an akinetic stupor which occurs in catatonic schizophrenia and severe depression. It is a condition of stuporous immobility in patients who remain in concious contact with their environment as shown by the movements of their eyes.

the patient is in *coma*, the deepest stage of unconsciousness. The only spontaneous movements such patients still show are slow movements of the eyes from side to side and respiratory movements which vary from a deep and stertorous activity to a superficial and sighing breathing.

Acute Physical Trauma

When an acute physical trauma suddenly disrupts psychoneural processes, it causes immediate coma. The trauma may consist of a cerebral concussion, an electric shock to the brain, an epileptic seizure, or an intracerebral haemorrhage. The resulting coma is of varying duration, and as the patient recovers from it, his responsiveness improves so that he passes, more or less quickly and in reverse order, through the various stages of clouded consciousness just described, until he either sinks into a normal sleep or becomes conscious of his environment, and perhaps also of a dulling of his mental capacities, a painful head and a feeling of nausea.

If the acute physical trauma has not caused localized neurological lesions in addition to the functional interference with diffuse psychoneural processes, the patient can recover completely.

After a cerebral concussion, there may remain, in some predisposed persons and for a varying length of time, certain clinical residuals. Among such post-concussional symptoms[359, 360, 490] are an increased tendency to headaches, occasional attacks of a momentary clouding of consciousness (generally described by the patients as giddiness or black-out), difficulty in sustaining mental concentration, increased irritability, and a reduced tolerance of noise, bright lights and alcohol. There are also indications that among post-concussional residuals there is occasionally a predisposition to develop the kind of altered consciousness that is found in hysterical trance states.

When persons suffer repeated concussions (e.g. boxers who are frequently knocked out), there may be an accumulation of post-concussional symptoms. If warning signs are not heeded in time, the end result may be the chronic disease of *punch-drunkenness*[102]. It consists clinically of memory disturbances, dulling of intellect, slurring of speech, a reeling gait, and coarse tremors.

Chemical Traumas: Toxic Substances

The physiogenic aetiology of a psychoneural pathology may also be due to chemical traumas, or toxic substances. Some of these traumas are precipitating events, others also have a predisposing component; some toxic substances are generally pathogenic, others are only idiosyncratic causes of psychopathological reactions in susceptible people.

Cerebral anoxia, however caused, is a precipitating and generally pathogenic cause of psychiatric symptoms. It may develop so rapidly that the patient loses consciousness with such speed that he cannot realize his danger and take evasive action. This happens, for instance, when a coal miner accidentally puts his head into a cavity filled with methane gas, or when a worker climbs down the shaft of a well whose bottom is covered with carbon dioxide. Following such an incident, there is often also a delayed effect occurring several hours after rescue and recovery; it consists of headache, nausea, and emotional lability. It is reminiscent of the hang-over after excessive indulgence in alcohol. When the onset of cerebral anoxia is gradual, as in mountaineers[200], for instance, the symptoms which develop can be very similar to those caused by a gradually increased intracranial pressure. There may be headache, nausea, vomiting, and a subjective awareness of mental dulling. Often there is a discordance between subjective and objective symptoms; in particular, individuals may not be aware of their mental dulling, their reduced perceptual contact with the environment, the slowness and inaccuracy of their responses, and their weakened judgment. They may thus behave in a foolhardy way that invites disaster. When they are given oxygen in time, the sudden increase in the clarity of perception and thought comes as a surprise to them. During mild anoxia, the mood may change to elation, depression, suspiciousness, stubborness, or irritability, and there may be unpleasant emotional outbursts. As anoxia increases, the patient becomes increasingly disoriented, delirious and drowsy, until he eventually shows the ominous signs of unconscious stupor and coma.

Among toxic substances, there are some which produce no untoward reactions when they are administered once or twice in small doses. Yet they may be generally pathogenic, if the small doses are frequently repeated so that cumulative and eventually pathological changes occur. Some substances of this kind interfere with psychoneural processes and can thus cause mental disease. An example of such a substance is mercury which was widely used in the manufacture of felt hats in the last century. There was then no adequate protection of workers against the inhalation of mercury vapours. As a result, the psychiatric disease of mercury encephalopathy developed in many hatters. The patients became emotionally disturbed, anxious, depressed, irritable, aggressive, and sometimes also deluded and hallucinated. They had marked muscular tremors and twitches to which the name 'hatters' shakes' was given. The 'mad hatter' may thus have been a frequent reality before Lewis Carroll immortalized his caricature.

The best-known example of a toxic substance that is generally pathogenic and precipitates an acute onset of psychiatric symptoms is alcohol. In fact, the term 'intoxication', when used without a qualifying adjective, is commonly understood to mean alcoholic intoxication. The symptoms of acute alcoholic intoxication depend on the amount of alcohol contained in the blood reaching the brain (exogenous cause) and the psychoneural reactivity to alcohol (endogenous cause) of a particular subject. When the concentration of alcohol in the blood rises above 0·15 per cent, it invariably interferes with psychoneural processes[122]. The clarity of consciousness begins to be clouded, though this may not be subjectively realized. The reduction in alertness and responsiveness, which is the objective sign of a clouded consciousness, may not be immediately apparent because the flow of ideas and the fluency of speech may be speeded up for a time, especially in the presence of convivial and stimulating company. This increase in the speed of thought and speech is, however, only achieved at the cost of accuracy and self-criticism. Mood may become euphoric and self-confident, irritable and aggressive, or maudlin and tearful. Motor co-ordination suffers, and eventually the person's speech becomes thick and dysarthric, and his gait unsteady and staggering. As the alcohol content of the blood rises, even the most stimulating social environment fails to prevent the onset of sleep which may deepen into a drunken stupor and finally coma. This typical clinical picture is so familiar and so commonly encountered after alcoholic excesses that the disease entity has been given the aetiological label of 'acute alcohol intoxication'. Such an aetiological diagnosis may, however, mislead us occasionally because a very similar clinical picture can be caused by a variety of pathogenic events, like concussion, cerebral anoxia or the presence of other toxic substances in the blood. A motorist, for instance, may be wrongly accused of being under the influence of alcohol when he, in fact, shows concussional symptoms after an earlier car accident or has been overcome by exhaust fumes that had seeped into the car interior.

Sedative, hypnotic and tranquillizing drugs may produce psychiatric symptoms similar to those caused by alcohol because they also diminish the level of consciousness and make the patient somnolent. In excessive dosage, they can lead to unconscious stupor, coma and death. A similar lowering of consciousness follows after injections of insulin which reduce the blood sugar level and thus diminish the supply of glucose on which the adequate functioning of cerebral neurones depends. Mild degrees of such insulin hypoglycaemia occur in many diabetics who are not too careful about the dosage of insulin they inject or the amount of carbohydrates they eat. They may display a variety of emotional symptoms as their first reactions, ranging from anxiety, depression and truculence to agitation and aggressiveness. Their behaviour is often very similar to that of a person intoxicated by alcohol. A tremor develops and disturbs the co-ordination of fine movements. The patients look flushed and may perspire profusely. Eventually they become delirious, agitated, and may have epileptic attacks. The final stages consist in unconscious stupor and coma. Unless glucose is administered then, intravenously or by stomach tube, the patient may die.

The occurrence of mental symptoms after an excessive amount of alcohol or the administration of poisons has suggested to many ancient and modern physicians the possibility that other mental symptoms might also have a toxic aetiology. In the past, this toxic, or 'humoral' theory of insanity inspired therapeutic attempts which were aimed at removing the noxious 'humours' from the body through blood-letting, purging, vomiting, blistering, cutting and similar measures. Such treatments were, in fact, routine procedures in 'madhouses' up to the nineteenth century[243, 314]. The search for toxic substances in the blood of mental patients still goes on, though it has as yet yielded few definite results. In some organic psychiatric diseases, toxic substances indeed accumulate in the blood causing delirium or coma. This happens, for instance, when the toxins of invading micro-organisms affect the brain, or when the functions of the liver or the kidneys fail. In functional psychiatric diseases, however, no toxic origin has so far been established by investigations that are reliable and objective enough to allow independent confirmation.

A by-product of the search for a toxic aetiology of psychiatric disease has been the study of 'artificial psychoses'[16, 39, 41, 293, 339, 348, 486] after administering toxic substances which are less commonplace than alcohol. Particular favourites have been opium, hashish (Indian hemp, marihuana, Cannabis Indica), mescaline (obtained from a Mexican cactus) and lysergic acid diethylamide (LSD). These and similar substances have been grouped together as 'hallucinogenic' or 'psychotomimetic' substances. They cause a clouding of consciousness and an enhancement of visual imagery which varies in detail according to the personality of the subject and his expectations. For example, after taking mescaline, Havelock Ellis experienced kaleidoscopic visions in gorgeous colours and spoke of a 'new artificial paradise'. Aldous Huxley was not quite so enthusiastic, but he also experienced an enrichment of colours and a sense of living in a miraculous world. Others were less fortunate, and merely felt sick and uncomfortable. A similar range of sensations and visions has been reported after taking LSD. The effect of a single application of a 'hallucinogenic' drug, however, soon wears off and the patient returns to his normal self with no other adverse consequences than perhaps a mild hangover.

Effect of Individual Predispositions on Symptoms

The variable symptoms produced by toxic substances indicate how important the endogenous factor of individual predisposition is. This endogenous factor may be potentially so pathogenic that it causes an idiosyncratic mental reaction to substances which are harmless to the majority of a population. For example, sugar and other carbohydrates which are not only harmless, but even necessary, constituents of a normal diet are idiosyncratically toxic to a patient with *diabetes mellitus*. If he eats them in normal quantities, toxic substances may accumulate in his blood, causing eventually a diabetic coma. There are other, usually innocuous, substances which become idiosyncratic causes of brain disease in specifically susceptible individuals. We mentioned, in the last chapter, that a genetically determined fault in an enzyme in liver cells can cause a pathological susceptibility to the usually harmless amino acid phenylalanine[45] so that *phenylketonuria* and mental subnormality result. Mother's milk is generally regarded as the prototype of a suitable and wholesome food for babies, but there are babies who respond unfavourably to it. They may have become temporarily unable to digest it, or have acquired an allergic hypersensitivity to it. They may also have been born with a pathogenic gene and therefore lack an enzyme necessary for the normal metabolism of milk sugar so that *galactosaemia* results with consequent damage to the brain, liver and ocular lens[240].

Some diseases give rise to changes in the blood which interfere with psychoneural processes only in predisposed persons who then develop psychiatric symptoms and perhaps even 'symptomatic pyschoses'. Patients suffering from *pernicious anaemia*[128, 544], for instance, occasionally exhibit depressive and irritable moods, apathy, paranoid psychoses (often with tactile hallucinations) and deliria. *Vitamin deficiencies*[261, 489] are sometimes associated with mental manifestations. Pellagra may cause emotional disturbances, especially depressions, and deliria; deficiencies of vitamin B can have similar psychiatric consequences and also affect the patient's memory and intellectual capacities.

An increase of thyroid hormone in the blood in *Graves's disease*[124] produces occasionally the clinical pictures of hypomanic excitation, or an anxiously depressed state, or delirious disturbances. A reduction of thyroid hormones in *myxoedema*[6, 17, 258] causes, in certain predisposed persons, epileptic fits which may end in coma and death, or psychoses with hallucinations and delusions of a paranoid or depressive kind. Some symptoms may not completely disappear after a successful cure of the myxoedema, and the patients may be left with a definite degree of dementia and memory disturbance.

The reduction of sexual hormones during *menopause* may be associated with emotional instability, anxiety and depression. Hormonal changes preceding menstruation may be accompanied by a *premenstrual tension state* in susceptible women who then complain of headache, nausea, dizziness, insomnia, irritability, anxiety attacks and depression[90, 107, 108, 109, 143, 201, 372, 417]. Hormonal changes in *early pregnancy* may be responsible for some symptoms, such as peculiarities of appetite ('pica'), emotional lability, depression and early morning sickness. The hormonal upheaval in the *puerperium* may be the idiosyncratic cause of psychiatric diseases which begin at that time in about one out of a thousand women. Puerperal psychoses often consist of a mixture of depressive, schizophrenic and delirious symptoms, and they may leave invaliding residuals behind. Even without a manifest puerperal psychosis, there are occasionally marked changes in personality after childbirth. If these changes include the development of sexual frigidity and a fear of intercourse, marital disharmony may result[12, 142, 212, 444, 497].

Toxic substances in small therapeutic amounts may also become the idiosyncratic pathogenic causes of psychiatric 'side effects' in specifically vulnerable people. Occasionally, a relatively small amount of alcohol can give rise to a delirious picture. Such patients can become aggressive, rowdy and even murderous, but have no recollection of their behaviour when they recover from this *pathological drunkenness* (or *mania à potu*)[350, 369]. Another kind of idiosyncratic response to small doses of alcohol is artificially induced for therapeutic purposes. This is done by administering the drug *antabuse* (disulfiram) which prevents the normal metabolic breakdown of alcohol in the body, causing an accumulation of acetaldehyde in the blood which gives rise to unpleasant toxic symptoms, such as headache, flushing, perspiration, nausea, vomiting, and sometimes even an alarming circulatory collapse[209, 253, 254].

Atropine in therapeutic doses is a useful drug that does not normally interfere with psychoneural processes. Many patients, undergoing eye surgery, for example, receive regular eye drops of 1%

atropine sulphate without showing any psychological ill-effect. There are, however, some patients with an idiosyncrasy to atropine. A few of them respond with severe psychiatric symptoms, become excited, confused and delirious. There are others whose reactions are much milder. They may merely show emotional lability or slightly confused and disturbed behaviour, and are therefore liable to be diagnosed as having a neurotic reaction to the stress of the eye operation and the discomfort of the post-operative régime. Such a wrong diagnosis may expose them to critical and disparaging remarks, and the chance of an immediate recovery through discontinuing the atropine eye drops is often missed[21].

Idiosyncratic psychiatric symptoms are also encountered after other drugs. *Reserpine*, for instance, which is widely used in the treatment of high blood pressure and was, at one time, also recommended in schizophrenia and anxious-obsessive neuroses, may occasionally cause such a profound depressive mood of hopeless despair that the unfortunate patient is driven to suicide[435]. *Cortisone* and related preparations provide other examples. They are valuable drugs in the therapy of many illnesses, such as functional deficiencies of the adrenal cortex or the pituitary, rheumatoid arthritis, collagen diseases, and allergic disorders. They generally give rise to a psychological reaction of euphoria so that the patients' subjective feelings of well-being may be at variance with their objective clinical state. In some susceptible persons, serious psychiatric disturbances develop, such as restlessness, confusion and delirium. It has been shown that this response is due to a specific idiosyncrasy to cortisone and is unrelated to any predisposition to other psychiatric diseases. The past mental history of a patient can therefore not be used as a guide to forecast his response to cortisone[320].

Drug Addiction

Some toxic substances may include among their idiosyncratic effects a psychological residual in the form of a craving for the drug[295]. If the drug is readily available, it will be taken repeatedly and, in predisposed persons, the craving will gradually turn into an *emotional dependence* on the drug. The most characteristic symptom of such a dependence is a fear of being without the drug. If the drug is hard to obtain, the susceptible patient's whole life may become centred around ways and means of getting hold of it by hook or by crook. All social and ethical considerations may be jettisoned, and all activities subordinated to this overriding aim. With certain drugs, especially morphine and heroin, this emotional dependence is aggravated by a *physical dependence*. The patient's body so adapts itself to the repeated applications of the drug that its sudden discontinuance has a disastrous physiopathological effect and gives rise to harassing and dangerous *withdrawal symptoms*. Patients who are enslaved by their emotional and physical dependence on a drug, and whose well-being is threatened by withdrawal symptoms, are said to suffer from drug addiction. The term is, however, often loosely applied to indicate merely an emotional dependence on a drug which does not cause physical dependence and withdrawal symptoms.

Addiction to morphine, heroin and cocaine[74, 198, 249, 387, 503] is relatively uncommon in Britain, but it is a serious problem in the United States. Cocaine causes not only the symptoms of drug addiction but may give rise to delirious states, when the patients are hallucinated, hear threatening voices and feel small animals crawling on their skin. In hospital, the addiction to any of these drugs reveals itself, first of all, by the patient's emotional dependence on it, his fear of being deprived of adequate supplies, and by his manifold, and often ingenious, machinations aimed at obtaining an illicit stock of them. Characteristic of the success of such manœuvres is a recurrent transformation of such a patient from an anxious, preoccupied, complaining individual into a contented, carefree and perhaps even sparkling companion. Such a transformation is most suspect, when it occurs after a brief absence of the patient from sight, after a visit by friends, or after forming a close friendship with another patient who can leave the hospital occasionally or mix freely with visitors.

An addiction to barbiturates can develop in predisposed persons. Barbiturates are very freely and frequently prescribed by medical practitioners, but the number of susceptible people is not large, The most tell-tale sign of barbiturate addiction is a history of unexplained falls and bruises. The speech of these patients may be slurred, their gait unsteady, their hands tremulous, and their memory unreliable. They show the usual fear that the drug may be withdrawn, and, if they are abruptly deprived of the drug, may develop panic attacks, delirious states and epileptic fits.

Amphetamine[88, 282] and allied drugs, which are used to induce alertness and a mood of well-feeling, can also cause addiction. Predisposed patients become emotionally and physically dependent on the drug. The physical dependence reveals itself by a progressive increase of the dosage required and by withdrawal symptoms of sleepiness and depression. Some addicts can tolerate surprisingly high amounts of amphetamine without apparent ill-effects, others may develop restlessness, insomnia, perceptual and intellectual disturbances, transient delirious episodes, or paranoid ideas without obvious clouding of consciousness.

Alcohol[259] is commonly regarded as typically addiction-forming, yet it does so only in comparatively few people, and after at least ten years of habituation to excessive doses, or 'alcohol abuse'. In some wine drinking countries, as in France, there are people who take alcohol continuously, i.e. in the same way as drugs are taken by other addicts, every day and at regular intervals so that the alcohol content in the blood can never sink too low and cause withdrawal symptoms. Such continual drinkers often show no signs of intoxication, merely the signs of emotional, and perhaps physical dependence. For the most part, however, alcohol is taken episodically, and for the sake of its intoxicating effect. This habit of episodic drinking is often socially sanctioned or facilitated. There are occupations, such as that of publican or commercial traveller, which are particularly exposed to the temptation of episodic alcohol abuse. On the other hand, there are cultural groups, such as the Chinese and the Jews, who disapprove of drunkenness, except perhaps on certain festive occasions, and the incidence of alcohol abuse among their members is low.

People who abuse alcohol episodically increase their tolerance of it so that they can drink larger quantities than abstemious drinkers and yet escape being totally incapacitated. When alcohol abuse is transformed into alcohol addiction, patients lose control of their alcohol intake and can no longer prevent themselves from becoming totally incapacitated at every drinking bout. They may still remain 'bout drinkers', or 'dipsomaniacs', whose alcoholic sprees occur only on special occasions or when they feel depressed. Yet in every bout they reach a stage of clouded consciousness which leaves no memories behind so that they later have a 'memory black-out' for their experiences when drunk. When the bout has been severe and prolonged, the misery of their subsequent hangover may be complicated by epileptic fits and by the frightening and harassing visions of a brief *delirium tremens*[250, 333, 492]. When patients are forced by their hangover agony to keep on drinking to prevent withdrawal symptoms, they have become chronic addicts who are both emotionally and physically dependent on their supply of alcohol. They are afraid to be without a bottle of alcohol; they sneak drinks during the day and may have a drinking bout every evening, of which they remember little or nothing the following morning.

The chronic poisoning of the brain through alcohol, together with the dietary and vitamin B deficiencies that generally accompany alcohol addiction, eventually cause permanent structural damage in the nervous system, the liver, heart, and other organs. The damage to the nervous system reveals itself clinically by an almost complete dysmnesic inability to remember recent experiences, by muscular in-coordination and paralyses, and by the painful and disabling signs of a peripheral polyneuritis—the 'Korsakoff' and 'Wernicke' syndromes. Sometimes there is only a permanent functional disorder of psychoneural processes, which causes auditory hallucinations in a setting of clear consciousness (alcoholic hallucinosis).

CHAPTER 9

PSYCHOGENIC AETIOLOGIES IN PSYCHIATRY

Events which originate outside the psychoneural pool and are transmitted to it through sensory nerves so that they are perceptually experienced are both *psychogenic events* and, at the same time, *psychological experiences*. If such events cause suffering and concern, they are both *psycho-pathogenic events* and *pathological experiences* which give rise to clinical symptoms. Endopathological physical lesions anywhere in the body can be psycho-pathogenic events in this sense, when their perceptual experience is a sensation of pain, nausea, giddiness, blindness, or other *sensory symptom*. Similarly, an environmental event can be psycho-pathogenic in this sense, when its perceptual experience causes fear, depression, disappointment, hatred, or any other *emotional* and *motivational symptom*. Such sensory, emotional, and motivational symptoms can be generally characterized as psychological symptoms with a psychogenic aetiology. This rather lengthy expression is usually shortened to *psychogenic symptoms*. The abbreviation is both convenient and firmly established by custom. It has, however, the disadvantage of ambiguity as the same term 'psychogenic' is then used both for the causal event and the caused reaction. The same ambiguity applies also to other usages of the syllable 'genic'; it can be understood in either an active or a passive sense. To a physician, for example, the word 'pyrogenic' means 'causing fever'; to a geologist, it means 'caused by fire'. On the other hand, the word 'iatrogenic' is always understood in a passive sense as meaning 'caused by doctors'; we do not speak of an iatrogenic curriculum which produces doctors.

The usage of psychogenic both for the pathogenic event and the consequent pathological reaction has contributed its quota to the frequent error of not distinguishing the two. It is important to realize that, in psychogenic aetiologies, we never deal with objective events as such, but only with the psychological experience of the events. If the objective event, for example, is a prolonged loud noise, it can only be psycho-pathogenic when it is subjectively experienced. If this essential condition is ignored and the objective event as such regarded as pathogenic the psychogenic symptoms of a patient seem to be irritatingly erratic and capricious. He may, for instance, at one moment react with headache, nausea, tension and irritability, to a prolonged loud noise in the environment. Yet a short while later, he may be seen engaged in an animated conversation or absorbed in the solution of a crossword puzzle, being apparently unaware of the continuing noise and not obviously inconvenienced by it. If we then draw his attention to the noise, it may again become a pathogenic experience and revive his symptoms.

It is this dependence of psychogenic symptoms on the actuality of a conscious experience which is baffling to those who think of the brain as an organ that responds only passively to stimuli impinging on it. In many psychiatric and psychological theories, this mechanistic view of the brain as at rest, unless stimulated, is still implicit, although it is at variance with the findings of neurophysiology which clearly demonstrate that cerebral neurones are continuously active and that they are responsive only to a selected set of data at any particular time.

The selective responsiveness of the psychoneural pool is in marked contrast to the indiscriminate responsiveness of peripheral sense organs. For example, people who have to work in very noisy factories achieve a psychological adjustment to the ear-splitting din around them because their subjective awareness of it becomes selectively blotted out. The peripheral sense organ, in the inner ear, however, has no protection against the high-amplitude waves of a loud noise which may be literally deafening to it. There will eventually be a peripheral loss of hearing which, at first, affects only the sensitivity for high tones in the frequency range of 4000 cycles per second. Later on, acoustic sensitivity for lower frequencies can also become damaged, and as sensitivity in this frequency range is necessary for the hearing of the human voice, such damage naturally impairs the adequacy of a person's social functioning.

Distinction Between Psychological Symptoms and Psychiatric Symptoms

The psychogenic symptoms we have considered so far are really psychogenically produced psychological symptoms. For practical reasons, it is necessary to distinguish these symptoms from psychogenically produced psychiatric symptoms. The psycho-pathogenic events giving rise to psychological symptoms can be generally pathogenic, but those giving rise to psychiatric symptoms are only idiosyncratically pathogenic as they require the presence of adjuvant conditions in the form of pathogenic psychoneural predispositions. Psychoanalytic theories have most consistently stressed this fact and demanded that treatment should not aim at removing precipitating environmental causes, but at changing a person's reactive tendencies.

When human beings experience an event which signifies danger, they normally respond to this psycho-pathogenic event with the psychogenic symptoms of fear. Consider, for example, the passengers of an aircraft who are informed that, because of a technical fault, the pilot is forced to attempt a hazardous emergency landing. They are told what to expect at the moment of impact, what posture to adopt then, and how to behave afterwards. They cannot escape from the danger situation and may have to spend terrified hours picturing the possible dangers and injuries in store for them. Should they finally land without mishap, they are liable to feel exhausted, tremulous and tearful.

The psychological symptoms of fear from which the passengers suffer in the hours of danger correspond phenomenologically to the psychiatric symptoms of fear which many neurotic and psychotic patients report. It might therefore seem justified to regard the symptoms of the passengers as the manifestations of a temporary psychiatric illness which could be labelled perhaps a 'reactive anxiety state'. There is, however, an understandable reluctance to consider the aircraft passengers as psychiatrically ill. We know only too well that the majority of people, ourselves included, would react as they did. We may even try to rationalize our diagnostic reluctance by the argument that the passengers' fear reactions were objectively justified, whereas psychiatric fear reactions have no objective justification. This is, however, the very argument that cannot—or should not—be invoked in the case of symptoms with a psychogenic aetiology in which the objective situation as such is of no account, but only the psychological experience of it. It does not matter to the passengers whether their experience of danger is objectively justified or not; all that matters is their subjective conviction that it is. They would suffer the same symptoms of anxiety, even if the pilot had been wrong in coming to the conclusion that a dangerous emergency situation existed.

Accepting the psychological fact that all passengers are convinced of the presence of danger, we have no alternative but to regard their reactions of fear as justified and normal psychological symptoms. We can only speak of psychiatric symptoms in the case of passengers who respond idiosyncratically, and thus abnormally, to their conviction of danger. If somebody remains totally indifferent to the prospect of an impending catastrophe, or even becomes elated by it, he will certainly arouse concern in his fellow passengers and the suspicion of being psychiatrically abnormal. An even more definite diagnosis of psychiatric symptoms can be made, if somebody cannot respond to exhortations to control his fears, but bursts into wild screams and sobs, rushes about in aimless agitation, or shows even more obviously pathological reactions, such as attacks on others, attempts to commit suicide, epileptic fits, hallucinations, and so on. As these diverse psychiatric symptoms are obviously due to a psychogenic trauma, the diagnosis of an acute traumatic neurosis or psychosis might be made. The term 'traumatic' in this diagnosis is, however, very misleading; it can be mistakenly assumed to refer to a physiogenic trauma, or at least to an event that has a high morbidity rate.

Even if pathological experiences cause only temporary and normal psychological symptoms, they can yet be thought to leave behind a lasting pathogenic change of psychoneural reactivity, and thus act as the predisposing causes of psychiatric symptoms in response to subsequent pathogenic experiences of a similar kind. However, any such predispositions are usually only of a minor and transient kind. After their ordeal most of the aircraft passengers will feel undue anxiety at the prospect of boarding another aeroplane. Yet this anxiety is generally not strong enough to prevent them flying again, when air transport is convenient or necessary for them. Moreover, the increase of anxiety soon subsides when there is no recurrence of anxiety-provoking experiences in an aircraft. There is, however, a minority of passengers who will be left with such a strong and lasting increase of anxiety that they can never again enter another aeroplane. In this minority, the thought of flying has become the idiosyncratic psycho-pathogenic cause of a psychiatric symptom in the form of a disabling fear.

The general resistance against the predisposing pathogenic effect of distressing experiences is often thought to be an attribute of mature adult personalities. It may then be argued that the immature personalities of children are less fortunate because they cannot be expected to cope with distressing experiences, and must therefore be prone to develop psychiatric predispositions. If the additional assumption is made—and this is done by many modern theories on psychopathology—that the predispositions become deeply and permanently ingrained in the developing personality, then some paradoxical consequences result. As nobody can go through childhood without having many distressing experiences, it follows that the normal adult personality (normal by both population and individual standards) is also bound to be abnormal, by the same standards, because it invariably harbours predispositions to respond to certain experiences with psychiatric symptoms. At the same time, it becomes a foregone conclusion that psychiatric symptoms have a psychogenic aetiology in distressing childhood experiences which can always be found.

Experimental Studies of Psychopathogenic Events

The first systematic and experimental investigation of psychopathogenic events was carried out on dogs and other animals by the Russian physiologist Pavlov[389, 390], and many research workers have followed his lead since. Before Pavlov turned to this field of investigation he had received the Nobel Prize in 1904, when he was 55, for his physiological studies on normal alimentary reflexes.

The neural basis of a reflex consists of the reflex arc which can be divided into three parts: (1) afferent nerves which transmit nerve impulses from peripheral sense organs to the central nervous system; (2) a central chain of interneurones which may extend over many segments of the central nervous system, and which end around the cell bodies of lower motor neurones; and (3) efferent nerves transmitting nerve impulses from the lower motor cell bodies to peripheral effector organs, particularly glands and muscles. The physiological reflexes studied by Pavlov started in the sense organs of the alimentary tract, which were chemically stimulated by food. The central chain of interneurones could extend to the highest level in the cortex. The efferent nerves caused glandular secretions and muscular contractions in the alimentary tract.

In the course of these reflex studies, Pavlov had noticed that what he, at first, called 'psychic' stimuli could interfere with the functioning of alimentary reflexes. This 'psychic' interference was produced by exteroceptive stimuli which signalled the impending arrival of food. The term 'psychic', however, had implications that were unacceptable to Pavlov. Already in 1903, in a paper entitled 'Experimental Psychology and Psychopathology'[389], he argued that psychic stimuli were essentially comparable to physiological stimuli. They started as sensory nerve impulses in the distance receptors of the eye, ear or nose and were transmitted from there to the cortex of the brain, the presumed seat of the highest psychological functions. According to the phrenological theory that psychological functions have specific localizations in the cortex, it seemed plausible to assume that different cortical areas were excited by the interoceptive stimuli from the alimentary tract and the exteroceptive stimuli from distance receptors. If it happened repeatedly that exteroceptive stimuli arrived in the cortex before the arrival of interoceptive stimuli caused by the mastication of food, then a neural link was formed between the respective cortical areas. Under these conditions, the exteroceptive, or 'conditioned', stimuli activated alimentary reflexes before the advent of the usual interoceptive, or 'unconditioned' stimuli. Reflexes of this kind were called 'conditioned' reflexes.

Some observations indicated that 'extremely strong and unusual stimuli' could interfere with conditioned reflexes which had been firmly established before. For example, in 1924, Pavlov's dogs were nearly drowned during a thunderstorm that caused a flooding of the kennels. Most dogs soon recovered from the 'extremely strong and unusual stimuli' to which they were exposed on that occasion, but well-established conditioned reflexes remained disturbed for a long time in a few dogs, especially those of an 'inhibitable type'.

Systematic experiments soon showed that similar disturbances of conditioned reflexes could be obtained in other ways, for instance by exposing the dogs to a conflict of excitatory and inhibitory conditioned stimuli. In one such experiment, dogs were given food each time after they had been shown a circle. The circle thus became an excitatory conditioned stimulus that caused a flow of saliva. When the same dogs were shown an ellipse, they were never fed afterwards so that the ellipse assumed the character of an inhibitory conditioned stimulus which suppressed the flow of saliva. When the ellipse was gradually altered in shape so that it looked more and more like a circle, some dogs became disturbed. They began to howl and struggle, and their conditioned reflexes became utterly disorganized. The usual correlation between the strength and nature of a conditioned stimulus and the strength and nature of the conditioned response could no longer be observed. Some dogs now showed 'paradoxical reactions' because weak stimuli elicited strong reflex responses and strong stimuli weak responses. In other dogs there were 'ultraparadoxical reactions' because inhibitory stimuli elicited excitatory responses and *vice versa*. There were also some dogs whose general behaviour was disturbed not only in the experimental situation, but also in their kennels. This seemed to indicate that the disorganization of cerebral functions had become widespread. The symptoms which such dogs showed differed widely in kind, intensity and duration. Among them were restlessness, irritability, aggressiveness, tics, tremors, steretoyped movements, abnormalities of respiration, of urination and of sexual functions, apathy, abnormal playfulness and so on.

Pavlov spoke of 'experimental neuroses' and stated clearly that their occurrence depended on the type of nervous system an animal had. He distinguished four main types which he classified in Hippocratic terms as sanguine, phlegmatic, choleric and melancholic.

The last two types were regarded as unbalanced and therefore more liable to produce symptoms. The type of nervous system was thought to be largely inherited, but past experiences and present stresses were given due consideration. Animals were known to differ according to their upbringing (e.g. whether in a kennel or not), and their neurotic predisposition seemed to be enhanced by intercurrent infection, physical trauma and castration. At a later stage, Pavlov tried to apply his explanatory concepts of cortical excitation and inhibition also to the analyses of psychiatric disorders in humans. He believed, for instance, that there were excessive excitatory processes in the cortex of anxiety neurotics, and excessive inhibitory processes in the cortex of patients suffering from hysteria or schizophrenia. These explanations are, however, speculative and do not accord well with the findings of modern brain physiology[297].

There were only few dogs whose symptoms of experimental neurosis continued outside the experimental situation and became a chronic abnormality which seriously interfered with their lives. The same is true of human patients who suffer a psychiatric illness akin to an experimental neurosis, such as an acute traumatic neurosis in a danger situation. Generally speaking, when a pathogenic danger situation is over, neurotic symptoms disappear within a few hours. That an acute experience of danger does not usually cause chronic neurotic fears is perhaps best illustrated by patients who lived through an acute attack of coronary thrombosis and suffered pain of an agonizing intensity together with an ominous feeling of being at death's door. Even when they subsequently develop angina pectoris which constantly reminds them of the precarious state of their health, they do not develop neurotic anxieties, or experience the overpowering terror of imminent death through heart failure which overwhelms patients with neurotic cardiac fears, whose heart is objectively quite healthy[306].

Social Isolation

Another potentially pathogenic experience is social isolation. The normal reaction to social isolation is a distressing feeling of loneliness and nostalgia. Susceptible persons may, however, respond with a variety of psychiatric symptoms. Although the majority of people suffer psychologically, when socially isolated for a long time, they yet remain well psychiatrically. This was perhaps best shown in the prisons of the eighteenth century in which solitary confinement was the rule 'to induce that calm contemplation which brings repentance', as the official explanation of this form of punishment put it. Elaborate precautions were even taken to prevent prisoners from seeing each other at the obligatory religious services. This penal system did not, however, cause an epidemic of mental illness among the prisoners. An even more absolute degree of social isolation fell to the lot of some polar explorers and again no psychiatric disease occurred in the absence of starvation or physical illness. Alexander Courtauld[92] and Admiral Byrd[72], for instance, each spent a polar winter in complete solitude and recorded their psychological reactions. They missed human contact; they yearned, in Admiral Byrd's phrase, for human 'sounds, smells, voices and touch', but they were never psychiatrically ill in a way that might have hampered them in doing the many jobs necessary for their survival in these circumstances[322].

Only a minority of people become psychiatrically disabled when they are either completely deprived of human companionship or live as strangers in an alien community whose language and social customs they do not adequately understand. The latter circumstance has become a serious problem in many teaching centres which are attended by students from foreign cultures, of whom a small, but conspicuous, percentage fall ill every year with disconcerting psychiatric symptoms.

The potentially pathogenic nature of the experience of social isolation also becomes apparent when the established customs and traditions of a society are weakened, a condition which the French sociologist Durkheim called *anomie*[125]. The resulting social fragmentation and loss of communal cohesiveness is experienced as personal isolation by susceptible individuals. Durkheim's investigations at the end of the last century revealed that, in conditions of *anomie*, the rate of suicide tended to increase, a finding which has since been repeatedly confirmed[208, 433].

It seems plausible to assume that complete social isolation must have its most devastating effect on young children because, in the absence of any social stimulation, their emotional and intellectual development must be stunted so that they will fail to acquire normal human personalities. Before the age of two, no child can possibly survive without human care. Yet several examples have become known of much older children being found living like wild animals away from human habitation. Rumour and myth have then often asserted that such children were suckled and reared by animals—it was always wolves in India and bears in Russia—but there has never been any reliable evidence of this.

Linnaeus regarded children living a solitary wild life by themselves as a variety of the main species of *homo sapiens* and coined the name *homo ferus* for them which is today generally rendered as *feral children*[114, 553]. He described them as *mutus*, *tetrapus* and *hirsutus* to indicate that they could not speak, ran on all fours and were hairy. Most of these children were subsequently found to be mentally subnormal, and to defy special attempts to educate them. This was the case, for instance, with the 'wild boy of Aveyron' who was discovered in a tree by hunters in 1799 when he was about twelve. He was considered an incurable idiot by Pinel, the foremost French psychiatrist of that time. But Itard, one of the first physicians to teach children who were deaf and dumb or otherwise educationally subnormal, undertook his training, managed to improve his manners and make him use a few words.

There were, however, other feral children who responded well to education. The wild girl of the Champagne, whom Linnaeus described as *puella campanica*, was intelligent, learned to speak well and became a nun. The feral child who perhaps created the greatest stir was the mysterious Kaspar Hauser who appeared at the gates of Nurnberg in 1828 when he was seventeen. He had apparently been shut up in a cellar for many years, was barely able to walk a few steps and could only utter a few hardly intelligible phrases. He quickly learned to speak, read and write, and only his ability to walk remained defective. He even began to write his autobiography, but was assassinated because, as it was rumoured later, the autobiography might have revealed him as the rightful heir of the Grand Duchy of Baden. Among well-attested recent cases is a girl reported by Kingsley Davis[112] in 1947, who had been kept secluded in a dark room by her deaf-mute mother for the first sixteen and a half years of her life. When found, she was afraid of strangers, unable to speak, and regarded as feebleminded and uneducable. However, she learned quickly and, within two years, reached the level of linguistic attainment normal for her chronological age. She grew into a healthy, bright, and energetic girl.

The details of extreme isolation in infancy can only be studied experimentally in animals which are artificially reared. Harlow[220] has carried out such experiments on rhesus monkeys which were removed from their mother a few hours after birth and afterwards brought up alone in a cage by themselves. He found that, if the deprivation of all social contact continued up to the age of six months—which corresponds to the age of two to three years in a human child—the animals' ability to fit into social life later was severely impaired. When brought together with other monkeys, they kept at a distance. They often sat immobile, staring into space for long periods; sometimes they kept rocking backwards and forwards or compulsively pinching or biting the same patch of skin over and over again. An improvement of social behaviour occurred only in a group of these monkeys who were moved from the laboratory and allowed to lead a more natural life in the local zoo. But return to the laboratory caused a relapse.

The social deprivation to which these monkeys were exposed had two components: maternal and peer deprivation, i.e. the absence of any interaction with the nursing mother and the absence of any interaction with playmates. Maternal deprivation was shown to be of less significance for normal social development than peer deprivation. An opportunity to play with peers compensated for any lack of mothering, with only one exception: female monkeys did not learn the technique of mothering, unless they had experienced it themselves. If maternally deprived female monkeys became pregnant later, they could not properly nurse their infants.

Such extreme social isolation never occurs in human infants. Some authors have, however, maintained that even relatively mild and temporary forms of isolation from familiar environments, such as a child's admission to hospital, commonly cause permanently harmful distortions of personality development, and blight the future emotional and social development of the children without hope of redemption[55, 56, 470, 471, 473]. There is no convincing evidence to support extravagant pathogenic claims of this kind which, for theoretical reasons, take a very poor view of the self-regulatory and reparative power of growing organisms. All that can be said is that there are some children who, after such an experience, show prolonged emotional disorders or remain hypersensitive to later experiences of social isolation and rejection, real or imagined[242, 321, 401].

There is no doubt that a depressive nostalgic reaction to the experience of social isolation is common among both adults and children and can therefore not be regarded as a psychiatric symptom. Unusual and idiosyncratic forms of reaction which can be diagnosed as psychiatric symptoms occur in only a minority of people who are specially vulnerable to this experience. Such people may develop a depressive illness and become irrationally convinced that they are inadequate, unworthy or sinful, that they are physically ill, or that there is no glimmer of hope in their future. Others display clinical symptoms which are usually found in schizophrenic illnesses, such as paranoid suspicions that other people have evil designs on them, interfere with their thoughts and feelings, or broadcast slanderous statements about them.

In many patients, the psychiatric illness precipitated by the experience of social isolation does not continue for long, once the psychopathogenic cause has disappeared. This is also true, as we mentioned before, for many patients who develop an acute traumatic neurosis after experiencing a prolonged danger situation.

Just as there are some people with danger-seeking dispositions, such as mountaineers or racing drivers, so there are recluses and hermits who seek actual social isolation. A less complete form of social isolation is chosen by those peculiar individuals we call tramps and vagrants. They are generally regarded as psychologically abnormal but not as psychiatrically ill, because they do not ask for psychiatric treatment, and would not tolerate it if it were offered to them. In fact, society merely offers them the threat of curtailing their liberty, if they should become a nuisance to their psychologically normal fellow citizens. They generally take the hint and avoid trouble.

An experience of social isolation, often of a merely subjective kind, is desired by many schizophrenic patients who are less able than tramps to fend for themselves, less amenable to the threat of punishment, and more liable to become a nuisance by disturbing behaviour. Chronic schizophrenics may eventually succeed in finding the subjective solitude they seek in some crowded back ward of a mental hospital. Investigations have shown that their eventual discharge from hospital after several years is most likely to be successful, if a social environment outside the hospital can be found for them which does not encroach too much on the privacy and insulation of their mental lives. Patients who are discharged to the care of parents or spouses show an aggravation of their clinical state significantly more often than those who go to live with siblings or in private lodgings. If such patients are exposed, for instance, to the solicitude of a devoted mother all day long, they are more liable to suffer a relapse than those who have a daily respite from such close emotional ties because there is a regular occupation that takes them, or the mother, out of the house for a while[66, 76]. Observations of a similar kind have also been reported by authors who studied the 'ecology', the general social environment, of chronic schizophrenics living in the community. It was again noticed that some of these patients did best in the lodging-house areas of a town where they could live in subjective solitude, even if their social environment was physically crowded[123, 136, 182, 215, 216, 217].

Some degree of physical social isolation is a necessary requirement even for the most sociable and gregarious individuals. To be deprived of all chance of physical privacy is a distressing experience for people of normal psychological sensitivity. Dostoevski, who was exposed to this experience in a penal settlement in Siberia for four years, said of it: 'There is one more torture which is almost harder to bear than any other; this is the forced community life'[120]. Elie Cohen, after five years in Nazi concentration camps, echoed this: 'To live continuously in the company of others became agony'[85]. Similar statements have been made by prisoners of war, by people in refugee camps and by polar explorers who spent a winter in cramped living quarters in the company of colleagues. Under these conditions of social surfeit, emotional reactions commonly develop which take the form of irritability, suspiciousness and personal antipathies[383].

Existential Illness

The dependence of an illness on the continuance of a precipitating pathogenic cause is characteristic of only certain kinds of diseases, such as some acute infections or intoxications. For practical reasons, it is desirable to have a distinguishing term for diseases which can be cured by removing the offending cause, and prevented by forestalling it. In psychiatry, they are sometimes called 'reactive', but this has proved an unsatisfactory adjective for several reasons. It has, for instance, become customary to equate reactive psychiatric diseases with neuroses, and to contrast them with endogenous psychiatric diseases, such as functional psychoses—a distinction which has nothing to commend it except perhaps the desire to find some justification for the conventional differentiation between neuroses and psychoses. The adjective 'reactive' has also contributed to the confusing custom of equating observable symptoms with theoretical disease entities. A patient with a manic-depressive illness, for example, may react to some unavoidable difficulty in his life with despair when he is in a depressive phase of his illness, and with energetic optimism, when he is in a mildly elated phase. In either case, we deal only with reactive *symptoms* and not with reactive *illnesses* of depression or hypomania. Finally, 'reactive' has the disadvantage of being applicable to all illnesses in which we can discern some kind of precipitating event which need, however, be neither a salient nor an exogenous cause (exogenous to the organism).

If an illness is dependent on the continuance of a salient, exogenous and precipitating event, we may characterize it as an existential illness—an illness that does not affect the 'essential' physical structure of an individual, but merely a mode of his existence. In the words of German existentialist philosophy, an existential illness does not affect a person's *So-sein* (his being *as* he is, his constitutional essence) but his *Da-sein* (his being-in-the-world and reacting to the things in the world). A purely existential illness thus excludes the occurrence of prolonged pathological changes. An illness in which a prolonged pathology is in the foreground can be distinguished as an *autonomous disease*. A bone fracture, for example, is an autonomous disease which continues after the precipitating event has ceased to be active because of the structural damage caused by it. The repair of the damage has to run its own autonomous course. In practice, there are no pure existential or autonomous diseases. In particular, new functional reactivities and predispositions are often established by existential diseases and may persist autonomously for a long time. After infectious diseases, for instance, there may be immunities or allergic hypersensitivities, and after an acute traumatic neurosis there may be an increased or reduced tolerance of future danger situations.

PART II
DESCRIPTIVE PSYCHOPATHOLOGIES

CHAPTER 10

THE PSYCHOPATHOLOGY OF PERCEPTION

We know next to nothing as yet about the physiological nature of psychoneural processes and about their physiopathological reactions to pathogenic events of a physiogenic or psychogenic kind. We therefore cannot yet speak of a psychoneural pathology, but it is possible, and customary, to speak of psychopathology. By this is often understood today a particular variety of psychopathology, a so-called 'dynamic' psychopathology, which is, in effect, no psychopathology at all, but a psycho-pathogenesis based on an intuitive construction of meaningful connections between subjective experiences of the patient. It serves the purpose of providing us with the satisfying feeling that we 'understand' how observed psychopathological manifestations came about. As Karl Jaspers pointed out[257], such an intuitive psychopathogenetic understanding refers to no objective reality, but merely to the conceptual reality of an 'ideally typical mind'. It is therefore not surprising that there are many theories of dynamic psychopathology which do credit to the ingenuity of human intuition, though their respective validities cannot be objectively tested. The main advantage of the various dynamic psychopathologies has been a pragmatic one: they encouraged psychotherapeutic techniques which have all had a measure of success. They all had their origin in the psychoanalytic theories of Freud which will be discussed later.

Another variety of psychopathology is concerned with the descriptive analysis of morbid psychological dysfunctions. This 'descriptive' psychopathology is, in psychiatry, often identical with clinical symptomatology, or semeiology, because there often are no significant endopathological changes which can be observed and described. In this and the following chapters, the term 'psycho-pathology' will be understood in this descriptive sense.

By perception we may mean the conscious subjective awareness of objects and events in the environment (exteroception), in one's own body (interoception), and of phenomena in one's own mind (introspection). However, when we deal with disorders of perception, it is customary to exclude all introspective and most interoceptive experiences. 'Disorders of perception' thus refer only to anomalies in the subjective awareness of objects and events in a patient's environment and in those parts of his body which are distinctly observable by him.

93

Sensory Anomalies

The sensory channels which transmit information of events to the psychoneural pool are those of the five exteroceptive senses, and also the proprioceptive and labyrinthine channels which convey the interoceptive information required for the awareness of the position and shape of one's body, and of the relative positions of one's head and limbs to each other and the trunk. Disturbances in sensory channels cause sensory anomalies which, although they naturally interfere with perception, are to be distinguished from perceptual disorders occurring when sense organs and the sensory pathways outside the brain are intact. Physical damage to a sensory channel may cause not only a diminution of the particular sensation concerned, but also a disorder of any movements which are cybernetically controlled by the missing sensations. Thus damage to the eyes or optic nerves may render a person blind and also affect his locomotion in space. Similarly, damage to proprioceptive channels may deprive a person of the ability to perceive the position of his limbs—unless he uses other sensory channels, such as sight or touch—and also disorganize his limb movements so that they are ataxic and uncoordinated.

It can happen that the stimulation of one sensory channel spills over into sensory experiences normally connected with different channels. This phenomenon is called *synaesthesia*[460] and occurs especially with auditory sensations which are then experienced together with visual or tactile sensations. The symptom is most commonly caused by a screeching or scratching sound, for example the high-pitched noise that can be produced by moving chalk quickly across a blackboard. It can stimulate, in susceptible persons, unpleasant sensations caused by muscular vibrations, such as shivers sent down the spine or teeth set on edge, and sometimes also visions of colour and movement. Some drugs, such as mescaline and lysergic acid (LSD), are known to increase the occurrence of visual synaesthesiae.

Sensory hypersensitivity is found in both functional and organic psychiatric diseases, after certain drugs, and immediately after a prolonged period of 'perceptual deprivation' in an environment with unpatterned sensory stimuli. There may then be complaints that even dim lights are glaring and dazzling, and colours too luminous and glittering[44, 232]. Other patients are hypersensitive to sounds; they experience the quiet closing of a door, the creaking of boards, the distant rumbling of traffic as irritating and disturbing because they are for them too loud and jarring. There are also patients to whom the weight of garments or bedclothes is an intolerably heavy burden, and others who find an average room temperature unbearably hot or cold. Patients who complain of *sensory hyposensitivity* report that everything is seen as in a dull haze, heard as muffled and distant, felt as numb, or tasted as insipid.

Percepts

When we speak of a sensation, what we have in mind is an abstract concept derived from the existential experience of sensations. But a sensation by itself can never form the content of an existential experience, only a field of sensations can do that. This field is usually divided into a distinct entity and an indistinct background. The distinct entity is called a percept, which, on analysis, is found to be composed of various sensations; in existential experience, however, it is a unitary object-phenomenon. It stands out as an entity for various reasons: because it has a distinctive or familiar pattern, because it moves in a stationary environment, because it fits in with our expectations or is unexpected, or because it has attracted our attention in one of many other ways. If it is existentially experienced as just a sensory configuration without recognition, it is simply a *sensory* percept. When it is recognized as something familiar, it becomes a *meaningful* percept[1].

A nucleus of simple sensory percepts may be present from birth. This is suggested by studies of instinctual behaviour and, more recently, by investigation in the field of ethology which is a branch of animal psychology dealing with the behaviour of animals in fairly natural situations rather than artificially contrived laboratory conditions[233, 329, 330, 331, 499, 504]. Ethologists have shown that newborn animals react instinctively to certain sensory configurations which they have therefore called 'instinct releasers'. For example, if a model looking like the silhouette of a single-engined monoplane is moved about the heads of newly hatched game birds in the direction in which such an aeroplane would normally fly, the birds respond with fear reactions. This congenital capacity to react specifically to such a moving silhouette is of biological advantage because the silhouette resembles the shape of a short-necked bird of prey in flight. When the monoplane model is moved in the opposite direction, it resembles a harmless long-necked waterfowl in flight, and produces no fear reactions. Similar instinct releasers may also play a role in newborn human babies. It seems, for example, that any configuration, resembling the shape of a mother's nipple and stimulating the baby's lips and mouth, could be an instinct releaser which initiates sucking and swallowing movements.

The conversion of sensory into meaningful percepts is a long and gradual process of which the foundations are laid in infancy, and which adults can no longer remember. Occasionally, however, we may gain an inkling of difficulties involved. For example, persons who were born blind live in a world in which meaningful percepts are haptic in nature—that is, derived mainly from tactile and kinaesthetic percepts. When such patients acquire vision after an eye operation later in life, they are confronted with the task of translating haptic percepts into visual ones, and of constructing meaningful percepts of a visual kind[421], [446]. At first, their visual field consists chiefly of a confused mixture of lines and colours in which object-phenomena only stand out if they are clearly differentiated from the environment. Some visual configurations belonging to external objects of common occurrence are however soon acquired and their meaningful relation to the corresponding haptic configurations learned. Yet it takes very much longer to learn to recognize the visual configuration of percepts whose meaning is of a more abstract kind. The patients find it hard, for instance, to distinguish visually between a triangle, a square, and a circle. The distinction is easily achieved by touch, but visually it can only be accomplished by looking for angles or straight boundary lines and then counting them.

In unusual circumstances, normal people can be diverted from recognizing the meaning of certain percepts so that all they become aware of are sensory percepts without meaning. If a long prose passage, for instance, is read to normal subjects and they have to pronounce the words as soon as they hear them, they succeed in copying the sensory percepts of the passage verbally, but cannot grasp its semantic content.

The conversion of sensory into meaningful percepts can be disrupted by brain lesions. The localization of the lesions varies with percepts of different sensory modalities.

Agnosia

The inability to convert the sensory percepts of some modality into meaningful percepts, and thus to recognize them, was originally called 'imperception'[58] by Hughlings Jackson, but Freud later renamed the symptom 'agnosia'[147], and this is the preferred term today. It is typical of agnosic patients, if they are not handicapped by additional brain damage, that they can copy a meaningful pattern, for example the schematic drawing of a house, quite correctly, and yet fail to recognize its meaning[26]. When agnosia is acquired and neuropathological in origin, it is often not complained about by the patients who may, in fact, even deny or conceal the symptom. The nature and extent of their agnosia must then be ascertained by clinical testing, and this may yield results which are variable and unreliable. The reason for this is that some patients feel anxious and worried in a test situation, and therefore do not do themselves justice. Others, however, exert themselves specially and succeed in tasks which are beyond them in more humdrum circumstances. One also has to take into account that the consciousness of brain-damaged patients is easily clouded, that they have a tendency to perseverate, and that they tire quickly.

Patients with *tactile* agnosia (or astereognosis) cannot recognize an object that is placed into their hands, while their eyes are shut. They may, however, correctly identify various tactile qualities of the object, such as its size, shape, weight, and texture. Bilateral tactile agnosia in right-handed persons may be due to left-sided lesions of the parietal lobe, especially in the region of the supramarginal gyrus. Left-sided tactile agnosia in right-handed persons may be associated with right-sided parietal lesions or damage to the corpus callosum[100, 105].

We speak of *visual* agnosia when a patient with adequate eyesight cannot recognize familiar objects visually, but identifies them easily when allowed to touch them. The symptom is generally limited to small objects, though the complexity of an object also plays a role. The total meaning of a picture may, for instance, not be recognized, but only individual details in it (simultanagnosia). If the agnosia applies particularly to the faces of people which should be familiar, the term 'prosopagnosia', from the Greek *prosopon*, face, is used. Sometimes the appreciation of space is affected more than the recognition of objects in it (space blindness). Such patients have difficulty in distinguishing directions (above–below, right–left, far–near), in setting the hands of a clock, in drawing the map of a room or in orienting themselves on such a map.

Dyslexia

When the visual agnosia of a brain-damaged patient affects mainly the recognition of written and printed language, his ability to read is impaired (acquired dyslexia, or word-blindness). He may fail to identify single letters (literal dyslexia) or only flounder in the task of combining letters to form a word (verbal dyslexia). It is often easier for him to read numbers, even if they consist of many digits. A patient, for instance, who stumbled over such simple words as 'house' or 'evening' read the figure 45,360,471 correctly and with little hesitation[479]. The explanation of this difference may be that numbers can be read piecemeal because each digit is completely identified by its shape and decimal position without requiring reference to other digits or the number as a whole. Typical cases of acquired dyslexia have no difficulty in writing spontaneously or from dictation, but they are liable to make mistakes as they cannot check what they have put down. They may also succeed in copying details of written or printed words, but without grasping the word as a whole.

The physical lesions in patients with acquired visual agnosia are generally found in the region of the dominant occipital and parietal lobe, interrupting fibres from the visual cortex of both sides to the neighbourhood of the angular gyrus of the dominant side. The lesions are often due to an impairment of circulation in the posterior cerebral artery.

Dyslexia also occurs in young children in whom no physical damage to the brain can be detected. This *specific developmental dyslexia*, or *specific reading disability*[106, 144, 210, 248, 364], must be distinguished from retarded reading ability due to poor intelligence, or emotional disturbance[231]. It has been estimated that about ten per cent of schoolchildren are retarded readers, but only perhaps one to two per cent can be classified as specifically dyslexic. The deficiency occurs about four times as often in boys as in girls, and many of them have a family history of slowness in learning to read, write or speak. Many such children, but by no means all, have a poorly established right- or left-handedness; they use the right hand for some skilled activities and the left hand for others; or they are right-handed, but left-footed or left-eyed. This may indicate a disturbance in the normal development of the brain so that the left hemisphere does not become fully dominant, and the person therefore not clearly right-handed[193, 194, 420].

Many dyslexic children have a right–left disorientation in space so that **d** and **b**, or **q** and **p**, cannot be distinguished. For the same reason they do not know what clockwise means, and cannot read the clock. When presented with an unfamiliar word, they do not read consistently from left to right, but mix up the sequence of letters. Similarly, when they have succeeded, after much practice, in memorizing the letters which make up a word, say the word 'rose', they may write it down as 'sore' or 'reso', or repeat a syllable ('rereso'), leave out some letters and add others ('sre' or 'repso'). Many dyslexic children are of good general intelligence, as evidenced by their good scholastic progress in response to auditory teaching. Most of them overcome their disability to a greater or less extent by the time they reach the age of 15, especially if they receive special remedial teaching, but some grow into adults who can, at best, read their own names and perhaps a few three-letter words.

Visual agnosia may also affect the ability to distinguish colours. This symptom of *colour agnosia*, or *achromatopsia*, is an acquired symptom, generally due to cerebral lesions, in contrast to colour blindness or weakness which is a sex-linked genetic disability affecting mainly men.

Brain-damaged patients with *auditory agnosia* have normal hearing, but cannot recognize familiar sounds, such as the jingling of coins, the rustling of paper, the ringing of bells, or the melody of familiar tunes. The greatest handicap for patients with auditory agnosia is their difficulty in recognizing speech, called *sensory aphasia* or 'word-deafness'[59]. They may be able to distinguish speech from other sounds, but it remains to them as confused and senseless as an unfamiliar foreign tongue. In typical cases, the disability is limited to auditory recognition, and does not affect reading and writing. Speech tends to be faulty as it lacks auditory feedback control. The patients are likely to mispronounce words or use the wrong terms (paraphasia). Their sentence structure is liable to suffer (paragrammatism), and, in severe cases, speech disintegrates into a meaningless jumble of expressions (jargon aphasia). Many patients with sensory aphasia also have a tendency to be extremely voluble (logorrhoea). In many patients with acquired auditory agnosia, lesions are found in the posterior part of the first temporal convolution of the left hemisphere.

Infantile word-deafness is a rare inherited handicap that occurs five times as often in boys as in girls. No cerebral lesions have been found to account for it. Such a child fails to develop normal speech, but may eventually evolve an idiomatic language of its own (idioglossia, or 'lalling') which conveys some sense and meaning only to those who are in close touch with him. His intelligence is generally normal, but he has to be taught by the same visual and tactile methods as deaf children. Children with 'high-tone deafness' can be mistaken for children with infantile word-deafness.

Some patients with lesions in the right parietal lobe of the brain suffer from an agnosia of the left half of their body. They pay no attention to that side, and may even feel that it belongs to somebody else. If they are pricked with a pin on the left side, they either disregard this or report a pinprick on their right side (alloaesthesia). This half-sided agnosia of the body is most grotesquely shown, when patients become hopelessly entangled in trying to put on a garment (dressing apraxia)[100].

Schematic Percepts

A meaningful percept is a sensory percept that is recognized as something familiar, yet it is not just a sensory percept to which a meaning is attached[202]. By becoming meaningful, the whole configuration of the sensory percept may undergo a change; it may turn into a schematic percept which has a configuration that agrees with a meaningful schema in the observer's mind rather than with the actually perceived sensory percept. For example, the purely sensory percept may be a rhomboid plane. If the plane is recognized as a table top, this meaning converts it into a schematic percept that is seen—actually seen—as a square or rectangular plane, since past experience has provided us with the knowledge that four-sided table tops are hardly ever otherwise than square or rectangular. If we are asked to draw what we see, we are likely to draw the schematic percept. The first drawings of children are schematic drawings; they have to be taught about perspective before they become aware of their sensory percepts as such.

When an object is perceived on different occasions, it can cumulatively acquire new facets of meaning so that the percepts to which it gives rise may run through a progressive series from sensory to schematic and even more highly conceptualized percepts. If the real object (or the class to which a particular real object belongs) corresponds, in fact, to the schematic, or even more highly conceptualized percept, there is correct recognition. However, when a discrepancy occurs, we deal either with an illusion or a misidentification of the object—that is, an error of recognition.

ILLUSIONS

We speak of an illusion, when an object is correctly identified, but its properties misperceived[410]. For example, if a specially constructed table with a rhomboid top is presented visually in an environment devoid of clues concerning depth perception, observers may have the illusion of a square table top—an illusion which will be recognized as such, and corrected, when closer examination of the table is made possible. There are many normal illusions which are either due to conditions in the environment such as a mirage, or a Doppler effect; or to innate or acquired perceptual habits, for example, the perception of movements when two still pictures are presented at short intervals, or the perception of three-dimensional depth in a two-dimensional drawing. If a person wears spectacles, for several weeks, which turn the world upside down, or transform vertical lines into lines curved to the right, he will, at first, see the world in the way the spectacles distort it, and know that his perception is distorted[294, 487]. As other people do not share the distorted perception of form with him, we may say that he has *abnormal illusions*. However, after a few days, the abnormal illusions are automatically corrected by auto regulatory psychoneural processes which bring them into line with information obtained through other sensory channels. When the person eventually discards the distorting spectacles, the correcting psychoneural processes do not immediately disappear so that he again has abnormal illusions for a while, seeing the world upside down for the second time, or vertical lines curved, though to the left this time.

Some psychiatric patients complain of *pathological* illusions which they know to be abnormal both by population and individual standards, and which cause them suffering and concern. They may complain that objects look abnormally big (macropsia) or abnormally small (micropsia), or that the structural properties of objects are distorted in more complex ways (metamorphopsia). Vertical walls may be seen as tilted; floors as curved, moving or slanting; the world as flat and without depth; rooms and corridors as unusually narrow; open spaces as unusually wide. Everything may appear tinged with a strange colour. An object may be seen further or nearer than it is known to be, or approaching and receding, moving up and down, shifting sideways or rotating, though it is known to be stationary and still. A single object can be seen double (diplopia) or multiple (polyopia); the speed of moving objects can appear altered just as in slow-motion or quick-motion films[32, 37]. Such pathological illusions usually occur in a person whose consciousness is changed through intoxication, brain damage or epileptic processes. They do not have the same pathological significance, when they occur during the process of falling asleep or waking up in an otherwise healthy person.

Illusions in the proprioceptive field cause patients to misperceive the shape and position of their body, or of parts of it. We then speak of *disorders of the body image*[37, 98, 101, 442]. Patients complain of distressing proprioceptive percepts they know to be false from the evidence of other senses. They have the experience that their whole body, or a part of it, grows bigger or smaller, or feels abnormally light or heavy. A dizzy person who closes his eyes loses his illusion that the world rotates around him, but exchanges it for the illusion that his body is rotating or floating. Many anxious neurotic patients are distressed by the proprioceptive illusion of a shaking or nodding head. After some 'hallucinogenic' drugs, such as mescaline or LSD, and in some other states of altered consciousness, the body image may expand in an illusory identification with parts of the external world or even the whole world (mystical experience or oceanic feeling). Many people past middle age retain a body image in which the changes caused by aging have not been registered, they therefore have the illusion of looking younger than they actually do.

There are also pathological illusions which affect more abstract elements of the penumbra of meaning surrounding conceptualized percepts of either the exteroceptive or interoceptive variety. The environment may appear abnormally real; or, conversely, more dreamlike and unreal (feelings of unreality). The body image may also be perceived as unreal (feelings of depersonalisation)[5]. Situations may be transiently experienced as having occurred before (*déjà vu* phenomenon, illusion of familiarity), as being premonitions, or as occurring for the very first time (*jamais vu* phenomenon, illusion of unfamiliarity).

Because illusions are percepts which are wrongly conceptualized, it is understandable that, in certain circumstances, beliefs and expectations will give rise to transient normal illusions, or modify those which have already occurred[68]. When we strongly hope and expect, for instance, that our name will soon be called, we are likely to have an illusory hearing of our name, when that of somebody else is called out. The influence of expectations on existing illusions has been neatly demonstrated with the help of an illusion to which the name 'autokinetic phenomenon'[453] has been given. This illusion is normally experienced, when a dimly-lit and stationary point of light is watched in an otherwise completely dark visual field. The point of light is then seen to move, but the direction and extent of movement varies individually. However, if persons are informed of the direction and extent of movement observed by other people, they expect to have the same experience and their own autokinetic phenomenon will tend to be in line with that belief.

It is therefore plausible to assume that psychotic delusions, which are held with an absolute and incorrigible conviction of their truth and a confident expectation that they will be confirmed, may give rise to *delusional illusions*, such as the perception that the environment has acquired a sinister and threatening aspect (delusional atmosphere or mood) or that everything that happens in the environment has a special reference to the patient (delusional illusions of reference). It is, however, often difficult to distinguish delusional illusions from delusional expectations which have not caused illusions.

Delusional illusions of the body image can be very disturbing and persist against all evidence provided by reason or close observation. Such patients may be irrevocably convinced that their body, or some part of it, is so deformed as to be repulsively ugly. They experience themselves as too tall or too short, too fat or too thin, looking too old or too young, having a nose or ears of the wrong shape or size, a chin that protrudes or recedes too much, teeth that are discoloured or irregular, a skin that is full of blemishes, lacking hair where it should be, or having hair where there should be none. These patients often clamour for cosmetic or plastic operations, but if these are performed and even if the results are objectively excellent, the patients' distress is not alleviated as the delusional illusions of the body image usually persist in undiminished strength. Neurotic patients may have similar body image illusions, but are only half convinced about them so that reassurance can bring about a transient amelioration.

In most textbooks, illusions are simply—and inadequately—defined as 'false percepts'. A percept can, however, be false in two ways: it may misidentify an object, or misperceive the properties of an object. Typically, the name illusion can only be applied to the second alternative, but the over-simplified definition of illusions as false percepts has encouraged a tendency to regard some misidentifications of objects as illusions. This is never done when the misidentification is due to agnosia or a disturbance of memory, but some misidentifications caused by powerful beliefs have been called illusions at times; for instance, when a person fearful of being attacked in a dark street mistakes every shadow for a lurking robber, and every sound behind him for the footsteps of pursuers. Delirious patients who similarly misidentify objects in the room, and perhaps mistake a flower or a wallpaper pattern for menacing beasts, have also been diagnosed as having illusions in an effort to make a pseudo-exact distinction between illusions and hallucinations.

The tendency of psychiatrists to equate misidentifications with illusions is, however, not consistent. Many other misidentifications by psychotic patients are conventionally classed as hallucinations. For example, when a schizophrenic patient misidentifies the noise of an aeroplane, or of running water, as the sound of voices, he is generally said to be hallucinated. Sometimes the term 'functional hallucinations' has been used for these obvious misidentifications of objects. The frequent report of paranoid schizophrenics that they passed a group of strangers in the street and overheard them make personal remarks about them is also generally diagnosed as a hallucination, though it is likely to be no more than a misidentification of sounds perceived at the time of passing the group of strangers.

It is often clear that the misidentifications of these patients are in agreement with their delusional preoccupations.

HALLUCINATIONS

A hallucination is an exteroceptive or interoceptive percept which does not correspond to an actual object[467]. In this respect, it differs from both misidentifications and illusions. A person who hallucinates an exteroceptive percept may realize that his experience is a hallucination either from unusual attributes of the percept or from the fact that other people present cannot observe the same object.

It is often thought that hallucinations are always pathological symptoms and never occur in normal people. This is, however, very far from the truth. We are, for instance, all familiar with the phenomonenon of after-images. When we have looked fixedly, for a while, at some bright object and then look away, we perceive an *after-image* which no longer corresponds to any object in our central field of vision and is therefore a hallucination which may even obscure objects present in our direct line of vision. The brightness of the original object is then usually reversed, and its colour transformed into a complementary colour so that we experience a negative after-image. After-images are easily recognized as hallucinations because they change their position with the movements of our eyes, and because they increase in size as we look at a distant surface, and shrink in size when the surface is closer to us. It seems that after-images are due to processes in the peripheral sense organ and as these are only of short duration, after-images are short-lived phenomena.

Positive after-images of a more central origin are also frequently experienced by normal persons. It seems best to distinguish them by a separate term, and we shall call them *perseverated images*. Some of them are very transient, such as those in the auditory field. We may, for instance, suddenly become aware that a question had been addressed to us to which we had not listened. But it is possible to listen to the perseverated image of the question which is perceptually available for a short while. Image perseveration of longer duration can occur, when the original objects were brightly lit and attentively watched for many hours. For example, people who had spent a day sailing, motoring or skiing may, in the evening, experience perseverated images which persist vividly against their will and interfere with other visual activities, such as reading.

An analogous phenomenon which is, however, largely subject to voluntary control, and not universally present, is the ability to experience *eidetic images* (from the Greek word *eidos*, shape)[174]. The ability is present in about 5 per cent of children up to the age of 12, but in only a few adults who, like some painters and sculptors, may have kept it alive through constant training. Eidetic images are the more or less accurate perceptual replicas of objects which had been attentively observed. They are, like after-images, seen as exteroceptive percepts and recognized as hallucinations. They differ, however, from after-images in that they are more persistent, can be deliberately revived after several minutes, do not change their size with changes in the distance of the surface on which they are projected, and contain a striking number of details present in the original object. If the original object was a picture, the eidetic image of it may allow the subject to ascertain details in retrospect he had not noticed before, such as the number of trees present or the sequence of letters in a foreign word. Eidetic images are, however, not photographically correct replicas; they are generally some items missing, and others that had been added unconsciously.

Normal hallucinations also occur regularly during sleep—they may be remembered as dreams—and in the transition from waking to sleeping (hypnagogic state) or from sleeping to waking (hypnopompic state)[57, 338]. In these transitional states, visual and auditory hallucinations occur not uncommonly, but as they are quickly forgotten again, it is difficult to be certain about their frequency. They can be responsible for accidents in the course of some monotonous activity, such as night driving. A hallucinated obstacle in the path of the car may make a driver swerve suddenly, and cause an accident. Normal hallucinations are generally recognized as purely subjective experiences either at the time of their occurrence or in retrospect. The same applies to many pathological hallucinations, such as those in delirious states, but the hallucinations occurring in functional psychoses are fortified by a delusional conviction of their reality. Such *delusional hallucinations* do not lose their reality character when it is realized that they are not shared by others. The patients may then keep their hallucinatory experiences to themselves or try and convince others that the hallucinations are real.

Pathological hallucinations can occur in several sensory channels at the same time, though one or the other channel is usually predominant. *Visual* hallucinations can be very simple percepts which obliterate part of the visual field (positive scotomata), such as the flashes and 'stars' seen after a blow on the head, or the scintillating luminous zig-zag shapes perceived during a migraine attack (fortification spectra, teichopsia). Other hallucinations are of objects which fit naturally into the environment and are therefore not recognized as unusual. They are generally of human beings, and such 'apparitions' can have all the characteristics of solid bodies which are opaque, throw a shadow, are stopped by furniture and walls, and so on. Other apparitions, however, are less like natural percepts and may be ghost-like, transparent and not subject to the laws of physical bodies. Sometimes the visions are of tiny people or animals, vividly coloured and moving fast (Lilliputian hallucinations)[7, 188, 316]. A striking visual hallucination is the sight of oneself —or rather one's double. This symptom of *autoscopy*[323, 332] has been reported by normal people, including some well-known writers and artists, as a brief occurrence at times of stress and fatigue. In patients with recent organic brain damage, it may persist for several days[116]. They may then even occasionally see their double outside the boundaries of the visual field, perhaps standing behind their back or moving about in another room (extracampine hallucinations).

Auditory hallucinations may consist merely in the perception of bangs and whistles, or of vague speech sounds which cannot be clearly understood, but they may be interpreted in the light of prevailing delusions. Other patients, however, report clearly heard sounds which come from a particular direction and convey specific meanings, such as the sound of a howling and groaning group of people entombed beneath the floor. Auditory hallucinations often consist of voices which can be more or less definitely understood and perhaps even identified as male or female, young or old, English or foreign, known or unknown. Sometimes there are several voices in conversation with each other, discussing indifferent topics or referring to the patient; sometimes it is only one particular voice which conveys messages to the patient, commands him to perform certain actions which he may feel forced to obey, teases and ridicules him, or comments on everything he thinks or does. The hallucinated voice does not always come from the environment: it may be an exteroceptive percept located in various parts of the body, but most often in the abdomen or the head. A schizophrenic patient may hear his own thoughts as they occur (thought hearing), and may feel that they are audible to other people as well who thus eavesdrop on the working of his mind and learn everything about him.

Patients with *gustatory* hallucinations often complain that their food has a peculiar taste, especially when they have delusions about being poisoned. Such delusions can also give rise to *olfactory* hallucinations, but simple gustatory and olfactory hallucinations can also occur in the absence of such delusions, especially in epileptics whose seizures begin with a temporal lobe disturbance. Some schizophrenic and depressive patients have delusions that they stink, perhaps because of a pathological conviction that their body is rotten and decomposing, and they may then have intero-ceptive olfactory hallucinations.

Patients with *tactile* hallucinations complain of being touched, especially in the genital and anal region, of feeling insects crawling on their skin, of noticing blasts of hot or cold air, currents of elec-tricity, or waves of peculiar rays which are specially directed at their body. *Motor* hallucinations are common in some schizophrenic patients who have the objectively unjustified proprioceptive percept of having moved their facial muscles and assumed particular facial expressions. They may watch themselves in the mirror to discover these hallucinated movements, and often engage in grimacing to study their facial expressions in the mirror. Motor hallucinations are also common in dreams and may be partly turned into actual motor innervations causing the dreamer to jerk, to perform rudi-mentary actions (licking of lips, groping), to speak in his sleep, or to enact more complicated somnambulistic acts.

It can happen that a deluded and hallucinated patient has such a convincing and domineering influence on relatives and associates with whom he shares a secluded life that the latter begin to develop *induced* hallucinations. They may taste the peculiar flavour in the water which, according to the patient, is poisoned; they may smell the gas sprayed through the window, and perhaps even hear the neighbour make threatening remarks.

To an observer, a hallucination appears as an object falsely added by the patient to their joint perceptual field. Patients may, however, also have experiences which, to the observer, appear as falsely removing an object from the joint perceptual field. The term 'negative hallucination' has been used for this symptom, but it is doubtful to what extent it is justified. A patient who, let us say, sees a hallucinated person in the room takes care not to walk into the apparition. By analogy, one might expect a patient with a negative hallucination of a person in the room to walk into the space occupied by the invisible person. Yet he always takes care not to do this. If we accept the patient's perceptual experience as genuine, then his apparent negative hallucination seems to be no more than an agnosia or misidentification of the person concerned.

After the amputation of a limb or of some other part of the body (breast, eye, nose, penis, rectum) adult persons can have *proprio-ceptive* hallucinations of the missing part (phantom limb phenomenon) which cannot be corrected by exteroception. In time, the phantom limb of, say, an amputated arm shrinks in size until eventually the absent hand is felt dangling directly from the shoulder.

CHAPTER 11

THE PSYCHOLOGY OF INTELLECT

The terms 'intellect' and 'intelligence' can be used interchangeably, if they denote 'that faculty of the mind by which one knows and reasons' (*O.E.D.*). The term 'intelligence' is, however, often also given a specialized meaning today which does not refer to mind in general, only to the relative ability of individual minds to know and reason better or worse than is normal by the population standard of their society. Reasoning enables man to create a theoretical world, composed of meaningful concepts, or ideas. Each concept is a logical class having certain 'defining properties' which characterize all its members. Conceptual classes are of varying generality and membership. The class of living persons without heads is a null-class having no members; the class of a particular person at a particular time has only one member; the class of the same person at any time of his life is a more generalized concept; the class of living human beings has as its members all living organisms having the defining properties of the human species; the class of mankind has as its members all the past, present, and future human beings; and so on.

The intellectual process which produced concepts of increasing generality is known as *inductive reasoning*. Meaningful percepts are transformed by it into *perceptual*, or *descriptive*, *concepts*. By a process of *inventive reasoning*, we can also construct concepts which have no counterpart in perceptual reality; they may be merely presumed to exist hypothetically because they explain the causal or functional relationship between events. These *explanatory concepts* are the raw material from which explanatory theories are built. The dynamic theories of psychopathology are of this kind, using such explanatory concepts as mind, Unconscious, instincts, mental mechanisms, and so on.

Some defining properties of concepts can be expressed as universal propositions. From the defining properties of the concept of mankind, for instance, the universal proposition follows that all men are mortal. Reasoning which starts with such universal propositions or premises, as they are called in syllogistic logic, and arrives at particular conclusions is known as *deductive reasoning*. It is often regarded as superior to inductive reasoning because its conclusions must be as true as its premises, as long as we remain within the 'universe of discourse'.

Universal propositions which appear to be self-evidently true axioms are derived from descriptive concepts which were generalized and idealized from a particular set of observations. With a change of the observational set, the self-evident truth of the axioms may change. From observations on separate particles, for instance, it emerges as obviously true that, by adding one particle to another, we obtain two particles. The universal proposition that $x + x = 2x$ has thus become one of the axioms of common algebra.

However, from another set of observations, different generalized concepts are obtained by inductive reasoning. For example, adding one drop of water to another may still leave us with only one drop of water. The same result is obtained, when we add one mental concept to itself. Each concept is uniquely characterized by its set of defining properties. No duplication is therefore possible. To call a concept by two different names does not add a new concept to a theoretical reality. To speak, for instance, of humanity and mankind is equivalent to speaking merely of humanity; or algebraically expressed, $x + x = x$.

From the formula $x + x = x$ and similar axioms, George Boole constructed, in the middle of the nineteenth century, a special kind of algebra which has since become known as Boolean algebra. As the human mind reasons with the help of concepts, Boole hoped that his system of algebra would prove a useful instrument in the study of "the fundamental laws of those operations of the mind by which reasoning is performed", and that he might obtain by its use "some probable intimations concerning the nature and constitution of the mind"[54]. This hope was destined to be disappointed, but his algebra has since become the starting point of the various modern systems of symbolic logic.

In the nineteenth century, it began to be recognized by mathematicians and logicians that the derivation of axioms from perceptual realities was a handicap to the purity of deductive reasoning. It was therefore agreed that axioms had no longer to be self-evident: they were merely to be considered the unproved statement forming the basis of mathematical and logical systems of thought, and had no basis outside the intellectual domain in which they were stated. As Bertrand Russell put it: 'Mathematics may be defined as the science in which we never know what we are talking about nor whether what we are saying is true'[34]. Mathematicians, however, began to develop their own criteria of truth which dispensed with any reference to perceptual realities. They spoke of a logical truth, and meant by it that theorems, derived from a suitable set of axioms by the use of appropriate rules of combination, are true because they are certain and cannot be contradicted by other theorems obtained by the same rules of combination from the same set of axioms. Their truth and certainty was, of course, strictly limited to their own universe of discourse; observations in a perceptual reality might easily be at variance with them. In the words of Einstein: 'As far as the laws of mathematics refer to reality, they are not certain; and as far as they are certain, they do not refer to reality'[340].

Yet even the certainty of purely logical and mathematical reasoning is not as securely established as had been imagined. Its certainty, as was said, depends on the demonstration that no contradictory theorems can be deduced from a basic set of axioms. In 1931, however, it was convincingly shown by Gödel[187, 376] that an axiomatic system can only be shown to be consistent if it is incomplete because, for the proof of its consistency, propositions are required which cannot be derived within the axiomatic system. Thus the certainty of mathematical systems cannot be supported by strictly deductive reasoning, but mainly by the far less reliable process of mathematical intuition. Gödel's proof has been 'clarified and confirmed by the work of subsequent metamethematicians' (that is, mathematicians concerned with the logic of propositions *about* mathematics), to quote from Braithwaite's Introduction to the English translation of Gödel's original paper.

In spite of the intrinsic flaw thus revealed in logical systems, and in spite of the discrepancies which demonstrably exist between logical and perceptual realities, the rationality and logic of thought has remained the criterion of an ideally normal mind. Irrational and illogical thought is still widely regarded as an indication of an abnormal or diseased mind. Yet most of the explanatory theories about perceptual realities, held by even the most normal and gifted persons, are far from rational or logical in their origin; they are, for the most part, derived from the theories, beliefs and convictions prevailing in some of the social groups of which they are members.

COLLECTIVE BELIEFS OF SOCIAL GROUPS

When given enough time, social groups always develop explanatory theories of their own which range from the idle rumours of personal gossip to serious ideologies about one or the other reality. This is the case, no matter whether the social group is a neighbourhood community, an ethnic body, a religious fraternity, a political party, a professional organization or a sovereign state. Adults always belong to several social groups and may therefore accept theories and beliefs which are contradicatory. When the cohesion and corporate existence of a social group depends on the strength with which its members adopt characteristic theories and beliefs, social groups resort to measures of indoctrination which are more or less deliberately organized. The most powerful of these measures is *prestige suggestion* which exploits a normal human propensity to believe in the truth of statements pronounced with the power and pomp of established authority, or the force of single-minded persistence. The readiness to be convinced by authority (prestige suggestibility) is normally more marked in children than adults. The second measure of social indoctrination is *persuasion* and *education*. It uses reason and rational argument to inculcate collective beliefs and 'general knowledge'. The third measure relies on procedures which reward the acceptance of customs and beliefs, and punish deviations from them. It is a *conditioning procedure* which employs a form of 'instrumental conditioning' that is an elaboration of Pavlov's classical procedures.

The conservatism of collective opinions and of social indoctrinations often perpetuates false knowledge for many generations, even if it could have been contradicted by simple observations. The history of medicine furnishes a remarkable example of this. For over 1000 years, the knowledge of human anatomy was dominated by the authority of Galen who had dissected mainly monkeys and pigs. His textbook therefore contained a description of anatomical features which do not occur in man. Yet generations of physicians dutifully 'saw', at anatomical demonstrations of human bodies, structural details which were not there to be seen, such as a liver with five lobes, a sternum with seven segments, a double bile duct, or a horned uterus. When Vesalius, in the sixteenth century, described what he really saw, and attacked the venerated authority of Galen, he was nicknamed Vesanus (meaning 'out of sanity', cf. *insanus*, 'without sanity'). When it eventually became clear that Vesalius was right, attempts were made to save Galen's prestige by the assumption that the human body had changed in the intervening centuries[3].

Beliefs and customs established by social indoctrination are shared by all the orthodox members of a social group. They are therefore normal phenomena by the population standards of that group. To a social outsider, however, they may appear irrational and superstitious because he judges them by collective beliefs he himself accepts as unquestioningly rational and true. The beliefs and customs of alien groups may thus seem strange, irritating, bad, and perhaps even wicked. This is bound to give rise to friction between neighbouring social groups. There may be physical clashes and open warfare. There even looms above us today the spectre of world destruction by hydrogen bombs because the collective belief in capitalism is irreconcilable with the collective belief in communism.

Collective beliefs can thus cause much suffering and concern. Yet one cannot regard them as psychopathological. They are normal psychological phenomena in spite of the pathological consequences they may have.

Cognitive Dissonance

When individuals entertain conflicting beliefs which prompt contradictory courses of action, they are in a state of conflict, imbalance, or—to use the name employed by Festinger and his colleagues—cognitive dissonance[137]. Such a state of cognitive dissonance can be dissolved by making a definitive choice which, once made, may be defended with every possible argument in its favour in order to prevent a revival of the tension that goes with the vacillation of opposing beliefs. In its most trivial form, we may notice this effect in a person who has, after a period of wavering, decided to buy one particular article of value rather than another which had been equally attractive, but for different reasons. After the purchase, the attractions of the unbought article normally fade in the person's mind, whereas all the virtues and advantages of the bought article become inflated, and are likely to be stressed by him, whenever he finds a listener.

The intensification of beliefs after the dissolution of a cognitive dissonance can have odd consequences. On one occasion, Festinger and his colleagues joined a group of believers who had gathered around a modern prophetess in the United States[138]. She had announced that the world would be destroyed by a great flood on a particular day. So great was the faith of some of her followers that they had given up their jobs and spent their savings in anticipation of the prophesied event. But the day came and went, and there was no cataclysm. The prophetess was shaken for a while, but she soon rallied and triumphantly announced a message from outer space that the world had been spared because of the great faith of her followers. Some of her followers dissolved the cognitive dissonance created by this incident, and conceded that they had been wrong in putting their trust in the prophetess; they may have pleaded extenuating circumstances, and perhaps stressed the virtue of not shirking a personally embarrassing admission of error. Others, however, especially those who had been with the prophetess in the critical hours and thus under her suggestive influence, felt an increasing faith in her, and the result was that they redoubled their efforts to spread her fame and to win new disciples for her. It has been contended that a similar situation existed among some of the early followers of Jesus, who believed he had proclaimed that he was the Messiah destined to become King of the Jews in his lifetime. When this belief was disappointed, they did not lose their faith in him, but increased their apostolic zeal to spread his gospel.

Self-verifying Beliefs

Collective beliefs are psycho-social phenomena which by themselves produce no change in inanimate nature. Whatever the explanatory theories are in a particular society at a particular time about, say, the shape of the earth, the movements of the stars, or the nature of fire, physico-chemical reality remains unaffected. The same, however, cannot be said about psychosocial realities. Collective beliefs, and the action based on them, can fundamentally alter the properties of social institutions or human personalities. Karl Popper called this alteration an 'Oedipus effect'[407], because the Oedipus Saga demonstrates how a belief in the accuracy of Delphic prophecies induced Oedipus to make decisions which caused the prophecies to come true. Popper argues that, because of the Oedipus effect, the analysis of the social forces responsible for past historical events shed no light on the effect of the same social forces in future. If the analysis is generally accepted and thus becomes a collectively believed theory, steps will be taken which either hasten or prevent the emergence of the same historical results in the presence of similar social forces at a future date.

When collective beliefs have the effect of bringing about psycho-social events which would otherwise not have happened, we may speak of self-verifying beliefs, or 'self-fulfilling prophecies' as the sociologist R. K. Merton[352] has called them. If, for example, a false rumour is widely believed that a bank is going to fail, there will be a run on the bank, and it may actually have to suspend its transactions. Similarly, when a social minority is collectively believed to be untidy and unintelligent, measures will be taken by the social majority to keep minority members out of good residential areas and to curtail their educational opportunities, with the result that they will indeed appear untidy and unintelligent. There are, of course, also *self-falsifying beliefs* in the psycho-social field. The collective belief in the untidiness and unintelligence of a minority is bound to act as a spur and challenge to them, and, if social conditions become favourable, they will exert themselves to prove the collective beliefs of the majority wrong.

Individual beliefs about the qualities of other persons can also have a self-verifying or self-falsifying effect. This is particularly true of the individual beliefs of psychotherapists with regard to their patients. In suggestive and inspirational forms of treatment, the psychotherapist conveys positive beliefs in the patients' abilities, which become self-fulfilling, if they succeed in buttressing the patients' self-confidence and determination. In psychoanalytic forms of treatment, on the other hand, the therapist conveys derogatory beliefs about the patients' symptoms and behaviour in the treatment situation. Such beliefs may challenge the patients so that they become determined to falsify them as best they can.

Absolute Convictions and Half-beliefs

When theoretical beliefs are held with an absolute certitude of their truth or untruth, they are absolute convictions. No shadow of doubt can fall on them. The opposite convictions are unthinkable, irrational or preposterous. People who are absolutely convinced, for example, that one form of religion or political ideology is better than another, have no understanding or tolerance for people with other convictions. The solidarity of a religious, political or ethnic group can be measured by the strength and universality with which orthodox convictions are collectively held. In a solidary community, weakened and deviant convictions are heresies and threats to the security and continuance of the social group, and may therefore be treated with ruthless suppression.

There are also, in every social group, collective convictions which were once regarded as absolutely true, but have gradually come to be recognized as absolutely false. Such a conversion of a collective conviction from truth to falsehood is most obvious in the case of those transitory social phenomena known as fashions or vogues. They exist not only in the sartorial world, but in every walk of life. There are, for example, many therapeutic fashions which spread through the medical world like a minor mental epidemic until many doctors are convinced that a new and true cure of a particular ailment has arrived. Then, gradually, doubts and disappointments make their appearance and, in due course, the doctors change their opinions again, become convinced that the method of treatment was false and forget about it[395].

However, the conversion of collective convictions from absolute truth to absolute falsity can be a prolonged process and pass through a lengthy intermediate phase when the majority of people half believe and half disbelieve that the theories are true. Such ambivalent convictions, or half-beliefs, may still be powerful enough to enforce compliance with the propositions, customs and rules based on them. The compliance may be motivated by a desire to adhere to traditional beliefs and to conform to the general usages in one's social group. It may, however, also be inspired by lurking magic fears that infringement might bring down punishment and ill luck. Half-beliefs that are perpetuated by such fears are superstitions which can be subjectively recognized as such by the people who timidly obey them. We may thus talk of 'self-recognized superstitions' to distinguish them from collective convictions that are only diagnosed as superstitions by an outsider, but believed to be true by an insider.

In the absolute collective convictions of the Jewish and Catholic religions, for example, masturbation has always been regarded as a major sin that required expiation. Until the second half of the eighteenth century, however, physicians did not believe that masturbation was especially injurious to health, though there had been some occasional speculations that excessive sexual activity of any kind might produce certain physical diseases. It then gradually became a medical axiom that masturbation was the disgusting and inevitable cause of many physical and mental evils[219]. In the nineteenth century, there was hardly a voice of doubt raised in the general chorus of condemnation by doctors, clergymen and lay people alike. They were all absolutely convinced of the pernicious effect of masturbatory activities on body and mind. Towards the end of the nineteenth century, the absolute convictions of many physicians changed into half-beliefs as they began to realize that masturbation did not inevitably lead to physical disease. Psychiatrists followed suit and began to absolve masturbation from responsibility for insanity, but they still held fast to the belief that it produced a variety of neurotic disorders. Eventually, even this belief had to be abandoned in the face of evidence to the contrary. Kinsey and his collaborators[283, 284] have demonstrated beyond doubt that the physical act of masturbation is not pathogenic. Their investigations of more than 5000 American men and nearly 2800 American women, published in 1948 and 1953, revealed that 92 per cent of the men and 56 per cent of the women had masturbated to the point of orgasm at some time in their lives. The incidence was even greater among educated persons, namely 96 and 63 per cent respectively. Yet physical or mental damage resulted in only 'exceedingly few cases', if at all, and it was of no relevance how early in life regular masturbation had begun.

The collective belief of psychiatrists today is that masturbation, though not the cause of psychiatric disorders, may be a symptom of them. This diagnosis is generally made when masturbation is preferred by an adult to what is, in our culture, regarded as a more normal sexual activity in circumstances in which sexual partners are freely available and intercourse with them not restrained by a variety of moral and social injunctions. There is, however, a time lag between the adoption of convictions in progressive medical quarters and in the more hidebound circles of the general public. The latter still more than half believe today in the depravity and health-destroying consequences of masturbation. This still causes much secret heartache and fear; it may even cause frankly neurotic reactions in predisposed persons. Thus, although the physical act of masturbation has been shown to be harmless, the superstitious half-belief in its danger is still strong enough in many sections of the population to become a self-verifying belief that produces some of the ill-effects it confidently expects.

When collective superstitions are powerful and widely observed regulators of social behaviour, there is an understandable tendency to deny their irrationality, and to come forward with some explanations which give them, at least, a semblance of plausibility. It is, for instance, a superstition, widely observed and indeed prescribed in medical practice, to dab a patient's clean skin with alcohol before giving a hypodermic injection. This may be explained as an antiseptic measure designed to kill any pathogenic bacteria in the skin area chosen for the injection. It is true that, in the test tube, alcohol can destroy pathogenic microbes, but it does not have the same effect on microbes in the skin. The pre-injection ritual is thus no more than a superstition which many doctors fear to disregard, though it is rather like an attempt to exorcise evil spirits by touching the patient with clean spirit.

Customs based on collective superstitions may be enforced by the power of public opinion so that any desire to disregard dubious traditions is counteracted by a superstitious fear of ill luck and a very real fear of social disapproval or condemnation. To many Jews and Moslems of today, for example, circumcision is merely a ritual ordained by religious tradition, but is devoid of medical or hygienic justification. Yet they comply with the custom, partly for fear of exposing their sons to a potential, even if unknown, peril and partly for fear of offending the public opinion of co-religionists. It is a strange fact that the superstitious custom of circumcision has been adopted by a surprisingly large number of Christian families in English-speaking countries, but apparently nowhere else[171]. False assumptions about the retractability of the foreskin in infants and other doubtful medical considerations have been advanced to lend an air of reasonableness to the custom. Certainly many unnecessary circumcisions have been performed in England for many years. An investigation in 1949 revealed that 60 per cent of the male students at Cambridge University had been circumcised. The proportion rose with the social class of the students' parents so that in the sub-group of 'students coming from the best-known public schools' it was as high as 84 per cent.

Many superstitions are taboos rather than prescribed activities. One of the most compelling taboos concerns the use of four-letter Anglo-Saxon words, especially those for the genital and anal regions and for sexual and excretory activities. They are considered as the obscene verbal equivalents of public indecency because, in superstitious half-beliefs, words are magically identified with the objects and events they signify. To use collectively tabooed words can thus arouse disgust, embarrassment and feelings of outrage in the social environment. The superstitious fear of the offender that his words may be visited by punishment is reinforced by the knowledge of these social reactions. To make the superstition even more self-verifying it has been embodied in Acts of Parliament which threaten with legal sanctions those who flagrantly violate the taboo. Yet the words are used with impunity in certain sections of our society in which they have become the most favoured adjectives for everyday activities and the most popular swear words so that constant familiarity with them has robbed them of all obscene significance. When the tabooed words happen to be reported in some Court case as the remarks of an accused person, newspapers could not print them in full, but had to resort to a code consisting of the initial letters followed by dots. This coding was as easily understood by readers as if they had been presented with the original words spelled out fully. Only when the tabooed words occurred in a work of undoubted literary and aesthetic merit was their obscenity regarded by the Law as purged, and the words could then be printed in their uncoded form.

In many self-recognized collective superstitions no kernel of truth can be discovered and yet many people feel bound by them, though perhaps with an air of self-mocking embarrassment to excuse the irrationality of their actions. It is, for instance, a common superstition that it is unlucky to walk under a ladder leaning against a wall. In a recent casual observation in a provincial town in

England the behaviour of people, confronted with a ladder over the pavement, was recorded. Nobody was standing on the ladder so that there was not even the spurious excuse that something might be dropped or spilled on those rash enough to venture underneath the ladder. Yet, of 51 people, 37, or 72·5 per cent, stepped into the road and walked around the ladder[181].

CHAPTER 12

THE PSYCHOPATHOLOGY OF INTELLECT

The term 'intellect' is used here to connote both a person's intellectual ability to think and reason, that is, his intelligence; and the premises from which his thinking and reasoning start—his beliefs and convictions.

A person's intelligence is the resultant of innate abilities which are shaped, facilitated or impeded by acquired attributes. Genetic potentialities, combined with events affecting the developing brain before, during, and shortly after childbirth, are responsible for a person's innate intelligence. The innate intelligence of some persons is abnormally low by population standards. Such *innate intellectual deficiency* is not necessarily a psychiatric disease, but it turns into one, if it causes suffering and concern to the person's social environment because he cannot reach the levels of adjustment to the world around him which are normal for successive stages of his mental development. The diagnosis of intellectual deficiency can be quantitatively refined with the help of intelligence tests which are standardized by population norms. A person's usual level of intelligence is lowered by processes which affect his psychoneural effectiveness. When this happens, he functions below his individual intellectual norm. This occurs transiently in states of altered consciousness, such as those caused by somnolence or intoxication, or in states of temporary emotional preoccupation.

ACQUIRED INTELLECTUAL DEFICIENCY

When a person's normal level of intelligence is more permanently reduced, we speak of dementia. A mild degree of dementia is not necessarily pathological. In fact, it is usual in normal senescence which is characterized by a weakening of judgment, reasoning power and memory, by an egocentric narrowing of interest, and by perseverative tendencies which cause an adherence to routine, a desire for sameness in the environment, and increasingly conservative attitudes[8, 529]. In spite of these limitations and the reduction of adaptability and versatility, a healthy senescent person is well able to lead an independent life and to look after himself. He often even peevishly rejects offers of help for fear of having his routine upset.

Senile Dementia

In senile dementia[310, 408, 430], the patient's contact with the environment is temporarily or permanently blurred by an obfuscation of consciousness which may make him appear restless and confused at night and somnolent during the day; which may cause automatisms and bring him into conflict with the law through dull-witted improprieties, or involve him in loss of money through extravagance or ill-judged financial schemes. The intellectual deterioration of senile patients may be aggravated by an intercurrent infective or manic-depressive illness[280, 409], by cerebral arteriosclerosis, perseverative tendencies, and by memory disorders either of the dysmnesic kind, which impairs the reminiscence of recent events, or of the linguistic kind, which interferes with the recall of words (nominal aphasia)[59]. In advanced states of senile dementia, the patients lose all initiative and lead an almost brainless existence, apparently empty of thought or concern, mute and hardly responsive[8]. Senile dementia generally occurs in people over the age of 70, and seriously reduces the life expectancy of the patients. Some investigations suggest the possibility that the disease is due to the inheritance of a dominant gene[310]. In the relatives of senile dements, the incidence of senile dementia occurs about four times as often as in the general population. Neuropathological findings do not always accord well with the severity of the clinical picture. Some severely demented senile patients show little overt damage or atrophy in the brain; conversely, quite pronounced pathological changes of the brain may be present in people with no more than the clinical signs of a normal senescence[279, 431].

Dementia may also make its appearance at an earlier age than senility. This may be associated with degenerative changes in the brain as in Huntington's chorea or presenile dementia (Pick's and Alzheimer's disease). Other causes of earlier dementia are infections (syphilitic encephalitis causing G.P.I., acute virus encephalitis occasionally causing not only parkinsonism, but also dementia), cerebral arteriosclerosis, hypertension, vitamin deficiency, head injury, brain tumour, and prolonged cerebral anoxia (perhaps during an operation under general anaesthesia).

Schizophrenia

Intellectual deficiency occurs in schizophrenic illnesses, especially those which make their appearance in the first three decades of life. In childhood schizophrenia[64, 94, 95], the foremost symptoms are an (often irregular) impairment of intellectual development (in which speech is either lost or never acquired) an egocentric narrowing of interest diminishing emotional contact with others, and perseverative tendencies causing an adherence to routine and a desire for sameness in the environment. The majority of childhood schizophrenics remain permanently handicapped both socially and intellectually.

In adolescent schizophrenia, the dementing process can be most prominent and disconcerting, especially when it cuts short the career of a promising pupil who, quite unexpectedly, fails his examinations, begins to waste his time in idle inactivity or futile pursuits, and becomes unfit for any employment, except perhaps for occasional unskilled routine work. The emotional and intellectual contact of such patients with their environment is loosened, even when their consciousness is alert and lucid. They become engrossed in thoughts which are dominated by egocentric fantasies rather than considerations of reality—thoughts that have, for this reason, been labelled 'dereistic' or 'autistic'[50]. The upshot is that the patients appear apathetic, oblivious of social and emotional requirements, and careless of their personal comfort. Left to themselves, they soon look dirty, unkempt, and neglected. It was this intellectual, social and emotional deterioration which decided Kraepelin to use the the name *dementia praecox* for this group of diseases. In adolescent schizophrenics of a 'simple' type, thought processes gradually dry up, and the patients may complain of a poverty of thought or an inability to form clear ideas or images. But complaints and other signs of mental initiative may fade away. Then the patients spend most of their time standing, sitting or lying about, looking away from people, out of the window, or at their own mirror image. They rarely speak spontaneously, and when questions are put to them, their replies are so monosyllabic and uninformative that no conversation develops.

Incoherent Talk

A symptom, related to poverty of thought, is thought blocking. A sequence of ideas is suddenly interrupted and leaves a mental void. The symptom is similar to the abrupt disappearance of intended thought that occasionally afflicts a speaker who is anxious, badly prepared or tired. Even the most practised speaker may suffer from it, when a question is put to him at the end of an exhausting discussion; he sets out to answer, following a train of thought, but realizing after a while that he can no longer remember what he intended to say or what the question had been. Such thought blocking causes embarrassment to a normal person. The dementia praecox patient, on the other hand, whose thoughts become blocked, may merely stop in mid-sentence, quite blandly and unembarrassed.

There are, however, also patients who continue to speak, oblivious of thought blocking, following a devious and disjointed ideational path. They then show the symptom of incoherent talk. This was, at one time, attributed to a pathological disruption of the postulated associational links between ideas. E. Bleuler saw in this dissociation of ideas[50] one of the primary features of dementia praecox, and therefore proposed the alternative, and today preferred, name 'schizophrenia'.

There can be several psychopathological causes of incoherent ideation and speech[104]. Thought blocking is merely one of them, when it blots out the intended goal of reasoned thought, causing the patient to lose himself in irrelevancies or word play, until he adopts another equally inconstant trend of thought which again evaporates into airy nothings. Other patients manage to hold on to their intended meaning by speaking in brief sentences, or even in ungrammatical strings of words. But when a particular thought has found its terse expression, the matter is ended for the schizophrenic, and a completely different thought may come next in succession. Speech thus becomes capriciously incoherent and has been compared to the knight's move in chess: two steps forward and one aside.

In the beginning of a schizophrenic illness, patients often notice that their thought processes are no longer under their intentional control. Occasionally they complain about it. A patient, for instance, wrote to his sister: 'I have to control myself continually so as not to write too much nonsense. . . . You must not take my letter too literally. . . . I must stop now, my thoughts have become unbridled'[239]. Later, when the patient's contact with reality has deteriorated further, he may attribute such psychopathological experiences to outside powers which put ideas into his mind, or take them away (passivity feelings).

Thoughts can become so nebulous and peculiar in the course of a schizophrenic illness that the current meaning of words no longer fits them. Patients then give idiosyncratic meanings to ordinary words, or resort to esoteric terms; their speech not only becomes obscure, but stilted and euphuistic. When the most unusual words no longer serve as a vehicle for schizophrenic thoughts, the patients create *neologisms*, or verbal monstrosities of their own, perhaps to indicate that they feel 'sporched in a filtrum' or surrounded by 'radiomittic conspirationists'. The verbal communications of many schizophrenics appear like a hodge-podge of nonsense in which one

can discern less meaning than in Lewis Carroll's *Jabberwocky* or *The Hunting of the Snark*.

Even a schizophrenic whose speech is intelligible, taken sentence by sentence, may still leave his audience guessing because there is too little redundancy in the information he conveys. Each bit of his information is contained in a mere skeleton of words. There is no background to put the audience properly in the picture. For example, an unmarried patient may merely state that he said this or that to 'her', not bothering to identify her, or his relationship to her. When he is interrupted and asked who she is, he may perhaps reply: 'the wife', and then continue on another tack, leaving the audience still puzzled. Further questions may elicit that 'the wife' refers to his landlady, but by then the thread of the original information may have been hopelessly lost. To take an adequate history from this kind of schizophrenic patient can be an arduous or impossible task. There is always a barrier of communication around a schizophrenic patient, making it difficult to penetrate into the peculiar world he lives in.

An acceleration of thought is experienced in schizophrenia as an unpleasant crowding of thoughts. It is a symptom, however, that is much more characteristic of a manically elated patient in whom it is called flight of ideas. If the schizophrenic patient expresses his crowded thoughts in speech, a disjointed babble results which is incomprehensible, and usually called incoherent; if the manic patient does the same, he is equally disjointed, but not usually called incoherent because he creates a communion of good spirits which is a bond that endows his disconnected utterances with a semblance of intelligibility. Yet when his words are written down, their meaning is whittled away for we can no longer see from his behaviour, gestures and facial expressions what impresses him from moment to moment, though we may still feel amused by his rhyming and punning.

Retardation of thought and speech occurs in schizophrenic patients without any obvious justification, and in depressive patients in whom it seems justified because we have an intuitive understanding how grief and misery so utterly absorb them that they no longer wish to live, to think or speak. Of course, we also understand intuitively why other depressive patients are so utterly miserable that they have to reveal their suffering to the whole world in agitated lamentations.

Circumstantiality of thought and speech occurs in some mentally subnormal people, some chronic epileptics, some paranoid schizophrenics who have to mention every redundant detail of suspected events, and in patients with nominal aphasia, who replace the missing words by a verbose use of others that still come to their mind.

DELUSIONS

Delusions are usually regarded as the most characteristic symptoms of disordered thought in psychotic illnesses. The general definition of a delusion is that it is a false belief. This definition, however, is more suitable for the so-called delusions of normal people, or 'normal delusions', than for psychotic delusions. The term delusion has entered common parlance in a non-technical sense to indicate that somebody is harbouring false beliefs, though this does not necessarily suggest that he is also insane. We may call our political opponents deluded because their propositions are untenable in our eyes, we may even call them mad, but we do not really mean that the proper place for them is a mental hospital. We are similarly likely to speak of delusions, when we hear statements made by followers of scientific theories which are to us nothing but arrant nonsense. Yet all we mean by the term delusion in the simple sense of false belief is that people start reasoning from preconceptions and beliefs which are self-evidently true to them, and equally self-evidently false to us. They therefore deduce conclusions with which we cannot possibly agree.

A psychotic delusion, however, means more than just a false belief. In the first place, the word 'belief' is not quite adequate. It has lost much of its original meaning of absolute faith, and can be used today to express no more than a tentative opinion. Yet the salient feature of a psychotic delusion is that it is inspired by an absolute and incontrovertible conviction of the truth of a proposition. At the very least, therefore, a psychotic delusion must be regarded as a false conviction.

A psychotically deluded patient may be absolutely convinced that he is the victim of witchcraft, that he is spied upon and persecuted by his neighbours or by a secret fraternity, that he is God or the Devil incarnate, that he has committed unpardonable sins for which he is eternally doomed, that he has changed his sex, that his body has rotted away, that his thoughts can be read by others, that he can raise the dead, that he will never die, that his legs consist of wood or his brain of glass, and so on. A psychotic delusion is false because it seems to us absurd and irrational. It makes the same impression on other people and even on other psychiatric patients with psychotic delusions of their own. If, for example, a number of psychotically deluded patients are assembled for the purpose of group psychotherapy, each patient will point out that the delusional convictions held by others are rationally untenable, yet each patient will defend his own psychotic delusions as obviously and unshakeably true.

The criterion of irrationality must be used with caution in psychiatry. After all, irrationality means no more than our inability to seè how certain propositions can be right; and yet our inability may be merely due to the fact that the propositions are derived from convictions that are culturally conditioned and happen to be different from ours. Thus, before making the diagnosis of irrationality and falsity we must decide whether another person's statements are in line with convictions held in his social or cultural environment. For example, a patient's conviction that his illness is the result of witchcraft does not automatically stamp it as a psychotic delusion. It becomes a psychotic delusion only if the patient belongs to a social and cultural milieu in which there is no overt belief in witchcraft as a pathogenic cause of disease. A psychotic delusion therefore must not only appear false, it must also be unshared or idiosyncratic.

A second characteristic of psychotic delusions is that they are ego-involved. By this is meant that they are infused with a sense of great personal importance, that they refer to realities with which the patient's ego is closely concerned. Yet the two characteristics of idiosyncrasy and ego-involvement are still not enough to allow a definite diagnosis of psychotic delusions because normal persons have convictions which are idiosyncratic and ego-involved without being psychotic. They have convictions which are so delicately and intimately private that they cannot be easily discussed with others, not even in the confidential atmosphere of a psychotherapeutic interview. This is particularly the case with many of the opinions an individual privately holds about his personal attributes. He may, for instance, regard himself as more popular or unpopular than others do, as socially more dominant or submissive, more attractive or ugly, more skilful or clumsy, more intelligent or dull, and so on. In the contexts of therapeutic groups, it has even been possible to obtain measurements of the extent to which a person's ego-involved estimate of his social popularity or dominance idiosyncratically deviates from the reality of his status, as collectively assessed by other group members[494]. If some aspects of a person's normal, but unshared, ego-involved convictions are too much at variance with the assessments by others, he is likely to become aware of this discrepancy sooner or later even in a very tactful and considerate environment. This may jolt him into changing his opinion of himself, though he may fight a rearguard action by avoiding critical test situations which can expose his self-deception. It is, for instance, quite common for people to cling to a body image of themselves whose youthful appearance and physical prowess deviates increasingly, with advancing years, from objective reality. However, normal people generally succeed in keeping the deviation within reasonable limits so that they do not run the risk of social discomfiture.

Apart from idiosyncrasy and ego-involvement, the most important characteristic of psychotic delusions is their (incorrigibility by psychological means.) In normal people, even lifelong, ego-involved and absolute convictions can be changed by an abundance of contradictory evidence or by forms of indoctrination which cunningly combine the tricks of conditioning procedures with powerful coercions, persuasions and suggestions[325, 439]. It is believed that these 'brain-washing procedures' were applied in Stalinist Russia to political prisoners with such success that they not only renounced political convictions for which they had worked and suffered all their lives, but declared in open court and with all the signs of genuine sincerity that they had never truly held such convictions and had always plotted to undermine them in others. There is, however, no form of indoctrination, no matter how cunning, resourceful and ruthless, that has ever succeeded in removing psychotic delusions. The treatment (if this is the correct word) of psychotic patients in past centuries provides horrifying proof of the incorrigibility of their delusions. Shameful neglect and degradation, painful punishments and torments, brutal intimidations and the weakening effect of incarceration, bleeding, purging and undernourishment were of no avail against the stubborn tenacity of psychotic delusions.

Finally, psychotic delusions are often characterized by their preoccupying power. When a psychotic illness is in an acute or active phase, delusions monopolize a patient's mind to the virtual exclusion of everything else. In more quiescent and chronic phases of a psychotic illness, patients are able to attend to other business, even if delusions continue to hover at the back of their minds and retain their force of absolute conviction. A preoccupying psychotic delusion cannot be hidden from the environment. At the very least it shows itself objectively in a brooding rumination or in behaviour that is odd and unpredictable. When the patient talks about his delusion, he soon realizes that he is disbelieved and perhaps even ridiculed. He may react in different ways to this realization. He may try to convince others of the truth of his beliefs, he may withdraw into a deluded private world of his own and pay no regard to the discrepant views of other people, or he may weave the disbelief of his social environment into the net of his delusional system and suspect that all the people around him try to deceive him.

In summary, we may thus characterize a psychotic delusion as an absolute conviction of the truth of a proposition which is idiosyncratic, ego-involved, incorrigible, and often preoccupying.

Self-verifying Psychotic Delusions

We have mentioned before that normal convictions can be self-verifying in certain circumstances. The same is true of psychotic delusions; there are therefore apparently self-verifying psychotic delusions which, by the very act of self-verification, lose their delusional character and become objectively true. This is sometimes most spectacularly demonstrated by paranoid patients with delusions of persecutions. Such patients, as will be described presently, may entertain the absolute conviction that every person they meet, socially or occupationally, is ill-disposed and hostile towards them. To this conviction, which is initially false, they are likely to respond by being hostile and antagonistic on their part. People around them are thus stung to retaliate in the same coin. Wherever such a paranoid patient goes, neighbours, workmates, employers or subordinates are sure to turn against him as he had delusionally predicted and expected. Hence the patient is, in fact, universally disliked, avoided and reviled. He can bring chapter and verse to prove the truth of his self-verifying psychotic delusion.

Some paranoid patients learn in time that, if they wish people to believe them, they had better talk only about the self-verified part of their persecutory delusions. However, if they can be induced to give reasons for the general hostility against them, their explanations are expressed in terms of delusional propositions which are not verified and therefore easily recognized as idiosyncratic, ego-involved and incorrigible convictions. Yet there are many patients who have become experts in revealing nothing to you but real and verifiable events, the unpleasant tricks neighbours have really played on them, the rude letters actually received by them, the visible damage done to their property, and so on. It may then need a sharp ear to detect the gaps in the patient's narrative, to discover how neatly they are covered up, and how persistently we are prevented from uncovering them.

It happens very occasionally that a paranoid patient succeeds in convincing one or two susceptible persons that his psychotic delusions, whether self-verifying or not, are true. He is most likely to be successful with persons who live with him and have little contact with the outside world. They are thus exposed to a barrage of continual indoctrination and have little chance to hear the views of unbiased outsiders. In the end, they may succumb to the patient's indoctrination, and wholeheartedly embrace his psychotic delusions. They may thus become as absolutely convinced of a neighbour's nefarious plots against them. They may also smell the poison gas the neighbour pumps into the house, feel the electric rays he sends through the wall, hear him tiptoe through their house at night, and see his shadowy figure leave through the gate. Such encapsulated collective convictions are readily recognized as delusional by all outsiders. It is customary to speak then of a *folie à deux* (or *à trois*, etc.)[117, 199, 542] or of an 'induced insanity'. These names are not aptly chosen as they are based on the false belief that the indoctrinated person, by adopting the patient's psychotic delusions, has himself developed a psychotic disease. Yet the presence of a clinical symptom, especially of a psychiatric symptom, is never a pathognomonic indicator of a specific disease entity. It can, in fact, be easily shown that almost all the indoctrinated persons have retained their sanity. All that is needed is to remove them from the patient's company and domination. It soon becomes apparent then that their delusions are not psychotic, and lack the characteristic of incorrigibility. The persons who had merely adopted the delusions of a psychotic patient then gradually begin to doubt their truth, and eventually realize how unjustified and false they were. A *folie à deux* is thus not usually an induced psychotic illness, but merely a shared delusion which is of the incorrigible variety only in the psychotic patient.

Forms Taken by Psychotic Delusions

Psychotic delusions can assume many forms. They may falsify the objective reality of only certain areas of a patient's life, perhaps only the reality of his health, or of his social relations with erotic partners, or business associates. A patient may have various delusions which are each of an independent and perhaps contradictory kind (isolated delusions) or are logically integrated into a consistent delusional system (systematized delusions). Delusions may be mainly centred on the patient's own body, morality and fate, or they may involve a particular person, or group of persons, in his environment, or a vague and anonymous body of people in the world at large. The great variety of psychotic delusions has been divided into a small number of categories which are, however, not pathognomonic for any particular group of psychotic diseases. Any one of the various delusional categories may be found in different organic or functional psychoses. The presence of one or the other type of psychotic delusion does not therefore, by itself, justify a particular psychiatric diagnosis. Yet it is also true that there is a definite tendency for some types of delusions to occur more frequently in one functional psychosis than others.

Paranoid Delusions

The largest delusional category is that of paranoid delusions which occur especially in schizophrenic patients, but are also present in many organic and depressive psychotics. The greater the age of a psychiatric patient, the greater the likelihood of his showing some paranoid features, though not necessarily of delusional intensity and incorrigibility. If paranoid delusions are in the foreground of a schizophrenic illness, we speak of a 'paranoid schizophrenia'. It typically occurs after the third decade of life, and as the personality of the patient is by then firmly established, signs of dementia, or deterioration of conduct, are less in evidence. Because of the wide range of paranoid delusions they have been sub-divided into delusions of persecution, reference, and jealousy, and into litigious and erotic delusions.

Delusions of *persecution* constitute the most characteristic form of paranoid delusions. They convince a patient that he is the innocent victim of a malevolent plot, directed and planned by an anonymous power, or a particular organization (Communists, Nazis, Jews, Freemasons, etc.), or by certain persons in the office, at home, or the neighbourhood. They may be convinced that their doctor's treatment is deliberately designed to ruin their health; that their solicitor purposely neglects their interests, that their business partner secretly deceives them, that their employer gives them the worst jobs, that a prominent public personality uses his influence to harm them; that they are followed and spied upon; that their thoughts are read and broadcast; that they are made to think particular thoughts and to perform particular actions; that their physical health is undermined by arcane means; that electricity, rays, and radiations are focused on them to stimulate them sexually and to sap their strength; that poison gas is sprayed on them, and toxic substances added to their food. It is no wonder that such patients, when living in the community, are constantly in conflict with neighbours, colleagues and superiors. They change their addresses frequently to escape persecution, or go from job to job in a vain effort to find employment where they will not be victimized, ridiculed and shunned.

A patient with delusions of *reference* finds ego-involved meaning in everything that happens around him. There are signs and clues everywhere of mischievous machinations directed against him, and of clandestine messages about him being passed between strangers. He sees a sinister purpose in the gestures of people he meets, in their facial expressions, their tone of voice, the way they smile or frown, the clothes they wear, the remarks they make. Somebody yawns to signal to others that they should think of the patient as lazy; they scratch their heads to reveal to all and sundry that he is mad; they rub their hands to draw attention to his masturbation; they stand with their backs to him to spread the lie that he is a homosexual. In short, there is hardly anything in the behaviour of other people that cannot convey a delusionally distorted meaning to the patient. He is convinced too that he is slandered and libelled in many other ways, that hidden information about him is published in the newspapers, on the wireless and television. Even the questions he is asked by his doctor seem to have the ulterior purpose of showing up his ignorance or of maligning his character.

Another form of paranoid delusions are delusions of *jealousy*[451] which start with the preconceived and unshakeable conviction of the infidelity of the patient's spouse. All evidence to the contrary is dismissed as deceptive, but the most irrelevant observation is eagerly seized upon, if it can be twisted into a possible sign of unfaithfulness. A female patient may be convinced that it is proof of her husband's infidelity that he had talked to her, and thus diverted her attention, just when they passed a woman in the street; or that he had bought himself a new tie; or that there were some hairs on his coat. A male patient may be similarly deluded that it is a sign of his wife's infidelity that he had seen her speak to a neighbour; that the window cleaner had been in the house; that he noticed some men who walked rather slowly past the window of their sitting room; that there were creases in his wife's skirt; or that there were peculiar spots on the bedlinen when he woke up in the morning after a heavy sleep, which meant that she had drugged him so that she and her men friends could enjoy a night of love by his side. Even the most harmless incident can be grist to the mill of a patient with delusions of jealousy, and spark off violent rows and accusations. Such patients generally refuse hospital treatment as they suspect it to be a ruse to get them out of the way. When they are actually committed to a psychiatric hospital, they stage an early recovery and declare, with every sign of sincerity, that they have realized now how groundless their jealous suspicions had been. They insist on an early discharge from hospital, but when they get home, their jealousies reveal themselves again with a vengeance.

Sometimes delusions of jealousy are, or appear, self-verifying. A wife, in her desperation, may eventually agree to her husband's incessant demands to tell him with whom she is in love. She may speak of somebody to whom she is secretly attracted, or with whom she had an affair before she knew the patient, or into whose arms she had actually been driven by the husband's intolerable jealousy. He may react to such confessions, or to discovering his wife *in flagrante delicto*, with an explosion of murderous fury, or break down in self-pitying tears, or suspect that a trick is played on him to put him on a false trail so that the real lover, or lovers, should remain unmolested. Delusional worlds can be so far out of touch with the world of reality known to us that the usual rules of proof no longer apply.

Another variety of paranoid symptoms are *litigious* delusions. Such patients constantly appeal to lawyers and law-courts for protection against the wrongs and torts done to them. They often acquire an extensive knowledge of the law which they interpret entirely in their own favour. They are incessantly engaged in legal wrangles and correspondence, and are a source of vexation and bother to the legal profession and to anyone who crosses their path and impedes them.

Erotic delusions are paranoid manifestations which seem to be the obverse of delusions of persecution. Instead of feeling harassed and annoyed by a person, patients are convinced that they are loved and desired by him. They may never have met the other person who may be a man of fame in the world of public affairs or entertainment, or an anonymous girl they happen to pass regularly in the street or on public transport; but often the person is some one they meet in a social context, perhaps their doctor or employer. Neutral events are interpreted as messages of ardent love from the person delusionally chosen. Hallucinations and dreams may fan the fervour of their convictions that there is a secret bond of tender passion between them and the loved one. When the patients eventually act upon their erotic delusions and assure the loved persons that the affection is mutual, and that the intended marriage can take place, they naturally cause surprise, embarrassment, and indignation. This may be delusionally explained away, perhaps as shyness on the part of the beloved or a cowardly fear of having their love made public. Then the loved person continues to be pursued with importunate avowals of affection. His (or her) home may be invaded by the patient who demands to be shown the delusionally expected love and devotion, and perhaps insists on being treated as the rightful wife (or husband), ordering the legitimate spouse out of the house. It can, however, happen that the erotic delusions of a patient eventually turn into delusions of being deliberately jilted. The result is either a depressive reaction that can reach suicidal intensity, or a reaction of malice which does its spiteful best to prove that 'heaven has no rage, like love to hatred turned nor hell a fury, like a woman scorned'. If a psychiatrist or psychotherapist becomes the object of a patient's erotic delusions, he is well advised to let a colleague look after the patient instead of running the risk of being, at first, incontinently importuned and, later on, pursued with abuse, personal attacks, and perhaps a legal action for misconduct or professional negligence.

Grandiose delusions can form part of a persecutory delusional system; they explain, to the satisfaction of the patient, the enmity of his social environment. He is sure that he attracted the attention of his adversaries because he came into the possession of some special knowledge, or because he had made a commercially successful invention which was somehow stolen and exploited by others, or because he is of noble descent, but was deprived of his birthright by a swindling gang of blackguards. Grandiose delusions are also found in manically elated patients who are confident that they are stronger, wealthier, healthier and cleverer than everybody else; that they can do no wrong and are invariably lucky and successful. If grandiose delusions occur in an organic dementia that is in G.P.I., they are often grotesquely exorbitant. The patients may brag and bluster of billions and billions of riches, and promise fortunes to those who help them; they may identify themselves with divine beings or with personages of fame and distinction; they may boast of their power to kill thousands by a mere nod of their head, to cure all ills in the world, to stop the sun in his tracks, or to perform some similar miraculous feat.

Depressive Delusions

Depressive delusions have their basis in psychotic convictions of personal failure that has been lifelong, extending from a mis-spent past to an inevitably doomed future (delusions of guilt and unworthiness). The patients accuse themselves of offences, ranging from trivial to serious and atrocious, which they may have committed in fact, or could not possibly have committed. Their memories and their expectations are steeped in dark gloom with no ray of light anywhere. They are willing to do penance, to accept their deserved punishment, and yet they shrink from it in fear of its inevitable severity. They are convinced they should be outlawed, imprisoned, deprived of all comfort; they are not worthy to have food, to sleep in a bed, to remain among decent people; they should be killed. They may be certain that their punishment has already been decreed and set in motion; that they have already been stripped of everything they ever possessed; that they will starve and die a lingering horrible death, and that the same fate is in store for their families. Some patients are even convinced that they are already dead and that only the material husk of their bodies continues to exist in a world that is no longer real (delusions of nihilism). There is often an air of grandiosity and megalomania in depressive delusions. Patients feel that they are stricken with some foul and pestilential disease which will destroy the health of the whole world. They blame themselves for all the ills on earth and all the misfortunes reported in the paper or witnessed in their environment. They may be afraid to pass water lest the world will be flooded, or to eat lest their bodies expand and choke everyone in the ward.

Hypochondriacal Delusions

Hypochondriacal delusions occupy an uncertain position among delusional categories. This is perhaps partly due to the over-simplified definition of delusions as mere 'false beliefs', from which the justification has sometimes been derived that wavering false beliefs which are transiently corrigible may be included in this category. The diagnosis becomes less uncertain, if a strict definition of psychotic delusions is applied and only those false beliefs of bodily ill-health regarded as hypochondriacal delusions, which are absolute, unshared, ego-involved and incorrigible convictions. Hypochondriacal delusions in this strict sense occur in organically determined disorders of the body image, in states of clouded consciousness, and in schizophrenia and depression.

In depressive patients, hypochondriacal delusions are associated with delusions of inevitable doom, and therapeutic measures are viewed as hopeless and perhaps even resisted; on the other hand, in schizophrenic patients, such delusions tend to be expressed with bland unconcern and no requests for treatment. The hypochondriacal delusions of functional psychotics are thus in contrast to the typical picture of non-psychotic hypochondriacs who are importunate in their demand for medical attention, go from doctor to doctor, and respond with an initial glimmer of hope and optimism to every new form of treatment they are given.

Hypochondriacal delusions about the physical state of internal organs are often of a crude and absurd kind because the patients' lay ideas about the inside of their bodies are very hazy. There may be assertions that their blood has turned to water, their spinal cord dried up, their brain shrunk, that their bowels are completely blocked with faeces, or their bodies decaying. Patients can have convincing sensations of foreign bodies in their inside, for instance, of water in the brain or around the heart; of stones, metal or animals in the stomach; of an ulcer or cancer in a particular part of the body; of a hole in their back; of a change of sex; or of a transformation into an animal.

CHAPTER 13

THE PSYCHOPATHOLOGY OF AFFECT—
FUNCTIONAL PSYCHOSES

Schizophrenic Symptoms

In schizophrenia, affective changes are usually regarded as less important than disturbances of thought and motility. Yet pathological emotions are often very conspicuous in schizophrenic patients. Many of them exhibit a *poverty of emotions* (analogous to their poverty of thought); they are apathetic and indifferent even to the extent of being neglectful of personal hygiene and comfort. They may soil themselves and smear their faeces about without caring; they may stand or sit immobile in freezingly cold and draughty conditions without showing signs of distress; they may bruise, cut or scald themselves without complaining of pain or guarding the injured parts. Their emotional poverty extends also into the field of interpersonal relations so that they are emotionally out of touch with their environment and seem to live in an unfeeling solipsistic world of their own.

Yet behind the façade of apathy and indolence, affect-charged experiences may exist of which we only obtain glimpses, when they occasionally break through to the surface in a display of feelings for which there is no objective justification. Most common in young solitary patients is a mirthless *schizophrenic giggle* or a dry chuckle of embarrassment for which the patient can give no adequate explanation. The usual apathy of such patients may, however, also be interrupted by unexpected *outbursts of temper* and senseless acts of aggression and destruction. There may also be an *incongruity of affect* in the sense that joyful events elicit a morose sadness, and depressing events an attack of giggling. Young schizophrenics, in the beginning of their illness, sometimes show *feelings of perplexity* which may be an understandable reaction to the puzzling intrusion of pathological thoughts and experiences into consciousness. There is also often an increase of *auto-erotic sexual feelings* that find an outlet in frequent masturbation in which patients may indulge quite openly in the presence of others.

In paranoid schizophrenics, there is generally no emotional poverty, but a wide variety of affects can occur which are usually in harmony with delusions and hallucinations. Persecutory delusions are accompanied by feelings of suspiciousness and depression; delusions of grandeur by feelings of superiority or missionary zeal; delusions of jealousy by feelings of distrust, despair, and hatred; erotic delusions by feelings of amorous affections; and litigious delusions by feelings of self-righteous indignation.

MANIC-DEPRESSIVE SYMPTOMS

The pathological affects of paranoid schizophrenics seem to follow in the wake of delusions. In manic-depressives, on the other hand, the pathological mood appears to be primary and to determine whatever thoughts, memories and delusions can occur. As the affects of manic-depressive patients are overtly displayed and evoke an emotional resonance in their social environment, their thoughts, memories, and often even their delusions are intuitively understood and therefore apt to be falsely accepted as justified, not only in the world of intuitive fiction, but in the world of objective reality. This error is not so likely to be committed when the manic-depressive illness is severe and its symptoms obviously psychotic, and thus abnormal both by population standards and by the individual standards of the patients' premorbid personality.

In milder degrees of manic-depression, however, the symptoms can remain almost within the limits of population norms, though they deviate, of course, from the patients' individual premorbid norms. It is then that the illness is often overlooked, and the patients' symptoms attributed to other causes, such as an abnormal, but psychiatrically healthy, personality.

A patient with *manic* symptoms of psychotic severity is continuously on the go, flitting from one activity, or trend of thought to another so quickly that nothing is ever completed. As a new fancy strikes his mind, or a new event distracts his attention, he has to deal with it then and there, either verbally or by manipulation, or both. He does not get enough nourishment because he cannot help interrupting his meals, when he has hardly begun them; nor does he get enough sleep for he is too restlessly active to remain in bed. He is never silent, but pours out a torrent of words in which a fitful flight of ideas is more conspicuous than any steadfast meaning; no train of thought is verbally expressed for long before it is hustled aside by remarks that go off at a tangent; and when ideas fail, the production of words can go on, though they are strung together for the most casual reasons, perhaps because they rhyme, have a similarity of sound, or convey a precarious pun. The mere utterance of words is often not enough; the patient has to shout, roar, scream or sing at the top of his voice. To add to the decibels of noise he can produce orally, he may engage in banging, stamping, clapping, clattering or any other ear-splitting manœuvre. He button-holes other people to make them listen to him, gives them commands, pushes them around, and misses no opportunity to make personal, and often rude and offensive, remarks. His mood is usually one of boisterous hilarity which radiates cheerfulness through gestures of *bonhomie* and through laughter that is hearty, loud and infectious, but the geniality is as fickle as his thought. Anger flares up quickly when he cannot get his own way. Insults and abuse are then hurled at those who oppose him; blows and missiles can follow. Yet the ill-temper generally evaporates as suddenly as it arose; while the victims are still smarting from the attack on them, he cheerfully suggests letting bygones be bygones. In many manic patients, however, the mood is not so much joyful as bumptious, boastful, critical, interfering and demanding. In others, the mood of elation is spiced with the occasional pleasures of some self-pitying tears and remarks.

It is obvious that an unruly manic patient cannot carry on with his work, nor can he be looked after by relatives. Medically, there is also the danger that his over-activity, combined with lack of proper sleep and nourishment, will undermine his physical health, and cloud his consciousness so that the clinical picture becomes aggravated by the addition of confused disoriented activities, and perhaps of delirious hallucinations. Admission to a psychiatric ward is then imperative so that shock treatment and tranquillizers can tone down the acuity of the manic condition and make the patient amenable to expert nursing care.

Most manic episodes last for a number of weeks or months and then clear up spontaneously. There is, however, a tendency for manic attacks to recur, perhaps interspersed, or alternating, with depressive attacks. The interval between the attacks can be many years, but it tends to become shorter with the number of attacks that have occurred, and in a few patients, a chronic manic condition develops eventually which requires continual supervision and treatment.

Hypomanic Symptoms

Hypomanic symptoms exceed the limits of a population norm of conduct, but are not sufficiently dramatic to suggest to the inexperienced layman the symptoms of an illness. Physicians may also be misled because they are often under the misapprehension that a manic illness is a psychotic disease even in its hypomanic form. They therefore miss the diagnosis in patients whose sanity is quite obviously intact since they are in touch with reality, even though their behaviour transgresses the ideal norms of law and convention. To make the diagnosis of hypomania it is necessary to appreciate that the patient's usual personality (his 'premorbid' personality) has undergone a change, that his present personality is abnormal by his individual standard of normality. Yet the appreciation of a change of personality is difficult, when the patient has had previous hypomanic episodes. During such episodes he is more outstanding in every respect and his characteristics therefore more memorable. As a result, his social environment is likely to assert that there has been no change in his personality, and the patient may concur because, in his elated mood, he also tends to remember events that happened in previous episodes of elation rather than those that occurred in his humdrum normal life. It needs skilful history-taking to uncover such a patient's normal personality. Everything conspires to lead one astray so that the diagnosis of an abnormal personality is made instead of the diagnosis of recurrent hypomania.

A hypomanic change is in the direction of increased mental and physical activity, greater self-confidence and more aesthetic relish. How far this change goes, depends on the severity of the illness, the frequency of its recurrence, and the premorbid personality traits of the patient. His movements become quicker and more determined; his gestures more lively so that his elbows are usually some distance away from his body; his conversation is more witty and original; his inventiveness, creativeness and judgment more acute; his energies and interests more unflagging and varied; his mood more optimistic and adventurous. The hypomanic patient however, cannot control, or put to profitable use his increase of drive, self-confidence and aesthetic relish. His drive may be dissipated in activities which are socially and morally objectionable, his self confidence may express itself in overbearing and critical behaviour, and his aesthetic zest may find a self-indulgent outlet in bouts of over-eating and over-drinking. He may feel conceited enough to think himself above the constraints of prudence and morality, and pursue his own selfish advantage in blatant disregard of law and honesty. He may get involved, through dare-devil bravado or a gambler's trust in his good luck, in a risky or risqué enterprise which may cost him his life, livelihood, reputation or fortune. A hypomanic girl may be 'nymphomanic' and indulge her heightened sexual appetite indiscriminately without paying attention to the possibility of an unwanted pregnancy or a venereal disease. A hypomanic man may ruin his business and his marriage; he often provokes legal proceedings against himself for civil or criminal offences, and his hypomanic illness cannot be pleaded as an excuse, even if it were correctly diagnosed, as it is not a psychotic illness and does not, in the eyes of the law, remove his liability for his actions.

When the heightening of energy, self-confidence and aesthetic relish is only moderate, and the person retains sufficient self-control to gear his overbubbling drive to productive and creative work, to the organization of social and sociable activities, to the pleasure of savouring a mutual erotic friendship, and the sensuous enjoyment of beauty in art and nature, there are no clinical symptoms as there is no suffering and concern. There is only a *hyperthymic condition* which is useful and welcome to the patient and society. Such normal and socially valuable hyperthymic conditions can, however, be the forerunners of later episodes which are manic-depressive, and thus socially and clinically precarious. It is not uncommon to encounter middle-aged manic-depressive patients who have had a successful career as enterprising businessmen, politicians, musicians, writers, or painters because of early hyperthymic conditions, when they had laid the foundations for brilliant achievements and reputations in their chosen domain.

Hypothymic Condition

When a person's mood dips below his individual norm, but remains within the population norm, he is in the grip of a hypothymic condition. He is not overtly depressed, but his enjoyment of pleasures is muted, his initiative blunted, and his self-confidence undermined. He may then have an increased need to be appreciated by friends and colleagues, and make special efforts to gain their goodwill by presents or offers of help. He defers to their better knowledge and judgment, thus giving them the gratifying feeling of superiority. A hypothymic person of this kind is very popular with his colleagues, a fact that may escape casual observers to whom he is a colourless, unobtrusive person in the background. When he develops a more intensive depressive episode and has to be admitted to hospital, his popularity is shown by the number of friends and colleagues who visit him and are genuinely concerned about his progress. This popularity can be a valuable diagnostic pointer. In his own family, however, a hypothymic person is not as popular as a rule. The family members are critical of him because they suffer from his listlessness and complaints, his inability to show positive and warm feelings, his irritable outbursts, his withdrawal from family affairs and—most of all perhaps—from the fact that he can change into an affable person, when visitors are present.

Hypomelancholia

When a hypothymic condition becomes more marked, the person's working ability suffers, and the change in his personality is then clearly abnormal by both individual and population standards. We then deal with an illness that might be called hypomelancholia in analogy to hypomania, but unfortunately this term is not in common use. Instead such vague and theoretically misleading expressions are employed as mild depressive reaction or neurotic depression. Yet the illness need not be a reaction to an antecedent experience; nor is it justified to use the word 'neurotic' with all its manifold implications, when all that is meant by it is 'non-psychotic'—or more correctly, an illness that has not reached psychotic dimensions.

The essential constituents of hypomelancholic symptoms can be, but need not be, the exact opposites of the essential elements in hypomanic symptons: there is usually a decrease in mental and physical activity, in self-confidence and in the enjoyment of pleasure. The patient lacks energy and intitiative in general, or only with regard to important and responsible functions of life. The usual clinical picture is that, after a night of curtailed sleep, he has no desire to get up in the morning, and is disheartened by the prospect of starting another day of emotional gloom. His mind is sluggish, and his speech sparse, short, and without sparkle: his movements are measured, his gestures few, and his elbows near the body. He gets through the day with a minimum of exertion, though he may shed some of his indolence in the evening. He may be scolded for being a laggard and idler, or receive sympathy for being 'out of sorts'. When he is regarded as merely lazy and inadequate, the treatment he receives is criticism, reproof, advice to show more interest and application, exhortation to continue with his work, or even disciplinary measures of one kind or another. To such therapeutic efforts he may react with annoyance and irritability because the demands exceed his powers to conform and add to the burden of his suffering.

Physical symptoms may be in the foreground of the clinical picture and the patient may be accepted as ill. When he complains of such symptoms as headaches, palpitations, indigestion, constipation, or a variety of localized pains, an organic diagnosis is often tentatively made, investigations started and different forms of medical, or even surgical, treatment tried. With good luck, the depressive episode clears up spontaneously in the course of one or the other investigation or treatment. But with more prolonged hypomelancholic episodes, the diagnostic hypotheses return to the psychiatric field, the depressive nature of the symptoms may be recognized and antidepressant drugs applied with usually good results. Alternatively, some other assumptions are made which can range from nervous debility to an immature, dependent or otherwise inadequate personality, and the patient is left to his own devices then, or given prolonged psychotherapy until the depressive episode comes to its natural end[301, 349, 525, 526].

When the depressive patient's self-confidence is at a low ebb, he agrees with the critical views others have of him, no matter whether the views are expressed candidly or hidden behind the diagnosis of an abnormal personality. He is then willing to accept any kind of psychotherapy, however costly, time-consuming, and emotionally harassing, for the alternative is far worse: it is the gloomy prospect of unending disapproval by his family, of dragging hours of inertia, self-critical worry, and unrelieved pessimism. If psychotherapy is not available for him, he may give up the unequal struggle and resign himself to his fate of being good for nothing, inferior, inadequate, dependent, immature, and useless. He is then likely to stay in bed much of the time, lounge about, avoid company, and begin to think of what seems to be the only escape from constant misery: suicide. There are more than 5000 annual deaths through suicide in England and Wales, which amounts to 11 to 12 deaths in any random sample of 100,000 people. This is about twice the death rate of tuberculosis today, and most of the suicides are caused by depressive delusions. The mortality of depressive illnesses is therefore far from negligible[125, 208, 433, 482, 483, 484, 549].

The lowering of self-confidence and the associated feelings of self-criticism and worthlessness are often the most characteristic signs of mildly depressive episodes. The patients even feel responsible for the symptoms of their illness, and blame themselves because they cannot cope with the problems of life or shake off their inertia, pessimism and dejection. They feel guilty and sinful, and their memory takes up all the peccadilloes they ever committed. They may have an urge to confess past misdeeds, and the consequences can be ruinous to their reputation, their friendships and married life. But depressive feelings of guilt and self-accusation are not always prominent in hypomelancholic episodes. Other affective symptoms may be more conspicuous, such as, for instance, the inability to enjoy pleasures. This may show itself as a loss of interest in hobbies and aesthetic pursuits. Music, literature, art or congenial company no longer elicit positive feelings in the patient; amusing and witty conversation leaves him unmoved; he cannot even feel love and affection for his family or an erotic partner.

In other patients, continual feelings of apprehension are in the foreground, or attacks of nameless terror for which there is no rational justification. There may also be a hypochondriacal over-concern with bodily functions, and a self-centred and querulous demand for getting personal attention from family members, nurses and doctors. This is often interspersed with profuse protestations of gratitude for the help and attention received. There are also patients who seek solace in an illicit love relation that is likely to bring as much guilt and anxiety as comfort and relief; and other patients who try to drown their depressive sorrows in alcohol or drugged sleep. Sometimes patients display a mixture of hypomanic and hypomelancholic symptoms, often in the form of a diurnal variation with depressive symptoms in the morning and a hypo-manic euphoria in the evening, or *vice versa*; or the presence of hypomanic or depressive symptoms may depend on the social situation and the degree of responsibility contained in it. The patient may thus be carefree and cheerful when he is at play, but anxious and hamstrung when he is at work.

Reactive Depression

When a depressive episode is preceded in time by a hypomanic spell—an occurrence that is not uncommon as the name manic-depressive illness indicates—there is much on which the patient's feeling of guilt and self-blame can fasten: wasteful expenditure of energy, neglect of proper rest and sleep, rash or dubious enterprise, financial loss, an illicit sexual adventure, or the estrangement of a loved partner who could not tolerate the patient's change of mood. To our intuitive understanding, the feelings of anxiety, worry and guilt, exhibited by the patient in his depressive phase, seem justified by the events for which he was responsible in the weeks or months, when he was hypomanic.

We may then feel inclined to speak of a 'reactive depression' because we have an intuitive understanding of the patients' emotional state, and agree that he has grounds for feeling depressed. It happens quite commonly that we mistake our intuitive under-standing for an aetiological diagnosis. We do not like to admit then that our diagnosis has come from the patient, that we merely agreed with him. After all, it should be the doctor who makes the diagnosis and conveys it to the patient. We therefore condescendingly admit that the patient agrees with us (not we with him), and we express this by saying that he has 'insight' into the origin of his reactive illness. But, as Karl Jaspers[257] has repeatedly stressed, our intuitive understanding of meaningful psychological connections is only true for ideally typical minds and may be wide of the mark for the minds of our patients. The same may, of course, be said of the patients' so-called insight which is only a mirror image of our own understanding.

Physicochemical Processes in Manic-depressive Illness

When a manic-depressive patient swings from a hypomanic to a hypomelancholic state, our intuitive understanding is only a fiction that has the semblance of truth. The real aetiological truth lies in a *primary* change of mood due to some unknown physico-chemical process that affects relevant psychoneural functions. The assumption of unknown physicochemical processes is, however, widely unpopular among modern psychiatrists. This may be an intuitively understandable reaction against the proliferation of such assumptions among the neuro-psychiatrists of the nineteenth century. It is also understandable that this reaction may have gone too far. Why assume something unknown, so the argument runs, when we intuitively understand the psychological processes behind depressive symptoms? To which the proper reply seems to be that we can have the same intuitive understanding of manic-depressive symptoms which have no psychogenic aetiology, but are demonstrably due to definite physicochemical causes. There certainly are some known physicochemical disorders of brain function which can give rise to mood changes of a manic-depressive kind which are primary in the sense of being without psychological antecedents. They happen, for instance, in such disorders as G.P.I., disseminated sclerosis, epilepsy, cerebral arteriosclerosis, or brain tumour. They can also occur after certain drugs, such as reserpine which can elicit severe depressive moods in predisposed persons[435].

There is thus no reason to deny the possibility of an endogenous manic-depressive illness with a primary physicochemical origin, although we cannot observe the physicochemical pathology directly and have to content ourselves with noting its psychological consequences. Physicists, who cannot fall back on claiming an intuitive understanding of the processes they study, have no hesitation in admitting that their explanatory concepts are not directly observable. Nobody can directly observe the nature of gravitational, electromagnetic or strong nuclear forces. Newton refused to make speculative guesses about the nature of gravitation *'Hypotheses non fingo'*, he said. He was satisfied with the force of gravity as an explanatory concept that accounted for observable, and measurable, consequences. For the same reason, psychiatrists need not feel inhibited in using the explanatory concept of endogenous physico-chemical processes, though their nature is today still completely unknown. Even when we succeed one day in identifying these processes—which may entail an examination of intraneural proteins and a co-ordination of findings with the help of electronic computers whose intellectual capacity far exceeds in speed and compass that of the human investigator—we should still be in need of explanatory concepts which are outside the realm of direct observation.

With the meagre knowledge at our disposal today, we still can say that it is not likely that all depressive illnesses are due to primary disturbances of mood. Some obviously have their origin in secondary disturbances which were precipitated by appropriate affective stimuli[385]. Yet, even then, we have to postulate a special affective predisposition to explain why the reactive depression, however justified as such, is more intense and prolonged than the milder grief reactions after similar affective stimuli in normal people. For the most part, the special predispositions are no more than ex-planatory concepts. Occasionally, however, they can be identified as particular diseases. A patient, for example, who eventually turned out to have an incipient G.P.I., developed a very strong depressive reaction after killing a child in a motor accident. There is little doubt about the psychogenesis of this reaction, but its undue intensity was a function of the neuropathological processes of the incipient G.P.I. It is even possible that the accident was not entirely fortuitous, but had a psychogenic origin in organically disturbed psychological functions, such as a lack of attention, carelessness, poor judgment, or delayed motor response.

Psychotic Depression

Depressions of endogenous or organic origin are often of psychotic severity. Patients with such a psychotic depression, (or 'melancholia') are so enveloped in their gloom that their contact with reality suffers. They are preoccupied with depressive delusions which are idiosyncratic, ego-involved and incorrigible. Some sit or stand quietly and silently by themselves, wholly given up to utter dejec-tion; some mutter about their sins and the punishments in store for them; some seek an audience to whom they can confess their abject wickedness and wretchedness; some walk about in agitated despair, wringing their hands and bewailing their fate. The danger of determined suicidal attempts increases with the depth of the psychotic depression; and so does the danger of homicidal attacks on dependent relatives whom the deluded patients wish to see dead rather than innocently exposed, through the patients' wickedness, to torments and miseries which, in the patients' mind, are psychotically amplified to unspeakable dimensions.

Severe psychotic depressions are not as common and sustained today as in past decades because of the effectiveness of modern forms of treatment, especially electric shock therapy and antidepressant drugs. This therapeutic advance makes it all the more imperative to improve our success in diagnosing depressive illnesses, whether they are of psychotic or merely 'neurotic' severity. Unfortunately, there have always been psychological difficulties which prevented the recognition of depressive illnesses, and some of these difficulties loom very large today.

Diagnostic mistakes are most readily understandable, when hypomelancholic symptoms take the form of physical complaints, such as dyspepsia, constipation, headaches, fatigue, and the like. It is also understandable that depressive self-blame is so often misinterpreted as justified repentance for past sins. It is a very human, though not very likeable, tendency to assume that malefactors must be treated as scapegoats and must suffer for their misdeeds, at least by feeling guilty and contrite. We are therefore prepared to overlook the fact that depressive patients feel unduly guilty and for an excessively long time. We are prone to condemn them at least in our intuitive understanding, if they provide us with chapter and verse for their feeling guilty. The gap between misdeed and self-reproach often has to be very large before we notice its existence. When a patient is convinced that he does not deserve to be among the living because, some decades before, he had stolen sixpence from his mother, the gap is too great to be overlooked. But when the patient's self-accusation has another object, such as an offence that is collectively regarded as unforgivable, or intuitively understood as culpable, then we have a blind spot for the gap. We may agree with the patient's self-accusation, when he points to the mischief he committed in a hypomanic state, to the hateful thoughts he entertained before the death of a close relative, to the masturbation in his youth, or to some other collectively tabooed act.

Changing Collective Convictions in Psychiatry

The collective convictions of psychiatrists can transform depressive delusions into self-verifying convictions. We see this most clearly with collective convictions that have gone out of fashion today, such as the mediaeval convictions about the power and wickedness of witches and sorcerers. When mediaeval depressive patients accused themselves of having had secret truck with the Devil, and of having cast evil spells causing sickness, blight and accident to the person and property of enemies, it was all too often believed that the patients' confessions were true, and that their malpractices called for the severity of the ecclesiastic and secular law rather than the compassion of the physician. When it is asserted today that depressions are rare in underdeveloped tribes, one feels sceptical in view of the possibility that cultural convictions, like those asserting the pathogenic power of witches, may effectively camouflage the existence of depressive illnesses. In the nineteenth century, collective convictions in our cultural milieu asserted that masturbation was the root of many evils, including mental illness. Patients whose depressive delusions led them to confess that they had indulged in the 'solitary vice' of masturbation were often condemned out of hand. Henry Maudsley, the leading English psychiatrist of the second half of the nineteenth century, once said of a chronic masturbator: 'The sooner he sinks to his degraded rest, the better for himself and the better for the world, which is well rid of him'[219]. However, he later abandoned this harsh moralistic attitude and admitted that chronic and excessive masturbation is likely to be a symptom of psychiatric disease rather than its cause.

Today, collective convictions obtaining in many psychiatric circles have tabooed the concept of endogenous disease entities and put in its place the concept of healthy personalities with abnormal reaction tendencies. Two theoretical schools of thought have brought about this collective attitude: clinical psychology and psychoanalysis.

The clinical psychologists of today have turned away from the study of mind-in-general with its antiquated tangle of metaphysical speculations, and have concentrated instead on the study of mind-in-particular, which they call 'personality', and of the differences between individual minds, or personalities. In this, they have followed the lead originally given by the phrenologist Gall. Mind-in-general is a supra-individual concept which comprises all varieties of psychological processes and abilities, such as thinking, feeling, willing, remembering, or traits, attitudes, habits, intelligence, temperament, and so on. Personality, on the other hand, refers to an individual's characteristic endowment with different psychological abilities and to their individually varying organizations. Some clinical psychologists have stressed that the organization of abilities and traits in individual personalities changes in the course of time and in response to external influences[10]; others, however, have emphasized that an individual personality is a 'more or less stable and enduring organization'[131].

The collective convictions embodied in psychoanalytic theories also postulate that the essence of a personality is permanent because it is thought to be mainly determined by 'unconscious mechanisms and complexes' which are laid down in early infancy and continue to affect a person's mental processes for the rest of his life. These unconscious mechanisms and complexes are believed to constitute 'a psychopathology' that is present in every human being and becomes overt in everyone occasionally, though to a different degree. Thus, the depressive symptoms of a patient are not the symptoms of a disease to many psychoanalysts, but merely depressive reactions determined by unconscious mechanisms and precipitated by the loss of a loved object. The article on psychiatric depression in the *Encyclopædia Britannica* of 1961, for example, begins with the following words: 'Depression (in psychiatry) is not an illness. . . . There is no clear line of distinction between normal and abnormal in depression; degree of intensity determines whether a depression is pathological. It is a type of emotional reaction with distinctive characteristics the root of which exists in everyone.' This means, in other words, that everyone has a predisposition to respond with depressive reactions to depressive experiences, and that the predisposition of different persons ranges imperceptibly from one causing normal grief to one causing the abnormal manifestations of hypomelancholia or melancholia.

A morbid predisposition can remain unrevealed either because it is too mild or because there are no suitable, or suitably strong, precipitating causes to activate it. Depressive experiences, however, are precipitating causes that are frequently encountered in everybody's life; they are experienced whenever a loved person dies or leaves us, whenever our self-love suffers because we have failed in a competition or examination, whenever our ambition is disappointed, and whenever we meet a setback. A person with a morbidly strong depressive predisposition is therefore liable to reveal it so commonly that a depressive mood and its consequences would be salient features of his personality.

If such morbidly depressive personalities really existed, they would have to be depressed, more or less continuously, from childhood. Yet this has never been established by objective investigations. On the contrary, it is well known that depressive symptoms tend to occur only in episodes in which perhaps hypomanic features may also be present at certain times. But the episodes are usually separated by intervals of years or months. A constantly depressive personality exists primarily in the subjective memory of many depressive patients who can only recall instances of culpable behaviour, lack of confidence, loss of initiative, inability of coping with the tasks of life, feeling of despondency, insecurity, and anxiety.

The patient's subjective belief in his hopelessly defective and inferior personality may be self-verifying because it is also adopted by his relatives who are exasperated with his incessant self-reproach, indolence, and egocentric moodiness. In their annoyance, they forget about the patient's past merits and achievements, and about his long intervals of normality; they only remember how the patient had failed, at times, to cope adequately with the normal routine of life. They cannot be expected to know that the patient's inadequacies are due to a recurrent psychiatric illness, and cannot be blamed, if they conclude that his personality has been constantly abnormal for many years. If, for example, a depressive patient had three previous episodes of depression in the preceding ten years, each episode lasting about a year, his relatives are likely to overlook the seven years of normality and to report that he has been abnormal for ten years. Accurate history-taking will, of course, elicit from the relatives that there had been seven years, when the patient had functioned normally. Even the patient himself may come to admit that there had been seven years during which he had worked and found time for hobbies and interests, though he may do his best to belittle his activities and achievements in periods of mental normality.

Unfortunately, not all depressive patients recover completely in the intervals between their episodes of depression. This happens in only about one third of them. In many others there remains a residue of subjective complaints such as feelings of anxiety, irritability, self-consciousness, obsessional urges[317, 480]. Such patients and their relatives are therefore justified in stating that there had been no period of freedom from *subjective* complaints since a depressive episode that had happened several years before. Still, even in those patients, the intervals are generally free from *objective* symptoms of depression so that strangers, colleagues or workmates often notice nothing amiss, and the patients are not prevented from following their occupation or engaging in the pursuit of their hobbies and interests. Moreover, it is possible to learn from the relatives that the patients' abnormal personality had not started in childhood, that there had been a definite change in their personality after a depressive episode.

All this is emphasized because of the present-day inclination of many psychiatrists to assume that the personality exhibited by depressive patients, either during the depressive episodes or in the intervals, is their 'normal' personality. If such psychiatrists take full histories of their patients' past lives, they can obtain contradictory statements. They may find, for instance, that a patient is said to have always been shy and tongue-tied in company, and yet he was also a successful commercial traveller for many years and the life and soul of parties; that a patient who describes himself as friendless has scores of people solicitously enquiring about his health; or that a patient whose personality is pictured as indecisive, puritanical and over-meticulous has had hypomanic periods of self-assured determination, moral laxity, or daring enterprise. Yet theoretical convictions often prove stronger than the knowledge of such personality changes. If theory denies the existence of disease, then the patient's present personality is regarded as typical, and he may be labelled as dependent, immature, inadequate, psychopathic, hysterical and the like. To add injury to these insults, he is not given the antidepressant treatment which might speedily restore him to health.

CHAPTER 14

THE PSYCHOPATHOLOGY OF AFFECT—
ANXIETY-DOMINATED NEUROSES

There is no sharp dividing line between functional psychoses and anxiety-dominated neuroses; the distinction between them has always been arbitrary and conventional. Both disease groups have this in common—that they occur in the absence of any organic pathology which can account for the clinical symptoms displayed by the patients. They differ, however, with regard to their attitudes to certain beliefs which are idiosyncratic and, therefore, unshared. Psychotic patients are absolutely and delusionally convinced that those beliefs are true, but anxiety-dominated neurotic patients are ambivalent about their truth. This difference is usually expressed by saying that psychotic patients have no insight into the truth, or untruth, of their idiosyncratic beliefs, but anxiety-dominated neurotic patients have.

From this differential criterion of insight, many aetiological and pathological theories have been derived. In past centuries, for example, there were theories which maintained that the lack of insight shown by psychotic patients was due to 'a disease of the Mind or a defect of Reason', whereas anxiety-dominated neuroses were thought to originate in a general disturbance of the nervous system. In due course, the philosophical concept of an immaterial mind with various faculties was abandoned by medicine so that the expression 'a disease of the Mind or a defect of Reason' lost its original meaning and justification.

It was then theorized that there were certain unknown processes in the brain—or psychoneural processes, as we termed them—of which a person could become introspectively conscious as subjective psychological experiences. It was further theorized that, in functional psychoses, there were unknown biochemical abnormalities which affected psychoneural processes to such an extent that some subjective cognitive experiences no longer corresponded to events in objective reality. In anxiety-dominated neuroses, on the other hand, no unknown biochemical abnormalities were assumed to interfere with psychoneural processes. It was thought that the latter did not function normally because they had acquired a lasting pathological habit by the usual process of learning through experience; but the experience must have been a special one, consisting of the perception of external events which had a pathogenic impact. This meant that the anxiety-dominated neurotic should have a knowledge of the events that had caused his illness. Of course, it was possible that he might remember the events, but not realize that they had been (and continued to be) pathogenic. This might happen, for instance, when the events had gradually become the conditioned stimuli of neurotic reactions. He was most likely to recognize the pathogenicity of an external event, when it had aroused, at the time, disturbing affective responses. Such an external event could be called 'psychogenic trauma'. The unfortunate fact was that many anxiety-dominated neuroses occurred in the absence of anything that could be called a conditional stimulus, or be interpreted as a precipitating psychogenic trauma. This difficulty was, however, overcome by the additional assumption that the pathogenic conditioning, or psychogenic traumatization, had occurred so many years before that the memory of the relevant events had become 'unconscious' and could be no longer recalled.

This kind of argument often led to a theoretical differentiation of anxiety-dominated neuroses and functional psychoses on presumed aetiological grounds. Neuroses were believed to have a psychogenic exogenous aetiology, and psychoses a physiogenic endogenous origin. In other words, anxiety-dominated neuroses were thought to occur through the influence of a pathogenic environment, but functional psychoses through endopathological changes. The main flaw in this argument is that the psychopathogenic aetiology of anxiety-dominated neuroses can be found, if at all, only in the retrospective analysis of unreliable memories. In prospective studies, neurotic habits, established through a course of conditioning, quickly disappear when circumstances change and there is no further reinforcement; and the affective consequences of traumatic experiences are also only transient in normal subjects.

Neurotic symptoms which are prolonged and stubbornly resist simple therapeutic measures, can only be viewed as reactive psychogenic responses to traumatic experiences, if we also assume that the few people who fall neurotically ill after such experiences are idiosyncratically sensitive to them. It may be speculated, as psychoanalytic theories have done, that this idiosyncratic sensitivity was caused by traumatic predisposing experiences at an early age. However, when a patient's past is diligently searched for possible traumatic experiences, the time inevitably comes, when concepts of hereditary constitution have to be introduced to account for differences in psychogenic reactivity. Attempts to avoid such concepts have only the effect of forcing the pursuit of presumed traumatic experiences further and further back to the earliest days of an individual's post-natal existence until the decision can no longer be avoided whether finally to admit a hereditary determination of psychogenic reactivity, or to postulate that the event of being born was the first pathogenic experience. But if the second alternative is adopted, then why does not everybody react with the same neurotic predisposition to this birth trauma? If the answer to this question still has to avoid concepts of genetic determination, then speculations about traumatic experiences by the embryo in the uterus become inevitable. In the theories of some psychoanalytic schools this trend of postulating earlier and earlier traumatic experiences is very clearly noticeable.

Yet there is a limit even to the most determined anti-genetic and anti-constitutional attitudes of psychodynamic diehards. Sooner or later, the existence of genetic-constitutional factors in determining individual differences of psychological reactivities has to be faced; and these differences must have a biochemical basis. However, this destroys the theoretical belief that there is a physiogenic endogenous aetiology only in functional psychoses; a comparable aetiology must then also be present in neuroses. Of course, the biochemical abnormalities which are respectively responsible for neuroses and functional psychoses are likely to be qualitatively different. There are, however, some clinical indications that this may not always be so— that quantitative variations of the same biochemical abnormality may produce gradations in the severity of clinical symptoms and thus give rise to the impression that the same patient can alternate between neurotic and psychotic episodes which have sufficient similarity and continuity to suggest the same psychoneural pathology. Patients who recover from a schizophrenic psychosis, for instance, may be left with a *schizothymic personality*, characterized by an emotional and social insulation, by interests in abstruse topics and solitary pursuits, or similar peculiarities which, however, all remain within the boundaries of population norms. There are, of course, also individuals with this kind of schizothymic personality who have apparently never suffered from a schizophrenic illness.

Recovery from schizophrenia may also leave certain neurotic *schizoid symptoms* behind, which are abnormal by population standards and cause suffering and concern. Such patients may have distressing difficulties in their relations with society in general and people in particular, they may have peculiar fears concerning their physical and mental well-being, entertain odd suspicions, behave in unexpected ways, show strange sensitivities and uncertainties, are gratuitously offensive or uncouth, pick unwarranted quarrels and arguments, and run into many other social difficulties which make their life emotionally hazardous and worrying. Again there are many neurotics with such schizoid symptoms who have apparently never had a definite schizophrenic psychosis.

Variations in the clinical picture are especially common in the manic-depressive sphere. There are many patients who exhibit, at different times in their adult life, hyperthymic or hypothymic features, hypomanic or hypomelancholic symptoms, or frankly psychotic signs of mania or melancholia. We have already mentioned that hypomelancholic illnesses are often regarded as reactive, and therefore as psychogenic and neurotic. This does not happen to hypomanic patients who are more likely to be classed as abnormal but healthy personalities than to be diagnosed as neurotically ill. The clinical picture of hypomelancholia is not restricted to the triad stressed in the previous chapter: decrease in mental and physical activity, decrease in self-confidence, and decrease in the aesthetic enjoyment of pleasures. There are also frequently attacks of fear and panic for which there is no obvious justification, and which may dominate the clinical picture to such an extent that, instead of a decrease of mental and physical activity, there is a restless fear-inspired agitation. Such attacks of anxiety are regarded as neurotic in hypomelancholic patients, and as psychotic when they occur, as is so often the case, in involutional or senile episodes of melancholic insanity.

Symptoms of neurotic anxiety may continue after melancholic or hypomelancholic episodes. It then seems that such episodes are followed by an anxiety-dominated neurotic illness, which may continue unchanged for many years[317]. It may perhaps disappear occasionally during a hyperthymic or hypomanic interlude, but return with redoubled intensity during the recurrence of a hypomelancholic or melancholic illness. If the original depressive illness has remained undiagnosed, as happens frequently, the anxiety-dominated neurosis appears to be a disease *sui generis*[480]. Anxiety-dominated neuroses are not a homogeneous group of illnesses; some of them, it seems, derive from personalities with specific neurotic predispositions; others occur apparently in the wake of functional or organic psychoses. Clinically, they may be divided into anxiety neuroses proper and obsessive-compulsive neuroses. This distinction does, however, not indicate two separate disease groups with different pathologies and aetiologies. The symptoms of either neurosis may occur in the same neurotic patient; they may also emerge during functional psychoses, during senile personality changes or in post-encephalitic conditions.

ANXIETY NEUROSES

Anxiety neuroses are also called *phobias* (from the Greek *phobos*, fear). They are characterized by attacks of unwarranted fear, or phobic attacks, which sometimes arise without obvious precipitation, as in depressive illnesses, but more often after the perception of certain objects or situations which are conventionally called phobic objects or situations, though it would be more correct to speak of 'phobia-stimulating objects'. The patients are well aware that the objects and situations which are the source of their phobic attacks are either entirely harmless, or contain a threat that is so unlikely and remote that it arouses no anxiety in normal people. Normal people develop anxieties in situations in which everybody is convinced of the possibility of imminent danger. These anxieties are, however, not comparable with the anxieties of phobic patients who only half believe in the possibility of imminent danger. It is only the self-recognized, and thus insightful, superstitions of normal people which are similar in many respects to phobic anxieties.

One of the main distinctions between such superstitions and phobias is that the former are overtly collective and, therefore, known to be shared to a greater or less degree by other members of the same cultural group, whereas the latter are not overtly collective and, therefore, not generally known to be shared by others. Both superstitions and phobias may, however, be viewed as half-beliefs, or ambivalent convictions, of imminent danger. Superstitious fears which are known to be shared by others, may be disclosed to others in the expectation of meeting a degree of understanding and sympathy in them. But as superstitious convictions are ambivalent, the understanding and sympathy aroused may be blended with an air of patronizing amusement that is more or less genuine.

People who admit to having a fear of the number thirteen, to being disconcerted by the breaking of a mirror, or to feeling obliged to say 'touch wood' (perhaps combined with a need to actually touch wood) whenever they mention a stroke of good luck, are not regarded as neurotic and odd by their social environment. They can count on being accepted with good-natured tolerance as having failed to reach the level of rational enlightenment which their audience may believe themselves to have attained. People who disclose a superstitious fear of dead bodies or ghosts are likely to find a rather more wholehearted understanding and sympathy in an audience that may 'pooh-pooh' this superstition in broad daylight, but is uneasily aware that it may feel similarly frightened when alone in a churchyard or mortuary at midnight. People who confess to having a fear of mice, large spiders, harmless snakes, great heights, or walking alone across an empty dance floor in full view of everybody can be certain of so many kindred spirits in their audience, that there is not only full and genuine understanding and sympathy for their fears, but also a collusive tendency to deny the superstitious nature of the fears by assuming some dubious threat or danger. After all, one might be bitten by mice, spiders and snakes, one might feel giddy at a great height and come to grief, and one might become the target of critical tongues on the empty dance floor.

Superstitious fears are never persistently disabling, but cause only transient disturbances. Moreover, the feared objects are not very common or can be avoided with a little ingenuity and the connivance of others. Urban people do not often come across mice or snakes, and they are not often required to handle spiders or dead bodies. It generally does not require much skill and determination to keep away from dizzy heights, the centre of deserted dance floors, or a room with the number thirteen (which, in fact, does not exist in many hotels).

Phobic fears, on the other hand, are always more or less disabling. Many phobic objects are of common everyday occurrence and cannot easily be avoided. The life of a patient with phobias of cats or horses, of crossing streets or bridges, of being in a crowd, or in an enclosed space, or of travelling on a bus or train, can be seriously disrupted. The more common and familiar the phobic objects are, the greater is the incomprehension and lack of compassion which the plight of the anxiety-neurotic arouses in normal people. It surpasses the intuitive understanding of normal people how anybody can be scared of a purring cat, of going outside his home, or of crossing a bridge, or riding on a bus. Surely, he merely pretends or exaggerates; he should pull himself together or be forced to do so.

Phobic patients are aware of the intolerance and lack of understanding among normal people. They themselves half know that their fears are senseless and ridiculous; they are themselves ashamed and critical of them. Yet the attitude of the environment adds a new dimension to their fears: the dread of being harshly judged and derided by others. Many patients thus suffer in silence and hide their symptoms from an unsympathetic environment. Their illness only becomes manifest, when their fears can no longer be secretly fought and suppressed in a continuous effort to save face. Even then they may try to complain only of symptoms which are secondarily caused by their anxiety, such as headaches, palpitations, diarrhoea or fatigue. Eventually, however, the time may come, when they have to tell some relative or friend of their ridiculous phobias of harmless objects or situations. Because of this secretiveness of phobic patients, the casual observer may not become aware of their feelings of anxiety. The trained observer, on the other hand, may notice some of the tell-tale physiological concomitants of fear. He may notice restless, fidgety movements, tremors and twitches, or rigidly tensed muscles in some people, while others show their anxiety by sagging limply at the knees so that they have difficulty in keeping upright. The upper eyelid is often retracted and the sclera becomes visible above the cornea. When this is combined with a reduction of blinking, the eyes seem bulging and staring. In other people, however, there is an increase of blinking and an over-secretion of tears. A mottled blush often rises from the neck to the cheeks, but the area around the mouth remains white. Beads of perspiration appear on the forehead, nose and upper lip, and sweat may pour freely from armpits, hands and feet. But the skin may also be dry, cold and covered in gooseflesh. When the patient's lips and mouth are dry, they have to be licked frequently, and his speech thickens. Speech may also become tremulous and stammering. The respiration can assume a slow, irregular sighing rhythm which may end in sobs and screams, or a fast respiration rate develops with marked overbreathing. Pulse rate and pulse pressure are raised, often causing visible carotid pulsations in the neck. Gastric and intestinal activity is often reduced; but it can also be increased and give rise to belching, vomiting, audible borborygmi, flatulence and diarrhoea. There may also be an increased urge to urinate, perhaps combined with polyuira. Genital reactivity is sometimes enhanced to the point of spontaneous or premature orgasm; or it is reduced so that impotence and frigidity results.

The tendency of phobic patients to keep their fears secret has a social side effect that usually occurs when people privately and surreptitiously deviate from norms they publicly profess. An out-sider who enquires into some norm, such as an overtly tabooed activity, may be told by members of a social group that it is un-thinkable for any of them to violate the taboo. Yet this may be far from the actual truth. A social psychologist, for instance, who investigated individual attitudes in a small rural community in which the Methodist Church was dominant, did not meet anybody at first who approved of playing cards, or of drinking alcohol, or who admitted having done so; but before he left, he had secretly played cards and drunk cider with many individuals[438]. F. H. Allport[9] has given the name 'pluralistic ignorance' to this social phenomenon. The activities, secretly performed by many individuals may hence be called 'pluralistic events'. They exist in clandestine isolation and are thus distinguished from collective activities which are publicly manifest. The phobias of anxiety neurotics obviously belong to this category of pluralistic events. Most patients are convinced that nobody else suffers from the same irrational fears, except perhaps some outcasts who are depraved or mentally ill. When they meet other patients with the same phobic symptoms for the first time on a psychiatric ward or in a therapeutic group, they realize with great relief that they are not alone in their suffering, and that the other patients look quite normal and not like freaks.

The pluralistic isolation of phobic patients can thus be partially lifted so that some degree of overt sharing results. No such overt sharing of symptoms is usually found in patients with psychotic delusions. They do not feel relieved on meeting other patients with the same delusion. They do not join forces with them as they have no insight into being ill. Each psychotic patient continues to be convinced of the truth of his own delusion, but to denounce the delusions of others as false. There are, however, limits to the sharing of neurotic anxieties. Such sharing only occurs in patients with the same phobic objects. A patient with a phobia of crossing bridges, let us say, has a fellow-feeling for patients who are similarly afraid of crossing bridges, but his understanding and sympathy fails when he meets a patient whose phobic objects are, let us say, stuffed animals or pencils.

It is characteristic of psychotic delusions that they are incorrigible; it is equally characteristic of collective superstitions that most people can overcome them, if and when this becomes necessary. Most medical students, for instance, lose their initial superstitious fear of corpses when they learn human anatomy and receive instructions in dissection. Phobic symptoms are intermediate in their corrigibility between collective superstitions and psychotic delusions. Phobic patients cannot shed their half-beliefs as easily as normal superstitious persons can; on the other hand, the half-beliefs are not as resistant to psychological pressure as psychotic delusions. In extreme adversity, when survival is hard and dependent on constant vigilance and exertion, psychotic patients perish because they cannot compromise, but phobic patients lose their neurotic anxieties and exchange them for collectively shared, or shareable fears. Kral, for instance, reported that, in the Jewish Internment Camp of Theresienstadt in Nazi-occupied Europe, in which over 120,000 people (86%) died, or were sent east to extermination camps, phobic symptoms 'either disappeared completely or improved to such a degree that the patients could work'[300].

No new cases of anxiety neurosis occurred in the camp, though schizophrenia, manic-depression and other psychiatric disorders developed in some people. Several months after liberation and return home, 'some of the old neurotics who had been free of complaints during their stay in the camp again developed their former symptoms'.

The most diverse objects and situations may acquire the power of precipitating phobic attacks in anxiety-neurotic patients. Some patients respond to only one phobic object, but others react to several and are, to that extent, more generally handicapped. Among the most common phobic objects are those which are potentially dangerous in exceptional circumstances. Here belong the widespread superstitious fears of such animals as mice and spiders (they might bite) or snakes (they might be venomous). Patients with *animal phobias* can react with panic feelings to any kind of innocent creature, even those that are pets to normal people: cats, dogs or horses, even when seen at a safe distance; some birds even when caged; hens, frogs, butterflies, earthworms, and even human babies.

Potentially injurious objects and situations can be the source of phobic attacks: the sight of sharp instruments, from pins to carving knives; travelling in fast-moving vehicles (buses, trains); leaving firm ground (swimming, sailing, heights, aeroplanes); the perils of the elements (lightning, thunder, rain, wind); the possibility of concealed dangers such as walking through shallow waters or long grass, exposing the body to draughts or overheated rooms or sunlight, taking drugs, coming into contact with dirt or seminal fluid or menstrual blood or disease-carrying objects; being in narrow and confined spaces (the claustrophobia of tunnels, tube trains, lifts, long corridors, streets flanked by high buildings, the pressure of crowds); having one's freedom of movement curtailed by having to wait in a queue or a shop or at traffic lights, having to sit still at the hairdresser, sitting in the middle of a row of seats in the theatre or cinema, being in a room where all doors and windows are closed, being in locked bedrooms or toilets or bathrooms, travelling on buses or trains which do not stop frequently; attending a doctor or dentist (such phobic patients have their minor ailments treated by lay practitioners of all sorts and consult doctors only when forced by emergencies).

Phobic objects are often reminiscent of injury and illness. Among these are the sight of sick people, cripples, beggars, accidents, wounds, blood or vomit.

Objects and situations may become phobic because they suggest *separation* from home and familiar company. Many patients cannot leave their home at all; others can move about within a limited area outside their home, especially when accompanied by a trusted person and during daylight so that all familiar landmarks are visible. The boundary of the area in which such patients can move is often marked by a river; they are then unable to cross the river by bridge, boat or any other way. If the boundary consists of roads or wide open spaces such as squares or parks, the patients suffer from *agoraphobia*. They react with fear, when they venture into what is to them an empty, threatening and foreign space beyond the pale of familiar territory. Many phobic patients find it impossible to board a bus or train, though some manage to travel on transport that stops frequently so that they can get out and, if necessary, return home. For the same reason, patients with travel phobias may have no difficulty in covering long distances, provided they can cycle or drive their own car.

Many situations are phobic because they evoke in the patient a fear of being exposed to adverse criticism. This happens only in social situations and we may therefore speak of *social phobias*. These patients often avoid all competitive activities, such as examinations or games; they may be unable to talk to superiors, to appear in front of an audience (stage fright), to eat in a restaurant or even at home when another person is present, to sit opposite others on a bus or in a tube, to have people walk behind them, to walk past a queue of people, to look at themselves in a mirror. They may be unable to write, or to carry on with any routine activity, when they feel themselves under observation. Some can only leave their house when it is so dark or foggy that they cannot be easily seen. Some have a fear of blushing or of attracting attention by behaving awkwardly or fainting. They may be afraid that their hand will tremble, when they are watched while writing or eating; they may, in fact, tremble in these circumstances so that their writing becomes a scrawl, their teacup rattles against the saucer, or soup is spilled when they raise the soup-spoon to their lips. They may also be afraid of a shaking or nodding head, but this fear is not as readily actualized as the fear of trembling hands.

The physiological functions of their body become phobic objects to some patients. They then develop *hypochondriacal phobias* which are sometimes indistinguishable in content from hypochondriacal delusions, but are, of course, neither absolute nor incorrigible convictions. Fears of constipation, body odour and halitosis are fairly common superstitious fears which are fanned by the assiduous advertisement of commercial interests. In predisposed persons, the relatively mild concerns of normal people about the functions of their bowels, and the odour of their body and breath, become phobic symptoms which are sufficiently strong and persistent half-beliefs to cause suffering, and to interfere with normal life activities.

Many hypochondriacal phobias revolve around sexual functions. Women may develop phobic half-beliefs of being pregnant because they had been kissed or had some even more innocent contact with a man. Even intelligent and knowledgeable women, like medical students and nurses, may fall prey to this irrational fear. A phobic half-belief that the intromission of the penis may cause physical damage can lead to the avoidance or refusal of intercourse. Phobias of pregnancy, of childbirth, or of bearing a deformed child are the reason why some neurotic women shun all sexual contact with men, or take excessive contraceptive care. Men can have phobic half-beliefs that their sexual organs are anatomically abnormal, or that their sexual functions were damaged by masturbation or seminal loss. Phobic anxieties about sexual functions often cause impotence because they interfere with normal genital reactions, so that the patient has insufficient erections or premature emissions when he has to prove his potency. Such patients can be helped by removing fear from the sexual situation. They may be authoritatively told that they should indulge in sexual caresses, but avoid seminal emission and refrain from intercourse. If they have an understanding and co-operative partner, normal genital reactions re-establish themselves, and normal intercourse becomes possible.

Other physiological functions are also often the content of hypochondriacal phobias. Patients may have the half-belief that they cannot breathe deeply enough, or they may feel a constriction or lump in their throat, a *globus hystericus*, which might choke them or make swallowing impossible. Other patients feel that their heart beats irregularly, too fast, too slow, too strong, too weak, or causes palpitations as a sign that it is seriously diseased; the result may be a panicky fear of death. However, the reverse may also be true in many patients; the panicky fear of death is primary and the felt irregularities of the heart are merely the vegetative equivalents of this fear. Psychological abnormalities can also form the content of hypochondriacal phobias. There are many patients with the phobic fear of going mad or of losing consciousness. The mere thought of a previous panic attack or of an imminent contact with a phobic object can be a phobic object itself—a symptom that has been called 'phobophobia', the irrational fear of an irrational fear. A travel-phobic patient, for instance, who knows that he cannot avoid going on a train journey is very likely to suffer temporarily from phobophobia.

OBSESSIVE-COMPULSIVE NEUROSES

In general parlance, the term 'obsessive', or its equivalent, 'obsessional', is used to characterize phenomena which 'obsess', preoccupy, or monopolize the mind of a person for some time. It is, therefore, quite legitimate to say that some psychotic patients are obsessively preoccupied with delusional ideas. Yet it would be quite wrong to infer from such a remark that the psychotic patients have obsessional symptoms.

The reason for this *non sequitur* is that obsessional symptoms are conventionally regarded as non-psychotic. This semantic custom may go back to demonological theories which distinguished between 'obsession' and 'possession'. In an 'obsession', evil spirits were supposed to harass and haunt a patient from the outside (the term derives from the Latin *obsidere*, to besiege). In a 'possession', however, they were thought to enter his body, and thus to dominate him completely. This demonological distinction between obsession and possession is, in modern theories, reflected by the distinction between neurosis and psychosis, between having and not having insight into being psychiatrically ill, or between holding morbid half-beliefs and entertaining absolute delusional convictions.

Today, the term 'possession' has completely dropped out of the psychiatric vocabulary because of its too obvious connection with discredited demonological views. The term 'obsession', however, continues to be used to indicate a preoccupation with certain ideas. Yet the preoccupying ideas are not necessarily neurotic; they need not even be morbid. It is quite normal to be obsessed with some ideas which are highly valued and highly attractive. An erotically infatuated person, for example, can be said to be obsessed with a greatly idealized version of his beloved who appears to him as a paragon of all the virtues. Comparable obsessions with over-valued ideas of high attractiveness are shown by people who are dominated by an absorbing interest in activities and ideologies which fill their whole life and leisure time.

Obsessions with absorbingly attractive and over-valued ideas are more than mere mental preoccupations; they have an element of compulsion attached to them. Yet it would be misleading to call them obsessive-compulsive manifestations because this expression has acquired a very technical sense in psychiatry today. Preoccupations with highly attractive ideas are not resisted, but enjoyed; and compulsions to entertain these attractive ideas, and to engage in any activities encouraged by them, are not dictated by fear; they are motivated by the temptation of expected pleasure. We are dealing here with a *self-indulgent obsession* rather than an anxiety-dominated obsessional compulsion in a narrow sense. In general parlance, the term 'mania' is often used to denote such a self-indulgent obsession instead of the elated phase of an affective illness, which is its more usual current meaning. When we say of a person that he has a 'mania' for collecting stamps, let us say, we mean that he has a self-indulgent obsession to do so. The term 'mania' has also survived in some compound expressions which refer to self-indulgent obsessions of a morbid and socially opprobrious kind: for example, dipsomania, (recurrent bouts of alcoholic over-indulgence), nymphomania (sexual over-indulgence by women), kleptomania (self-indulgent obsession with stealing), bibliomania (self-indulgent and unscrupulous collection of books), pyromania (self-indulgent obsession with incendiary activities), and trichotillo-mania (self-indulgent obsession with tearing out one's hair).

When 'obsessive-compulsive' is used in a narrow technical sense, the obsessional ideas are also over-valued, but not highly attractive; the compulsion to entertain such ideas, and to behave in accordance with them, is not experienced as a pleasurable self-indulgence, but as an onerous duty or a harassing obligation. Such oppressive compulsions are often the main components of anxiety-dominated obsessive-compulsive manifestations. It is then usual to speak merely of compulsive neurotic symptoms, leaving out any reference to obsessions. Instead of 'compulsive' a Greek equivalent can be used, as is often done in German psychiatry, namely the term 'anankastic' (from the Greek *anankasmos*, necessity, compulsion)[119].

Tendencies to abbreviate the cumbersome hybrid expression 'obsessive-compulsive' are understandable, but they carry with them the risk of adding extraneous components to the category of obsessive-compulsive manifestations. When such manifestations are merely called obsessive or obsessional, then it may seem that self-indulgent obsessions should be included; and when the manifestations are merely called compulsive (or anankastic), then it may seem that such symptoms as motor tics also belong here. Yet in self-indulgent obsession, there is no oppressive compulsion, and in pure motor tics, there is no obsessional preoccupation with ideas. Keeping these risks in mind, there seems to be no harm in following the usual custom of using, for the sake of simplicity, the term 'obsessive', or 'obsessional' to stand for 'obsessive-compulsive'. Obsessional manifestations, in this narrow technical sense, occur as normal traits in 'obsessional personalities' and as morbid symptoms in 'obsessional neurotics'.

Obsessional Personalities

The obsessional traits of a normal personality derive from preoccupations with over-valued ideas of what is right and wrong conduct. The standard of rightness is provided by the general customs, laws and morals, prevailing in the society to which the person subjectively belongs. Any deviation from the over-valued standard of right conduct rouses a punitive reaction in the obsessional personality. If other people deviate, his reaction is 'extra-punitive'; if he himself commits the wrong, his reaction is 'intra-punitive' causing him to feel anxious, guilty and worried, and forcing him to do everything in his power to put matters right. This excessive social conformity of the obsessional personality requires no outside pressure or threat. He is driven by his intra-punitive tendencies to make sure that he knows what is right, and to avoid any thought or action that he knows to be wrong.

The dread of being, or doing, wrong is, of course, not the prerogative of obsessional personalities. It is present to a greater or less extent in all people—a fact that is expressed in the ancient concept of conscience, and its modern psychoanalytic counterpart, the superego. The concept of conscience is, however, not entirely adequate in this context because it is usually regarded as that part of the mind which is somehow the repository of eternally true moral laws and values, and also the guardian of their observance. If that were true, the conscience of all human beings would be the same, and obsessional personalities would only have more of it.

Yet consciences differ with the standards of right conduct in different societies. An obsessional person, who bears allegiance to a society whose standards of conduct deviate from our moral laws and values, may regard conduct as right and ethical that is usually denounced as wrong and wicked. In a Nazi concentration camp, for instance, an obsessional official, steeped in Nazi laws and values, might have considered it his duty to perfect means of torturing and killing prisoners who, in his belief, were enemies of his own over-valued ideas. Similarly, a patriotic and obsessional wartime soldier of whatever nationality may feel in duty bound to carry out some savagely murderous orders to the last word. In peacetime and normal circumstances, the obsessional personalities of our culture live up to the expectations of our traditional moral and social customs. Of course, not all the many customs are adopted as lodestars of behaviour by every anankast. Individual differences are unavoidable. But the greater the number of moral and social customs which are obsessionally observed, the more typical and pronounced the obsessional personality.

Obsessional personalities are conventional and conscientious in some or several areas of their social functioning. They are virtuous and righteous according to their lights, correct in the manner, dress and speech of their social circle; they are diligent and persistent in perfecting the knowledge expected of them or idiosyncratically chosen by them; they are orderly and tidy in some areas of their life which implies disorder and untidiness in others; they are reliable, scrupulous, precise and pedantic in what they do; their time schedule follows a strict and punctual routine; their work schedule is carefully regulated so that time is not wasted; they are temperate and money-conscious; they are disciplinarians and hard task masters, who strive for perfection in their own achievements and expect such striving from others; they are circumspect and do not take risks, but try to calculate the consequences of their actions beforehand. In short, the obsessional personality can be a model citizen who obeys laws and customs, and applies himself with plodding perseverance to his duties. In order to abolish the obsessional dread of being wrong, he carefully checks his actions. He checks his arithmetic, the style, grammar and spelling of his letters, the correctness of his dress and manners, and the accuracy of all the tasks he has performed. But the checking activities of a normal anankast remain within reasonable limits. He trusts the accuracy of his checks. Generally speaking, obsessional personalities make excellent book-keepers and ledger clerks; they are often brilliantly successful in tasks requiring single-minded devotion, precision and patience.

Obsessional Neurotics

One of the main distinctions between a person with an obsessional personality and a person with an obsessional neurosis lies in the different standard of rightness by which they judge their thoughts and conduct. A normal obsessional person adopts a collective standard of rightness. He makes sure that he knows what is collectively regarded as right, and he makes sure that his conduct lives up to that standard. But an obsessional neurotic cannot always attain this certainty. He is forever doubtful about the right standard of some thought and action, because his neurotic standards are not sanctioned by collective beliefs; they are unshared, unrealistic and half-believed standards which provide no guidance that this way is right and that way wrong. He, therefore, dare not make a quick decision since it may be false, and bring ill-luck and ruin in its train.

Having to make a decision can be a phobic experience to an

obsessional patient, but he cannot escape from it in the same way as an anxiety-neurotic by doing everything possible to get away from the phobic object in his environment. The obsessional patient is not as fortunate; he cannot remove himself from his phobic experience. The only way out is a right decision. But this is just what he cannot do because it presupposes a knowledge of what is right, and he lacks this knowledge. He thus falls prey to prolonged spells of anxious indecision. He suffers from the symptom of obsessional doubt. Because of the predominance of this symptom in obsessional neurosis, this illness is sometimes labelled *folie de doute*, though this name has become almost obsolete today. As there are no objective criteria by which to resolve his obsessional doubts, the patient takes refuge in fanciful half-beliefs about the workings of his mind and the nature of trancendental forces in the world. He half believes and half fears that the world is governed by powers which respond magically to the ritual of his thoughts and actions, so that the right ritual will be followed by favourable results in the social and physical world, and the wrong ritual by disastrous results.

These magic half-beliefs of the obsessional patient are idiosyncratic, vague and uncertain, but they are essentially akin to magic beliefs of a collective and definite kind, which play a significant role in some metaphysical doctrines as well as all religions, mythologies and occult theories. Such collective magic beliefs have found their most influential expression in the doctrine of *Logos* which inspired, for example, some of the religious tenets of the Old and New Testament, and some of the cosmological speculations of the Stoic school of philosophy. *Logos* has been variously translated as Word, Reason, Power, God, or Creative Intelligence. Note, for instance, the opening statement of the Gospel according to St. John: 'In the beginning was the Word (*Logos*), and the Word was with God, and the Word was God.' In many philosophical systems, *Logos* appears as an entity that gives reason, order and intelligibility to the physical world. From such a doctrine even the belief of scientists is derived that the universe is governed by natural laws which can be discovered and comprehended by the human mind.

In prescientific views of the world, not only the mystic power of a cosmic mind (or cosmic minds) is exalted, but also the supremacy of processes in individual minds over matter in general. The thoughts, words, and deeds of individual persons are believed to be endowed with magic qualities, turning them into charms and spells which alter physical processes: into prayers and supplications which beseech divine and occult forces; or into transgressions and sins which incur the wrath of supernatural beings.

ANXIETY-DOMINATED NEUROSES

The half-beliefs of obsessional patients are similarly steeped in assumptions that their thoughts, words, and deeds may be magic charms and spells, magically right or wrong, the magic instruments of finding salvation or suffering damnation. The similarity is so striking that Freud called this neurosis a 'private religion', but it is a private religion in which fears are more conspicuous than hopes. In this last respect, it differs from the private religion of gamblers in which hopes of attracting good luck through auspicious thoughts and deeds loom very much larger than fears of inviting misfortune through ill-starred actions. The magic tenet of the gambler's private religion that the desires of his mind can influence chance events in the physical world has been taken seriously enough in recent times to be subjected to empirical tests. This was done by Rhine and other investigators of so-called 'psi-phenomena'—psychological phenomena of a magic-psychic, or 'extrasensory' kind. They claim to have found evidence that the desires of the mind can indeed influence physical chance events, such as the fall of dice. The influence has been called 'psychokinesis', or PK; it is minute, yet alleged to be observable in large series of tests with gifted subjects[180, 423, 424, 533, 543].

Whether psychokinesis exists or not, the obsessional patient could be said to be afraid of it. He is afraid that the mere possibility of having an evil thought will force him to concentrate on it obsessionally; and that the mere thinking of an evil thought will have evil consequences in the physical world or his own mind. He may be afraid to think ill of people, because such thoughts might obsess him against his will and magically harm the people, or induce him to kill them, either in an unguarded and forgotten moment, or through an overwhelming impulse which he has no power to resist. Yet evil thought may be provoked against the patient's will, perhaps by certain external situations. A church service, for example, may perversely call out obsessional thoughts of an obscene and blasphemous kind. This drives the patient frantic with the fear that his thoughts will have an evil effect on others in the congregation; or that he may inadvertently divulge them, or even shout them out at the top of his voice. Other patients are affected by fears that they might take off their clothes in public, lose control of their bladder or bowels at the most inopportune moment, injure themselves or others with sharp instruments they happen to handle, throw themselves or others in front of a fast-moving vehicle, look ostentatiously at the genital region of passers-by, make lewd suggestions to strangers, indulge in unremembered sexual intimacies with them, insert scurrilous remarks unwittingly into letters, use every pen or pencil to draw obscene pictures, and so on.

The external objects and situations which thus provoke evil thoughts in an obsessive-compulsive patient become phobic objects for him. Their presence produces phobic attacks. He will, therefore, anxiously seek to avoid such objects in his environment, just as phobic patients do, but he will go to much greater length in his avoiding manœuvres. He has to guard himself, not only against perceiving the phobic object, but also against the magic dangers inherent in the mere thought of it. An anxiety-neurotic patient with claustrophobic attacks in church, for instance, simply has to stay away from church services. An obsessive-compulsive patient for whom the church is a phobic object, does not only have to stay away from it, but may also have to avoid contact with other church members so that there is no opportunity of his revealing his obscene and blasphemous thoughts unwittingly or through an irresistible impulse. An anxiety-neurotic patient with a phobia of pins is forced by his fears to keep away from any pin he happens to notice, but an obsessive-compulsive patient has to go to greater pains because, after accidentally seeing a pin, he is beset by the fear of somehow having used it to injure others. An anxiety-neurotic patient with a phobia of dirt takes good care to keep away from anything dirty, and if he has been in touch with a dirty object, he is driven by his panic to cleanse himself immediately and thoroughly. An obsessive-compulsive patient with a similar phobia has to keep away even from objects that look scrupulously clean, because the mere thought that they are dirty may magically make them dirty and also contaminate him, even if he cannot remember having touched them. His magic fears also make his cleansing procedures more prolonged and vigorous.

Compulsive Rituals

In the private religion of the obsessional patient, there are not only fears of doing wrong and causing evil, but also hopeful half-beliefs of finding salvation through thinking or doing what is right and redeeming. Such hopeful half-beliefs, however, have to battle against the inveterate tendency to doubt, and, in the process, they become compulsive rituals which have to be religiously observed to an exacting magic standard of rightness before they can achieve a resolution of obsessional fears. The purpose of the rituals is often difficult or impossible to discern; they are, like many charms and spells, magic formulae and gestures which have no logical foundation and no practical justification. The patients have insight into the absurdity and irrationality of their compulsive rituals, but this does not liberate them from the fear-driven necessity of observing them accurately and painstakingly. There are two kinds of compulsive rituals, which are often combined: a mental variety which consists entirely of thought processes, and a motor variety which has to be overtly enacted. They hold out the same promise of hope and redemption to the obsessional patient as prayers and sacraments do to the pious and devout. But the reward is not as easily earned by the obsessional patient as by religious people who have full trust in the power of prayer and sacrament; he cannot have full trust because he is consumed by doubt whether his private rituals had been the right ones, and whether he had not slipped from the proper standard of rightness in observing them. So he is forced to repeat them and check them with unflagging attention before he finds eventual relief from his fears and uncertainties.

Compulsive *mental* rituals may consist in rehearsing alternatives of intended actions in the mind until one action appears to be magically right. The most trivial decisions may thus be kept suspended as the patient compulsively wavers between alternatives before he can make up his mind. Yet the problem may be merely whether he should put his right or left foot on the floor first when getting out of bed in the morning. Many patients find themselves obliged to pursue compulsive ruminations, hoping that they will act as lucky charms, and fearing that the slightest slip will turn them into sinister spells. The ruminations cannot come to a satisfying end until they have reached a privately acceptable standard of magic rightness. Patients may have to repeat in their minds some prayers, poems, prose passages, and even senseless phrases; they may have to count up to a 'lucky' number, repeating the process a 'lucky' number of times; they may have to perform some mental calculation and mentally check its accuracy; or they may have to call up the image of some experienced or imagined scene until it has reached a certain level of clarity and detail. The compulsive ruminations of many patients revolve around problems for which there is no adequate answer. The problems are of a semi-philosophical kind (What is the purpose of life? Who am I? What is nothingness?) or are utterly trivial (What was the name of the shop passed an hour before? Why is this door painted green? Why are these children in the playground?). Many compulsive ruminations concern incidents in the patient's past. He may have to review in his mind what he had been doing in the past hour or day, making sure that there is no ominous gap in his memories during which he might have committed some wrong; or he may have to recall all the relevant happenings of the past weeks to see that they tally. This kind of mental checking is not only compulsively undertaken, but also compulsively prolonged because it is judged by an arbitrary though exacting standard of rightness. When compulsive mental rituals are elaborate, they have to be performed in conditions of absolute privacy. Every interruption spoils the magic promise so that the patient, to his despair and irritation, has to begin the ritual all over again.

The simplest compulsive *motor* rituals consist in the enforced performance of alternative actions so that a 'to-and-fro' activity, a 'doing and undoing', results. For example, the patient may at last have succeeded in breaking through the deadlock of compulsive indecision when getting out of bed in the morning. He puts one foot on the ground. Immediately he is beset by the obsessional fear that this was wrong. He is forced to undo his action and to lift the foot again. This sequence of indecision–doing–undoing–indecision may repeat itself several times.

Compulsive indecision and the anankastic ritual of to-and-fro activity can seriously interfere with the patient's life. It may take him an unconscionable time getting through even the simplest tasks of everyday routine. His dressing in the morning, his undressing in the evening are usually prolonged ordeals of indecision, followed by vacillating actions and perhaps by elaborate motor rituals. The mere walking through a door can be a distressing lengthy performance. There is first the mental ritual of ruminating about alternatives. Should he, or should he not, walk through the door? Eventually he does. But was it right? He is forced to come back and the cycle begins once more, and then again and again.

Patients do not like being observed in these time-wasting, anxiety-dominated activities. Many of them are, therefore, carried out in the privacy of their bedroom or in the lavatory. When strangers are present, patients often succeed in speeding up their mental and motor rituals so that they can appear no more than slow and indecisive to outsiders. One of the most harassing and incapacitating undoing rituals is compulsive washing. It is intended to undo a wrong that only happened in the patient's magic half-beliefs, a wrong that caused the obsessional dread of having been contaminated. But the magic contamination can only be removed by a magic ritual of washing and washing again, so thoroughly and frequently that the whole day is taken up by purification procedures, which have to be performed, even though they are made painful by chapped and inflamed hands.

The most frequent rituals against the obsessional fear of having done some wrong are compulsively prolonged activities of factual checking. Their form depends on the nature of the obsessional fear they are meant to dispel, but their enforced repetition rests on the obsessional fear that the previous checking did not come up to a magic standard of rightness. The patient may have to check several times that a cigarette is properly stubbed out, that the gas taps are all switched off, that all the windows are closed and all the doors locked, that there was no error of style, grammar or spelling in the letter written, and so on. Sometimes the checking has to be combined with a doing and undoing of the original act. The cigarette then has again to be stubbed out, the gas taps again turned on and off, the windows again opened and shut, the letter again written. Factual and mental checking often complement each other. A patient, who is obsessed by the anxious half-belief that he picked up a pin in the street and pushed it into a baby's head, has to go back and look for the pin and the baby. But if such factual checking is not possible, or the pin and the baby can no longer be found, mental checking has to reassure the patient that there is no gap in his memories, that he can recall everything he did after passing the pin and the baby in the street.

When obsessional doubts undermine the magic promise of compulsive rituals, the patient is forced to resort to ever more exacting and fastidious ceremonials which have to be slavishly executed in all detail, and their correctness minutely checked and rechecked. Before going to bed, for example, the patient may have to divest himself of his garments in a ritually prescribed order, fold each garment carefully, and arrange them all in a hair-splittingly accurate geometric pattern. Prolonged and repeated cleansing procedures and ablutions may have to follow before he finally manages to get into bed, but his plight need not be over yet. He may still have to visualize all the objects in his room, and then perhaps go through an exhaustive mental check of all his activities during the day.

When compulsive rituals are performed by psychotic patients, they are openly displayed and not concealed from the environment. Schizophrenic patients, for instance, may spend their whole waking day carrying out the same bizarre ritual over and over again without minding in the least that they are observed by others. Melancholic patients may similarly spend their day in overt repetitive activities, perhaps rocking and wailing in agitated despair. Obsessive-compulsive neurotics, on the other hand, make a secret of their anxiety-dominated compulsive rituals because they are acutely aware how ridiculous and absurd their compulsive behaviour looks to the eyes of common sense. But they cannot completely hide all their obsessive-compulsive peculiarities from members of their family or from other patients on the ward, who are, therefore, allowed to witness those rituals which cannot easily be concealed. Moreover, one or the other relative or friend is often treated as a trusted confidant, and perhaps even turned into a partner who has to assist in the execution of rituals. These assistants may have to perform the final check that all objects are in their ritually appointed places, that there are no forbidden objects in the patient's environment or pockets; and they may have to reassure the patient that he has observed all compulsory measures to the last dot, that he had not misbehaved in any way while in company, and so on.

Counterphobic Compulsions

There are usually no conflicts between the phobic and obsessive-compulsive symptoms of a patient. Occasionally, however, the two kinds of symptoms are at odds. In particular, the phobic anxiety kindled by an external situation may become the experience that arouses obsessional fears of being wrong and in magic danger. The patient may then develop a fear-driven compulsion to undo the wrong and obviate the danger. Such a counterphobic compulsion may force the patient into the vicinity of the phobic situation, if it is his obsessional fear that it is wrong to surrender to an absurd phobic anxiety that urges him to keep away from the situation. When the phobic compulsion to keep away and the obsessional compulsion to go near are fairly evenly matched, the patient becomes involved in a prolonged to-and-fro activity of advancing and retreating. If he has a phobia of the sea, for instance, his counterphobic compulsion eggs him on to spend as much time as possible by the sea, going as close to the water as he dares, perhaps even allowing the last ripple of a quiet wave to lap briefly against his feet, before hastily putting a safer distance again between himself and the water. Similarly, a patient with a phobia of speaking in public may be counter-phobically compelled to join a discussion group, and perhaps even succeed in making an occasional, carefully rehearsed, contribution.

It can even happen that counterphobic compulsions score a therapeutic success against a phobic anxiety by gradually familiarizing the patient with the phobic situation until it loses its fear-provoking quality. The phobic situation may then, at least for a while, become an over-valued object of high attractiveness. The patient who once had a phobia of the sea then turns into an enthusiastic swimmer and sailor, and the patient who once had a phobia of public speaking seizes every opportunity to address a public audience.

CHAPTER 15

THE PSYCHOPATHOLOGY OF AFFECT—
EMOTIONAL PSYCHOPATHY

There are many patients with signs of a psychopathology of affect who cannot be easily allotted to psychotic or neurotic disease categories. Such patients are usually called emotional psychopaths, or psychopaths for short. As their main disorder is an abnormal emotional reactivity, the name 'emotional deviant' or 'thymopath' might also be applied to them. Emotional psychopaths are characterized by three special attributes: (1) they are not psychotic; (2) their abnormal emotional reactivity leads to self-indulgent actions; and (3) these self-indulgent actions are condemned by society.

Psychopaths are distinguished from pyschotic patients because they have no idiosyncratic delusions, are not hallucinated, and do not misinterpret their environment. In other words, they are 'in touch with reality' in the sense that they share the collective convictions and knowledge of their social environment, and do not live in a conceptual world that differs significantly from that of other people. In particular, they know the moral and legal code of their society, and are aware of the significance of their actions.

Self-indulgence

Psychopaths are also distinguished from patients with depressive or anxiety-dominated neurotic symptoms. The latter patients are a prey to oppressive emotions, and driven by them to strive for a goal that promises relief from their emotional distress. A psychopathic patient, on the other hand, tends to be governed by emotions which are usually not oppressive, and to be excessively driven by them towards a goal that is pleasurable to most human beings or only pleasurable to him. It is the attraction of this pleasurable goal which tempts and incites the psychopaths to engage in self-indulgent actions, disregarding the possibility that this may be detrimental to others, or, in the long run, to themselves.

We have already considered some self-indulgent actions of this kind; namely, hypomanic behaviour which submits to the lure of every passing emotion; dipsomanic behaviour which succumbs to the recurrent temptation of alcoholic abuse; the nymphomanic behaviour of women, which is motivated by excessive sexual emotions; kleptomanic behaviour, which expresses a variety of emotions, especially a desire to gamble with danger; and some other similar forms of abnormal behaviour. There are many other self-indulgent emotions and actions, which fall into this category, though they are not characterized by the suffix '-manic'. In fact, psychopaths might be classified according to the kind of emotion in which they excessively indulge. One might thus distinguish aggressive, assertive, submissive, hyperkinetic, hypokinetic, inquisitive, sexual, gambling, hoarding, and many other varieties. Such varieties can be further subdivided according to whether the emotional self-indulgence manifests itself chronically or episodically. There are, for example, some aggressive deviants who are chronically pugnacious thugs and others who have only occasional outbursts of violent temper; there are some alcoholics who chronically drink too much and others who do so only periodically; there are some homosexuals whose emotional deviation is constant and others in whom it is variable.

The self-indulgence of episodic psychopaths may be related to the stimulating effect of certain situations. A person may, for instance, give rein to aggressive emotions only when dealing with particular persons (e.g. spouse, underling), only at home, or only in commercial negotiations. The form which such aggressive emotions then take is usually dictated by the situation and can vary from nagging, pestering, threatening, harrying, sarcastic criticism and persecution to actual physical violence. Sometimes the connection between a situation and the emotional self-indulgence aroused by it is unjustified, incongruous and perverse. Such reactions are comparable to the incongruous relationships that exist between harmless situations and the phobic fears provoked by them. In psychopathic patients, however, the emotions that are excited by particular situations are not those of fear; they are usually those of aggression or erotic attachment. There are occasional psychopaths, for instance, who develop murderous desires in the company of defenceless and trusting persons, such as children. Such desires are pleasurable to them and may give rise to what appears to be a motiveless murder. There are other psychopaths, mostly women, who become erotically tied to persons who misuse, maltreat, and exploit them unscrupulously.

Obviously, not every self-indulgent action is a psychopathic response; only those which society denounces as immoral, wicked, asocial or antisocial because they deviate from some ideal norm and transgress some moral or legal code. As these norms and codes vary in different societies, the concept of psychopathy is inevitably variable too. To indulge in overeating, for instance, was once one of the seven deadly sins, but comes today near to a status symbol among businessmen. The drinking of moderate amounts of alcohol is accepted in our society nowadays with as much tolerance as the smoking of tobacco, but the use of hashish (marihuana) is branded as illegal. In some Moslem countries, this relation is reversed: alcohol is forbidden, but hashish tolerated. Male homosexuality was exalted as a virtue in ancient Greece, but is today a criminal offence in many countries, even when it is practised by consenting adults.

There is thus no doubt that, in making the diagnosis of emotional psychopathy, one has to take the ideal norms and the moral and legal codes of particular societies into account. What is psychopathy in one society, may be no more than a respectable, or perhaps slightly suspect, form of emotional self-indulgence in another. It is obvious that the majority of adult members of a society succeed in keeping within the limits of law and social custom. This suggests that persons with normal emotional reactivities find it possible to adjust to the requirements of their society. It has, however, to be kept in mind that large communities are never uniform; they contain minority groups of an ethnic, religious or political variety which have their own social norms and *mores*. Thus there always are people in large communities whose conduct deviates from that prescribed by the *mores* of a dominant section, not because of abnormal emotional reactivity, but because of membership in a deviant minority group. This argument also applies to members of deviant minority groups whose *mores* sanction a criminal or parasitic way of social life[184, 226]. Such people may have grown up in families or neighbourhoods in which stealing from strangers and despoiling wealthy citizens is regarded as justified, provided it remains undiscovered and unpunished. Other people may have chosen crime as an occupation or craft because it promised to be more profitable than a more respectable form of livelihood. Such people do not have an abnormal emotional reactivity or any other mental disorder; they are professional or opportunist criminals.

Psychopathy and Crime

Psychiatrists are not required to deal with normal criminals, but they may be asked to assist in establishing the diagnosis of psychological normality or abnormality. The presumption of psychological abnormality is suggested mainly in two conditions: (a) when the law is violated so openly and with such unconcern in detection that arrest is practically inevitable; and (b) when an offender continues his lawless pursuits despite repeated experience that the possible advantages accruing to him are minimal compared with the likelihood of being detected and punished. The first alternative, the open commission of a crime, occurs only with conspirators who have resigned themselves to martyrdom, and with people who are insane. Most of the people in this category of crime are, in fact, insane. But how insane must a person be in the eyes of the law to be regarded as not responsible for his crime?

This was a question that was decided by fourteen judges of the House of Lords in 1843. The deliberations of the judges had been occasioned by a famous murder trial. In January, 1843, one M'Naghten (or McNaughton to use the correct spelling of his name)[373] shot and killed the private secretary of the Tory Prime Minister, Sir Robert Peel. The murderer stated on his arrest: 'The Tories . . . follow and persecute me wherever I go . . . They have everything in their power to harass and persecute me. In fact, they wish to murder me. It can be proved by evidence.'[264] At his trial, he was found not guilty on the ground of insanity, and eventually sent to Bethlem Royal Hospital, where he spent most of his remaining years.

There was a public outcry against the verdict of 'not guilty' and this led the judges in the House of Lords to lay down the so-called M'Naghten Rules, by which the responsibility of insane criminals was to be assessed. Essentially, there were two criteria (or 'limbs' as they are often called). The defence might succeed in establishing the fact that the accused was so insane, at the time of committing the act, 'as not to know the nature and quality of the act he was doing'. For example, M'Naghten would have been not guilty on the ground of insanity, if he had been suffering from such a clouding of consciousness ('a defect of reason from disease of the mind' was the actual wording) that he did not know he was handling a gun and directing it at a human being.

The alternative criterion became applicable, when the accused had, at the time of committing the act, not been so insane that he did not know what he was doing, but had been so deluded 'that he did not know he was doing what was [legally] wrong'. If M'Naghten's delusion had been such that he feared an immediate attempt on his life, he could have shot the delusional assailant, knowing that, in this extreme danger-situation, such an act of self-defence was legally permissible. If, on the other hand, his delusion had been that his good reputation was being libelled and slandered by the other person, there would have been no legal justification for the crime because he would have, or should have, known that defamation did not entitle him to take the law into his own hands and kill the detractor.

The M'Naghten Rules are a very severe test of insanity. As was said by a nineteenth-century judge (Lord Bramwell): 'Nobody is hardly ever really mad enough to be within the definition of madness laid down in the judges answers' (i.e. the M'Naghten Rules)[462]. The Rules have other defects. They contain, for instance, the phrase: 'from disease of the mind'. This phrase could be understood to exclude patients who have had a defect of reason all their lives. Such a defect of reason may be considered constitutional and not caused by an (acquired) disease of the mind. But the main shortcoming of the Rules is their identification of insanity with an acquired defect of reason, or dementia. Insanity due to an acquired psychopathology of affect is completely disregarded. This exclusively intellectualist approach by jurists to the concept of mental illness is very much at variance with the views of modern psychiatry. It can happen that a paranoid schizophrenic, let us say, who reasons logically and does not display his delusions too conspicuously, is declared legally sane in a court of law, even when there is expert psychiatric opinion available, and uncontested, that the patient is undoubtedly insane.

English lawyers have been fighting a rearguard action against widening their concept of insanity. But, in the course of time, there have been some concessions on their part which admit the possibility of diminished responsibility in certain patients who, though insane, do not fully satisfy the M'Naghten Rules. The first breach in the legal bastion came with the Infanticide Act, 1922, (now replaced by the Infanticide Act, 1938). It acknowledged that a woman who killed her child before it was twelve months old, might have done so while 'the balance of her mind was disturbed by reason of her not having fully recovered from the effect of giving birth to the child, or by reason of the effect of lactation consequent upon the birth of the child'. The Homicide Act, 1957, went even further. It explicitly introduced into English law the defence of diminished responsibility, a defence which was already well established in Scottish law. Section 2(1) provides that 'where a person kills or is a party to the killing of another, he shall not be convicted of murder if he was suffering from such abnormality of mind . . . as substantially impaired his mental responsibility for his acts and omissions in doing or being a party to the killing'. Section 3 of this Act also considerably widens the defence of emotional provocation, which may be set up by a person accused of murder.

Resistance against these concessions to psychiatric thought has, however, never been silenced. As Barbara Wootton put it: 'Once we allow any movement away from a rigid intellectual test of responsibility on McNaghten lines, our feet are set upon a slippery slope which offers no real resting place short of the total abandonment of the whole concept of responsibility[546].' She felt uneasy about the kind of circular reasoning which seems to be acceptable occasionally in some psychiatric quarters. A person who commits a crime may be regarded as mentally ill, by some psychiatrists, though there is no other evidence of mental illness, but the commission of the crime. Similarly, an accused may be regarded as having committed a criminal act under the influence of an irresistible impulse, though there is no other evidence but the fact that the impulse was not resisted. There is a danger that this sort of justification of a preconceived idea by a foregone conclusion may abolish the boundary line between offenders who are responsible for their act and therefore deserving of punishment, and offenders who are not fully responsible for their act, through a mental disorder, and therefore deserving of sympathy and treatment.

Another criterion which may suggest that an offender has a mental disorder is his persistent recidivism despite repeated experiences that the possible advantages accruing to him are minimal compared with the likelihood of being detected and punished. This is not another piece of circular reasoning because recidivism despite punishment is characteristic of some offenders only. Such a diagnostic criterion of mental disorder has, however, the disadvantage of being *ex post facto*; the patient has to be punished first, before his illness can be diagnosed and treatment attempted. There is also another objection: this approach can be taken as an encouragement of recidivism. Barbara Wootton[546] has expressed this objection forcibly: 'If you are consistently (in old-fashioned language) wicked enough, you may hope to be excused from responsibility for your misdeeds; but if your wickedness is only moderate, . . . then you must expect to take the blame for what you do.'

It must also be admitted that recidivism despite punishment cannot be regarded as a pathognomonic sign of mental disorder; it may merely indicate that the offender got into a social rut from which he cannot extricate himself without external help, because he knows no other means of livelihood but crime. However, if the punishment of offenders is tempered with attempts to rehabilitate and reform them, those with a normal personality may succeed in eventually establishing themselves in new ways of life, which are more advantageous to them and less obnoxious to society. There is still a large group of recidivists who are neither improved by punishment nor by opportunities of rehabilitation, and yet show no sign of a psychotic illness. To assume that they deliberately choose a hazardous and ruinous life of crime and rebellion in preference to the advantages open to a law-abiding and adaptable citizen, is to credit them with a gratuitous degree of perversity. We have no intuitive understanding of such perversity, if we postulate an ideally typical mind that is reasonable and responsible, and therefore capable of exercising a free choice between right and wrong conduct. However, we succeed in understanding such recidivists intuitively, if we attribute to them a mind of diminished responsibility and self-control. If this diminished responsibility and self-control is not due to a defect of reason through delusions, hallucinations, a clouding of consciousness and the like, then its origin must lie in a disordered emotional reactivity.

The idea that a person's responsibility may be diminished not only by intellectual, but also by emotional, defects is not of recent origin. It happened that, in the year before the M'Naghten Rules were formulated, this idea was put forward by the Bristol physician J. C. Prichard, in a book entitled *On the Different Forms of Insanity in Relation to Jurisprudence*. Prichard remarked: 'It seems on the whole to be settled doctrine of English Courts at present, that there cannot be insanity without delusion, . . . that is, without some particular erroneous conviction impressed upon the understanding, the affected person being otherwise in possession of the full and undisturbed use of his mental faculties. . . . A man is supposed to be mad on one point, and sane in every other particular; a state in itself most incredible.' In opposition to this legal view of insanity, Prichard emphasized 'that mental derangement, in almost every case, not only involved a disordered exercise of the intellectual faculties, but . . . implicates more remarkably the moral affections, the temper, the feelings and propensities'[314].

The class of mental derangements in which the 'moral affections' were predominantly disordered, Prichard called 'moral insanity'. It was an unfortunate name that has been variously interpreted. By the adjective 'moral' Prichard did not refer to a special moral sense, but to emotional experiences in general. The noun 'insanity' was understood by him in a very wide sense; he denoted by it all three varieties of the psychopathology of affect, which we have distinguished as psychotic, neurotic and psychopathic. When the concept of moral insanity is applied to offenders, it is possible to differentiate those who are psychotic or neurotic because they show specific psychological dysfunctions in addition to their antisocial behaviour. The offenders whom we call psychopathic today also have an additional dysfunction, but it becomes apparent only with the lapse of time: their antisocial behaviour is not improved by the likelihood of punishment.

In the Mental Deficiency Act of 1913, the assumption was made that psychopaths have not reached mental maturity, and are not only emotionally disordered, but also mentally defective. In fact, they were called 'moral imbeciles' and defined as 'persons who from an early age display some permanent mental defect coupled with strong vicious or· criminal propensities on which punishment has had little or no deterrent effect'. It should be noticed that the terms 'vicious and criminal' were vague enough to cover almost any kind of immoral, depraved and antisocial conduct. 'Permanent mental defect' was not clearly defined either. It was not specified as an intellectual defect, measurable perhaps by intelligence tests. On the contrary, the implication was that intellectual shortcomings could be inferred from the inadequacy of social adjustment, that moral imbeciles were 'incapable of managing themselves or their affairs' and needed 'care, supervision and control for their own protection or for the protection of others'.

In 1927, these definitions were amended in England, though not in Scotland. The term 'moral imbecile' was softened to 'moral defective'; his emotional propensities were still characterized as before; but his mental defectiveness was no longer described as permanent; it was defined as a 'condition of arrested or incomplete development of the mind existing before the age of eighteen years, whether arising from inherent causes or induced by disease or injury'. The age of eighteen seems to have been chosen to signify the point at which adult mental maturity was attained. It followed that a person, who developed strong vicious or criminal propensities for the first time after the age of eighteen, through some intercurrent disease or injury of the mind, was yet responsible for his actions, unless the excessively severe M'Naghten Rules could be applied.

In the Mental Health Act of 1959, all reference to moral imbecility or moral defectiveness has disappeared. Psychopathy has been acknowledged as a 'persistent disorder or disability of the mind' which occurs before the age of 21, but is not necessarily coupled with any 'subnormality of intelligence'. Yet not every psychopath is, in the eyes of the law, a patient in need of treatment; only some of those who persistently display 'abnormally aggressive or seriously irresponsible conduct'. Those whose misbehaviour consists 'only of promiscuity or other immoral conduct' have been specifically excluded from the category of patients who might be in need of medical treatment. It seems that moral indignation and condemnation won the day, when the motives of misbehaviour could be easily imagined by the legislators. Parliament obviously had an intuitive understanding of people who indulge their immoral and promiscuous sexual leanings for the sake of immediate pleasure. Such people were thus considered normal and culpable; but the motives of people with abnormally aggressive and seriously irresponsible conduct were less readily understood; they were thus considered as possibly in need of medical treatment rather than legal punishment.

Not only judges and legislators have ambivalent attitudes towards emotional psychopaths. Psychiatrists have similar difficulties, which reveal themselves mainly in the question: Is psychopathy an illness or a personality disorder? There are many psychiatrists who prefer to think of psychopathy as a personality disorder, occurring in a healthy person who has become abnormal (but not ill) through the acquisition of bad emotional habits. Such psychiatrists argue that disease can only be diagnosed, when endopathological lesions exist. Followed to its logical conclusion, such an argument would deny the status of disease to all functional psychiatric disorders. There have been some psychiatrists who have indeed gone as far as that, but it has been more usual to make a gratuitous distinction between functional psychosis on the one hand, and neurosis and emotional psychopathy, on the other. Patients with a functional psychosis have then been credited with an endopathology that is as yet unknown. They have therefore been believed to be both abnormal and ill personalities. No such assumption of endopathological changes has been made in neurotic and psychopathic patients; they have therefore been believed to be abnormal, yet (physically) healthy, personalities.

We do not have to accept arguments of this kind. We can leave speculations about endopathological changes aside, and concentrate on the concept of clinical disease. This is diagnosed by the presence of morbid clinical symptoms; that is, by the presence of manifestations which give rise to suffering and concern in the patient or his social environment. We deal with a personality disorder only, when acts of abnormal emotional self-indulgence are not followed by morbid symptoms; and with a clinical disease, called emotional psychopathy, when such acts give rise to morbid symptoms. If there are no morbid symptoms, we cannot speak of an illness. It does not matter, however, whether the symptoms arise from physico-chemical causes, as in the case of drug addiction, or from the reactions of society, such as the unhappy interpersonal relations the psychopath creates, or the social condemnation and punishment he encounters. In either case, there will be morbid clinical symptoms in the patient, which justify us in regarding emotional psychopathy as a clinical disease due to the physiopathological or sociopathological consequences of an abnormal emotional self-indulgence.

Sex and Psychopathy

Among the various kinds of emotional self-indulgence, which can become abnormal and then perhaps give rise to an emotional psychopathy, those of a sexual nature stand out in importance and deserve a special analysis. Adult sexual emotions consist of several emotional strands. The most basic among them is an emotion that is closely linked with certain psychosomatic changes in the genital organ, changes which are required as a normal prelude to the adult sexual act. The psychosomatic changes consist primarily in a tumescence of the external genital organ and increased secretions by genital glands. The genital emotions which are associated with such genital reactions, consist in self-indulgent desires to derive pleasure from a stimulation of tumescent genital organs.

Genital reactions of a rudimentary form, and some equally rudimentary genital emotions, are present already in infancy. Even very young children show occasional genital reactions in the form of tumescence, but not in the form of increased genital secretions[211]. These infantile genital reactions are capable of arousing some genital emotions and a tendency to enhance the emotions by manipulations of the genital organ. The presence of genital reactions and emotions in infants has never been a secret in communities with little privacy. In the mediaeval household, for instance, where every room could serve as a communal bedroom, children knew as much of the sex life of adults as the latter knew of the genital pleasures of children. In fact, it was usual then for adults to fondle the genital organs of children and to joke about this.

This mutual knowledge disappeared with the introduction of private and personal bedrooms. With the advent of the sexual prudery of Victorian times, the collective conviction could therefore spread that children are sexually completely innocent. All evidence to the contrary was disregarded and denied. Freud regarded it as one of his main achievements that he rediscovered the primitive sexual reactions of children. In fact, the external genital organs became for him only one among several 'erotogenic zones'. The sexual experiences of infants were predominantly auto-erotic. They began with sensations in the erotogenic zones, aroused genital (or pregenital) emotions, and ended with self-indulgent activities which enhanced the pleasurable sensations from the erotogenic zones.

Freud, whoever, paid little attention to the completely new elements which were added to the sexual life of individuals at puberty, elements which had not been present in earlier childhood at all. Yet the transformation occurring at puberty is all too obvious. Physiologically, the shape and functioning of the whole body are fundamentally altered so that the post-pubertal mature individual has little in common with his infantile immature past. He is also psychologically quite different. Before puberty, sexual emotions are auto-erotically aroused by sensations which originate in eroto-genic zones. The child does not respond with genital reactions to objects and events in its environment, which are sexually exciting to adults. Love stories do not attract it, sexual jokes do not amuse it, and the sight of sexual charms leaves it indifferent. But after puberty, allo-erotic percepts and information become a source of sexual excitement. In men, such percepts and information arouse genital reactions more readily than in women. That is the reason why there are strip-tease performances for men, but not for women. Women tend to respond to allo-erotic stimuli primarily with seductive sexual emotions and behaviour.

The change-over, at puberty, from auto-erotism to allo-erotism is never quite complete, but it is a psychological revolution which is as considerable as that which occurs in the physiological field. There is no doubt that the physiological changes of puberty are genetically determined. There is also no doubt that the new psychological functions, the allo-erotic act-phenomena, are similarly determined by genetic influences. But what about the allo-erotic object-phenomena? Theoretically it is possible that the object-phenomena which become linked to allo-erotic act-phenomena are mainly selected by chance experiences or deliberate indoctrination. This is possible, but it is not very likely. After all, it is of biological importance that the object-phenomena should be such that they are suitable for the achievement of sexual intercourse and the propagation of the human race.

Innate Releasing Mechanisms

The object-phenomena which we are considering here are, in the language of the ethologists, sexual 'instinct releasers'. The act-phenomena are assumed to originate in certain psychoneural structures, called innate releasing mechanisms, or IRMs. The theory is that IRMs are inherited structures which are responsive to particular instinct releasers from the moment of birth, or become so at a later stage in life.

We have already mentioned earlier that newly hatched game birds respond with signs of fear and efforts to conceal themselves, when they, for the first time, perceive an event that resembles the overhead flight of a bird of prey. The game birds are therefore credited with inherited IRMs of fear, which are specifically attuned to particular instinct releasers, such as the shape of a bird of prey flying overhead. In that case, the linkage between act-phenomena and object-phenomena is obviously due to genetic determination. The two kinds of phenomena could not have been linked by means of learning through experience or instruction. With IRMs that become responsive later in life, there is always the possibility that their inherited responsiveness was unspecific, and the linkage between them and particular instinct releasers is therefore not entirely due to inheritance, but partly the result of learning through experience or instruction. This may apply also in the case of the sexual IRMs which become allo-erotically responsive at puberty.

The present-day popularity of psychoanalysis has encouraged tendencies which try to discount genetic influences and to lay stress on the importance of learning through experience. It is true that Freud's analysis of the mind was begun in the hope of finding significant experiences in a person's past, which were responsible for psychological abnormalities. Yet his theories have, at the same time, always been firmly anchored to the concept of instincts and their genetically determined maturation from an oral, through an anal, to an ultimate genital stage of infantile sexuality. He even pointed out that there were allo-erotic precursors during the otherwise auto-erotic phase of infantile libido. In the genital phase, for instance, the allo-erotic precursors consisted in the observation of, or fantasy about, sexual copulation, especially the so-called primal scene of parental sexual intercourse. Yet these allo-erotic precursors did not produce overt genital reactions or sexual advances on the part of the infant because it had 'Oedipal fears' of punishment by castration. According to this theory, when allo-erotism becomes overt at puberty, the Oedipal fears and taboos of incest continue so that family members, and especially parents, remain excluded from the list of sexually exciting object-phenomena.

Generally speaking, the functions of an organism are determined by both genetic influences and life events. Therefore, instead of asking an 'either-or' question about the origin of allo-erotic instinct releasers at puberty, it seems more helpful to consider some instances in which the relative influence of genetic effects and life events can be separated. The usual allo-erotic object is a person of the opposite sex. IRMs therefore tend to be predominantly heterosexual in their sensitivity. There is, however, a considerable proportion of people in whom genital reactions can be excited allo-erotically by persons of the same sex. The homosexuality of these people (or lesbianism as it is sometimes called in the female sex) is either exclusive or occasional. Because homosexuality is often disparaged in our society, psychological pressure is likely to reduce the number of exclusive homosexuals.

Kinsey and his collaborators have systematically investigated the sex life of American men and women[283, 284]. They found that about 63 per cent of adult men and about 87 per cent of adult women were exclusively heterosexual in their overt activities, though many of these people had subjective erotic feelings occasionally in response to members of their own sex. Four per cent of adult men and a smaller percentage of adult women were exclusively homosexual. Thus about a third of adult men and about a tenth of adult women were capable of responding with genital reactions to either sex, and had had some homosexual activity to the point of orgasm in the course of their lives. Kinsey graded heterosexual and homosexual tendencies on a seven-point scale extending from grade zero (exclusively heterosexual) through grade three (equally heterosexual and homosexual) to grade six (exclusively homosexual).

The examination of monozygotic twins can throw light on the extent to which homosexual IRMs are genetically determined. Systematic investigations of this kind are, however, extraordinarily difficult because of the understandable reluctance of people to disclose their private sex life to strangers. So far only Kallmann has been able to publish a sufficiently large and adequately examined series[273, 274]. He found that the concordance with regard to homosexuality was almost 100 per cent among monozygotic male twins with a Kinsey rating of at least four. There have, however, been a number of reports in the literature which described an occasional discordance of homosexuality in monozygotic twin pairs[291, 296, 384, 412].

To clinch the fact that homosexuality is predominantly genetic in origin, it is also necessary to show that the concordance for homosexuality is much smaller in dizygotic twin pairs. It was indeed found that, in their case, the concordance is only about 12 per cent. In spite of this overwhelming evidence in favour of a genetic determination, there are psychoanalysts who believe that homosexuality can be caused by a special family constellation, namely a possessive and seductive mother to whom the patient is strongly attached, and an indifferent or hostile father. However, these beliefs are not very securely founded. They rely almost entirely on the retrospective exploration, in the course of psychoanalytic therapy, of the family constellation in the patient's infancy. Even if his reminiscences could be accepted as referring to an objective reality rather than to infantile fantasies, they would not prove that homosexuality is the result of a special family constellation. The patient's positive relations with his mother and negative relations with his father could just as well be due to infantile manifestations of his homosexual IRMs[534, 535].

Thus, although the causal significance of a special family constellation in a homosexual patient's infancy remains doubtful, it has been shown that other social influences in infancy can affect the allo-erotic feelings of people whose sexual constitution is weak or disordered. Such patients may be born with external genitalia, which are not typical of either sex. Their 'intersexual' genitalia may have their origin in a variety of endopathological conditions. They may be found, for example, in true hermaphrodites who possess both ovarian and testicular tissue; in female infants whose external genitalia have been masculinized through adrenocortical hyperplasia; or in male infants with testicular feminization. Intersexual infants of this kind may be assigned to the wrong sex at birth; wrong, that is, in comparison to their chromosomal sex. They are then subjected to a social indoctrination which prepares them for the wrong 'gender role'. Investigations have shown that in most patients in whom chromosomal sex and assigned gender role are at variance, social indoctrination for their gender role is the more important determinant of sexual orientation[214, 365, 366, 367]. However, there are exceptions.

The genetically determined sexual orientation sometimes proves stronger than the social indoctrination towards a wrong gender role. Such patients may reveal their chromosomal sex even before puberty by behaviour that does not fit in with the assigned gender role. Patients wrongly brought up as girls, for example, may be tomboyish and perhaps prefer to urinate in the standing position. By contrast, patients wrongly brought up as boys may like playing with dolls and perhaps prefer to urinate squatting down. In such patients, secondary characteristics of their true sex may develop at puberty. These may include an allo-erotic attraction to persons of their own gender role—an attraction, which appears to be homosexual merely because their true chromosomal sex had not been diagnosed at birth. This spurious homosexuality can be readily cured by an official change of the assigned sex and gender role. Surgical repair of the faulty genital anatomy is often possible, and such patients may then even enjoy a more or less satisfactory sex life[40, 115, 183].

Examples of this kind show that the sexual IRMs of some people can be so strongly heterosexual in their genetically determined reactivity that their sexual orientation overrides all social indoctrination towards what is, in effect, homosexuality. It is therefore also conceivable that some persons are born with IRMs which are genetically so strongly biased towards homosexuality that social indoctrination towards a heterosexual gender role is of no avail. Kallmann's investigation of homosexual twins shows that a genetic determination of the reactivity of sexual IRMs is quite common. This determination is, of course, quite independent of those influences which are responsible for intersexuality. The vast majority of homosexuals are not intersexes; their physical and genital constitution is quite normal and agrees with their chromosomal sex.

Persistent homosexuals are abnormal by population standards. For that reason, they may be said to have abnormal personalities. They do not, however, necessarily suffer from their abnormality. On the contrary, they are capable of enjoying their sexual orientation just as much as heterosexual persons, provided the society in which they live accepts homosexuality as a harmless, or even useful, variant of sexual orientation. In our society, for instance, female homosexuality is tolerated, but male homosexuality less so. There have, however, always been societies which tolerated homosexuality in both men and women. In ancient Greece, a largely idealized form of male homosexuality was perfectly respectable. Plato even suggested, in his Symposium, that homosexual lovers would make the best city councillors and the best soldiers because they would rather die than feel dishonoured in the eyes of their homosexual partners. Ford and Beach, in a study of 76 contemporary primitive societies, found that homosexual practices among men were accepted in 64 per cent of them, and were often even imposed by custom[141].

In societies like our own, in which it is an inveterate collective conviction that male homosexuality is a sin, an 'unnatural' vice, or a perversion, people of high Kinsey grades are bound to experience hardships. Inasmuch as they suffer from such hardships, they may be said to be psychiatrically ill. Social conventions and convictions therefore can have pathological consequences because they can convert a homosexual abnormality of personality into a homosexual psychopathy.

Sexual Anomalies

There are other kinds of sexual abnormalities which can turn into sexual psychopathies through social condemnation and persecution. Such sexual anomalies can be divided into three categories: (1)

the anomalous arousal of genital reactions by unusual instinct releasers; (2) the anomalous arousal of genital reactions by non-sexual emotions; and (3) the anomalous performance of the sexual act.

Anomalous arousal of genital reactions by unusual instinct releasers—The most common anomaly in this category is homosexuality, which has already been considered in some detail. Other unusual instinct releasers are garments worn by the opposite sex, such as shoes, stockings, underwear or rubber raincoats (fetishism), sexually immature bodies (paedophilia), old bodies (gerontophilia), dead bodies (necrophilia), statues (pygmalionism), animals (bestialism), or raging fires (pyromania).

Some persons derive sexual enjoyment from dressing in the clothes of the opposite sex. Such transvestism[237] is tolerated in our society when done by women. They can wear male clothes, cut their hair short, sport a collar and tie, and assume a masculine stride in low-heeled male shoes so that they are mistaken for a man at first glance, and yet they will arouse no more than surprise and amusement. Male transvestites, on the other hand, are more sternly judged and have to be more secretive. During the day, they may do no more than wear some female undergarments, which remain invisible to others. But in the evening, in the privacy of their home, they may go further—put on female dress and high-heeled shoes, and use lipstick and rouge. In this guise, they may even venture on an occasional outdoor stroll at night. If they are married, their wives often feel so disgusted and upset that they insist on a psychiatric investigation of their husbands. The only time a male transvestite can indulge his perversion in public and excite no other emotions but amusement is when he dresses up as a female impersonator on the stage or during a party game.

Some people obtain sexual pleasure from imagining themselves with the physical characteristics of the opposite sex. Occasionally the pleasure grows into an overriding desire for a physical change of sex (trans-sexualism)[36, 413]. They may develop a loathing for the sexual characteristics of their own body, and this may become so preoccupying that they desperately search for a surgeon who will agree to operate on them and change the physical signs of their sex. Men appeal for a castrating operation and the surgical construction of an artificial vagina, and women for the removal of their breasts. When their appeals are refused, they may suffer so desperately that suicide may seem to offer the only solution to them. Neither trans-vestites nor trans-sexualists are necessarily homosexuals or fetishists, though female trans-sexualists are usually lesbians.

Anomalous arousal of genital reactions by non-sexual emotions—Normal sexual pleasures are often enhanced by non-sexual emotions which play a contributory, though subordinate, part in the total experience. In some persons, however, such contributory emotions may become indispensable so that no full sexual satisfaction can be achieved without them. The non-sexual emotion may be a cruel desire to inflict pain and humiliation on a sexual partner (sadism), to have pain and humiliation inflicted on oneself by a sexual partner (masochism), to frighten women by the unexpected exhibition of an erect penis (exhibitionism), to secretly watch copulating couples or the intimate behaviour of women who feel unobserved in their bedrooms or lavatories (voyeurism, scoptophilia). The sexual pleasure of some persons can only be gratified by illicit affairs with married women (Don Juanism), or married men; by promiscuity; or by the seduction of inexperienced virgins of either sex. In some women, sexual emotions are only kindled by the non-sexual feelings of reconciliation after a period of estrangement. This anomaly has not received a special name, and is often overlooked, perhaps because the reconciliation of an estranged couple is something that is applauded as admirable rather than condemned as abnormal. The anomaly is, however, obvious in the matrimonial history of such women, which consists of episodes of furious quarrels alternating with times of mutual forgiving.

Anomalous performance of the sexual act—There have always been some societies in which any deviation from the natural coital position and activity has been officially denounced as abnormal. This denunciation applies particularly to all forms of extra-vaginal coitus, such as mutual masturbation, oral intercourse (fellatio), anal intercourse (buggery, or sodomy, a term that can also be understood in a wider sense, connoting bestialism, homosexuality and other deviations), or stimulation of the clitoris and vulva with the mouth or tongue (cunnilingus). The anomalies mentioned are not always acted out in reality. Many people gratify their deviant sexual desires in private fantasy only, often as a prelude to masturbation.

Eccentricities

Man has many instincts apart from those associated with sex. He must therefore have many non-sexual IRMs which may, for one reason or another, become sensitive to unusual instinct releasers. When this happens, individuals stand out from the common herd because of the idiosyncrasy of their interests and emotional reactions. If they are otherwise well endowed mentally, they may rise to heights of fame as leaders and originators in a special domain. Some may even be acknowledged as geniuses because they opened up new vistas in science, art, politics or religion, and obstinately indulged their own bent in face of the opposition of the traditionalists. This relation between genius and emotional individuality does not, of course, imply that geniuses are in some way mentally ill or psychopathic. They do not necessarily suffer through their unusual gifts, though they may encounter social difficulties because they are different from others and pursue a path of egocentric originality rather than one complying with established views. The originator who is accepted by his society may be hailed as a hero, sage or saint; but if he is rejected, he is likely to be denounced as a madman, traitor or heretic. The alternatives are particularly marked in the political sphere. If he succeeds, he may go down in history as a great man; if he fails, he may have to endure punishment that is often more savage than that meted out to 'antisocial psychopaths' of a non-political kind.

CHAPTER 16

THE PSYCHOPATHOLOGY OF MOBILITY

When the mobility of a patient is diminished, we speak of *hypokinesis*, or *akinesis*; when it is increased, of *hyperkinesis*. In many diseases, both hypokinetic and hyperkinetic manifestations occur. Depressive patients are often hypokinetic, especially when they are overwhelmed by feelings of despondency and gloom. They then present the clinical picture of a 'retarded depression'. When such patients become akinetic, they are said to be in a depressive stupor. They stand, sit, or lie immobile for long periods of time, but retain enough initiative to avoid soiling themselves. They do not speak spontaneously and, when asked questions, may remain mute, or reply only after a long pause with a few whispered words. But depressive patients, especially those past middle age, may also be hyperkinetic. They are then usually dominated by anxiety and despair. In this agitated depression, they are continually on the move, finding no peace anywhere.

The hyperkinesis of manic patients is different in origin. It is due to their increased reactivity, the elation of their spirits, and the flight of their ideas. In all psychiatric diseases in which fear is aroused, the patient usually becomes hyperkinetic, though hypokinetic reactions can also occur. The psychopathological source of the fear does not matter; it may lie in hallucinations, delusions, endogenous depressions, or neurotic phobias. If the overt manifestation of the hyperkinetic reaction is deliberately inhibited, it may still reveal itself in trembling hands and knees, or in a tremulous voice. Neurotic fears sometimes cause attacks of *tachypnoea* and *hyperventilation*. These attacks may be so prolonged that they give rise to tetanic symptoms in the form of carpopedal spasms.

Catatonic Schizophrenia

In catatonic schizophrenia, psychopathological changes of mobility are in the foreground of the clinical picture. Characteristic is a poverty of movement. Whatever movements do occur are stiff and awkward, even stilted and manneristic. Questions are answered, if at all, with an extreme economy of words. The immobility of the patients often leads to a swelling of their legs, and may contribute to the development of cold and cyanotic extremities. When total immobility occurs, apart from movements of the eyes and eyelids, the patients are said to be in an *akinetic*, or *catatonic*, or *cataleptic stupor*. Their consciousness is unimpaired, in contrast to the symptom known as 'unconscious stupor'. There is postural fixity so that the patients either resist any attempt to change their posture, or allow their limbs to be passively moved into peculiar positions, which are then maintained for some time (flexibilitas cerea). The patients often assume peculiar postures on their own initiative. They may lie in bed with their knees drawn up to their chin or rigidly stretched out, but with the head lifted off the pillow—a position normal people could not maintain for long; they may lie on their side with their mouth open and saliva drooling from it freely. The face is often drawn into a grimace; soiling is common; feeding is often a problem when the patients refuse to eat, or keep food in their mouth without swallowing it. Their lips are often pouting (snout cramp, '*Schnauz-krampf*').

Some catatonic patients squat about in an uncomfortable and bizarre posture. They resist efforts to change the posture, or resume it as soon as they are left alone again. Sometimes such postures are adopted only when the patients feel they are the objects of attention. A catatonic posture disappears during sleep. It can also be temporarily removed by the intravenous injection of barbiturates or other somniferous substances. Under their influence, the patient can talk and move with relative freedom for a while.

Catatonic schizophrenics may also develop episodes of *catatonic hyperkinesis* which often occur with disconcerting suddenness. Inactive or stuporous patients suddenly become vehemently over-active, tearing, pushing, shaking, kicking or destroying everything within sight, inflicting injuries on others or themselves. The hyperkinetic vehemence may end as suddenly as it arose. Another form of catatonic hyperkinesis consists in *reiterated stereotyped activities*. They present themselves as manneristic habits, or as compulsive rituals, which are openly and endlessly performed all day and every day. The patients may walk round and round along the same path, touching the same objects in the same sequence and manner, until they have worn away the floor and the places touched; they may scratch or bang the same part of their body until it is a bruised and bleeding mess; they may rub the same spot on their head until it is bald; they may tear their clothes and twist off buttons with never-ending persistence; they may masturbate openly; and they may play the same dirty tricks every day with their food, saliva or faeces.

The mobility of catatonic schizophrenics may also be distorted by a pathologically inflated *catatonic negativism*. When asked to open their eyes, they close them; when asked to show their tongue, they immediately shut their lips tightly; they refuse food put before them but help themselves from the food put before other patients; they do not reply to questions, until the questioner gives up and turns away; they do not open their bowels or pass water when they are put on a lavatory seat, but soil themselves on their return to the ward.

Catatonic patients may also show the opposite of negativism, namely *automatic obedience*. They carry out every requested movement, and may then maintain the resulting posture hypokinetically. Such a patient may, for instance, put out his tongue in response to a request, and then leave it out indifferently, even when the examiner pretends to push a pin into it. Automatic obedience may also take the form of echo reactions[79, 478]. The patients then copy the movements (echopraxia) or the words (echolalia) of another person, though in a slower and often slightly modified form. Such echo reactions are, however, also present in patients who are mentally subnormal or whose understanding of the environment is impaired through agnosia or a clouding of consciousness. There are also some rare, and perhaps today obsolete, forms of automatic obedience which are culturally determined habitual mannerisms. They will be reported later.

The mobility of some schizophrenic patients appears peculiar because of *ambivalent movements*. Such patients, and they are not always catatonics, begin to perform an action, but reverse it halfway through or before completing it properly. This is most typically shown in the so-called 'schizophrenic handshake'. The patient reacts to a hand stretched out to him by moving his own hand forward, but he stops prematurely and withdraws it before reaching the other hand or after touching it superficially, but before clasping it for a proper handshake.

Parkinsonism and Paralysis Agitans

In some diseases, hypokinetic manifestations are due to an increase of muscular tone. This is the case in parkinsonism and paralysis agitans, diseases which are associated with endopathological changes in the basal ganglia due to such causes as cellular degeneration, cerebral arteriosclerosis, toxic damage (for example, carbon monoxide or manganese), or virus infections (for example, epidemic encephalitis). The increase of muscular tone in parkinsonian diseases is not steady; it is an oscillating phenomenon. The result is that muscular resistance to passive movements is staccato in form (cogwheel rigidity). The movements of the patient are slowed up (bradykinesis). This may, in fact, be the first symptom noticed by him. He finds that he is no longer able to perform quick nimble movements, such as those required for playing the piano. His arms do not swing freely when he walks; his gestures eventually become fewer; his writing smaller (micrographia) and less legible; his posture stooping; his knees and arms flexed; his gait slow and shuffling; his eyes unblinking; and his speech sluggish and without modulation.

In post-encephalitic parkinsonism, 'oculogyric crises' occur, during which the eyes are held in an upward or, more rarely, lateral position by an increase of tone in the relevant muscles which may last for hours. The head may, at the same time, be held in a position of opisthotonus or (more rarely) torticollis. During these crises, the patient may be 'obsessed' with certain thoughts which he cannot banish from his mind. The obsession is, however, not necessarily accompanied by an anxiety-dominated urge to think those thoughts; if it is, the phenomenology of the symptom is indistinguishable from that in obsessional-neurotic patients.

The hyperkinetic features of parkinsonism and paralysis agitans consists mainly of coarse rhythmic tremors, which may be one-sided at first. They often begin in the fingers (pill-rolling movements) and wrists, spreading later to the ankles, head, lower jaws, and perhaps even the tongue. If the tremor of the arms is prominent, movements requiring a steady hand become impossible. Such patients cannot lift a spoonful of soup or a glass of water to their lips without spilling the liquid; they are thus forced to drink through straws. Tremors are increased by emotional excitement and generally disappear during sleep. Emotional excitement, or the sudden stimulus of an emergency, can, however, overcome the bradykinesis of the parkinsonian patient, and allow him to perform an unexpectedly quick movement, such as catching a falling object or, with a sudden jump, boarding a bus that threatens to move off.

In many parkinsonian patients, a movement that begins bradykinetically gradually gathers speed until its ends up hyperkinetically in a series of quick movements. This acceleration, or 'festination' as it is technically known, is often most noticeable in a patient's gait. When he starts walking, his slightly bent legs move forward in slow, short steps; then their speed picks up, until he hurries along with the same short steps at a quick run. The same festination may characterize the patient's speech which begins at a slow measured rate and ends in a fast and unintelligible mumble. Sometimes the voice production cannot come to a quick halt, but the last word is repeated several times (palilalia), or only part of the last word (logoclonia).

Hypokinesis and Hyperkinesis in Other Diseases

Hypokinesis is associated with a lowered muscle tone in some diseases. To some extent, this happens normally in states of fatigue and somnolence, when the persons concerned have to make a special effort to move along slowly or to say a few mumbled words. The lowering of the muscle tone may be pathologically exaggerated. This happens, for instance, in *narcoleptic* patients who suffer from repeated and overpowering attacks of sleepiness during the day[110, 404, 540]. Because of the lowered muscle tone, such patients may slump to the ground. This may also happen to them after some emotional experience (cataplexy).

Similar attacks which are as sudden, though not preceded by sleepiness or emotional experiences, occur also in old people. In such *senile drop attacks*[449], the patient falls down suddenly during some routine activity. He does not lose consciousness, but may sustain physical injuries and emotional shock. Those who are uninjured can often rise immediately afterwards and are none the worse for their fall. There are, however, also uninjured patients who remain hypokinetic for hours. They may be unable to rise by their own efforts, and relatives may not be strong enough to lift them, because they are such a 'dead weight' on account of the absence of tone in antigravity muscles, which normally sustain the erect posture of people. If the patients retain muscular tone in their arms, they may succeed in pulling themselves up on some heavy furniture, or in dragging themselves along the floor until their feet push against a firm surface. It seems that pressure on the soles can reflexly restore the postural tone in antigravity muscles. Senile drop attacks must be distinguished from other causes of falling in old people, such as tripping over unnoticed objects on the floor or becoming dizzy on bending back the head[539]. Old people also have hyperkinetic manifestations. Many of them are fussily overactive and restless, especially at night. Senile tremor is common. It is a fine and rapid tremor of the hands, or a nodding or shaking tremor of the head.

Many psychiatric and neurological diseases have characteristic tremors. In disseminated sclerosis, for instance, the beginning of an intentional movement is often accompanied by tremor (intention tremor). Some chronic intoxications cause tremors, such as cocaine or alcohol. In an alcoholic *delirium tremens*, the tremor is marked and coarse. There is also a familial tremor, which can occur in several, otherwise healthy, members of a family; it starts early in life and does not lead to other complications.

Among hyperkinetic manifestations, muscular spasms and twitches are often the leading clinical symptoms. Spasms can painfully interrupt such occupational activities as writing (writer's cramp)[382], typing, or playing a musical instrument (occupational neuroses). In some women, sexual intercourse is made impossible by the involuntary spastic contraction of the muscles of the vaginal introitus, which are reflexly excited by attempts to penetrate into the vagina (vaginismus)[2, 343]. Occasionally, the spasm occurs after penetration and prevents the withdrawal of the penis (penis captivus)[234, 428]. A common and harmless, but unexplained hyperkinetic symptom consists in restless legs which force people to get up from a sitting or lying position in order to move about. A more general urge to be restlessly active (akathisia), is sometimes experienced after medication with tranquillizers of the phenothiazine group. In such patients, parkinsonian symptoms may develop; among them, oculogyric crises, opisthotonus, torticollis and facial twitches.

In *choreatic diseases*, restlessness is combined with the occurrence of quick, irregular and jerky movements in various muscle groups. A choreatic child is often punished for three reasons, before the correct diagnosis is made: (1) because it cannot sit still, (2) because an unexpected jerk causes it to drop things, and (3) because it grimaces. Allied to choreatic symptoms are the localized spasmodic movements known as 'tics'[507, 552]. They may consist in spasmodic eye blinks, spasmodic movements of the lips, jaws or tongue, a spasmodic turning of the head (spasmodic torticollis), a spasmodic shrugging of one or both shoulders, or other spasmodic muscular contractions which cause the patient to produce such involuntary noises as coughing, spitting, sniffing, grunting, barking, or hiccupping. Many tics begin in childhood, sometimes after an attack of chorea, and continue for several years before they permanently or temporarily disappear. As the tics lose their compelling strength, it becomes easier to inhibit them voluntarily, at least for a time. At this stage, tics are often regarded as 'bad habits', and attempts are made to suppress them by punishment. The grunts and barks caused by tics can be so loud and unexpected that they frighten and startle other people. The voice of some patients is explosively strong at the beginning of a remark so that they sound angry and threatening, when they merely intend to say a few innocent words. In some patients, the vocal tic is elaborated into compulsively barked obscenities (Gilles de la Tourette syndrome)[53]. All tics become more marked in states of excitement and fear.

Hyperkinetic manifestations are often shown by mentally subnormal children. They may spend most of their waking hours in some such stereotyped activity as rocking rhythmically backward and forward or from side to side, swaying or bowing the body, banging the head, or sucking and biting their arm. More elaborate stereotypies occur in psychotic children who may be continually occupied in the routine of solitary and ritualized games, for instance, spinning objects around and around in the same way[94]. In some children with damaged brain functions, perhaps after epidemic encephalitis or through epilepsy, an 'infantile hyperkinetic syndrome' develops. Such children are ceaselessly over-active; they overturn, throw, spill or destroy everything they can lay their hands on; they tease and annoy adults as well as children, and may wantonly attack and injure them. They often seem to enjoy their unruly behaviour and, to the exasperation of their environment, laugh gleefully at their most unpleasant tricks. Attempts to discipline and restrain them, may be the prelude to violent outbursts of rage and anger. Phenobarbitones often have an aggravating effect on this infantile hyperkinesis, whereas paradoxically, amphetamines can damp down the overactivity.

Dyskinesis

The psychopathology of mobility can also consist in a disorganization of movement, or dyskinesis, in the absence of any sensory, perceptual or motor impairment that could account for the disorganization. The dyskinesis of purposive movements is known as *apraxia*. It may occur in otherwise healthy children (developmental apraxia) who are clumsy and awkward in their movements, and poor at drawing, dancing, gymnastics and ball games; their handwriting is an illegible and untidy scrawl; they look dishevelled and carelessly dressed with shoelaces untied and buttons undone; they are often inattentive and fidgety; and if their deficiencies are constantly criticized and punished, they may also show the pathological emotional reactions which are known as 'behaviour problems'. On intelligence tests, they typically have a higher score on verbal than performance tests. Developmental apraxia may be due to an unequal maturation of psychological functions; the symptoms then improve at puberty or in adolescence[522].

Patients with social phobias show a neurotic form of apraxia; they are so self-conscious that they become clumsy and 'all thumbs' when they have to carry out a skilful task under observation. Organic apraxias occur especially in patients with lesions in the parietal lobes or the corpus callosum. Purposive movements can be so disorganized that the patient is handicapped in the performance of routine tasks. Sometimes, however, apraxia only occurs when some action is carried out on demand and under observation, whereas there is no difficulty with the action when performed automatically in the course of some habitual sequence.

In *ideational*, or *ideo-motor apraxia*[59], the spatio-temporal sequence of an intended movement is so disordered that the purpose of the movement is not achieved, though there is no paralysis, agnosia or sensory ataxia which could explain the disturbance. The patient may find it impossible to innervate the correct muscle groups in correct sequence for the purpose of sitting or lying down (trunk apraxia) or of walking (apraxic abasia), even if he can carry out walking movements, when lying down[346]. He may find it hard to obey requests to smile, frown, blow, whistle, or show his teeth (facial apraxia); or to mimic how to use a key, comb or toothbrush, how to play the piano, drive a car, point at someone, salute, wave good-bye, or shake his fist. He may become hopelessly entangled, when asked to light a cigarette, and his fumbling may end with the match in his mouth and the cigarette vaguely encircling the matchbox.

In cases of so-called dressing apraxia[227], the term 'apraxia' is not wholly suitable, because the disorganization of motility is the result of a spatial agnosia. Such patients usually suffer from an agnosia of both the left half of their body and of spatial relations in their environment. As a result, they cannot achieve a congruence between the spatial relations of a garment and the spatial relation of their body. Similarly, in *constructional apraxia*[400], it is not the motor performance itself that is disorganized, but its guidance by perceived or imagined spatial relations. Patients cannot draw a schematic house, a simple map or a clock face; nor can they copy simple geometrical shapes with the help of paper and pencil, match sticks or suitable wooden blocks. They may declare themselves satisfied with constructions that are far from adequate.

A special aspect of the psychopathology of mobility concerns the expression of ideas by means of speech. In some children, the development of speech is delayed so that they do not utter recognizable words until after the age of two, or recognizable phrases until after the age of four. When deafness and childhood psychosis can be ruled out, we deal with a *developmental aphasia*[59, 371, 520]. This is most commonly due to severe mental subnormality. Occasionally, however, the condition is observed in intelligent children and is then attributed to a maturational delay of linguistic functions. The aphasia is then likely to disappear spontaneously in time. This was the case, for example, with Einstein who caused some concern to his parents because his speech was still backward at the age of four.

The condition is more common in boys than girls, and usually responds to early speech therapy, especially when there had been no incentive for a pre-school child to correct his linguistic deficiency, or *dyslalia*, because he had been understood in his family circle.

In *infantile psychosis*, or *autism*[94], speech is always impaired. Some psychotic children never learn to speak; some start late and then surprise their environment by an unexpected range of words and phrases; and some begin with a normal development of speech which disintegrates with the onset of the psychosis so that they then use only stereotyped phrases, or become entirely mute. The diagnosis can be made from the other symptoms of infantile psychosis: the anxious or stubborn withdrawal from the social environment, motor mannerisms and stereotypies, and a sustained resistance against any change in the narrow world of their existence.

Some self-contained and anxious children develop an *elective mutism*[434, 508]. They may speak at home, but not at school; or to some members of the family, but not to others. The symptom usually disappears in time. *Stammering* is a form of linguistic dyskinesis, which occurs more often in boys than girls. It generally appears at the age of three or four, but many improve after some time so that only traces of stammering are retained, which emerge in situations of anxiety or uncertainty. In many people, however, stammering continues throughout life as a more or less severe linguistic handicap. The severity of the symptom varies with adjuvant conditions; it improves in familiar company, when the patient sings or declaims, when he uses well-worn phrases, or when he cannot hear himself speak because of noise or because he speaks in unison with others.

Verbal dyskinesis can occur in adult patients as the result of a physiogenic interference with cerebral functions. Acute alcohol intoxication, for instance, can cause an *ataxic dysarthria*, which impedes the pronunciation of words so that the drunkard's speech is thick and slurred. A similar verbal dyskinesis is characteristic of G.P.I. In disseminated sclerosis, the smooth flow of voice production is sometimes broken up into a discontinuous series of brief phonations so that the patient's speech acquires a staccato quality that is known as 'scanning speech'. Other forms of verbal dyskinesis associated with parkinsonism and the Gilles de la Tourette syndrome have already been mentioned.

A special form of verbal dyskinesis occurs with neuropathological lesions, which usually, though not invariably, affect the left frontal lobe. It consists of an impaired motor expression of intended speech and is called *motor aphasia*[59]. The patient knows what he wants to say, but cannot form the right words and phrases. This disconcerting experience has been clearly described by some patients whose motor aphasia was only a transient and isolated functional disorder, unaccompanied by a clouding of consciousness. De Fouchy, for instance, gave this account of a brief motor aphasia suffered by him in 1783 at the age of 76. 'Towards the end of the dinner, I felt a little increase of pain above the left eye, and in the very instant I became unable to pronounce the words I wanted. I heard what I said and I thought of what I ought to reply, but I spoke other words than those which would express my thoughts, or if I began them I did not complete them, and I substituted other words for them. I had nevertheless all movements as freely as usual. . . . I saw all objects clearly, I heard distinctly what was being said. . . . This sort of paroxysm lasted about a minute.'[38].

In the same year and at the same age, Samuel Johnson had a similar experience one night, but his motor aphasia lasted some days and was accompanied by some dyskinetic difficulty in writing. This is how he described the incident two days later in a letter. 'I perceived . . . that my speech had been taken from me. I had no pain, and so little dejection in this dreadful state that I wondered at my own apathy. . . . I then wrote a card. . . . In penning this note I had some difficulty, my hand, I knew not how or why, made wrong letters. . . . I have so far recovered my vocal powers as to repeat the Lord's Prayer with no very imperfect articulation'[103]. As this illustration shows, motor aphasia can be associated with signs of *agraphia*. But agraphia can also occur in a relatively pure form and without much disturbance of spoken speech. Such patients may, however, learn to write correctly with the other hand.

When motor aphasia is a long-lasting disablement, it deprives the patient of all but a few words, and these are often mutilated and badly pronounced. He may, however, succeed in conveying some information with the help of writing and gestures, and also by varying the stress and inflection of the words still at his command. This last means of communication is not available to patients whose motor aphasia has altered the natural rhythm, inflection and stress of their native language. Such 'aprosody' can make them sound like foreigners.

CHAPTER 17

THE PSYCHOPATHOLOGY OF MEMORY

The term 'memory' has acquired so many meanings today that its unqualified usage is liable to be misunderstood. The term is not even confined to the mental domain any longer, although it is etymologically derived from the Anglo-Saxon word *gemynd*, meaning mind. For example, the part of an electronic computer, which stores coded data and makes them available for electronic scanning, is called a 'memory unit'. The 'memories' of the unit are not the original information but information expressed in a coded language for the computer's sake, and retained physically on punched cards, magnetic tapes or in electric circuits. Similarly, biologists speak of a 'biological (or racial) memory' and mean by it the transmission of genetic characteristics from one generation to another. In this case, the information consists of cell functions which are coded in the form of nucleotide sequences in DNA (desoxyribonucleic acid) molecules, and stored in the chromatin network of cell nuclei.

In its most typical sense, the term 'memory' refers, of course, to specific mental functions. The information with which this psychological memory deals are psychological experiences. These are coded in a way of which we have no definite knowledge as yet. But the final result of this coding is a transformation of the original information into some altered functions or substances within the brain, which are more or less stable and remain available for mnestic scanning for some time. These altered functions or substances constitute the so-called 'memory trace'.

We are ignorant about the details of these mnestic processes in the brain, but three kinds of physiological changes have been tentatively mooted. It has been theorized, for instance, that in an original experience discrete psychoneural circuits are activated, that this activation leaves behind changes in the neuronal synapses involved, which facilitate the reactivation of the same psychoneural circuits, and with it the mnestic reliving of the original experience. Thus, according to this theory, the original data are coded and stored in a language that consists of changes in synaptic transmissions. It is, however, not likely that the theory is correct. It is known that there is no part of the brain in which memory traces are specifically localized. The psychoneural circuits assumed would therefore have to involve a large part of the brain. Yet large parts of the brain can be destroyed without incurring a loss of memory traces. A comparable theory, tarnished by the same flaw, is based on the assumption that the memory trace consists in currents, which constantly reverberate in certain neural loops. In this case, the mnestic re-living of the original experience would occur when a connection is established between the neural loops and the rest of the brain's activities.

The most recent theory postulates a possible analogy between biological and psychological memory. If the biological memory consists of nucleotide sequences in DNA molecules, psychological memories might, in their coded form, consist of nucleotide sequences in RNA (ribonucleic acid) molecules which can be soluble and might therefore be diffused to many neurones[91, 246, 247, 336]. This would take account of the difficulty that memory traces are not localized, but the theory still leaves a host of other questions unexplained.

In contrast to the vastness of our ignorance about the physiological basis of mnestic processes, we are intimately familiar with the phenomenology of memory. We know from personal experience that mnestic phenomena can be differentiated into act-phenomena and object-phenomena. When we loosely talk of memory, we blur this differentiation. To avoid misunderstanding, we shall use the term 'memory object' (or just 'memory', when the context makes the sense clear) to denote mnestic object-phenomena, and the term 'remembering' to denote mnestic act-phenomena.

Memories

Memory objects can be of three kinds:

(1) rote memories, (2) impersonal memories, and (3) reminiscences (or personal memories).

Rote memories are the most elementary forms of memory objects. By themselves, they are devoid of meaning. When activated, they unfold mechanically. All motor habits and motor skills rest on rote memories. For example, having once learned the motor skill of riding a bicycle or driving a car, the rote memory of it is available automatically, when the need for it arises on some later occasion. Paying attention to the skilled movements may interfere with their automatic unfolding. With the help of motor habits, we are enabled to carry out several concomitant activities. Once the mind has initiated a motor habit, little attention is required to adjust it to minor situational changes. The bulk of our attention is then free for other tasks. We may thus take a walk, while our attention is almost completely preoccupied with the solution of some problem; or we may carry out the intricate motor habit of playing the piano and, at the same time, engage in some extraneous conversation.

Impersonal memories appear in consciousness in two forms: in a totally abstract form as meanings (ideas, thoughts, concepts) and in a more concrete form as words or images. The link between the two forms of impersonal memories can be very close, especially the link between a particular concept and the word naming it, for example the link between the concept of a canine animal and the English word 'dog' (or its synonym in a foreign language). Yet when we learn our mother tongue, the sound and sight of many words are often committed to memory before their meanings are grasped. In linking words and their meanings, dictionaries can serve as an alternative kind of memory which we can usefully consult, especially when we try to learn a foreign language.

Even firmly established links in one's memory between words and their meanings can be severed in special circumstances, for example in searching our mnestic stores for words that merely rhyme or alliterate. Similarly, when we have learned a whole sequence of words by heart, i.e. acquired a rote memory of it, we can reproduce it mechanically without paying attention to any meaning it may contain. When interrupted in such a rote activity, we have to retrace our steps until we find an opening into the mechanical sequence and begin again from there. Multiplication tables are rote memories which have been learned by heart. That is why most people have to do their arithmetic in the language in which they originally memorized it at school, even when they are conducting a conversation in a different tongue.

When the link between thoughts and their expressions, verbally or otherwise, is not firmly fixed, we are faced with the task of clothing our thoughts in suitable words, gestures or pictures. We can then give rein to our inventiveness and imagination. On different occasions, the same thought may thus be conveyed in different phrases, languages, actions or graphic illustrations.

Impersonal memories are built up from the experience of events on many occasions. They need have no association with any particular instance. In that case, we are aware of an impersonal memory only as something that has multiple roots in long-lost past experiences, something that is recognized as a familiar part of our memory store, and certainly not as something that has been newly created and invented by us then and there.

Reminiscences, or *personal memories*, are mnestic revivals of occasions we have experienced. When the reminiscences are still fresh in our minds, they can be accurately located in space, dated in time or at least fitted easily into a temporal sequence of occasions which had been personally experienced. As time passes, location and dating become more hazy, but approximations may still be constructed with some effort for a while, though with diminishing objective accuracy. Of the events which compose occasions, only those that have been experienced form part of a reminiscence and most of these soon fade away, leaving behind merely the more salient or interesting details. The meaning of the details in a reminiscence derives from their associations with cognate impersonal memories. Details devoid of such associations, e.g. foreign words or abstruse formulas, have no meaning and are therefore not understood.

Remembering

The act-phenomenon of remembering has the function of converting memory traces into conscious memory objects, and of evaluating the mnestic significance of any conscious phenomena. There are three kinds of remembering: (1) recall, (2) perceptual recognition, and (3) mental recognition. We speak of *recall* when a memory object is brought into consciousness either intentionally or incidentally. When an intentional recall is unsuccessful, a memory trace can often still be converted into a conscious memory through the perception of events, or objects, which are similar to those from which the memory trace had been built up. When perception thus brings back a memory, we speak of *perceptual recognition*. For example, when a person fails in an attempt to recall a foreign word with which he was once familiar, he may be presented with a list of foreign words. If one of these words arouses its own memory trace, the person has the experience of perceptually recognizing the mnestically wanted word.

Remembering is phenomenologically more than simply the conversion of a memory trace into a conscious memory; it also evaluates the mnestic significance of the resulting conscious memory. This is usually an automatic process that is experienced as a *mental recognition* of two attributes of the conscious memory: first, that it is a memory and not a percept or a completely new and original mental creation; and second, that it certainly, or probably, is (or is not) the correct memory that is mnestically wanted. A person for instance, who tries to recall the rote memory of the number that is the product of seven times eight may succeed in recalling the number 56, which he mentally recognizes as a recalled memory, and usually also as the correct memory. If such mental recognition should remain uncertain, rote memories of the 'eight times' multiplication table can be activated to remove the uncertainty.

Mnestic Retention and Decay

The phenomenology of memory begins with the awareness that new experiences are mnestically retained so that they can be remembered. Psychological investigations have shown that this mnestic retention of new experiences can be divided into two phases. There is, first, a short-term phase which follows immediately upon new experiences. During this phase, the new experiences are converted into memory traces, or 'consolidated' as the process is often called. This process of conversion seems to require the adequate functioning of the mnestic system of the brain. The system is associated with the limbic lobe, especially the hippocampus, fornix, mamillary bodies, anterior nucleus of the thalamus, and perhaps also the cingular gyrus. Bilateral lesions of any of these areas prevent the formation of the second, or long-term, phase of mnestic retention. Such patients retain new experiences only for a short while.

During the second and long-term phase of mnestic retention the memory traces formed are stored in such a way that localized lesions of the brain do not interfere with them. The memory traces, however, do not remain unaltered. Like all living products, they are subject to many transforming influences. In the first place, there is always an interaction with memory traces that had been formed earlier or were acquired later. As a result, the content of memory traces changes. They 'decay', as it is usually called. At the same time, they gradually lose their ready accessibility to the mnestic scanning process of intentional remembering.

The mnestic decay of the memory trace, and its developing *mnestic inaccessibility*, jointly contribute to the common experience of *forgetting* memory objects. The two components of forgetting, however, seem to affect different kinds of memory objects to a different degree. Rote memories seem to be less affected by mnestic inaccessibility than by mnestic deacy. A person, for example, who once acquired the motor memory of riding a bicycle, usually has little difficulty in reviving this memory, when mounting a bicycle for the first time again after many years. But the memory trace has noticeably decayed by then, so that he has to reacquire much of his former skill.

Impersonal memories that are not frequently activated may, on the other hand, be more affected by mnestic inaccessibility than mnestic decay. At first, such memories become inaccessible to the scanning process of intentional recall, but remain sufficiently intact to respond to perceptual recognition. Eventually, however, impersonal memory traces decay to such an extent that even perceptual recognition no longer succeeds. The continued presence of a decayed memory trace can then, however, still be demonstrated with the help of learning experiments because there is a saving of time on re-learning information that had been forgotten to the point of perceptual non-recognition.

Personal reminiscences seem to suffer primarily from mnestic decay rather than mnestic inaccessibility. The reminiscence of a particular occasion, consists, at first, of the memories of several events which are temporarily and spatially connected, and which are usually also integrated into a meaningful whole with the help of reasonable or plausible links. As the memory trace of a reminiscence decays, some attributes or associated events drop away. The correct calendar dating is often the first to go; but the dating of the reminiscence relative to other occasions, and its correct geographical placing remain intact for very much longer. Eventually, however, even relative dating and relative placing vanish from the memory trace. The reminiscence of an occasion then becomes the personal reminiscence of a partial experience that occurred at an uncertain time and place, and has uncertain associative links with other reminiscences[25].

Cryptomnesia and Paramnesia

Eventually, what was once a personal reminiscence may no longer be mentally recognized as such. It is then experienced as an impersonal memory; or it may no longer be mentally recognized as a memory at all, and is experienced as an original mental creation. Such cryptomnesia is a common occurrence, but it usually attracts no attention because the ideas which are left to the cryptomnesic person are rather homespun and humdrum. Sometimes, however, those notions and ideas have a wider interest and importance. Cryptomnesia may then have embarrassing consequences, which attract attention, especially when it leads to unconscious plagiarism.

In his doctoral dissertation, Jung examined cryptomnesic phenomena and reported his discovery of an example of unconscious plagiarism in Nietzsche's *Thus Spake Zarathustra*[266, 268]. Freud, in his *Psychopathology of Everyday Life*, described an incident, when he himself had been guilty of unconscious plagiarism through cryptomnesia. He had informed a close friend, one day, of a new psychopathological discovery he had made, namely that the problem of the neuroses could only be explained by assuming that all human beings are initially bisexual in their psychological disposition. To his surprise, the friend had replied: 'That's what I told you two-and-a-half years ago . . . but you would not hear of it then.' The following week, Freud succeeded in recalling the reminiscence of the occasion to which his friend had referred. He reflected ruefully: 'It is painful to have to surrender one's originality in this way.'

If a piece of remembered knowledge is collectively shared, an individual can readily check the accuracy of his memory. But how can he check the objective accuracy of some knowledge or reminiscence that is private and unshared? This is only possible, when an enduring non-mental record has been made at the time of acquiring the information. Such enduring records, however, do not always exist. People have to rely, for the most part, on the subjective truth-value of their mental recognitions. Yet the subjective truth-value of a mental recognition is no guarantee of its objective truth. This applies particularly to reminiscences. Psychological investigations have exhaustively shown that the testimony of people must be viewed with reserve, because of the frequency with which reminiscences, which are mentally recognized as absolutely true, turn out to be falsified memories, or paramnesias.

In one of his earliest experiments on the psychology of testimony, Stern[485] had asked his students to look at a picture for 45 seconds and to report immediately afterwards everything they could remember with certainty. Five per cent of their statements were found to be incorrect. Some weeks later the error had increased to 10 per cent. When the students were asked to underline the memories on whose truth they were prepared to take an oath, there were still one or two 'perjuries' in each individual's testimony.

The perceptual recognition of a reminiscence can be faulty because its memory trace had been changed through an incorrect interpolated recall. In one experiment, for instance, the subjects had to wait for two minutes, in a room with a poster on the wall facing them, before they were taken to the experimenter. One group of subjects, after performing some irrelevant psychological tests, were subsequently shown the poster and asked whether it was the same they had seen in the waiting room. 72 per cent recognized it without hesitation. A comparable group of subjects were given as their psychological test the task of recalling the poster. This reduced the percentage of subjects who later correctly recognized the poster to $12\frac{1}{2}$ per cent. The failure of the majority could be traced back to the introduction or omission of detail, which occurred when they attempted to recall the poster[33].

The unreliability of reminiscences is taken into account in judging the testimony of witnesses in court cases. In medicine, and particularly in psychiatry, however, we are too much in the habit of accepting the reminiscences of patients at their face value. How misleading this can be, was shown, for example, in an investigation of the reliability of the anamnestic interview, conducted by some Norwegian authors[207] on a group of 19 mothers. The mothers were first interviewed one month before delivery, and then again at successive intervals of six months, six years and two years. After six months, there was no statistical correlation between the mother's remembered attitudes to being pregnant and the original attitudes $(r = 0.02)$, but most of them could remember whether they had desired a male or female child $(r = 0.81)$. After eight years, there were poor memories for prenatal anxieties about childbirth $(r = 0.09)$ and about the child's normality $(r = 0.32)$. The memories were fair, though far from infallible, about the child's length $(r = 0.89)$ and weight $(r = 0.71)$ at birth, whether it was a full-time delivery $(r = 0.81)$, the length of breast feeding $(r = 0.77)$, and whether the child had been planned $(r = 0.83)$. The authors were struck by the 'general inaccuracy of the anamnestic reports given by many of the mothers', and they remarked: 'It appears that the anamnestic material did not reflect the mother's earlier experiences and attitudes so much as their current picture of the past.' Paramnesic reminiscences of this kind are, however, widely accepted today as true memories, and many personality traits and psychiatric symptoms are psychodynamically 'explained' with their help.

Even the reminiscences of highly reputable persons can be paramnesic, though they may swear to their accuracy and find support in the pseudo-reminiscences of relatives who have come to mistake a story they often heard for an experience they had actually witnessed. The apparition remembered by Sir Edmund Hornby, Chief Judge of the Supreme Consular Court of China and Japan in Shanghai, may serve as an example and a cautionary tale[206]. In the July number, 1884, of the monthly magazine *The Nineteenth Century*, two British psychiatrists published a paper on 'Visible Apparitions'. The most impressive story came from Sir Edmund who described himself as 'wanting in imagination and no believer in miracles'. His account was so strange, however, that the psychiatrists remarked it needed 'the high authority on which it comes to satisfy the reader he has not passed unaware into the region of romance'. They also added: 'Lady Hornby had kindly confirmed the above facts to us as far as she was cognisant of them'.

In brief, nine years earlier, the Judge had been awakened one night by the intrusion of a Shanghai reporter into his bedroom, who had demanded to be given a verbal summary of the judgment

Sir Edmund was going to deliver the following day. In order not to wake his wife, the Judge had complied, but had told his wife about the incident shortly afterwards. The following day, he learned to his consternation that the reporter had died the previous night before he had appeared as an apparition in the Judge's bedroom. Sir Edmund asked his wife to confirm what he had told her about the incident the previous night, and made a brief note of everything.

The publication of the Judge's story, however, had a sequel in the form of two letters in a later number of the magazine. The first came from a Shanghai newspaper editor who pointed out four inaccuracies, the most damaging of which was that the Judge had not been married on the day mentioned and had not married until three months later. The second letter came from Sir Edmund who did not deny the substance of the inaccuracies pointed out, but angrily insisted that both he and his wife continued to remember the story as it had been published. 'If I had not believed, as I still believe, that every word of it was accurate, and that my memory was to be relied on, I should not have even told it as a personal experience.' Many unlikely events—ranging from telepathy and clairvoyance to flying saucers—have, at various times, been trustingly accepted as true on no firmer evidence than somebody's subjective conviction that his memory was to be relied on.

Hypermnesia

The acquisition of memory traces correlates positively with intelligence. Intelligent persons memorize information more quickly than persons of average intellectual endowment, and the latter are better in memorizing information than mentally subnormal persons. Intelligent persons also, by and large, retain memorized information longer than average individuals, probably because they have a superior ability to organize memory traces into meaningful systems. The memorization and retention of information also depends on a person's particular interests and hobbies. His attention tends to dwell on information that arouses his interest, and the memory trace of such information is kept fresh by frequent reactivations.

A few memory giants have been described who showed an astonishing degree of hypermnesia even for abstruse and nonsensical information. They usually learned to improve their constitutional gift by mnemonic devices which converted unintelligible information into something that had meaning. From this meaningful code, the original information would then be reconstructed. The Moscow psychologist, Luria[334], had the opportunity to study such a hypermnesic person for over 30 years. The man, S. V. Shereshevski, had been originally sent for psychological investigation because his superiors had noticed the ease with which he could repeat, word for word, long and complicated messages he had been asked to deliver. Luria found that the man memorized 'without effort sequences or tables containing, 50, 100 and more figures presented to him aurally or visually. . . . It was just as easy for him to reproduce geometrical figures and formulae, the significance of which he did not understand. He also easily remembered musical motifs.' When he was asked after up to 20 years to recall certain series of words, lists of figures and formulae, 'he closed his eyes, raised his finger, slowly wagged it around and [after a few orienting introductory remarks] then and there quite rapidly he reproduced without hesitation the information which had been given to him many years before.' There were only occasional inaccuracies in his recall. The mnemonic devices he used consisted mainly in visualizing certain items of information, and in arranging others in the form of a scenic story, such as the story of a walk in which various incidents happened, each incident being a code signal for an item of information.

General hypermnesia is an abnormal personality trait because it is so uncommon, but it is not a psychiatric symptom as it does not cause suffering and concern, and occurs in people who are otherwise quite healthy. There are, however, certain forms of *specific hypermnesia*, which can be found in some psychiatric patients and occasionally give rise to suffering and concern. Such specific hypermnesia can occur, for instance, in litigious paranoid patients who, despite an otherwise poor education, have amassed a remarkable range of legal knowledge.

Specific hypermnesia may also be found in people with a neurotically inhibited learning capacity for the usual kinds of knowledge that are widely shared. They may develop compensatory interests in esoteric fields of knowledge and skill. If they are otherwise educationally and socially backward, this paradoxical proficiency may earn them the appellation *idiot savant*, though this term has today largely gone out of use as the patients are neither idiots nor savants. A young schizophrenic patient of mine, with a very poor school record, acquired for example, an extensive knowledge of the routes and timetables of trains and buses in and around London. This came to light, when, during the formal testing of his memory, he was asked to repeat digits. He achieved the surprising feat of easily repeating up to 15 digits backward. The explanation was that he had grouped the digits into up to five bus routes which he could, without effort, keep in his mind and reproduce in reverse order. In other patients of this kind, the specific hypermnesia takes the form of retaining accurately dated and placed reminiscences for several years. The patients may be asked about their experiences on a specified date—what day of the week it had been, what the weather had been like, whom they had met, and similar questions. Their replies, when checked, are usually found to be fairly accurate.

Other Deficiencies of the Mnestic Functions

Apart from these few examples of specific hypermnesia, the bulk of the psychopathology of memory consists of deficient and irregular mnestic functions. These may be divided into two categories: (a) mnestic disorders due to a failure to establish lasting memory traces and (b) mnestic disorders due to a failure to reactivate established memory traces.

A relative failure to establish lasting memory traces occurs in people of low intelligence. A similar reduction of learning ability may also be found in very intelligent people, if they are so preoccupied with over-valued or disturbing ideas that they are too 'absent-minded' to concentrate on memorizing extraneous information. This may happen to children threatened with insecurity through parental discord, to adolescents engaged in revolt against authority, or to adults caught up in the emotional tangle of a love affair. The memory traces they form of new experiences are soon altered and obliterated because subsequent experiences and thoughts of a more arresting nature exert a 'retroactive inhibition'.

The information experienced during states of somnolence or clouded consciousness is, for the most part, of such a fleeting and vague nature that it forms no definite memory traces. The few and fragmentary memory traces, which are formed during sleep or mental obfuscation, and survive afterwards, are usually quickly abolished, when mental lucidity recurs, because of the retroactive inhibition exerted by new experiences. Some of them are, however, elaborated into meaningful, though paramnesic, memory traces which can persist for some time. We certainly can have hazy memories of dreams at the moment we awake from sleep, but a few minutes later they can no longer be recalled. The occasional reminiscence of a dream that is retained changes into a paramnesic memory that is more definite and elaborate than the original dream experiences could have been.

The same happens to memory traces retained by patients recovering from a period of clouded consciousness. The patients remember little or nothing of their obfuscated experiences, and whatever they remember is almost certain to be false and distorted in important respects. They may have carried out automatic activities of greater or less complexity, when their consciousness was clouded, but there is an 'amnesic' gap for the activities afterwards. The patients cannot remember what they did while their mind was obfuscated. They have a *post-confusional* or *post-traumatic amnesia* of which they are subjectively aware.

A confusional episode due to physical or toxic interference with psychoneural functions leads often to an amnesic gap that extends to occasions experienced before the onset of the organic cerebral disturbance. After a concussion, for instance, there is not only a post-concussional amnesia for experiences during the post-concussional confusion state, but also a *retrograde amnesia* for experiences ante-dating the concussion. The patient may, therefore, not be able to describe the events that preceded the concussion[347]. Such retrograde amnesia seems partly due to an interference with the functions of the mnestic system of the brain so that information received before the physical trauma is not consolidated into long-term memory traces. There can be little doubt, however, that the retrograde amnesia is also partly due to a breakdown of mnestic accessibility—a breakdown that may be only temporary.

A severe post-confusional amnesia (or many minor amnesic episodes of this kind) may turn into a *dysmnesic* or *amnesic syndrome*[238, 319, 491], which is characterized by a chronic failure to retain any new experiences, even though they occur during complete mental lucidity. The syndrome may make its appearance after an acute cerebral catastrophe (severe concussion, severe asphyxia after strangulation, prolonged cardiac arrest, or carbon monoxide poisoning) or after repeated minor cerebral insults (through chronic alcoholism, repeated knock-outs, cerebral arterio-sclerosis, or senile disorders). However, when a dysmnesic syndrome is caused by tumours in or around the third ventricle, it usually does not follow a post-confusional amnesia, but pre-cedes it.

When the cerebral damage is mainly limited to regions of the mnestic system, the patients are not demented. They can think rationally and have no difficulty in recalling memories they had acquired long before the onset of their illness. This is the clinical picture of the dysmnesic syndrome which Korsakoff originally des-cribed in his, mainly alcoholic, patients. 'The patient gives the impression,' he said, 'of a person in complete possession of his faculties; he reasons about everything perfectly well . . . makes witty remarks, plays chess or a game of cards.'[518] That his memory for new experiences is severely defective becomes obvious only on closer acquaintance with him. One may therefore speak of a 'Korsakoff dysmnesic syndrome' to distinguish these patients from others with a dysmnesic syndrome that is combined with signs of dementia and with transient periods of mental confusion. This last combination is usually found in geriatric patients with progressive brain damage that is not restricted to the mnestic system.

Dysmnesic patients have an 'amnesia for recent events' as it is usually called; that is, they have no reminiscence of their recent past. This amnesia extends back to the onset of their illness, and often for many years beyond through retrograde amnesia. When the dementia of dysmnesic patients is progressive, they have not only a retrograde, but a *retrogressive amnesia*. Reminiscences and pieces of knowledge, which are still available to recall, then come from progressively earlier stages of the patients' life. Dementing senile patients may thus eventually live with the memories of their youth, ask about the welfare of people long since dead, use their maiden names, or do not recognize their own children[8].

Dysmnesic patients often do not even remember that they have no recent memories. They are not aware of memory gaps. When asked about recent events, they may make no reply at all or relate some recent experience which did not happen. These fabricated reminiscences are technically known as *confabulations*. With prodding and encouragement, some patients may be made to produce quite fantastic and impossible confabulations, and yet apparently believe that they are telling the truth.

Because the forgetting of recent memories is so quick in dysmnesic patients, they show some of the mnestic vagaries of normal people, but after an unusually short interval of time. A senile patient may still remember some interesting piece of information he had heard, perhaps from us, a short while before, but may no longer have a reminiscence of the occasion on which he had heard it. He may therefore, a few minutes later, convey the same information to us as an item of news, and perhaps repeat this performance at short intervals, always forgetting, in between, that he had already told us the story before. This symptom is a form of 'partial crypto-mnesia'.

Among other consequences of the quick forgetting of dysmnesic patients is their difficulty to orient themselves properly in geo-graphical space and calendar time, when put into a new environ-ment, for instance, sent to a hospital. They are then bound to lose their way and wander about aimlessly. Such patients never have any idea of calendar time, and may be far out in their estimates of the month or even year. Other difficulties in temporal orientation are aggravated by the patients' poor recognition of recently acquired information. Normally, we measure the passage of time, at least to some degree, by the ease with which we can put recalled or recognized events into a wider reminisced context. When a dysmnesic patient meets a person for a second time after a short interval, his recognition of the person is without reminiscence of the occasion when the first meeting occurred. He then has the impression that a long time must have elapsed since he had last met the other person. The patient's recognition may even be so uncertain that he concludes he must have once met someone looking very much like the other person, perhaps his twin (reduplicative paramnesia)[398, 550].

CHAPTER 18

THE PSYCHOPATHOLOGY OF CONSCIOUSNESS

All our existential experiences are conscious phenomena. We are consciously aware of them at the moment of their psychological existence. To speak of unconscious existential experiences would therefore be a contradiction in terms. Yet there is much talk today of 'unconscious experiences'; of experiences, *nota bene*, which are not stated to be existential. But this expression is largely a misnomer. It does not refer to mental experiences generally, but only to object-phenomena, which had been experienced in the past, yet cannot be recalled and made existentially conscious in the present. 'Unconscious experiences' are therefore no more than repressed past object-phenomena.

'Consciousness' is, however, also used in a completely different sense that has nothing to do with existential object-phenomena, but is a variable attribute of existential act-phenomena. In particular, it refers to the reactivity of the psychoneural functions which are manifested as existential act-phenomena. When the reactivity of the mind is high, this is subjectively experienced as full, clear, or lucid consciousness. Sometimes the term 'sensorium' is used to avoid the ambiguity of the term 'consciousness'. A lucid sensorium is objectively noticed as a state of alertness, attentiveness, or vigilance. If a person's subjective responsiveness is reduced or limited in any way, he is said to have an altered consciousness, or sensorium. There are three types of altered consciousness: sleep, obfuscation, and trance. Sleep and obfuscation will be considered in this chapter; trance in the next.

SLEEP

Sleep is physiologically regulated, at least in part, by the functions of the ascending reticular formation, a network of interneurones that reaches from the mesencephalon to the cortex. When the activating processes in this neural formation are diminished, a clear sensorium is gradually replaced by the state of somnolence and, eventually, sleep. The subject need not be existentially aware that he is in a state of somnolence or sleep, but after his wakefulness has returned again, he may realize retrospectively that he was somnolent or asleep.

Objectively, the sleepy or sleeping person shows a slowed respiration, a lowered muscular tone, a closing of eyelids, and a diminished responsiveness to external stimuli. The EEG is also a helpful indicator of the depth of somnolence or sleep present in a subject. The greatest sleep depth is usually reached in the first few hours after falling asleep. Reactions to external stimuli are at a minimum then, and not necessarily accompanied by EEG signs of arousal. There are frequent variations of sleep depth during the rest of the night[381].

Dreaming occurs mainly during special phases of sleep, which are characterized by bursts of rapid conjugate eye movements and special EEG features. Dream thoughts differ from waking thoughts. The latter are, for the most part, made up of trains of imageless and unverbalized notions. Such notions may be present also in dreams, but they are then outnumbered by trains of images to which all sensory modalities may contribute though visual, auditory, and kinaesthetic images generally predominate. There are usually no imaged reminiscences of special occasions and events experienced before, but most dream phenomena are fantasy creations built up from independent pieces of imaged knowledge.

Sometimes, however, there are dream phenomena which are close to imaged reminiscences of special events. This can happen after some prolonged waking activity. After a lengthy period behind the wheel of a car, for instance, imaged vistas of roads and traffic can intrude into dream thoughts; they may even appear during the state of somnolence that precedes sleep. Such an intrusion may ruin the peaceful transition from wakefulness to sleep. The same disturbing effect can be produced by the autonomous recurrence of imaged snatches of music in a person who had spent the day in the rehearsal of an orchestra, or by recurrent snatches of thought, which had intensely occupied a person before retiring to bed. Similarly, after frightening experiences, dreamed reminiscences may occur during the process of falling asleep, or in the middle of the night, causing nightmares and other disturbances of sleep.

When a person is asleep, dream images are usually experienced as representing reality, since no other reality is perceived, or thought of, at the same time. Dream images are thus hallucinations, which have only a subjective existence in a person's experience, but no objective existence outside his psychoneural pool of interneurones. Their hallucinatory character can be, and usually is, recognized in retrospect on awakening, when another reality is perceived and differentiated from the remembered dream experience.

The natural selectiveness of existential experiences is increased in the sleepy and sleeping state so that hardly any exteroceptive or interoceptive sensations penetrate into consciousness, and hardly any intended actions issue in enacted intentions. There are, as it were, inhibitory barriers between the somnolent and sleeping psychoneural processes and the neural structures connecting them with the external world. It is usual to speak of a 'dissociation' between the sleeping mind and sensori-motor innervations.

Partial Sleep

The dissociation is, however, never quite complete. Even during sleep, a person seems to have some awareness of exteroceptive and interoceptive sensations, though he may fail to recognize their meaning; instead he may fit them meaningfully into the world of his dream images. Most people are familiar with dreams in which, let us say, the ringing of a bell occurs as part of a dream sequence, or in which they go in search of a toilet, only to wake up eventually with the realization that the bell belongs to an alarm clock by the bedside, or that the search for a toilet originated in sensations from an overfull bladder. In these examples, stimuli from an objective reality intrude into the dream world and are assimilated by it. The situation may, however, also be reversed and the dream world may partially intrude into an objective reality in which it is an alien element.

When such intrusions into an objective reality occur, we speak of partial sleep. In conditions of partial sleep, a subject may have the impression that he continues to be awake, though he has already lost meaningful sensory contact with many aspects of his environment; or, conversely, he may have dreams of intended actions, which are already to some extent converted into performed actions. Phenomena attributable to partial sleep may therefore be reported by the subject himself as abnormal experiences during supposed wakefulness; or they may be reported by objective observers as abnormal reactions in a sleeping subject. In either case, the manifestations are more or less maladapted to the subject's total environment. Manifestations of partial sleep occur so frequently in the transition from wakefulness to sleep, or from sleep to wakefulness, that they must be considered normal by population standards. They are characterized as *hypnagogic*. Sometimes, however, a distinction is made between hypnagogic and *hypnopompic* manifestations, the former occurring while falling asleep, and the latter while waking up.

In the initial stages of falling asleep, dream images may invade a reality-oriented consciousness. This can happen to a person engaged in a monotonous task, or in an activity that can be performed semi-automatically at the fringe of attention. A dream image of partial sleep can then be taken as real, and the person's performance become objectively faulty. When this happens to people carrying out skilled actions, the resulting *skill fatigue* as it has been called, may be the cause of accidents. A long-distance lorry-driver, for instance, may suddenly and unexpectedly brake at some crossroads in the country because he saw a non-existent red traffic light, or he may swerve dangerously because of the dream image of an obstacle in his path. *Hypnagogic hallucinations* of this kind are very transient; their unreality may therefore be quickly recognized, though sometimes not quickly enough to avoid an accident.

Hypnagogic hallucinations occur, of course, also, when a person goes to sleep intentionally. When he closes his eyes, he may see moving geometric patterns, sometimes highly coloured; flashes of light; landscapes; faces or other objects which often change their size, and perhaps seem to recede or approach; he may hear his name called; a bell ringing; the report of a shot; twanging sounds or animal noises; he may have the bodily sensation of falling or levitation, of growing partly or wholly to a big size or shrinking to minuteness; or he may experience an oppressive weight on his chest. The last-named hypnagogic phenomenon has given rise to the name 'nightmare' in which the second part derives from an Anglo-Saxon word with the same meaning as 'incubus', the oppressive night fiend.

Hypnopompic hallucinations in the drowsy state of awakening are recognized as unreal, when a fuller stage of wakefulness has been reached. The waking person may, on opening his eyes, see a person stand by his bed or an angel hover above it, but the apparitions disappear, when a closer look is taken at them. When hypnopompic hallucinations occur in the middle of the night, the sleeper may not fully wake up, but return to sleep and have no reminiscence of his nocturnal experience the next morning. But observers may have noticed his partial awakening during the night, his watching of some hallucinatory scene with open eyes, and his display of emotional reactions. Many of these nocturnal hallucinations are frightening and disturbing. When they occur frequently, the term *sleep hallucinosis* is used[57].

In partial sleep, the dissociative barrier between motor intention and the psychomotor apparatus may be incomplete. Falling asleep is often disturbed by sudden jerky movement, which occur before the sleep barrier to motor intentions has become strong enough. Such *nocturnal jerks*[380, 381] vary from slight twitches to tossing movements or kicks. They may wake the sleeper with a sudden jolt, but

THE PSYCHOPATHOLOGY OF CONSCIOUSNESS

he may have forgotten the incident the following morning. The incidence of nocturnal jerks is therefore greatly underestimated, yet their occurrence is very common as can be established by enquiries from married couples.

When nocturnal jerks cause arousal, the subject may have the impression that they occurred at the end of a dream sequence which made a sudden jerky movement necessary, such as a dream of missing one's footing on some stairs, or of landing with a bump after a fall. It is possible that this impression is illusory and that it was the motor jerk that came first and caused the arousal. The dream sequence would then have been elaborated in the interval between the jerk and awakening, and it would have assumed a meaning which made the appearance of the jerk intelligible. It is, however, equally probable that the dream did, in fact, come first, and that a motor intention in the course of it broke through the psychomotor barrier to be converted into an actual movement. In any case, this is the more likely explanation, when the activity of a partial sleeper is more prolonged and co-ordinated, as occurs in sleep talking and allied manifestations.

Sleep talking varies from a few grunting and groaning noises to the mumbling of a few dysarthric words and the clear enunciation of some short sentences. When the sleeper is awakened at this point, the verbal activity of sleep talking is found to express words spoken in the context of dream thoughts. *Sleep masturbation* is similarly associated with sexual dreams, though these can also cause orgasm and copulatory movements during sleep without direct physical stimulation of the external genital organs. According to Kinsey[283,284], sexual dreams ending in orgasm were reported by 99 per cent of his sample of American men with a college education, but by only 37 per cent of his comparable sample of American women. It is interesting that the dreams which cause orgasm are not always of a frankly sexual nature; they may be about events which seem to have no more than a symbolic connection with sex, such as driving a car or climbing a ladder (though both these activities sometimes also cause sexual feelings in waking subjects through a physical stimulation of the genital region by vibrations or pressures).

There are other dream enactments which, unlike dream talking and dream masturbation, are beyond the limits of normality, and must be regarded as psychiatric symptoms because they are uncommon by population standard and cause suffering and concern. Chief among them is nocturnal bedwetting, or *enuresis*[52, 356], which can occur during periods of superficial sleep, and is then not simply a passive voiding of urine because it is accompanied by the contraction of some voluntary muscles, such as the *recti abdominis*. Maturational and educational deficiencies, as well as emotional disturbances, play the main role in the causation of this symptom, and also in the causation of the much rarer symptom of nocturnal defecation, or *encopresis*[15].

The dreamed reminiscence of a frightening incident can be coupled with a motor re-enactment in partial sleep. A soldier, for instance, who had seen his friend burn to death, when their car had caught fire, and who had himself suffered burns in the accident, relived the event in frightening dreams during which he jumped out of bed, tore off his pyjamas and other imaginary garments, rolled about the floor beating out imaginary flames, and shouting for help to imaginary companions. He did not fully wake during these paroxysms, but returned to bed, when they were over, and was soon fast asleep again. Such enactments of dreams also occur in patients who did not suffer a recent emotional trauma, but are generally distressed by events in their life. This happens particularly in children who are emotionally more labile than adults. It is not surprising therefore that dream enactments can be observed, occasionally at least, in many children (sleep-walking or somnambulism).

The contact of a sleepwalker with his environment is precarious; he may overlook or misinterpret hazards in his path, and perhaps come to grief by falling down some stairs or dropping from a window. Sleepwalkers who are intercepted do not always wake up fully, even if they resist attempts to take them back to bed. In a few cases, crimes, and even apparently unmotivated murders, have been committed by sleepwalkers. Partial sleep connected with sleepwalking can also occur in other circumstances. It has long been maintained that sleep-deprived soldiers may partially fall asleep and yet continue to march. EEG investigations have shown that repetitive habitual actions can be performed by a subject, who is either in partial sleep or fluctuates between it and wakefulness. He may not be aware of his periods of 'micro-sleep', but believe himself to have been more or less awake all the time. However, as the acquisition and retention of information is poor in such conditions, he may subsequently remember little or nothing of what had happened on such occasions[381].

Sleep Rhythm

Periods of sleep are necessary for the normal functions of the brain. Wakefulness and sleep therefore alternate at fairly regular intervals; and in adults a rhythm is generally established in which wakefulness predominates during the day, and sleep during the night. When the sleep rhythm has to be altered, because of a change from day to night work perhaps, or after a long-distance East-West flight, a period of adjustment is required during which neither complete wakefulness nor a satisfying sleep may be achieved, with a consequent fall in a person's working capacity and emotional stability.

Organic lesions, which interfere with the rostral parts of the reticular formation can also cause disturbances of the sleep rhythm. There may be an excessive need to sleep (hypersomnia) so that patients merely alternate between sleep and drowsiness, or their daylight hours of wakefulness are punctuated by a frequent and often irresistible urge to go to sleep (narcolepsy). Either symptom can, however, occur also in patients in whom no organic complication can be found, and it is then usual to speak of 'idiopathic hypersomnia' or 'idiopathic narcolepsy' [110, 404, 540]. The narcoleptic urge to go to sleep may overpower patients while they are engaged in everyday activities. They may fall asleep in the middle of a conversation; while driving along a road; during a meal; in the act of sexual intercourse; or when walking in the street, so that they then bump into people or obstacles. Their sleep may only last a few minutes, or it may continue for hours, if they are left undisturbed.

Narcolepsy may be accompanied, and often preceded, by frequent attacks of *sleep paralysis*[195]. This may occur on falling asleep, when the patients, on being aroused notice that they perceive everything that is going on around them, but are unable to move or speak for several seconds. The same may happen to them in the morning on waking up from a nights' sleep. The combination of sleep paralysis and narcolepsy is found four times as often in male as in female patients. There may be other symptoms of partial sleep present as well, such as sleep hallucinosis.

Sleep paralysis by itself can occur in normal persons during partial sleep. It is not uncommon among night nurses, for instance. After sitting at their desk during an uneventful period in their ward, they are surprised by the visit of the night sister. They want to rise and speak, but are unable to do so straight away (night nurses' paralysis). Similar experiences have been reported by naval officers on night watch, and also by healthy persons on awakening from sleep. The period of paralysis is generally brief, but, in the subjective estimation of the subjects, it seems to last some time. It can be associated with a nightmarish sense that something is going on in the environment that is weird, spooky and threatening.

Narcolepsy is also often connected with another manifestation of partial sleep: a loss of muscular tone. This may happen without warning, while the patient is fully awake; very often, however, such attacks are preceded by a strong emotion, such as laughter, fear, anger, surprise, or erotic feeling. Some patients just feel weak during the attack, but others slump to the ground, remaining limp and helpless for a minute or two. These symptoms are called 'cataplexy' or 'cataplectic attacks'. It is peculiar that, in patients with both narcoleptic and cataplectic attacks, organic neuropathological lesions have only rarely been found.

In some patients, an *inverse sleep rhythm* develops; they tend to be awake by night and asleep by day. The symptom may occur in epidemic encephalitis and in senile patients. In the latter, the existence of an inverse sleep rhythm may, however, be illusory, and due to the patient's inability to have sufficiently long periods of restful sleep either during the night or during the day; at night, however, their spells of wakefulness are more noticeable, and, by day, their short naps.

Many patients complain of some form of insufficient sleep, or *insomnia*. They may have difficulties in falling asleep, be awake for long periods during the night, or wake up prematurely in the morning. Objectively, such patients are often asleep for very much longer than they believe, even when they subjectively feel sleep-deprived.

Some anxiety-neurotic patients have a *sleep phobia*. They are afraid to fall asleep for a variety of reasons: they may dread the occurrence of night terrors, the possibility of enuresis, of nocturnal orgasm, or simply the loss of conscious control over their actions so that they might unknowingly commit some forbidden act.

OBFUSCATION

The alteration of consciousness in sleep is due to normal cerebro-physiological processes of a somniferous kind. The manifestations of partial sleep may merely indicate that these normal somniferous processes are disordered in some way. But when an altered sensorium assumes the form of *mental* obfuscation, or mental clouding, its cause lies no longer in cerebro-physiological functions or their disorders, but in endopathological cerebral processes. When such cerebro-pathological processes are acute, but relatively mild, the clinical picture that results is so similar to that of partial sleep that it is often characterized by such expressions as sleeplike, or 'oneiroid'.

The most common acute variety of clouded consciousness is that due to alcohol intoxication. A similar clinical picture is obtained by oxygen deprivation or sleep deprivation. The patients' judgment of reality situations suffers, their manual skills are reduced, they look groggy, their gait is staggering and ataxic, and their speech thick and dysarthric.

When dreamlike hallucinations make their appearance, they further falsify the patients' obfuscated awareness of their environment. We then speak of a 'mental delirium', or an 'organic twilight state'. The hallucinations are mostly visual in kind, and tend to become more florid in the evening and during the night, when somniferous processes add their share to the alterations of the sensorium. The hallucinations are often nightmarish and may provoke a mixture of distressing emotions, especially fear, mistrust and irascibility. Pleasurable emotions of elation, joy, and even ecstasy may, however, also occur occasionally.

Many delirious patients are agitated and restless. They toss about; groan and mutter; their hands and fingers are fussily over-active, rubbing or scratching parts of the body, plucking at bed-clothes and wallpaper, or pulling and tearing whatever they get hold of. The patients may get out of bed to totter about in a be-mused and befuddled way. Sometimes they wander off in an obstinate pursuit of a hallucinated goal, resenting and resisting all interference. As they are only hazily in touch with their environment, and unsteady on their legs, their capricious roaming may end in an accident.

Delirious activities are *automatisms* because they are inspired by a mind which is out of touch with reality. Patients in an alcoholic delirium tremens often enact 'occupational automatisms' because, in their hallucinations, they are back at work. Thus the delirious navvy may shovel imaginary clods of earth, and the delirious bar-man give a faithful imitation of pouring out imaginary drinks and handing them round to imaginary customers. Twilight auto-matisms may, however, assume less innocent and amusing forms. The patient's hallucinatory dream world may be full of enemies; he may respond to them by trying to hide in out-of-the-way places, by running away, or by turning aggressively against the people he meets. He may come to harm by such behaviour, or cause injury and even death to others. Self-mutilation and suicide are possible; they have been known to occur especially when the patient experi-enced hallucinatory threats and provocations which came from inside his body. When delirious experiences have an erotic tinge, there may be amorous approaches to people, ranging from lascivious remarks and salacious pawing to sexual assaults.

When the brain-pathological processes responsible for acute and chronic states of obfuscation are very pronounced, their interference with psychoneural functions blots out all existential experiences, even those of a delirious kind. The patients are then in an *unconscious stupor* that may be followed by *coma* and death. When the brain-pathological processes of obfuscation are gradual in their onset and chronic in their course, the clinical picture is less dramatic, unless it is interspersed with acute delirious episodes.

Organic-Confusional State

The most superficial form of chronic obfuscation presents clinically as an organic-confusional state. It used to be called a 'toxic confusional state' at one time, when the aetiological significance of intoxications and infections was overrated. The simple term 'confusional state', which is also in vogue because it is short and convenient, is best avoided as it is too all-inclusive and can be applied to most maladapted thinking and acting, whether it is of organic origin or not. The term 'subacute delirium' has been suggested, but as these patients are only occasionally delirious, it does not recommend itself as appropriate. The expression 'organic-confusional state' seems to be the best compromise term at present.

Organic-confusional patients are in much better contact with the environment than delirious patients. In fact, they often present the deceptive appearance of having a lucid consciousness. Whereas delirious patients tend to be restless and emotionally excited, organic-confusional patients often display a surprising indifference and unconcern despite a reality situation that might worry and disturb a normal person. Indeed when organic-confusional patients become really lucid, their equanimity usually disappears and gives way to justified emotions of embarrassment, concern and distress.

The organic-confusional patient is, however, not always in a state of stolid equanimity. He is liable to have emotional outbursts. These may sometimes be due to a temporary deepening of the obfuscation so that a delirious depth is reached. They may, however, also be directly due to special neuropathological dysfunctions which manifest themselves clinically by a seemingly spontaneous affective lability. Without obvious precipitation, organic-confusional patients can exhibit fits of laughter or crying which is unintentional, and as embarrassing to them as to onlookers. In many patients, indifference to their own clinical condition is coupled with a disturbance of mood in their social relations, which makes them peevish, irritable, suspicious, and sometimes inanely jocular or fatuously euphoric.

Apart from these apparently unjustified changes of affect, organic-confusional patients can be also emotionally ruffled, when it is brought home to them that their nonchalance in the face of severe physical or psychological handicaps is unwarranted. This emotional disturbance has been called a 'catastrophic' reaction. K. Goldstein, who introduced the term, gave a graphic description of it in a patient with a frontal lobe lesion, who had failed to solve a simple arithmetic task. 'Just looking at him, we can see a great deal more than this arithmetical failure. He looks dazed, changes colour, becomes agitated, anxious, starts to fumble. . . . A moment before amiable, he is now sullen, evasive, exhibits temper, or even becomes aggressive.'[191] It takes some time for a catastrophic reaction to subside. The patient may be apologetic afterwards, and is likely to do his best to prevent a recurrence of similar incidents in future; he may refuse to take further tests or secretly practise the answers to them.

There are few reminiscences, or none at all, of events experienced in states of clouded consciousness. The patients therefore show more or less marked signs of a *dysmnesic syndrome*, and put forward all sorts of excuses to explain away their failure to recall recent events. Their dysmnesic syndrome is, of course, clinically different from that in typical Korsakoff patients whose consciousness is lucid, and who can therefore apply themselves consistently and intelligently to practical tasks, which are perceptually guided, such as playing chess or finding their way about in familiar surroundings.

The combination of a clouded sensorium and a dysmnesic syndrome gives rise to the most characteristic signs of organic confusion: *disorientation* in time, place and person. Disorientation in time is usually the most obstinate symptom, and the last to go in patients whose organic confusional state is gradually clearing up. They do not only make surprising blunders with regard to calendar time, but also find it hard to put remembered events into their correct chronological order. Disorientation in place shows itself mainly in a failure to perceive and remember spatial relations, or to distinguish right from left. As long as their memory functions are disturbed, patients may be quite unaware of their geographical location. Disorientation as to person is mainly due to dysmnesia so that the patients do not remember the individuality or social role of people they meet repeatedly. Another constant sign of an organic-confusional state is the tendency to *perseverate*. This symptom may have its origin in a sluggishness of psychoneural processes. In a test situation, for instance, patients may find it difficult to rouse themselves sufficiently to fix their attention on the examiner's remarks.

When they have responded to him, they return to their original state of placid indolence. If the examiner now requests another response, they cannot easily readjust to the new demand, but give the quickest possible response which is a repetition of the preceding one. Thus if they are asked to put out their tongue and do so correctly, the next request to close their eyes may merely evoke another tongue movement or a combined tongue and eye reaction.

Brain-damaged senile patients

The organic conditions responsible for a clouding of consciousness occur most often in old age, when cerebral functions are liable to be hampered by the ageing of neurones, the precarious variability of the blood circulation in the senile brain and similar pathological defects. Brain-damaged senile patients are likely to show signs of obfuscation either permanently or periodically. The intensity of their obfuscation is changeable; it is aggravated, when normal somnolence intervenes or because intercurrent diseases throw an extra burden on psychoneural processes. When the patients are in a state of organic confusion, they behave in an incompetent and blundering way, either complacently neglectful of everything, or fussily and circumstantially persevering with some activity to the detriment of more pressing tasks. When they lapse into a twilight condition, their conduct becomes decidedly odd, inconsequential and even irresponsible because they are hallucinated and only hazily and capriciously in touch with their environment. In a muddled and absent-minded way, they may turn on gas taps without lighting them, walk into the street only half dressed, or get into a bath only half undressed. They mislay objects and may suspiciously accuse others of having stolen them; they become slovenly and dirty; they are inclined to hoard all sorts of rubbish, and to fly into a temper when the rubbish is removed; their nutrition suffers because they forget to prepare food; they may noisily potter about in the middle of the night to the annoyance of neighbours; or go on scatter-brained errands and lose their way.

If their lucid moments are sufficiently long, brain-damaged senile patients sometimes succeed in counteracting their muddle-headedness by turning themselves into a caricature of an obsessional personality. They become creatures of habit whose life is anxiously and obstinately organized along the same unchanging lines. They develop a rigidly regular routine, and become so excessively punctilious and orderly that every activity has its right time and every piece of their belongings its right place.

Epilepsy

Another group of illnesses, in which clouded consciousness is a dominant feature, has its origin in an epileptogenic neuropathology[84, 118, 235, 344, 393, 405, 406, 447, 538]. This is characterized by the development of abnormally synchronous electric discharges in cerebral neurones, which manifest themselves in the EEG as waves of excessive voltage. The clinical symptoms produced by these discharges vary with the parts of the brain affected, the speed with which the cerebral disturbance spreads, and the type of abnormally synchronous electric discharges which is exemplified in EEG abnormalities.

When the epileptogenic disturbance remains confined to a relatively small part of the brain, there is no clouding of consciousness. The subjective and objective symptoms which appear depend on the localization of the disturbance. When motor neurones are excited by the electric discharges, there is a clonic (rarely a tonic) contraction of the corresponding muscle groups. Subjectively, the patient has the impression that these contractions occur involutarily or even against his will. This happens, for instance, in the later stages of *myoclonic epilepsy*, a rare familial disease, in which the patient suffers from shock-like contractions of the same muscle groups on both sides of his body. In *Jacksonian epilepsy*, the muscular contractions, which are generally clonic, can be restricted to a particular muscle group on one side of the body; or they may spread to other muscle groups on the same side, and eventually involve the other side as well. Consciousness is only lost when the epileptogenic disturbance of the brain is so widespread that clonic muscular contractions occur on both sides of the body.

There are many other clinical symptoms which are caused by circumscribed epileptogenic disturbances in the brain. The patient may experience unpleasant visceral sensations in the pit of his stomach, or painful irritations in some other part of the body; he may have simple hallucinations of taste, odour, sound, or of lights which can be white or coloured, still or scintillating; he may also have organized hallucinations of scenery, music, or of performing some actions; he may, in fact, carry out some vague, fumbling movements or start to run, to hit out, to laugh, or to shout. There often is a feeling of *déjà vu*, and when this is combined with a scenic hallucination, the patient may be convinced that he is experiencing a reminiscence. When such a *hallucinated reminiscence* seems to encompass the whole of his past life in a moment of existential experience, it becomes a 'panoramic memory'. Exteroception and interoception may alter in many ways; objects, for instance, may assume illusory forms, perhaps grow or shrink, approach or recede. The meaning of percepts can change so that the patient has the subjective experience of derealization, depersonalization, or of a 'dreamy state'. Thoughts may break off; particular ideas or delusions may come to obsess his mind. Emotional anomalies occur frequently, developing gradually or with paroxysmal suddenness. There may be feelings of depression, which can reach suicidal intensity, and feelings of rage or hatred, which unleash murderous attacks. A few patients have feelings of ecstatic happiness and mystic joy, but most patients complain of unpleasant feelings of irritability, anger, anxiety, hypochondriacal worry, and so on.

When one or several of the symptoms just mentioned develop gradually, they may be *prodromata* of an epileptic seizure, and disappear afterwards. When the symptoms develop suddenly, they constitute an *aura* that is often immediately followed by an epileptic attack. As the symptoms of the aura occur in a setting of relatively clear consciousness, the patient can recall them later, even if a fit has supervened. The aura of individual patients is usually characteristic for them, and can serve them as a warning sign of an impending loss of consciousness.

An epileptic fit may, however, also occur without prodromata or aura. It may consist only of a sudden and momentary state of unconscious stupor, generally and loosely called a loss of consciousness. During such an attack of minor epilepsy (*petit mal* or *absence*), the patient falters in what he is doing or becomes motionless; he does not respond to questions, looks pale and has a blank staring expression. Sometimes there are a few muscular contractions; there may also be a loss of muscular tone so that the head sinks forward or he slumps to the ground for a second. The whole attack is over quickly[506].

In major epilepsy (or *grand mal*), there is a more profound disturbance of brain functions; the seizure lasts longer, and the patient takes longer to recover from it. It begins with an immediate loss of consciousness and a generalized tonic contraction of muscles. The patient falls to the ground so vehemently that he can sustain severe injuries. His respiration stops and his face becomes cyanotic. This tonic phase is followed, after 10 to 30 seconds, by a phase of clonic muscular contractions. Breathing returns and is often stertorous. Frothy saliva collects at the mouth and may be bloodstained, if the tongue is bitten during a clonic spasm of the jaw muscles. Incontinence of urine, and sometimes also of faeces, may occur. The clonic spasms gradually become less frequent, and cease after a few minutes. The patient then passes into a state of clouded consciousness, which gradually becomes more and more lucid, or turns into a sleep that may last for hours.

Another form of epilepsy is commonly distinguished today by the name of *psychomotor epilepsy*, or *temporal lobe epilepsy*. It consists of a variable combination of symptoms encountered in the other two forms of epilepsy. There are both psychological and motor manifestations, namely an aura with a variety of subjective symptoms together with some semi-purposive movements. Consciousness is clouded to a variable extent, but is completely lost when a major seizure follows.

Other episodes of clouded consciousness occur in epileptic patients either spontaneously or after a seizure. They usually do not last longer than half an hour, but, while they last, the patient may act in an odd or objectionable way without retaining a memory trace of his behaviour. He may, for instance, undress in public, pass water in a busy road, steal articles without any attempt at concealment, become threatening and abusive, and sometimes dangerously and violently aggressive (epileptic furor).

Occasionally, the episodes of obfuscation in epileptic patients last for several days and even weeks or months. Their behaviour then is very variable. They may be torpid and dull, extremely slow in all their movements and in their responses to questions. But there can be emotional explosions, when the patient is seized by panic, rage or lust, and commits crimes for which he has no subsequent reminiscence. Some patients can verbally communicate the delusional and hallucinatory experiences which fill their clouded consciousness; others merely reveal them in their behaviour which, together with their disorientation, can give rise to an epileptic fugue (from Latin *fuga*, flight); they may walk or travel long distances, but their obfuscation is apparent in their slow fumbling behaviour, and they are sometimes wrongly accused of being drunk.

Apart from these delirious or twilight psychoses, epileptics can also develop schizophrenia-like psychoses in a setting of clear consciousness. This happens only occasionally in epileptics of more than 10 years' standing (though sometimes after a much shorter time). The clinical picture resembles that of paranoid schizophrenia with paranoid and hypochondriacal delusions, auditory hallucinations, and thought disorder. The affective reactivity of these patients seems to be better preserved than in genuine schizophrenics. Slater and his collaborators have shown that these occasional psychoses in epileptics of long standing can be distinguished from endogenous functional schizophrenia; they seem to be symptomatic schizophrenias caused by a chronic epileptic disorganization of psychoneural functions[29, 186, 464, 465, 466].

PART III

DYNAMIC PSYCHOPATHOLOGIES

CHAPTER 19

THE PSYCHOPATHOLOGY OF TRANCE STATES

It is perhaps still due to the philosophy of Descartes that there is a tendency, even today, to regard the mind as indivisible, and mental processes therefore as forming an interrelated and integrated unity. Yet existential experiences are divided into those at the centre of attention and others at its fringe. Those in the centre of attention are clear and detailed, and it may be that they are determined by a redundancy of psychoneural processes; those at the fringe of attention, on the other hand, are vague and shadowy, and it may be that they are determined by only a minimum of psychoneural processes. When the mind is alert, attention can easily and quickly shift from one set of phenomena to another so that what was on the fringe of attention at one moment can be in the centre at the next. This flexibility of attention may give the impression of a fundamental unity among mental phenomena. Yet when the phenomena at the centre of attention are preoccupying, phenomena at the fringe may receive no special attention for a long time. The mind then seems to be divided into experiences which are fully conscious and deliberate, and others which are half-conscious, automatic and absent-minded. Such a condition may be described as partial absent-mindedness.

Partial Absent-mindedness

A person who is partially absent-minded performs two simultaneous mental activities; a fact that can be most convincingly and objectively demonstrated, when one of the simultaneous activities is an overt motor performance. He may be lost in thought and, at the same time, engage in an automatic activity, such as walking or eating or dressing. The automatic activity must, of course, not be thought of as an entirely mechanical and predetermined rote activity. Walking, for example, is adjusted to the environment, even when it is automatic. The automatism is auto-regulated so that obstacles and dangers are avoided with only a minimum of conscious attention. Normally this works well, but because of the scarce attention the automatism receives, and because of the diminished redundancy of psychoneural processes involved in the automatism, errors are more likely to occur. The person whose centre of attention is preoccupied with disentangling some knotty problem may walk into danger or lose his way.

It is only when such errors occur that the person becomes aware, retrospectively, of the division of his sensorium and his partial absent-mindedness. To the outsider, the partially absent-minded person sometimes seems to engage in some purposive yet senseless, rash, or even foolish, action. He may, for instance, undress and go to bed, when he merely meant to change his suit before going out in the evening; or he may, as legend reports of Newton, boil his watch and blindly stare at an egg in his hand.

The kind of absent-minded automatism, just mentioned, may be said to have been started intentionally and then left to run its own auto-regulated course. But there are other manifestations of partial absent-mindedness which start unintentionally, and whose automatic course can be interrupted only with difficulty. This applies to all habitual mannerisms which accompany purposive behaviour, such as, for instance, the gestures and gesticulations usually associated with speech. Some of these mannersisms are the result of collective indoctrinations, and therefore perhaps characteristic of some ethnic group. The typical gesticulations of Italians and Jews, for example, can be easily distinguished, and both can be differentiated from the reserved speech behaviour of the typically non-gesticulating Englishman. Every individual, however, has also his own mannerisms which are typical of him alone.

Usually people are not aware of their unintentionally induced and automatically regulated mannerisms, but if they are ridiculed because of them, they may try their best to prevent or stop them though not always with success. It is then that mannerisms may be regarded as abnormal and perhaps even pathological. Various abnormal mannerisms have been described as ocurring with particular frequency in certain cultural groups. Beard[30], for instance, reported in 1880 that, among the members of a strict religious sect in Maine and the adjoining parts of the U.S.A. and Canada, there were some whose response to startle stimuli had earned them the name of 'Jumpers'. When they were frightened in some way, perhaps by merely having a finger pointed at them, they jumped and rolled on the ground. They also had a mannerism of automatic obedience, and had to obey unintentionally when they were given a sharp word of command. They could thus be made to dive into water fully dressed or to slap a friend. Often they also had to repeat the word of command ('manneristic echolalia'). Not surprisingly, the Jumpers dreaded startle stimuli, and were annoyed with companions who amused themselves by evoking these automatic mannerisms.

Similar mannerisms were also observed in other parts of the

world, especially in the Far East. They were called *latah* in Malaya and 'arctic hysteria', or *miryachit*, in Siberia[129, 213a, 548]. The mannerisms included not only unintentional obedience and echolalia, but also manneristic echopraxia. Individuals afflicted with this mannerism responded to startle stimuli by copying the behaviour of others. The afflicted women, for instance, began to imitate the dancing steps of a bystander who deliberately provoked them, perhaps by a strip-tease performance. They were angry when they were thus held up to ridicule, and often accompanied their manneristic echopraxia with an outburst of cursing and swearing which may have relieved their feelings, but was not effective in removing the ingrained manneristic habit. Collectively determined mannerisms can disappear, of course, when cultural conditions change. This may be the reason why neither the mannerisms of the Jumpers nor those of latah can be readily found in the modern world.

Following a state of partial absent-mindedness, the subjects have a reminiscence of those experiences which had been in the centre of their attention, but they have little or no reminiscence of either having intended an absent-minded activity or having regulated it. That this is so can be clearly demonstrated when the activity performed in partial absent-mindedness was not a habitual performance but a new and meaningful mental creation. A practised pianist has no difficulty in improvising a medley of tunes on the piano, while engaging at the same time in an animated conversation. Subsequently he will have a clear reminiscence of his conversation, but only a hazy memory of the improvised tunes. Even if his improvisation had been recorded and were played back to him, he would not recognize it as something he had creatively produced a short while before.

We are not in the habit of accompanying a conversation by writing that is improvised and meaningful. Yet this capacity can be trained. The result is *automatic writing*, which can differ in content from the simultaneous conversation. The subject has little or no reminiscence of what he had automatically written, and does not recognize it as his product, when it is shown to him. He may even deny having ever entertained the thoughts expressed in his automatic writing. If the subject disowns thoughts originated by him, he shows a phenomenon that is the obverse of unconscious plagiarism. Automatic writing received a good deal of attention in the last century because people in search of supernatural explanations saw in the more or less meaningful messages of automatic writing the influence of discarnate spirits. Today it is recognized as a phenomenon that is no more mysterious than the performance of the improvising pianist.

Complete Absent-mindedness: the Trance State

Automatic writing and other forms of automatic activity do not necessarily presuppose a divided sensorium. Some people can succeed in making their mind a blank by deliberately removing phenomena from the centre of their attention. If they are then still able to perform activities at the fringe of their attention, such as improvising tunes or writing automatically, they are in a state of complete absent-mindedness. All their mental processes then are vague and move only in a range that is narrowly associated with the motivation that dominates their fringe attention. If their attention cannot be easily heightened or readily directed to a wider range of phenomena, they are in a trance state. They subsequently have only a hazy reminiscence, if any at all, of what they did and experienced during their trance.

A person in trance is only in precarious contact with his environment. He may be almost entirely shut off from it, when his trance is deep and his fringe attention entirely absorbed by some phenomena in his mind. On the other hand, when his trance is superficial, he interacts with his environment in the same way that an absent-minded person walks past obstacles, but his interactions may be restricted to objects and events which are related to his absent-minded motivations.

Objectively, a person in deep trance has a diminished muscular tone so that the onset of his trance may be heralded by his slumping to the ground, where he lies motionless or tosses about in aimless contortions; his face is usually vacant and blank, but may be set in a grimace of fear or fury, or with an expression that is 'entranced', ecstatic and enraptured. The objective manifestations of a superficial trance state resemble those of partial sleep and organic twilight states; the person is capable of engaging in purposive activities, though he may show signs of not being fully alert and determined.

The resemblance between trance states, on the one hand, and sleep or obfuscation, on the other, does not indicate that they owe their existence to comparable psychoneural processes. On the contrary, there seems little doubt that the psychoneural basis of these three conditions of altered consciousness is different. This is most clearly revealed by the EEG which, in a person in trance, is indistinguishable from the EEG of a normal waking person, and is different from the EEGs of sleep and obfuscation.

In some social groups, the attainment of a trance has high prestige value. People with a facility to go into trance are then held in great esteem, generally because they are credited with the power of getting in touch with supernatural forces. Examples are the spiritualistic medium, the shaman or medicine-man, the Yogi, and other 'holy' men. People, who lack the facility of going into a trance easily often have recourse to special induction procedures. Some induction procedures, which have been employed in different cultures and at different times, rely on the excitation of strong emotions. This is generally done with the help of communal dancing, stamping, swaying and shouting to the rhythm of drums, the wailing of reeds, the twanging of stringed instruments and the blaring of brass. Primitive war dances may have had the same purpose because people in a superficial trance are oblivious of personal safety and impervious to pain. The same might perhaps be said of the bands, bugles, drums and bagpipes which raised the spirit of the marching columns of soldiers as they advanced to the battlefields. It is well known of the 'whirling' or 'howling' dervishes, the Mawlawis and Rafa'is, that their wild dancing and chanting produces a trance state in which they can gash themselves without fear or pain, and without shedding much blood. The Voodoo dances of Haiti end in even more dramatic trance automatisms in which the subjects enact their notion of being possessed by supernatural powers[436].

It is possible that trance states also played a role during the various dance epidemics which swept through mediaeval Europe, when large crowds of people left their homes and wandered from place to place to indulge in prolonged dancing frolics[228, 337]. The most remarkable epidemic occurred in the Rhineland in 1374. According to eye witnesses, the dancers, or 'choreomaniacs', 'when they had wearied themselves with leaping and dancing and such like exercises, suddenly rushed wildly from place to place, screaming fearfully, ranging like beasts over the land, and complaining of the most terrible internal pains'[20]. Even in the Europe of today, similar scenes can occasionally be observed[493]. When the rock 'n' roll dance was all the craze in 1957, the rumour spread that one had to burst into dancing, when one listened to the twelve-bar beat of the rock 'n' roll music. The rumour was self-verifying, and the resulting dancing revels sent some susceptible young people into trance states; they were 'gone' as they expressed it, and their facial expressions showed that they were in an enraptured trance.

The excitement of rapturous emotions through dance and song is not the only induction procedure of trances. Another procedure consists in stimulating emotions of fear and guilt. The revivalist preachers of the eighteenth century were adepts in this. Their stirring eloquence, which vividly portrayed the perils of eternal damnation and hell-fire torment, sent such thrills of fear and guilt through their congregations that trance states made their appearance. John Wesley, for instance, noted in his Journal for Friday, June 15, 1739: 'Some sunk down and there remained no strength in them; others exceedingly trembled and quaked; some were torn with a kind of convulsive motion in every part of their bodies, and that so violently that often four or five persons could not hold them'[436]. Similar trance states still occur in some evangelical sects today. Sargant[436], for instance, observed them in religious sects in North Carolina in 1947, in which fear was artificially whipped up by the ritual handling of poisonous snakes which were passed from hand to hand.

The manifest phenomena shown by people in superficial trances are varied because they express multiform motivations and thoughts. They are susceptible to social indoctrination, and can vary with the fickleness of fashions. It was reported[547], for example, of an eighteenth century revivalist preacher in Kentucky, who was a man of 'hideous visage and thunder tones' that many people, thronging to hear him, fell to the ground in trance convulsions. But later, the fashion in trance manifestations changed. There were times when the onset of the trance showed itself in histrionic and loud laughter which disturbed the religious service; and other times when people in trance danced wildly, or moved on all fours and barked like dogs.

Social indoctrination and example does not only shape the form of collective trance manifestations, it can also bring on a trance state in a susceptible person, who is constitutionally endowed with the facility to go into a trance. He may succumb, even against his will and professed inclinations, to the heterosuggestive and contagious power of the sight of people in a trance. This has often been dramatically demonstrated in revivalist meetings. People who had come to scoff and to express their indignation at the unedifying spectacle of trance manifestations were suddenly seized by a trance state themselves. There have been many reports of such occurrences. John Wesley regarded them as tokens of religious conversion. On July 30, 1739[436], for example, he mentioned in his Journal a woman who zealously criticized 'those who had cried out and made a noise, being sure that any of them might help it if they would. And the same opinion she was in still, till the moment she was struck through, as with a sword, and fell trembling to the ground. She then cried aloud, although not articulately, her words being swallowed up. In this pain she continued twelve or fourteen hours, and then her soul was set at liberty.'

Another method of inducing trance states makes predominant use of prestige heterosuggestions, which convey the belief to people that they will have trance experiences. If the people are in a susceptible frame of mind for such heterosuggestions, the conveyed belief becomes a self-verifying conviction, and the people go into a trance whose depth depends on their constitutional predisposition and on their previous training to achieve the altered consciousness of a trance.

Mesmer

Prestige heterosuggestions in the induction of trance states were introduced into modern medicine by the Viennese physician, Franz Anton Mesmer[505]. His flamboyant pretensions and extravagant therapeutic claims enraged his medical colleagues in Vienna. He therefore left that town in 1778 and went to Paris where he initially scored a great fashionable success.

Mesmer had an unfortunate theory to account for the manifestations which he undoubtedly produced in his patients. He thought he had discovered a special physical force, which he called 'animal magnetism', and believed that his results were achieved by 'magnetizing' his patients. It was not difficult for French scientists to disprove this theory. In their opinion, Mesmer's results were due to the imagination of his patients, by which they meant that they were imaginary and therefore unreal. Mesmer angrily defended his theory. He was convinced that the manifestations his patients showed were induced by a physical force, his animal magnetism, and were not just psychological imaginings. There can be no doubt today that Mesmer was the first modern psychotherapist, even to the extent of introducing useful remedial measures for the wrong theoretical reasons. It would, however, be untrue to say that Mesmer did not know that psychological forces contributed to his results. He knew that the patients' expectations were important for the success of his method, and he spoke of the necessity of *rapport*. He also knew that this rapport was increased by a display of prestige status on his part, by mystification and impressive ostentation. Yet by thus deliberately donning the mantle of the charlatan, he provoked the suspicions and the antagonism of the medical world.

The heterosuggestive convictions which Mesmer conveyed to his patients were often very vague. He believed that a therapeutic result required an initial aggravation of symptoms, an initial 'crisis' as he called it. What form the crisis would take was, however, not always specified by him, especially when he started group-therapeutic sessions in which several patients were magnetized at the same time. Patients therefore produced different reactions. The scientists, investigating Mesmer's claims in 1784, reported about his subjects: 'Some of them are calm, tranquil and unconscious to any sensation; others cough, spit, are affected with a slight degree of pain, a partial or a universal burning, and perspirations; a third class are agitated and tormented with convulsions. These convulsions are rendered extraordinary by their frequency, their violence and their duration. . . . They [the patients] are entirely under the government of the person who distributes the magnetic virtue; in vain they may appear in a state of extremest drowsiness, his voice, a look, a sign from him rouses them.' It will be noticed that, in this report, some patients were described as calm, tranquil, in a state of extremest drowsiness, and yet responsive to the magnetizer's voice, looks and signs. This particular 'magnetic' manifestation was specially investigated by one of Mesmer's pupils, the Marquis de Puységur, who spoke of artificial sleep and somnambulism.

When Mesmer disappeared from the public scene after the French Revolution, and spent most of the remaining 26 years of his life as an obscure country practitioner near Lake Constance, the interest of his followers concentrated on this artificial sleep, because it amplified a person's responsiveness to the influence of the magnetizer to such an extent that the most astonishing reactions could be produced. The absent Mesmer's name began to be used to characterize the 'magnetic' methods and the phenomena he had demonstrated, and such terms as 'mesmerism', 'mesmerist', and 'mesmeric state' became current. He even achieved the unusual distinction of having his name used as a verb: to mesmerize.* These eponymous expressions were replaced, after 1843, by the terminology of today which was introduced by Braid, a Manchester surgeon. Braid attributed the artificial mesmeric sleep to 'a peculiar condition of the nervous system' and spoke of 'nervous sleep'. Translated into Greek, this became 'neuro-hypnotism' which was shortened to hypnotism and hypnosis.

Hypnosis

A person in hypnosis is in a trance state and his contact with the environment is so narrowed that his absent-minded attention is entirely focussed on the communications received from the hypnotist.

* Only one other physician's name is similarly used: the name of the German psychiatrist, Ganser, who described hysterical symptoms caused by the autosuggestive conviction of being mad. Such patients are often said to 'ganser'. Pasteur, whose name is commemorated in the verb 'to pasteurize', was not a physician.

The hypnotist's suggestions, however, absurd, become absolute truths to the hypnotized person who is forced to obey them without demur. Hypnotic suggestions can continue to influence a person's perceptions, thoughts and behaviour even post-hypnotically, when he has regained full consciousness[461, 528, 541].

A person's heterosuggestibility in response to communications from the hypnotist remains amplified in the post-hypnotic state. Psychologists have developed tests to measure the degree of hetero-suggestibility in normal people[131]. They use, for example, the 'body sway test' in which a person, standing with his feet together and his eyes closed, has to listen to the constant and urgent sugges-tion that he will fall forward. The amount of body sway thus pro-duced in normal persons varies from as little as one inch to as much as six or seven inches. The extent of body sway is accepted as indicat-ing a person's susceptibility to prestige suggestions. This test, is, however, hardly applicable to persons in a hypnotic or post-hypnotic state. They are so sensitive to prestige suggestions coming from the hypnotist that even a casual remark by him, that they are falling forward, has the effect of prostrating them on the ground.

A hypnotist may suggest psychotic symptoms to hypnotized persons, and they will promptly give an exhibition of their notion of such symptoms. D. H. Tuke wrote a paper on 'Artificial Insanity' in 1866[513], which described the variety of apparently psychotic symptoms that can be produced in this way. A hypnotized person can be made to have hallucinations, to see apparitions, hear non-existent voices, or feel imaginary insects crawl over his skin. It is equally easy for the hypnotist to evoke delusions in his subject, convincing him that he is, let us say, a man of high rank and great wealth, or the victim of ill-will and persecution. Such artificial insanities, however, usually have a more histrionic tinge than genuine psychoses, and they do not last as long.

Tuke realized that heterosuggestions were not only of importance in the artificial insanity of a hypnotized person, but also in the genuine psychosis of a mental patient. He remarked: 'Indeed, with lunatics, the exciting agent of a particular delusion may come from without, and be truly a suggestion.' This is certainly true. The schizophrenics of the Middle Ages, for example, had delusions that they were influenced by daemons and witches, those of the nine-teenth century often accused electricity, and those of today radio-activity. But the difference between a psychotic patient and a hypnotized person is that the former has delusions on account of his mental illness, and it is only the content of delusions and hallu-cinations, not their very existence, which may partially originate in heterosuggestive influences. In the hypnotized person, on the other hand, both the existence and the content of delusions and hallucinations may spring from heterosuggestions.

We know today that a special variety of suggestions, namely autosuggestions, are of great aetiological significance in the neurotic disease of hysteria. We also know that heterosuggestions can produce symptoms of an artificial hysteria, which closely resemble those of genuine hysteria. That this is so was first shown by the French 'neuropathologist', Charcot, when, in 1878, he began to use hypnosis in the study of hysteria. It was through his efforts that this illness was eventually accepted in the medical world as a true disease, whereas previously medical opinion had been almost united in denouncing hysterical symptoms as the imagined or simulated fabrications of persons with a sexually overheated fantasy life.

To induce a hypnotic trance through heterosuggestions, the hypnotist repeats monotonously, but persuasively, such suggestions as: 'You are feeling relaxed and drowsy; you are falling asleep'. A susceptible subject, who is both heterosuggestible and capable of entering a trance, develops a hypnotic state of varying depth. In accordance with the hypnotist's suggestions he assumes the repose of a person in a quietly relaxed sleep. Yet when the hypnotist's suggestions change, the subject's behaviour shows a corresponding change. If required to do so, he will open his eyes and perform whatever actions are suggested. To the outsider, this appears to be a change from a condition resembling sleep to one resembling somnambulism. The hypnotized subject seems to be a completely helpless and obedient tool in the hands of the hypnotist.

Yet the helplessness and obedience are not as complete as they look; there are limits to the hypnotized subject's automatic compliance with heterosuggestions. Demands which arouse fear and alarm in him are not obeyed; they are either avoided by some compromise action, or the hypnotic trance comes to a sudden end. It is thus not possible to make a hypnotized subject commit suicide, injure himself severely and intentionally, or perpetrate a serious crime or sexual impropriety. For example, a credible story is told of a young girl in deep hypnosis who was told by the hypnotist during a medical demonstration at Charcot's hospital that she should obey the commands of a medical student, and the latter jokingly suggested she should take off her clothes. She came out of her hypnosis in an instant and walked off indignantly.

When a hypnotized subject is left alone, he usually falls asleep and eventually wakes up without any ill effects. When he is told by the hypnotist to wake up, he does so immediately. He then often has only a vague reminiscence or none at all, of his experience during hypnosis. This *post-hypnotic amnesia*[474] depends partly on the depth of the hypnosis, partly on the subject's autosuggestive expectation of a post-hypnotic amnesia, and partly on the hypnotist's suggestions during hypnosis that the subject will remember every thing afterwards or forget it all. Sometimes, a subject is amnesic only for a while after coming out of the hypnosis; but subsequently recovers some reminiscence of events during hypnosis; sometimes he remains amnesic until he is again hypnotized. The memory traces of experiences in hypnosis are thus retained, at least for a time, whether they can be easily reactivated or not. In the immediate post-hypnotic phase, such memory traces may even have a cryptomnesic effect on the subject's overt behaviour.

This becomes obvious when the hypnotized subject had been given a *post-hypnotic suggestion*. He may have been told that, after waking up and on being given a particular signal from the hypnotist he would perform a specified nonsensical act, such as pouring water on the carpet, without remembering that he had been given this suggestion under hypnosis. On receiving the signal in the post-hypnotic phase, the cryptomnesic desire suddenly obsesses the subject that he wants to pour water on the carpet. This is usually a a compelling obsession which he has to perform for his peace of mind, even if he is hard put to it to invent a plausible explanation for behaviour which he knows to be odd. The hypnotized subject may also have been given post-hypnotic suggestions which leave him with hysterical symptoms on awakening. He may, in compliance with such suggestions, have the cryptomnesic, though objectively untrue, knowledge that he is universally disliked, or the equally cryptomnesic, though objectively true, knowledge that his arms are paralysed. These symptoms are not likely to last for long, but while they last, they are indistinguishable from genuine hysterical manifestations.

The psychogenesis of such post-hypnotic symptoms has today provided the favourite prototype of theories of dynamic psychopathology, which attempt to understand and explain how neurotic symptoms originate. All hysterical, and sometimes also all other neurotic and even psychotic, symptoms are then regarded as having been partly caused by forgotten, and therefore unconscious, reminiscences, comparable to the forgotten reminiscence of receiving a post-hypnotic suggestion during hypnosis.

If this were exclusively so, it should be possible to cure psychiatric patients by making the unconscious and pathogenic reminiscences conscious again. This is, in fact, the aim of many modern psychotherapies. As the unconscious and pathogenic reminiscences are usually believed to refer back to infantile events, hypnosis is used by some psychotherapists on the assumption that, in hypnosis, a person can be made to 'regress' to, and relive infantile events, thus making them conscious again and removing their pathogenic power. There have been several attempts to prove that such age regression can actually take place in hypnosis. One such investigation[512] claimed that it had been possible to regress hypnotized subjects to their fourth year of age, and that 75 per cent of them then knew on what day of the week Christmas had fallen that year. Unfortunately, when this investigation was repeated, a negative result was obtained[22]. This was hardly surprising because it was also found that among four-year-old nursery school children in a comparable community, 70 to 80 per cent had no idea of how to distinguish between the days of the week.

The hypnotizability of subjects who are often hypnotized is increased. The speed with which hypnosis can be induced in them can be further improved by suitable post-hypnotic suggestions. They are told in hypnosis that they will, in future, sink into a deep hypnotic trance immediately they received a particular signal from the hypnotist, while they are reclining on a couch. It is important to emphasize that the signal must come from the hypnotist and will be effective only when they are reclining on a couch. Otherwise a chance encounter with the signal, even a very unusual signal, is possible and could have embarrassing results for the subject. From then on, the subjects can be hypnotized with extraordinary ease and speed in accordance with the post-hypnotic suggestions given.

With the help of suitable post-hypnotic suggestions, patients can even be taught to hypnotize themselves in order to achieve therapeutic results, such as the removal of pain or anxieties. Two German psychiatrists[285] have elaborated such a method of self-hypnosis which may be used, if necessary, several times a day. It has proved particularly useful in some patients suffering from chronic intractable pains for which they previously had to have large doses of analgesics. The method, of course, requires safeguards. To induce hypnosis, patients have first to perform several unusual actions. They may, for instance, have to put a rubber band, to which buttons are affixed in a particular pattern, tightly around one arm with the buttons pressing into the skin; they may have to set an alarm clock to ensure waking up after, say, ten minutes, instead of drifting from the hypnotic trance into a normal sleep that might last a few hours; and finally they may have to look at a card with an abstract and

vividly coloured design on it which, through post-hypnotic suggestions, has been made the precipitating stimulus of a hypnotic trance,
provided the sensations of the rubber band and the ticking of the
alarm clock are present.

To produce artificial psychiatric symptoms by purely psychological means, the induction of hypnosis through heterosuggestion
is not an exclusive condition. Heterosuggestion without hypnosis
can be equally effective, though only in persons with a suitable
predisposition; and it seems that this predisposition consists in an
ability to induce a state of mind that is similar to that of a person
enacting a post-hypnotic suggestion. It is a state of mind that
cannot be easily understood. To explain it, it is often assumed that
it is a divided mind of a special kind in which certain phenomena
are 'dissociated' from the centre of attention so that they are no
longer experienced, not even absent-mindedly. They are then
regarded as dissociated phenomena, which have become unconscious. People who can easily dissociate mental experiences, which
are then no longer available to conscious recall, have been said to
have a predisposition to form mental dissociations, or a *dissociative
predisposition.*

It is helpful to have an adjective with which to characterize a
particular predisposition, even if the explanatory theory behind the
adjective is of doubtful validity. If a hypnotized subject is given the
post-hypnotic suggestion that he will fall forward, when he gets up
after coming out of hypnosis, it is easy to see what is dissociated: it is
the reminiscence of the occasion when he received the post-hypnotic
suggestion. The information contained in the suggestion is not
dissociated; when he gets up after coming out of hypnosis, he
suddenly knows that he is falling forward, and this knowledge
is a self-fulfilling conviction. But what is it that the subject dissociates
who receives the same heterosuggestion in clear consciousness? He
knows that he is being given the repeated suggestion to fall forward.
If he is heterosuggestible, he realizes that he is beginning to sway
forward, but he will usually succeed in preventing a fall. Only if
he is heterosuggestible and has also a dissociative predisposition,
does he have the self-verifying knowledge that he is indeed falling
forward, and is unable, or unwilling to prevent it.

Individual differences in heterosuggestibility and dissociative
predisposition are highlighted during hysterical epidemics in which
the heterosuggestive influence comes from a rumour that certain
physical symptoms will make their appearance in a community.
Those members of the community, who have a dissociative predisposition may develop such symptoms, whereas those who are merely

very heterosuggestible are convinced that the rumour is true, but their conviction does not become self-fulfilling by the production of personal symptoms. An example of such a hysterical epidemic occurred, in September 1944, in Mattoon, a mid-western town in the U.S.A. with about 16,000 inhabitants, and it lasted for about twelve days[260]. The rumour started when a woman complained to the police that somebody had sprayed an anaesthetic gas through her open bedroom window, causing her and her daughter to feel ill and to have a partial paralysis of the legs. The local newspaper gave a dramatic account of the incident under a frontpage banner headline 'Anaesthetic Prowler on Loose. Mrs. X and Daughter First Victims.' It may have been the suggestive impact of the ordinal number 'first' that there were nine similar incidents within the next four days. The town was in an uproar. Armed groups of vigilantes roamed the streets nightly in search of the elusive anaesthetist. By the twelfth day, the police had proved that there was no such person, that the town was hunting a 'phantom anaesthetist'. The epidemic disappeared as suddenly as it had arisen. But, by then, 27 people in all had reported short-lasting hysterical symptoms, such as paralyses, nausea, vomiting, and the like[75, 475, 493, 495].

CHAPTER 20

THE DYNAMIC PSYCHOPATHOLOGY OF HYSTERIA

The meaning given to the concept of hysterical disease has varied throughout the ages. So have the theories about its causes. The very name 'hysteria' still indicates an obsolete theory about its pathology. The name comes from the Greek word *hystera*, meaning womb. In the medical folklore of ancient Greece the womb was regarded as the seat of sexual desires in women. When these desires were frustrated, the womb was believed to move upward and cause hysterical symptoms. The origin of this theory may have been the observation that sexually experienced women often had a prolapsed uterus, but rarely suffered from hysteria, whereas sexually frustrated young women often had hysteria, but rarely a prolapsed uterus.

Plato mentioned this theory in his *Timaeus*, when he said that the sexually frustrated uterus 'by straying all over the body and blocking up the passages of breath . . . cast the body in great distress.' This quotation seems to refer to a symptom which is still common in many psychiatrially ill women who complain that their breathing is blocked by a lump in their throat. The symptom is still called *globus hystericus*, although it is doubtful whether the adjective *hystericus* is really justified. Galen, who knew more about anatomy than Plato, realized that the womb could not stray all over the body. He also knew that sexual frustration could cause symptoms in men as well, which were analogous to those in hysterical women. He attributed sexual frustration symptoms to the accumulation in the body of undischarged sexual fluids which became toxic through decomposition.

Many psychiatric diseases, apart from hysteria, have since been ascribed at various times to sexual frustration and the treatment often suggested for them was sexual intercourse. Robert Burton, for instance, in his *Anatomy of Melancholy*, recommended this treatment for what he called 'love-melancholy'. In pre-Victorian days, such well-known psychiatrists as Chiarugi in Italy and Reil in Germany were of the same opinion. For them intercourse was a purely physical activity, though they knew that it could bring psychological harm to some patients. 'In insanity due to sexual desires, intercourse may act as a physical remedy', wrote Reil, in 1803, in his *Rhapsodies on the*

Application of Psychological Methods of Treatment to Mental Disorders.
But he added: 'Physical copulation sometimes affects the moral
sense of a patient to his advantage, sometimes to his detriment. The
idealistic recluse, who became insane because he endowed the
female sex with the shining virtues of higher beings, should be given
a brothel nymph as companion. I have no doubt that, if he can
respond to her, she will cure his misconception.'[419]

The prudery of the nineteenth century drove such blunt recommendations underground, though various young men continued to
be told, in private, that a sexual escapade might help them. The
therapeutic advice for hysterical young girls was more conventional:
they should get married, and, if that did not cure their symptoms,
they should have a child. It was Freud who eventually drew
attention to the frequency of such therapeutic suggestions and criticized their value. His criticism was not based on follow-up studies,
but on the psychoanalytic theory he evolved from his clinical findings. This theory presented the age-old views on the sexual aetiology
of hysteria in a completely new light by shifting the emphasis from
the frustration of adult sexuality to the frustration of infantile sexual
instincts.

The many theories and opinions that have gathered around the
concept of hysteria in the course of centuries have made its meaning
ambiguous. This applies particularly to the term 'hysterical' which
is today understood in two essentially different ways: as denoting (a)
a special category of neurotic symptoms, and (b) temperamental
and ostentatious behaviour. To avoid confusion between these
two meanings, we shall restrict the use of the term 'hysterical' to
a particular kind of neurotic illness and a particular variety of
neurotic symptoms; and the use of the term 'histrionic' to a particular kind of normal personality, characterized by temperamental
and ostentatious behaviour. Hysterical symptoms and histrionic
behaviour can occur quite independently of each other. In fact,
many hysterical patients display a very characteristic attitude of indifference to their physical symptoms, an attitude which is technically
known as *belle indifférence*—the very opposite of histrionic ostentation.

Psychoanalysts often use the hyphenated expression 'conversion-
hysterical' instead of simply 'hysterical' because of a theoretical
assumption that, in this form of hysteria, there is a pathological
conversion of psychological functions into such physical symptoms
as sensory or motor disorders. This assumption, however, leaves
out of account that among the most common hysterical symptoms
are disorders of 'unconverted' psychological functions, for example,
disorders of consciousness, memory, and emotions.

Hysterical Symptoms

Hysteria is a clinical disease concept that is composed of a great and bewildering number of clinical symptoms. It will be helpful to make a distinction between the dynamic psychopathology of the illness itself and that of the component symptoms. It is obvious that hysterical symptoms, like all other mental products, have many causal associations of a psychogenic and physiogenic kind. In the context of dynamic psychopathology, certain psychogenic causal associations are of particular interest, which appear in a different light to the patient and his doctor.

To the patient, hysterical symptoms consist in the observation that some of his mental or physical abilities do not function adequately, or at all. The symptoms have the same significance for him as organic symptoms. He is not aware of any difference; he does not feel responsible for the occurrence of either kind of symptom. In fact, he usually prefers an organic diagnosis, and may refuse to see a psychiatrist or psychotherapist because he is afraid that the origin of the symptoms will be attributed to him personally.

The observation of symptoms, whether hysterical or not, usually creates in the patient the conviction of being ill. Thus, a patient with a motor paralysis of his arms, whether hysterical or organic, observes that he cannot intentionally move his arms. He becomes aware of the conviction: 'I cannot move my arms; they are paralysed.' If a doctor diagnoses the paralysis as hysterical, he views the patient's conviction of being paralysed in a different light. To the doctor, the conviction does not appear to follow on the observation of symptoms; to him it is a self-verifying conviction which is the *cause* of the symptoms, and not a result of them. It is a hysterical conviction of a special kind, namely a hypochondriacal hysterical conviction. In the doctor's estimation, the patient is convinced that he cannot move his arms, and this conviction puts into action psychoneural processes which, without the patient's intentional co-operation, bring about its verification.

A similar endopsychic process, causing the self-verification of a conviction, can occur in hypnotized subjects. When the hypnotist suggests to them that some of their mental or physical abilities do not function adequately, or at all, this heterosuggestion is accepted as absolutely true, and turns into a conviction that verifies itself as a hysterical symptom. A comparable process seems to take place in hysterical patients. The main difference is that heterosuggestion plays no significant role in the genesis of their symptoms. Auto-suggestion takes its place.

Autosuggestion may be defined as the uncritical acceptance of the truth of some proposition or observation in the absence of any heterosuggestive assertion of its truth. In everyday life, we accept uncritically the truth of many propositions and observations. Life would be too cumbersome otherwise. There is thus no doubt that we make constant use of autosuggestion. When we recognize a clearly perceived and familiar object, for instance, we are autosuggestively convinced that our recognition is true. Autosuggestion is also responsible for the inductive conviction that a particular sequence of events that has often been experienced in the past will, when experienced again at some future date, occur in the same way. We thus, inductively and autosuggestively acquire the knowledge that water is wet and fire hot, that day is followed by night, and lightning by thunder. People, however, differ in their autosuggestive readiness to accept unusual propositions and observations as true. They thus differ in the personality trait of *autosuggestibility*, which can be assessed by suitable psychological tests. Subjects may, for instance, be asked to lift a series of ten identical boxes, which have been so arranged that the first five increase in weight by the same small, but noticeable, amount, whereas the last five are of the same weight. Highly autosuggestible subjects tend to form the conviction that the progression of weights in the first five boxes will be continued in the last five. When lifting the last five boxes, they will therefore report a non-existent regular increment of weight.

But a hypochondriacal proposition, even when accepted as true through the effect of heterosuggestion or autosuggestion, is still not enough to produce a hysterical symptom. The resulting hypochondriacal conviction must become self-verifying, and this can only be achieved in persons with a high dissociative predisposition.

We can find hysterical symptoms in any disease, quite apart from the disease of hysteria. But we can also find, in those diseases, the forerunners of hysterical symptoms, especially hypochondriacal convictions that manifest themselves clinically as hypochondriacal symptoms. In psychotic diseases, for instance, heterosuggestive and autosuggestive influences contribute to the development of hypondriacal delusions. The delusions can be in a form which could not possibly be self-verifying; for example, a psychotic patients' conviction that his head is shrunk or his blood turned to water. But if objective self-verification is a possibility, it depends on the patient's dissociative predisposition, whether hysterical symptoms make their appearance or not. If a patient is, let us say, delusionally convinced that there is no power left in his muscles so that he can no longer move, he does not necessarily exhibit this subjective conviction objectively in the form of a hysterical paralysis. On the contrary, in most psychotic patients with such a delusion, there is a discordance between subjective complaints and objective symptoms. In spite of their absolute, incorrigible, and perhaps preoccupying, conviction that they are paralysed, they continue to move. This discordance, incidentally, is not the sign of a schizophrenic incongruity, as it can also be met in severe melancholia and other psychotic disease. After all, delusional realities are idiosyncratic, and more or less completely divorced from objective realities.

In anxiety neurosis, there are also hypochondriacal convictions, though only half believed, which could not possibly be self-verifying. such convictions generally concern diseases, such as hypochondriacal fears of having a brain tumour, a heart defect or a venereal disease. Many hypochondriacal phobias are, however, potentially self-verifiable, and yet are not usually converted into overt hysterical symptoms. This is true of phobias of fainting in the street; of having audible borborygmi in polite company; of being overcome by an irresistible urge to pass water, wind or a bowel motion in embarrassing social situations; of having a shaking head, or similar symptoms.

There are, however, other hypochondriacal phobias which can be self-verifying in persons with dissociative predispositions. To this category belong hypochondriacal fears of blushing, trembling hands, shaking knees, sexual impotence, increased urinary and intestinal frequency, and the like. Whenever hypochondriacal phobias are self-verifying, the resulting symptoms are hysterical from the point of view of dynamic psychopathology. Yet the presence of such hysterical symptoms does not alter the diagnosis of anxiety neurosis.

However, not only neurotic fears are capable of producing hysterical symptoms. The same is true of fears which have a different origin. In acute danger situations, for example, the hypochondriacal conviction may establish itself that one is not actually involved, that the danger is a nightmarish unreality, that it affects someone else and not one's true self, which thus can stand apart as an external observer. This 'splitting of the ego' has been described by many people on their first exposure to the perils and brutalities of Nazi concentration camps. People of weak dissociative capacity could not advance beyond this stage of hysterical depersonalization and derealization. In others, the hypochondriacal conviction of standing apart developed into a hysterical trance state which, very rarely, was deep enough to produce hysterical fits and faints. For the most part however, the trance states seem to have remained superficial and objectively inconspicuous so that they did not attract potentially dangerous attention. Yet even a superficial trance was enough to blunt the impact of what was experienced. In particular, it could mercifully induce some degree of analgesia and an increase of stamina in standing up to severe trials of endurance.

It is possible that such superficial trances also occurred in some mediaeval suspects of witchcraft, who were subjected to a cruel physical examination by the Inquisition. What the Inquisition was searching for were *stigmata diaboli*, and foremost among these were insensitive spots in any part of the body, which could be pricked without causing pain or bleeding. The fear, torment and humiliation of the unfortunate suspects must have been such that susceptible women went into a trance, and thus developed the usual trance signs of analgesia and diminished bleeding.

In psychosomatic diseases, an aggravation of vegetative symptoms can be achieved by the arousal of strong emotions, especially those of fear and anger, without the interposition of autosuggestions and dissociations. Conditioned reflexes may also be responsible for some aggravations of symptoms. In a patient, for example, whose bronchial asthma is allergically caused by horse dander, the sight of horses has become the conditioned stimulus of asthma attacks. If he is merely shown the picture of a horse, he may begin to wheeze and feel short of breath. However, repeated viewing of the picture would have a deconditioning effect, because there is no reinforcement by the unconditioned stimulus, which consists in the inhalation of horse dander. On the other hand, if viewing the picture of a horse excites in the patient the autosuggestive conviction of an impending asthma attack, he will respond with dyspnoea, even if he has no marked dissociative capacities. Viewing the picture repeatedly would then not necessarily reduce his asthmatic reaction.

An asthma patient has been described[113], for example, who was allergic to aspirin. He developed asthma attacks, whenever he saw someone swallow aspirin, or only a tablet that he took for aspirin. In another patient, the sight of a goldfish in a bowl of water was the precipitating experience because it conjured up the idea that the fish had no air to breathe. This idea became autosuggestively the self-verifying conviction of being without air, which caused the asthma attack. It is, however, doubtful, whether these apparent inductions of psychosomatic symptoms through hypochondriacal convictions are genuine hysterical symptoms. It is likely that, in these patients, there is merely an aggravation of symptoms, which are so well established that they do not require dissociative capacities, but can be intensified by mere autosuggestive expectations.

One has the impression that physicians, who are particularly interested in the aggravation of psychosomatic symptoms through hypochondriacal convictions, are most likely to find one or two convincing examples. It is possible, and indeed probable, that their interests act as a heterosuggestive force on susceptible patients. But once the physicians' interest has waned, it is not longer so easy for them to find illustrative patients. That may be the explanation why nobody has as yet been able to publish more than one or two relevant cases.

Hypochondriacal Conviction

So far, we have considered the dynamic psychopathology of hysterical symptoms only. We must now turn to the dynamic psychopathology of the hysterical disease. It has its most immediate origin often in a conviction of being ill, a hypochondriacal conviction. People with a desire to be ill do not necessarily develop a hypochondriacal conviction. To achieve this, an autosuggestive capacity of sufficient strength is required. Without this capacity, a hypochondriacal desire leads, at most, to a malingered disease. Malingerers do their best to exhibit a disease with both subjective and objective symptoms[13, 509], but true malingerers are not often encountered.

It has been noticed that doctors with only a smattering of psychiatric knowledge have a predilection for making the diagnosis of malingering. The greater a doctor's psychiatric experience, the less ready he is with this diagnosis. Jung[267], for instance, reported that malingering was diagnosed in only 0·13 per cent among 8430 admissions to the Swiss mental hospital of Burghölzli. The stress of wartime can increase this percentage, but it still remains relatively small. A survey of the diagnoses made in American soldiers, referred for neuropsychiatric assessment during the Second World War, showed that experienced psychiatrists diagnosed malingering with a frequency that varied between 2 and 7 per cent[69, 351].

People who are sufficiently autosuggestible may succeed in converting a hypochondriacal desire into a hypochondriacal conviction of being ill, but this, by itself, is not enough to produce a hysterical illness. It leads, at most, to hypochondriasis. Hypochondriacal patients are so convinced autosuggestively that they are ill that they succeed in repressing all knowledge of their hypochondriacal desires. Their illness is a reality to them for which they feel in no way responsible. They have diverse aches and pains and indispositions, and clamour continually for new forms of medical and paramedical attention. Yet the subjective suffering of typical hypochondriacs is not confirmed by the evidence of objective symptoms. In this respect, they differ from malingerers who often go to great lengths to simulate objective symptoms.

People who are not only strongly autosuggestible but also have a strong dissociative capacity can succeed in transforming hypochondriacal desires into hypochondriacal convictions which are self-verifying both subjectively and objectively. They then suffer from a hysterical illness. They are like malingerers because they exhibit both subjective and objective symptoms, and they are like hypochondriacs because they have no memory of their hypochondriacal desires.

The autosuggestive and dissociative capacities of most people is, however, insufficient to maintain a hysterical illness for a long time. Hysterical illnesses may therefore improve in the course of time. As a result, the patient may become conscious of hypochondriacal desires. He may then deliberately aggravate whatever hysterical symptoms he still has, and may thus resort to the tricks of the malingerer. The whole malingered-hysterical mixture is then exhibited with histrionic ostentation so that it becomes difficult, if not impossible, for the psychiatrist to decide where hysteria ends and where malingering begins. Even the confession of such a patient, at a later time, that he had simulated a particular symptom in the past is of no help. The confession is likely to be influenced by conditions prevailing at the later time, and these conditions will also dictate the kind of reminiscence that is revived, a reminiscence that is more likely to be a distorted or invented paramnesia than a true memory.

Because histrionics and emotional fireworks are so characteristic of the patient with a mixed malingered-hysterical illness, there is a widespread medical belief that a histrionic personality, or demonstrative antics, are pathognomonic of hysteria. Such an assumption is, however, unjustified and may bring harm to the patient and embarrassment to the doctor, when it turns out that behind an emotional and ostentatious display of symptoms there was a serious psychiatric or physical disease: an agitated depression perhaps which ends in suicide, or an acute failure of the left ventricle, causing an agitated panic that hides the poverty of cardiac reserves. In either case, a rash diagnosis of hysteria can seriously damage a doctor's reputation.

Disease-rewarding Situations

Let us now consider the origin of hypochondriacal desires. At first sight, it may appear puzzling that a person should ever develop a strong desire to be ill. Yet the puzzle is solved, when we take into consideration the social situations in which hypochondriacal desires make their appearance. Such situations are distinguished by one common characteristic: they are all disease-rewarding. Generally speaking, disease-rewarding situations are unpleasant, threatening or stressful situations which can be avoided, terminated or mitigated by falling ill. These situations often arise within the family circle and tempt susceptible persons to desire an illness that will enable them to renounce onerous responsibilities, to escape from disliked duties, to claim the special privileges accorded to invalids, and perhaps to achieve the emotional subjugation of relatives who are sensitive to the accusation that they shamefully and callously neglect the suffering of a member of their family.

Disease-rewarding situations occur, of course, also outside the family. The danger of an examination, of criminal charges, imprisonment or military conscription can be very powerful instigators of hypochondriacal desires. However, the most typical disease-rewarding situations occur in wartime among front-line soldiers. To them, falling ill can bring the immediate reward of being moved from the combat zone to the comfort and security of a base hospital. If their illness is prolonged, it has the reassuring additional advantage that it prevents their return to the battle area. It is therefore not surprising that hysterical illnesses were common in the armed forces during both world wars, but not in prisoners of war to whom they could bring no benefit. The clinical symptoms produced varied with the theoretical expectations of the medical staff in different theatres of war. The symptoms received a variety of diagnostic names which often expressed the aetiological views prevalent at the time. In the First World War, for instance, it was, at one time, assumed that pressure waves from an exploding shell could cause molecular disturbances in the nervous system. The disease was therefore termed shellshock, but it consisted of an assortment of often bizarre hysterical symptoms, especially tremors, twitches and gait disorders. Later, emotional traumas were aetiologically inculpated, and such terms as traumatic neurosis or war neurosis came into vogue. In the Second World War, a combination of both physical and emotional stresses was postulated and the terms used were battle exhaustion or battle fatigue[272, 351].

In all these diagnostic terms, the aetiological role of pathogenic traumas is stressed rather than any disease-rewarding procedures. Patients, doctors and the general public jointly hold the collective conviction that illness must be due to something noxious and should not be attributed to measures taken with remedial and humanitarian intentions. Yet in the practice of modern warfare, the pathogenic role of disease-rewarding procedures has finally been recognized. Battle-fatigued casualites are nowadays treated with sedation, rest and sleep in the forward area so that the disease-rewarding evacuation to a base hospital is eliminated.

Before the Second World War started, the theory that war neuroses are caused by emotional trauma and stress led to the expectation that the bombing of civilian populations would be followed by many psychiatric casualities. In Britain, a large number of hospital beds were therefore set aside for them, but they remained largely empty. There were, of course, among the populations of bombed towns, a number of traumatic neuroses with hysterical symptoms, but the patients usually recovered quickly as there was no advantage in remaining ill. The same absence of chronic traumatic neuroses among civilians was found in all the belligerent countries of the Second World War, even among the survivors of the atomic bomb raids on Hiroshima and Nagasaki[272].

Chronic war neuroses thus were a prerogative of the armed forces, at least as long as disease-rewarding regulations kept them alive. Once the regulations became obsolete, most of the patients speedily recovered. At the end of the First World War, for instance, 2,500 American soldiers with shell shock were waiting to be shipped home, when Armistice was announced. Within a day or two, all but 400 of them had lost their symptoms[230]. But there were no miraculous cures in soldiers who received a disability pension for war neurosis. They tended to retain their disabilities. There was, however, a remedy for the vast majority of them as was clearly proved by Germany in 1926, when the payment of pensions to shell shocked invalids was stopped. The following, psychiatrically inspired, explanation of the decision was given by a German law court: 'When a disability is caused by the patient's idea of being ill, or by more or less conscious wishes, the preceding traumatic experience is not the essential cause of his disability, even if the traumatic experience elicited the idea of being ill or raised the hope of financial compensation.'

Compensation Neurosis

Disease-rewarding regulations exist also in peacetime, though the number of persons who succumb to their pathogenic power is very much smaller than in war. The hysterical illness which develops in these patients is generally diagnosed as 'accident neurosis' or 'compensation neurosis'[359]. Usually, there was some accident, often of a trivial kind, for which compensation can be claimed. The result is a mixture of malingered and hysterical symptoms, or a malingered-hysterical aggravation of some organic disability. No medical, surgical or psychological treatment can help these patients.

There is only one curative measure: the settlement of all compensation claims either by their outright rejection or by a lump sum payment. Unfortunately solicitors and doctors cannot see eye-to-eye in cases of compensation neurosis. Solicitors have to advise their clients against accepting a quick and final settlement because the doctor's prognosis might be wrong and the compensation eventually turn out to be inadequate.

Some compensation neurotics have acquired a certain fame in neuro-psychiatric literature because their unusual symptoms attracted the interest of clinicians who, after painstaking investigations, published their findings in great detail to prove that all the psychological anomalies they had uncovered were due to organic brain damage. Mr. Schn., for example, a German soldier, was wounded in the occipital region by mine splinters in 1915 and was subsequently unconscious for four days[191, 192]. He made a good physical recovery, but complained of dizziness and buzzing in his ears. After seven months, a small iron splinter was removed from the back of his head, but this only added headaches to the list of his complaints. Eventually he was transferred to a neuropsychiatric hospital for a complete investigation. There his behaviour was found to be fairly normal. Yet clinical examinations and carefully designed psychological tests revealed that he suffered from visual agnosia.

Mr. Schn. was unable to recognize individual letters by sight, whenever his visual agnosia was formally tested. It was, however, peculiar that, in spite of his handicap, he could read. A solution of this paradox seemed to offer itself eventually: Schn. read with the help of movements that traced the outline of letters. 'Careful observation disclosed that his "reading" was accomplished by a series of minute eye and head movements. . . . An especially interesting aspect of the case was the patient's own ignorance of his device. Even after our discovery, we found it difficult to *persuade* him that his procedure was not the customary one' (italics added)[191]. Mr. Schn. was discharged from the Army and received a 70 per cent disability pension. During subsequent clinical investigations, it was found that his statements were unreliable and contradictory[27, 270]. Although he was not obviously handicapped in everyday life, his behaviour in hospital always revealed complicated visual symptoms. Outside the hospital, he had no difficulty in running his own food shop, in working in a railway ticket office, or in performing the duties of a mayor in a small town[100]. Yet, in hospital, his vision was too poor for any of these occupations. Whatever may have been the nature of the original symptoms of Mr. Schn., there seems little doubt about the hysterical component in his later symptoms.

Another misdiagnosed compensation neurotic, who created quite a stir among German psychiatrists, was Mr. Br. In 1926, at the age of 24, he was overcome by carbon monoxide fumes while working on blast furnaces and was unconscious for an hour or slightly more. After a week in hospital, he was discharged fit for work at his own wish. However, a week later, he showed signs of a Korsakoff dysmnesic syndrome. He could not remember anything since the accident, was unable to retain new experiences, and had difficulty in orienting himself in space and time. Two months later, he was admitted to a hospital for observation, and afterwards given a disability pension of 100 per cent because of his memory disturbance and his forgetting of new experiences after three to five seconds. After his discharge from hospital, he and his fiancée (who was 11 years his senior), moved to their small Bavarian home town.

In the following year, he was examined by two professors of psychiatry at the University of Würzburg[203], who found that his symptoms were quite unusual and seemed to throw new light on the brain pathology of memory disorders. He did not show the usual constellation of symptoms characteristic of the dysmnesic syndrome. His only symptom was his inability, since the accident, to retain new memories for more than one to one-and-a-half-seconds, so that he lived in a continual present, as though his existence had been broken up into isolated, 'punched-out', seconds of being. He was shown as the man with the 'one-second memory' at meetings of German psychiatrists in 1930 and 1933, films were made of his peculiar reactions and behaviour, and newspapers carried his story to a wide public. He could not even repeat the German word '*Hass*,' but stopped at '*Ha—*' because he could not remember what he had wanted to say; he could only understand brief sentences, provided they were reiterated often enough; he referred to his wife (whom he had married in 1930) as his fiancée; he greeted her after the shortest absence, as though he had not seen her for a long time; he still thought that it was 1926 and that he was still employed at the blast furnaces.

Some psychiatrists expressed doubt, from the start, about the organic nature of this unusual clinical picture. However, nothing was done to clarify the diagnosis until the Second World War was over. In 1948, he was examined by a professor at the University of Erlangen, who rejected the previous diagnosis of an organic memory disorder and reported: 'His whole behaviour justifies a reasonable doubt in the organic origin of his symptoms and suggests rather a hysterical amnesia due to a psychogenic repression, a systematic dissociation of all experiences since the accident and of everything he continues to experience daily'[440].

The publication of this report in 1950, started a battle royal. The Würzburg professors sharply criticized it and sent some doctors to Mr. Br.'s home town, who found that he had moved to a new house, but that his whole condition was unchanged and could not, in their opinion, be regarded as hysterical[204]. In 1955, the Erlangen professor visited the patient's home town and collected information from reliable informants that Mr. Br. was capable of finding his own way to and from his new house, that he could join in normal conversation and make quick-witted remarks, that he had carried out such tasks as building a fence and a shed without having to consult special notes, that he in fact showed no signs of any memory disturbance in his everyday life[441].

When this new information was published in May 1956, the Würzburg professors sent two of their assistants along to disprove the accusation that Mr. Br. was shamming. The assistants acted like detectives. Under the guise of being tourists, they rented a room opposite the patient's house and kept him and his wife under observation for a fortnight. They also seem to have resorted to the ethically even more dubious device of secretly tape-recording conversations the patient had with his wife and other people. Eventually they visited the patient and disclosed their identity. They obtained from the wife an open admission that he had improved, but had exaggerated his symptoms when medically examined because, so the wife maintained, the doctors had expected him to have these symptoms[519]. There could be no further controversy. The Würzburg professors admitted that Mr. Br. may have shown a mixture of malingered and hysterical symptoms for years, but they re-emphasized their conviction that his original memory disorder had been of organic origin[205].

Self-indulgent Convictions

Finally, we must also take note of the fact that autosuggestion and dissociation may produce hysterical disorders which cannot be called illnesses because they are not composed of morbid symptoms that cause suffering and concern. Such hysterical disorders do not derive from hypochondriacal convictions and disease-rewarding situations, but from self-indulgent convictions and from social situations which promise to reward such self-indulgence. The most impressive illustration of self-indulgent convictions occurs in women who fervently desire to have a child and succeed in producing hysterical changes of bodily functions, which imitate the changes normally occurring in pregnancy.

Self-indulgent convictions can also give rise to changes of physical or mental functions, which appear curative rather than pathogenic, though the curative effect is usually ill-sustained. The social situations in which such hysterical reactions occur are often those in which a person fears that he will be made to suffer pain, or an increase of pain. Thus a person with toothache, who is forced to visit his dentist, fears the increased suffering that may be in store for him. His desire to have no toothache may turn into a self-verifying conviction. As soon as he enters the dentist's waiting room, he finds that the toothache has gone. This hysterical analgesia, is, however, hardly ever of sufficiently long duration to make the visit to the dentist unnecessary. Similar temporary analgesias occur also in other medical situations, and may seriously mislead doctors who carry out a physical examination of the patient.

Other self-indulgent convictions can give rise, in suitably predisposed persons, to hysterical manifestations which benefit them at the expense of their social environment. Such persons may succeed in convincing themselves of the truth of hysterical pseudo-memories, and are thus enabled to enact confidence tricks with the deceptive appearance of complete sincerity and assurance. The blatant exploitation of such hysterical paramnesias is, however, generally not accepted as the morbid symptom of an illness; it is usually condemned as an inconsiderate self-indulgence that deserves punishment rather than treatment.

CHAPTER 21

THE DESCRIPTIVE PSYCHOPATHOLOGY OF HYSTERICAL SYMPTOMS

As hysterical symptoms express hypochondriacal and self-indulgent desires, they can be protean in their variety and variability. To bring some order into the vast and wide-ranging field of hysterical symptoms, we shall therefore subdivide them into disorders of consciousness, memory, motility, perception, emotion and autonomic functions. The subdivision is obviously arbitrary because many hysterical symptoms could be listed under several headings.

Hysterical Disorders of Consciousness

The autosuggestive and dissociative capacity of hysterical patients often causes an altered state of consciousness, a *hysterical trance*. In its most dramatic form, a deep trance sets in with paroxysmal suddenness so that the patient loses contact with the environment very abruptly, and falls down unconsciously. Such a hysterical fit can manifest itself clinically in different forms. The patient, who is usually female, slides, slumps or crashes to the ground. There she may lie limp or rigid; or she may quake, jerk or writhe in epileptiform contortions, sometimes silent, sometimes screaming, moaning, crying or laughing.

A hysterical fit can be even more impressive and spectacular than a major epileptic seizure, but the hysterical patient does not bite his tongue, is hardly ever incontinent, and always escapes serious injury. Even if she seems to fall dangerously, perhaps hurling herself down some stairs, she sustains no more than superficial abrasions and bruises. The trance of the hysterical fit never reaches the depth of unconscious stupor in a major epileptic attack. Unlike epileptics therefore, patients in a hysterical fit show signs of purposive activity. This becomes most obvious when they actively resist attempts to be examined and, for example, tightly close their eyes as soon as they feel someone is trying to open them.

In another variety of hysterical trance, the patient lives in an autistic world which is largely populated by his own imaginings and fantasies. In such a hysterical twilight state, or *hysterical delirium*, the patient has florid hallucinations and may be able to remember them, when he returns to full consciousness after a few hours or days. Patients presenting this clinical picture are rare, and their diagnosis often remains uncertain.

Hysterical Fugue

In a superficial hysterical trance, the patient's behaviour may appear quite normal to casual observers, though he enacts a hypochondriacal and self-indulgent desire to lose his personal identity, so that he can get away from it all, escape from the hackneyed routine of his daily life or from the burden of social responsibilities and obligations. As he no longer remembers who he is or what he is, he leaves his home and duties for a holiday from himself. He is then in a hysterical fugue.

Sometimes the precipitating causes of such a fugue are intuitively easy to understand. The hysterical fugue of a soldier, for instance, may take him away from the battle zone to a place of comparative safety. It needs little psychological acumen to divine the motivations that activated the soldier, once he had succeeded in going into a trance and shedding his identity. In civilian patients, such motivations are not always as clearly discernible, but it seems that feelings of fear and guilt are often the precipitating causes. The feelings are sometimes objectively justified and sometimes due to a depressive illness[476, 477]. Neuropathological changes often appear to play a predisposing role because, among the patients prone to have hysterical fugues, there are many who had suffered from a serious clouding of their sensorium before, perhaps after a head injury or a prolonged alcoholic bout[42].

In a hysterical fugue, some patients wander long distances on foot, living rough for several days until their feet are blistered and they are physically exhausted; others travel in comfort as long as their money lasts; some have no obvious goal; others make straight for a particular destination. The few patients who were observed while they were in a fugue behaved unobtrusively, and reacted normally to their physical and social environment, except that they did not recognize friends or relatives, unless these were needed to provide money or temporary shelter.

When the fugue comes to an end and the trance state disappears, the patient is left with a more-or-less total post-trance amnesia for experiences during the fugue, and perhaps also with a retrograde amnesia, blotting out the reminiscence of events which happened before the onset of his fugue. The patient is aware of a gap in his memory and that some time must have elapsed between his last reminiscence and his present circumstances. He does not know exactly what he had been doing during the amnesic gap. However, he may on coming out of the trance regain the knowledge of his personal identity, and then has little difficulty in reorienting himself. He returns home, and the fugue episode is over. There may, however, be lingering memory disorders as an aftermath of a fugue.

Hysterical Disorders of Memory

When a hysterical fugue comes to an end, the patient often does not recover his knowledge of personal identity. He is in a quandary then. His retrograde amnesia blots out all the reminiscences of his former life. He is a man without a past, a man whose reminiscences, at best, extend back to the time he came out of the hysterical fugue. Nor does he know his name, address and occupation, recognize the relatives who come to fetch him or the home to which they take him. He is usually described in lay phraseology as a man who has 'lost his memory'. Yet this phrase is incorrect. He has merely lost his reminiscences and all knowledge that is associated with his personal identity. All other knowledge that he had learned in the past is freely available to him. He can converse in the languages he had acquired, use the currency of his country, do mathematical calculations, dress correctly, and behave in a manner that does not infringe social customs and mores. His memory defect is limited to a hysterical loss of personal identity.

It is characteristic of many hysterical symptoms, and also of many mental symptoms of organic origin, that they are neither consistent nor stable. The hysterical loss of personal identity is no exception. It is common for such a patient to have islets of reminiscence and of private knowledge associated with his personal identity. He may, for instance, recognize a neighbour and perhaps even address him by his correct name, even when his closest relatives and friends appear as total strangers whom he had never set eyes on before; or he may remember which bus to take from his home to the local cinema, though he does not recognize any of the streets leading to it. Such inconsistencies, however, do not disturb the patient. Even when they are critically pointed out to him, he does not try to explain them away for he is as puzzled by them as anybody else. In this respect, he differs from the malingerer who is aware that he is responsible for all his symptoms and thus also for inconsistencies which, he feels, might give his simulation away. The malingerer thus gets flustered, when inconsistencies are noticed by others, and tries to explain them away and cover them up as well as he can.

A few patients have been known who, after coming out of a

hysterical fugue, have a loss of personal identity, but do not recognize the loss and confabulate, as it were, a new personal identity. They start a new life as persons with their own confabulated set of reminiscences. In such patients, one can with justification speak of a *dual personality*—a term that was at one time rather freely used for personality changes caused by hysterical mood changes or hypnotic suggestions. The classical example of a dual personality is the Rev. Ansel Bourne, who disappeared one day from his home, after having withdrawn a considerable sum of money from his bank. Two months later, in a distant town, a man known by the name of A. J. Brown, the owner of a small confectionery store, woke up one morning and, to his consternation, did not recognize his environment. He knew that he was the Rev. Ansel Bourne, had never heard of a man called A. J. Brown, nor of his confectionery store. He was completely at a loss to explain how he had arrived at his whereabouts.

Hysterical patients may enact the hypochondriacal desire that they are mad, and therefore deprived of all previously learned general knowledge. They then present the clinical picture of a *hysterical pseudodementia*. The most characteristic symptom of this condition is a tendency to give approximate answers, when their general knowledge is tested. They may maintain that two and two is five, that two times two is 22, that there are eight days in the week, that a spoon is a shovel, or a shoe-lace a rope. They may even forestall any questions and, on meeting their doctor, spontaneously make obviously wrong statements. They may stand in bright sunlight and remark that it is rather late at night, and when Christmas decorations are very conspicuous in the ward, they may gratuitously explain that this indicates preparations for Easter. Answers and statements of this kind seem to imply that the patients know the truth, but deliberately talk past it—a symptom that is often denoted by the German word *vorbeireden* or its equivalent English expression 'talking past the point'. Some pseudodemented patients also lose their motor knowledge of acquired skills. When asked, for instance, to use a key, or strike a match, they behave in a way that looks like a theatrical imitation of an organic apraxia, fumbling about with the key or the match in all possible ways, except the correct one. Their behaviour then often gives the impression of deliberate clowning and buffooning.

Hysterical pseudodementia is also frequently called a 'Ganser syndrome'[178, 179, 189], and the patients are said to 'ganser'. Yet the picture described by the German psychiatrist Ganser in 1898 was of a pseudodementia complicated by an altered state of consciousness that caused disorientation and hallucinations. It may be of advantage to restrict the term Ganser syndrome to pseudodemented patients having this additional complication. The behaviour of pseudodemented, or gansering, patients conveys the very distinct suggestion that it is simulated because it is so very inconsistent. Yet the patients, unlike malingerers, are not upset by inconsistencies, and are not anxiously on guard all the time to avoid them. They are quite carelessly inconsistent. A wrong reply to a particular question is often followed, a few minutes later, and quite casually, by the correct reply to the same question. Similarly, they may have been fumbling about ineffectually after being asked to strike a match, and yet perform this task faultlessly a little later, when they wish to light a cigarette. This freakish and unconcerned fluctuation between a display of ignorance, *vorbeireden* and apraxia on formal testing and a competent unconcealed efficiency in dealing with the affairs of everyday life is certainly characteristic of the hysterical pseudodement, but not of his malingering counterpart.

Yet the suspicion that hysterical pseudodements malinger is often wrongly strengthened by the fact that they have something to gain from giving the impression of being *non compos mentis* and therefore not responsible for their actions. This is particularly the case when the Ganser syndrome develops in prisoners awaiting trial or in persons claiming compensation for the decline of mental powers after an accident. Moreover, when the critical situation is over, and there is no further need for the Ganser syndrome, it disappears. Yet this dependence of the syndrome on a critical situation does not allow a retrospective differential diagnosis between malingering and hysteria.

Some Ganser patients never recover. In their case, neither malingering nor hysteria was the correct diagnosis. They are most likely to impress the experienced clinician with the fallibility of his Ganser diagnosis, or perhaps only with the uncertainty of the prognosis in these patients. The patients who recover disappear from his ken; those who do not, remain in hospital and force him to recognize that a Ganser syndrome is sometimes the overture to a schizophrenic illness, organic dementia or epilepsy. It is therefore not surprising that some clinicians have become sparing with their diagnosis of pseudodementia because they remember the patients who had turned out to be 'pseudo-pseudodements'.

There are also patients who enact the hysterical desire of having regressed to a helpless state of infancy. They lose the acquired skills of walking, talking, or of observing adult codes of manners. They may then crawl on all fours, make inarticulate talking noises, eat with their fingers, and perhaps suck their thumbs and wet their beds. This condition is known as *hysterical infantilism*, or 'hysterical puerilism'.

Hysterical Confabulations

Another hysterical disorder of memory consists in the replacement of recent reminiscences by hysterical confabulations. There is no lasting amnesia of recent events as in Korsakoff patients; the reminiscences of recent events are merely temporarily replaced by 'hallucinated' reminiscences, which are true memories to the patient, at least for a time, and untrue fabrications to outsiders. The hysterical confabulations are often as obviously derived from hysterical desires and fantasies, as they are totally at variance with objective reality.

When a child has a tendency to report confabulated reminiscences as having actually occurred, we usually take a lenient view, and attribute the child's paramnesia to the liveliness of his youthful imagination. But when such hysterical confabulations are found in adults, an impartial assessment of the symptom is hampered by moral judgments. As a result, the symptom is sternly denounced as 'pathological lying', or *pseudologia fantastica*. The stories reported to us as true are indeed often fantastic. Patients may confess to having committed a murder that had hit the headlines, although they could not possibly have been implicated; they may boast of having just met some celebrity, of having carried out a daring rescue, of having won or lost large sums of money; they may describe how and where they had just seen a ghost; or they may accuse their father of having sexually assaulted them on many occasions, claim that their physician had made sexual advances, or report that they had just been raped by a stranger in a public park in broad daylight.

There are many patients with hysterical confabulations who derive no material advantage from them; at most, they have the gratification of an occasional audience that is impressed and emotionally stirred by their story. But even this pleasure is usually only short-lived, and followed by the humiliating experience of being treated as a liar. People who live and work with such a patient soon learn to discount his stories, even when they are related most convincingly and with a wealth of circumstantial detail. They come to disbelieve him, even should he happen to speak the truth about some unusual events. Occasionally, workmates rag such a patient mercilessly, and amuse themselves by extracting from him the account of some recent adventure which they know to be fictitious because they know that the patient had been working with them in the same factory at the relevant time.

However, not all patients with hysterical confabulations suffer from their capricious memory functions. Some exploit their skill in telling convincing lies, and deliberately deceive others to obtain personal benefits. They thus embark on the career of a confidence trickster[516]. When the malpractices of confidence tricksters eventually come to light, it often seems unbelievable that they should have succeeded in duping so many people for so long. We must, however, remember that hearsay stories about them cannot convey their spell-binding impressiveness or the aura of truthfulness with which they surround their most unlikely tales. Horatio Bottomley for example, managed to fleece a large section of the British public for over 30 years, before he was finally unmasked. Until then he had been a public idol who could do no wrong. He founded the weekly magazine, *John Bull*, was twice elected Member of Parliament for South Hackney as an Independent Liberal, and was unsurpassed as a patriotic speaker in the recruiting campagin of the First World War.

The greatest of all confidence tricksters was undoubtedly the Swedish 'match king', Ivar Kreuger. For 20 years, he succeeded in duping the whole world of international finance and business. Governments would have fallen and countries gone bankrupt, had he not lent them millions of confabulated dollars. When he eventually came under suspicion in 1932, he committed suicide. It took some time before the full story of his defalcations and forgeries was finally disentangled. In retrospect, it seemed incredible that among the financiers, big businessmen, and politicians of the world, who by reputation are supposed to be hardboiled and shrewd, there had been no one who had doubted Kreuger's integrity sufficiently to insist on the usual safeguards of the commercial world and to ask for an audit of his books. Psychiatrists rarely have an opportunity to examine such artists of fraud, and are as likely to be deceived by them as much as anybody else.

Hysterical Disorders of Motility

Among the most impressive symptoms of hysteria are *motor paralyses*. They may be restricted to a hand, a foot, or a limb; involve the whole of one side of the body (hemiplegia), or only the lower parts of the body (paraplegia), or both sides of it (diplegia). Hysterical paralyses of the face or tongue are rare. Fairly common is a partial paralysis of the muscles of the vocal cords which expresses the hysterical conviction: 'My voice has gone'. Patients with such a hysterical *aphonia* cannot raise their voice above a whisper. Yet, unlike patients with an organic paralysis of the vocal cords, they can cough because they do not connect the sound of coughing with the sound of their voice. Hysterical *mutism* occurs in patients with the hysterical conviction: 'My speech has gone'.

The tone of hysterically paralysed muscles is usually normal or flaccid. Muscular rigidity is, however, sometimes present, though it differs from the muscular rigidities due to neuropathological lesions; it is increased, whenever there is an attempt to move the paralysed part passively. Hysterically paralysed muscles show no reaction of degeneration and no wasting, although there is some diminution of muscle volume in longstanding cases. The skin of hysterically paralysed limbs may become shiny, cyanosed and oedematous.

Another hysterical motor disorder consists of *tremors* which are variable in their intensity and distribution; they may be fine or coarse, localized or general, continual or spasmodic. They are displayed with ostentation and unconcern, and differ in this respect from the tremors of patients with social phobias, which are anxiously concealed.

The co-ordinated performance of skilled movements can become hysterically disorganized. This applies particularly to the skilled movements of standing and walking. Patients with such a hysterical *astasia-abasia* have no muscular paralyses, but they flop to the ground either immediately on leaving the bed or after some faltering steps. Some of these patients manage to remain upright and to move about, as long as they can hold on to something, or merely have the slightest finger-tip contact with firm objects. Hysterical *gait disturbances* can be very bizarre and exhausting manœuvres. The most peculiar antics and gyrations, requiring much skill and energy, are often performed. Some patients walk, as though they had to keep a swaying balance on a tightrope; some move slowly and painfully in a squatting position; and some crouch precariously before they dart from one handhold to another.

Hysterical disorders of motility can also affect the normal rhythm of breathing. Attacks of hysterical *hyperpnoea* or *tachypnoea* develop especially in some young girls. They may be preceded by a feeling that a sufficiently deep inspiration cannot be carried out. There is no air hunger as in dyspnoeic patients, merely a fear that respiration does not provide enough air. If an attack of hyperpnoea develops, the patient looks distressed as the rate and depth of her breathing increases, but her distress can be distinguished from that shown by patients in an attack of bronchial or cardiac asthma. The hysterical patient does not support herself on her arm to facilitate respiratory chest extension; her head does not tend to move back with every inspiration; and her speech does not come in short gasps, but in sentences long enough to reduce the rate of respiration. If hysterical hyperpnoea is prolonged, too much carbon dioxide is removed from the blood and the resulting alcalosis can give rise to tetanic symptoms, beginning with tingling in hands and feet and progressing to typical carpo-pedal spasms.

In some patients, an episode of hyperpnoea is followed by a period of apnoea with the breath held in expiration for long enough to produce cerebral anoxia and loss of consciousness. Some patients learn to use this 'breath-holding trick' deliberately, whenever they wish to stage an impressive fainting attack[241]. In children under the age of four, breath-holding attacks occur quite frequently after a spell of crying. The children quickly become cyanosed and then usually resume breathing without further ill-effects. Occasionally, however, the resumption of breathing is delayed, and such children go limp, become unconscious and may even have an epileptic fit.

Hysterical Disorders of Perception

A hypnotized person may be given the suggestion that he cannot see a table in the middle of the room. In response to questions, he then maintains that there is no table, but when he is made to move about the room, it will be noticed that he carefully avoids bumping into the table that is allegedly invisible to him. This symptom has been called a *negative hallucination*, but it is doubtful whether that is the correct appellation for it. The hypnotized subject obviously does not experience a blind spot, or positive scotoma, that obliterates the region of the table. It is more likely that he sees something where the table is, but he does not recognize this something. In that case, it would be wrong to regard the hypnotized subject as blind with regard to the table; he merely has a *hysterical agnosia*, or *hysterical imperception*, for it. That would explain why he walks around the object which he does not 'see' because he has no cognition of it.

Hysterical imperception of a particular object is only encountered as a hypnotic or post-hypnotic symptom. But the symptom of hysterical blindness is encountered in the clinic, and we may also consider it a symptom of imperception rather than an actual loss of visual sensations, such as occurs in organic blindness. Similar considerations may also apply to hysterical deafness and a hysterical loss of taste or smell. The most common hysterical imperception concerns the cutaneous sensations of touch, temperature and pain. It is usual to speak of a hysterical anaesthesia or analgesia then because the patient does not recognize it, when he is touched or pricked in the skin area involved. This terminological inaccuracy, has, however, contributed its part to the misunderstanding of hysterical patients.

It can easily be shown that the so-called hysterical anaesthesia, is, in reality, a hysterical imperception. A patient with a hysterical anaesthesia of the left side of the body, for instance, may be instructed to close his eyes and to say 'Yes' when he feels touched, and 'No' when he does not. We then touch his chest at irregular intervals along a line running from right to left. As soon as we cross the midline of his body, his 'Yes's' become 'No's'. This test was, at one time, regarded as unmasking the deception of an unintelligent malingerer, or the self-deception of a naïve hysterical patient. The reasoning was that, if he had really been anaesthetic and felt nothing, he should not have known when to say 'No'. Yet the self-deception belonged to the examining doctor rather than the hysterical patient who felt something which he did not recognize as a touch, and to which he therefore responded with a 'No'.

Comparable observations have been made in hysterically blind or deaf patients. A hysterically blind patient shows a normal blink reflex when the doctor quickly and unexpectedly moves his hand towards the blind eye. A hysterically deaf patient behaves like a person with normal hearing and raises his voice when a Bárány noise box is put in his ear; his speech becomes disorganized like that of a normal person when he is made to hear a delayed feedback of his voice.

The skin area which is hysterically anaesthetic or analgesic can vary in size; it can extend over the whole surface of the body or over only a more or less well defined part. The borders of the anaesthetic areas are more sharply defined than in comparable organic anaesthesias. In organic hemianaesthesia, for example, the loss of sensation does not begin exactly in the midline, but it begins there in hysterical imperceptions of one side of the body. The hysterical imperception of a hand or a leg usually covers the area that corresponds to the idea 'hand' or 'leg', and is therefore said to have a 'glove' or 'stocking' distribution. The same distribution has, however, also been found in some organic patients suffering from polyneuritis or subacute combined degeneration. Anaesthesia of the cornea or pharynx is indicated by the absence of corneal or pharyngeal reflexes in response to touch stimuli. Their absence was regarded by Charcot as a stigma of the hysterical predisposition, but this assumption has since been abandoned as untenable.

Some hysterical patients have an imperception of postural sensations. They cannot indicate, with closed eyes, the position of a limb after it had been passively moved. The same inability is present as a clinical sign in patients with organic ataxia. But hysterical patients are not ataxic; their loss of postural sensations is not due to a proprioceptive anaesthesia which, through an impairment of neural feedback regulations, invariably causes ataxia.

Vaginal anaesthesia can be a hysterical symptom of imperception that contributes to a patient's frigidity. The imperception may be present with some sexual partners only and not with others. Similarly, some men suffer from a hysterical phallic anaesthesia during sexual intercourse with some partners and not with others, or only during intercourse, but not when masturbating.

A special variety of hysterical imperception occurs in some patients who strenuously deny suffering from some organic symptoms which are conspicuously obvious to others. A hysterical denial of organic symptoms can be present in young persons who,. for the sake of some much desired pleasure, temporarily succeed in suppressing all awareness of symptoms which threaten to spoil their chances of enjoyment. The symptom is more commonly and lastingly present in people of advanced age who deny the signs of senescence and cling to a body image of themselves that has been overtaken by time. It is often found in otherwise healthy people who develop insidious deafness. They often indignantly refuse to have a hearing aid, claiming that there is nothing wrong with their hearing, if only other people would stop dropping their voices and speaking indistinctly. A comparable hysterical denial of failing eyesight in otherwise healthy persons is not as common. The deterioration of memory with age is also usually recognized by a healthy senescent person and accepted with resignation.

Clinical interest in the denial of organic symptoms was first aroused by some brain-injured patients with a left-sided hemiplegia. Babinski[19] introduced the name 'anosognosia' for it in 1914. There are, of course, many other neuro-pathological symptoms for which an agnosia, or denial, can develop; urinary or faecal incontinence, involuntary movement, blindness, aphasia, alexia, and so on. Many neurologists regard anosognosia as an organically determined symptom because it occurs in organically brain-damaged patients. There have also been attempts to link it with lesions of the parietal lobe, especially that of the non-dominant hemisphere. It occurs, however, with lesions in many other parts of the brain, and it sometimes seems to depend on a clouding of consciousness. It has been noticed, for example, that, when anosognosia has disappeared in a patient, it can be reactivated by a lowering of consciousness through an intravenous injection of sodium amytal.

Hysterical disorders of perception can also consist in hallucitions. They occur particularly during deep hysterical trances and twilight states. They may be composed of several sensory modalities, but visual hallucinations are usually predominant. The hallucination of hysterical pain generally occurs in patients with a lucid sensorium. There is often a discrepancy between the patient's complaints and his relatively undisturbed behaviour, especially when his attention is diverted. On no account should the diagnosis of a hysterical pain be made exclusively dependent on the patient's histrionic and flowery description of his suffering. A histrionic personality will present even organic symptoms in this overdemonstrative way.

Hysterical Disorders of Emotions

When hysterical symptoms provide the patient with an opportunity to escape from a harassing social situation, the suffering and concern caused by his handicaps are tempered with a peculiarly bland indifference, a *belle indifférence*, about the significance and prognosis of his illness. In this respect, such a patient is the very opposite of a hypochondriac whose whole life is continually centred on his illness and his symptoms. A hysterical patient, for instance, who has lost his personal identity after a fugue is not as distressed as one would expect him to be. Similarly, a patient with hysterical pseudodementia may give the impression of being pleased, when he displays his ignorance, and he certainly does not get flustered by the baffling inconsistencies in his knowledge and behaviour.

Hysterical *belle indifférence* must be distinguished from the emotional apathy shown by many schizophrenics and by patients with a mild clouding of consciousness. The emotional unconcern of these non-hysterical patients extends to everything they are doing; very often, they are too indolent to do anything at all. They pay as little attention to any of their symptoms as to their environment, unless it becomes too obtrusive, when it may elicit irritation and negativistic responses.

Belle indifférence is, however, by no means the only emotional disorder that can be found in hysterical patients. Many of them have a 'histrionic personality' which is the very opposite of emotional blandness and unconcern. People with this personality can gain fame on the stage, the screen, or in occupations in which the enactment of artificial, and yet convincing, emotions is required. But the other talents needed for such careers, or the opportunities to embark on them, are not available to every histrionic personality. Socially less acceptable outlets may then be found. Such a person often tends to be conspicuous in social gatherings because he likes the limelight. In his personal relations he can be difficult, if he manœuvres people into situations which offer plausible outlets for his emotional displays. Only when such displays cause suffering and concern, is it justified to regard them as morbid symptoms and to speak of 'hysterical emotionality'.

Patients with hysterical emotionality can subdue and dominate their family and friends with demands for supplies of love and consideration, with angry scenes, temper outbursts, anxiety attacks, accusations, self-pitying depressions, and many other emotional demonstrations. But such temperamental histrionics do not last as a rule. When one set of feeling has been gratified, another set may take its place. After a storm of angry and destructive feelings, there may be an equally intense enjoyment of conciliatory and affectionate feelings. Some patients with hysterical emotionality are labile in their moods and continually dissatisfied because the bliss of any emotional gratification soon wears thin and stale. Such patients crave diversion and change at all cost, even at the cost of hurting and deserting those around them. The enjoyment of love, affection and sexual activity soon loses its initial appeal for them, and the spice of some novelty is needed to revive it. They may then experiment with perversions or new partners; or seek to heighten their enjoyment with the help of alcohol and drugs.

Normal histrionic personalities are not necessarily unstable in their mood. Nor are they domineering and assertive in their dealings with other people. On the contrary, they tend to be sociable, extraverted, charming, and helpful people. Yet their emotional expressions often leave an aftertaste of insincerity and artificiality. Many histrionic women are flirtatious and sexually attractive; yet they are often unable to react with sexual emotions. The men who are attracted by them have to content themselves with a promise of sexual intimacy that never materializes, or if it does, is a cold and heartless affair.

Many histrionic women indulge emotions of submissiveness. It is their desire to serve the emotional demands of others in a maternal or philanthropic way. They may thus be found among the entourage of a popular leader, subjecting themselves to his histrionic needs and manipulations; and they are often also attracted to such Samaritan professions as nursing or social work. When histrionic submissiveness becomes excessive, it turns into emotional bondage. The most typical example of this is the bondage that exists between a hypnotized person and the hypnotist. It is said to exist also between some prostitutes and their souteneurs. A temporary form of emotional bondage develops in people who are sexually so infatuated that they abandon a settled life, rebel against family ties and social propriety, and risk financial ruin or loss of prestige for the pleasure of being near their idol.

Emotional bondage is, however, not always of a positive kind. Aggressive elements may predominate and cause hysterical spite reactions. They are primarily directed against persons with whom the patient was in love once, and among these may be employers, doctors and psychotherapists. The patients viciously pursue their target, accusing and denigrating it with all the weapons at their disposal, including hysterical symptoms, such as emotional scenes, paramnesias, and pathological lying.

Hysterical Disorders of Autonomic Functions

In patients with dissociative capacities, hysterical convictions can produce a constriction of the arterioles and capillaries in discrete areas. This is, for instance, clearly shown by some patients in a hysterical trance who can inflict wounds on themselves which hardly bleed. There can also be a dilatation of arterioles and capillaries in discrete areas. The most frequent example of this reaction occurs in anxiety neurotics with a fear of blushing. When discrete hyperaemia is prolonged, urticarial weals are formed. A patient has been described who, in a somnambulistic state, re-enacted a conviction that he had, ten years previously, been restrained by having his arms tied with ropes behind his back so that he should not be able to walk in his sleep. He had nevertheless struggled free. During the re-enactment of this apparent memory in an artificially produced somnambulistic state ten years later, 'weals appeared on both forearms; gradually these became indented; and finally some fresh petechial haemorrhages appeared along their course'[368]. The patient was under close observation at that time, and trickery was ruled out. The hysterical rope marks remained visible for hours and could be clearly photographed.

In the pathology of urticarial weals, it is not only a dilatation of blood vessels that is involved, but also an increased exudation of fluid into the tissues, perhaps combined with petechial bleeding. The exudation of fluid can be marked enough to produce blisters, as investigations with hypnotic suggestions have indicated[121, 432]. Other investigations have similarly indicated that hypnotic suggestions can also reduce the exudation of fluid, for example after intracutaneous injections of tuberculin in previously Mantoux-positive subjects[48, 541].

It is possible, and indeed likely, that rubbing movements usually assist in the hysterical production of blisters and petechiae. They may also contribute to the hysterical creation of superficial skin erosions from which clear or bloodstained fluid oozes. Manifestations of this kind are subsumed under the general heading of *dermatitis artefacta*. The extent to which unconscious dissociative mechanisms and conscious malingering machinations respectively contribute to the genesis of dermatitis artefacta obviously varies from patient to patient and time to time.

Among the manifestations of dermatitis artefacta are some which are inspired by hysterical convictions of a religious nature. Such patients may develop the *stigmata of Christ* in the form of bloodstained erosions on their forehead, their hands and feet, and in the region of the liver. The first to show some of these stigmata was St Francis of Assisi in 1224. More than 300 cases of stigmatization have since been reported, most of them women. The manifestations generally appear on Fridays, and with special intensity on Good Friday. Among the best-known stigmatists of recent years have been Theresa Neumann of Konnersreuth in Germany and the Italian Capuchin monk, Padre Pio.

Hysterical convictions can also interfere with many other autonomic functions. The most common disturbance of gastric functions is hysterical vomiting. It consists in a rapid regurgitation of food during or after a meal. The patients do not appear to suffer from nausea, nor do they complain about it. When their fit of vomiting is over, they can resume their meal without any ill effect. They hardly ever lose weight. A hysterical retention of urine occurs occasionally in young girls, and has been known to lead to a minor epidemic of urinary retention in girls' schools.

Fear of being pregnant can cause hysterical amenorrhoea in many women. A greater dissociative predisposition is, however, indicated, when women with a hysterical desire to be pregnant develop amenorrhoea, and an enlargement of their abdomen and breasts so that they look just like pregnant women. The clinical picture of such a hysterical pregnancy, or *pseudocyesis* can be so convincing that even doctors are occasionally deceived by it. When the time of confinement arrives, the patient may develop rhythmic pains, indistinguishable from those of normal labour. One such patient has even been reported who narrowly escaped a Caesarean operation[47].

The pseudocyesis of some patients has acquired historical fame. Mary Tudor[313], for instance, believed herself 'quicke of childe' four months after her marriage to Philip II of Spain, and ordered thanksgiving services to be held in all the churches of the London diocese. Eigth months after her marriage, in April 1555, she retired to Hampton Court and made arrangements for her confinement. In May, letters were prepared to be sent to foreign courts by special ambassadors, announcing the birth of a child. But when June and July went by uneventfully, the truth could not longer be hidden that the signs of pregnancy in the Queen owed their origin only to a hysterical conviction and a fervent desire to bear a child.

Among patients with hysterical disorders of autonomic functions there is a peculiar group with a craving for medical or surgical attention, who repeatedly develop alarming symptoms which are partly due to genuine hysterical processes and partly to deliberate simulation and faking. The name 'Munchausen syndrome'[18, 23, 82, 224] has recently been introduced to characterize the variety of clinical pictures these patients can present. The choice of name is not very felicitous as Baron Munchausen was merely a pleasantly mendacious storyteller and not a person given to the production of hysterical symptoms. Yet the name has served its purpose to draw attention to this group of patients and the special problems they present. Many of them have had some training as nurses or acquired considerable medical knowledge in pursuit of their aim to feign a convincing medical or surgical illness. They do not shrink from injuring or damaging themselves secretly to add verisimilitude to the clinical picture. They may produce dermatitis artefacta by stealthy means, such as by the clandestine application of corroding acids or the furtive stabbing of the skin with dirty needles. They may keep operation wounds open by deliberate interference, cause hyperthyroidism by taking thyroid tablets, or produce pain and swelling in an arm by keeping a tight band around it which they remove and hide before a medical examination. They may falsify thermometer readings to simulate pyrexia, bang their nose until epistaxis occurs, or prick themselves to obtain enough blood to feign bleeding from the ears, the throat, or the urinary tract. Some of these patients lead ordered and obsessionally regulated lives in between their malingering episodes, others are unsettled wanderers with many aliases. Some are frequently admitted to hospitals as emergency cases with symptoms suggestive of serious abdominal, gynaecological, neurological or cardiac complications. Some have had repeated laparotomies for suspected perforations of peptic ulcers, intestinal obstructions, ectopic pregnancies, or because they had swallowed glass, nails or open safety pins[308]; some eventually admit their various deceptions, others adamantly deny them and become angry at the first indication of being under suspicion.

PART IV

RECENT DEVELOPMENTS

Since the original edition of this book some advances have been made in the field of psychopathology of which an account will be given here.

CHAPTER 22

DEFINITION OF DISEASE

Some consideration was given in the early pages of this book to the definition of clinical symptoms and of clinical disease entities. Clinical symptoms were provisionally defined as abnormal deviations from population and/or individual standards which are directly observable by the patient or his social environment and cause suffering and concern to them. Since clinical disease entities are constructed from clinical symptoms, this provisional definition also applies to them; they are symptom complexes which are abnormal by population and/or individual standards, are directly observable and cause suffering and concern to the patients and their social environment.

It has been remarked that the definition of disease is not just a problem of psychiatry, but one that concerns medicine in general (cf. McHugh, 1975). There have been few attempts to come to grips with this problem as it seems too intractable for a generally acceptable solution. Scadding (1967) attempted to formulate a definition which, in essence, proposed that a disease is composed of clinical and pathological manifestations which are abnormal by population standards in such a way that they gave rise to a biological disadvantage. Scadding was well aware that the concept of biological disadvantage was 'rather vague' and he therefore wisely refrained from trying to clarify it. An attempt at such a clarification was made by Kendell (1975) who stipulated that the concept of biological disadvantage 'must embrace both increased mortality and reduced fertility'. Unfortunately, this had some unusual implications. For example, it excluded conditions like post-herpetic neuralgia or psoriasis from the domain of diseases because they did not shorten life, and it included homosexuality because it reduced fertility.

I have been looking for a different kind of solution by means of expanding my provisional definition of clinical symptoms and clinical disease entities in such a way that it should become generally applicable at least to human diseases (Taylor, 1971–2, 1976, 1979). To achieve this, notice had to be taken of the established knowledge of clinical syndromes of which doctors are aware but not laymen, and of the diagnostically useful clinical signs which can be elicited by doctors and their paramedical colleagues with the help of special

279

investigations that may call on highly sophisticated technical procedures. To obtain the required expansion of my provisional definition a distinction had to be made between the concern aroused by disease manifestations in the patient himself or his social environment, on the one hand, and in his doctors, on the other. These two kinds of concern have been called 'therapeutic' and 'medical' respectively.

It is therefore proposed to define human diseases as consisting of manifestations which are not only abnormal by population or individual standards, but also characterized by at least one of the following criteria: (1) they arouse therapeutic concern for himself in the patient, (2) they evoke therapeutic concern for him in his social environment, or (3) they elicit medical concern for him in his doctors.

It must be admitted that this definition has its shortcomings since it relies so largely on the psychological reactions of therapeutic or medical concern. These are liable to be swayed by individual or cultural biases. In particular, the recognition of psychiatric diseases can vary at different times and in different places. Even today, many a chronic schizophrenic in the community who comes before a court on some minor charge will sometimes receive therapeutic concern and be sent to hospital and at other times fall victim to punitive views which land him in prison.

The proposed definition of disease can therefore not claim to provide definitive diagnostic criteria, yet it seems to come close to the actual practice followed in diagnosing disease.

CHAPTER 23

THE XYY SYNDROME

Among men with a trisomy of sex chromosomes, there are not only those in whom the X chromosome is doubled (it can indeed be more than doubled) to produce a sex complement of XXY and the clinical picture of the Klinefelter syndrome, but also men in whom the Y chromosome is doubled so that they have a sex complement of XYY. It seemed at one time that such an XYY complement had dire consequences in that it was always associated with a special clinical syndrome consisting of an emotional instability with criminal propensities, an abnormally tall stature and intellectual retardation (Jacobs *et al.*, 1965; Price *et al.*, 1966). Thus the possibility was considered that people with XYY chromosomes might be entitled to plead diminished responsibility, when accused of a crime. Pitcher (1971) cited three cases in which convicted murderers received relatively lenient sentences because their XYY chromosomes seemed to have been taken into account as extenuating factors.

In due course, it was, however, realized that this view of the effect of XYY chromosomes was largely mistaken. It had been formed because of the unexpected finding that there were quite a few men with XYY chromosomes in high-security prison hospitals and they tended to have an abnormally tall stature. But inferences drawn from findings in highly exceptional populations are almost bound to be biased and misleading. It is therefore not surprising that attention was soon directed to the existence of XYY males with an unblemished reputation, normal height, or a level of intelligence that was average and even occasionally superior. The upshot has been the realization that XYY men can be so inconspicuous that there must be many of them in the general population whose chromosomal peculiarity has gone undetected. On the other hand, there is certainly a tendency in many XYY men to be emotionally and socially unstable from an early age, and to be taller and less intelligent than their siblings.

Pitcher (1971), taking into account five independent investigations of 10,000 infants in Edinburgh and North America, calculated that there are about 1·5 XYY infants among 1,000 live male births. A similar frequency of 1·24/1,000 among adult males in Denmark was reported by Nielsen and Christensen (1974). These authors found that in Danish psychiatric hospitals, not containing criminals or mentally retarded patients, the frequency of XYY males was 3·21/1,000 which was not significantly higher than in the general population. On the other hand, the frequency of XYY males in Danish institutions for criminals was 8·76/1,000 and this was a highly significant increase (P < 0·001). In maximum-security prison hospitals, the frequency is apparently even far greater. According to a leader writer in the *Lancet* (1974), the incidence of XYY males among the admissions to four such hospitals in England, Wales and Scotland in 1972 and 1973 was 21/1,000, and 70 per cent of them were youths aged between 15 and 20 years. The same writer also mentioned that W. H. Price in an unpublished assessment had put the risk of being admitted to such a hospital during a life time as ten times greater for XYY males than for XY males, namely 1 per cent compared with 0·1 per cent.

CHAPTER 24

THE PREVALENCE OF PHENYLKETONURIA
(PKU)

Early investigations in South Sweden seemed to indicate that PKU occurred in about one child among 40,000 (Larson, 1954). This means that many people in a population must be heterozygous carriers of the PKU gene. The mathematics of establishing their number is fairly simple. If q is the proportion of the PKU gene in a population and p the proportion of the non-PKU gene in that population, then $p + q = 1$, if there is only this pair of allelic genes to be considered. Since q is very small in our example, we can regard p as being close to one. The proportions of the three possible combinations of the two genes is given by the well-known algebraic formula $(p + q)^2 = p^2 + 2pq + q^2$. The proportion of people with two PKU genes is q^2. If this proportion is 1 : 40,000, q is 1 : 200. The proportion of heterozygotes is 2pq and this approximates to 1 per cent of the population examined.

More recent and refined methods of establishing the frequency of PKU patients in the general population of the United States indicates that this frequency is greater than had been previously accepted. According to McCready and Hussey (1964), the frequency is 1 : 10,000. This means that 2 per cent of the population of the United States are heterozygous carriers. Partington (1964) found even higher frequencies in Canada which would indicate that 4 per cent or more of the population are heterozygous carriers. However, some caution in accepting these higher figures is advisable. It was shown (Stephenson and McBean, 1967) that in some children the liver enzyme that transforms phenylalanine into tyrosine (namely phenylalanine hydroxylase) becomes fully active only some time after birth. Therefore, if infants are tested too early, they may be wrongly diagnosed as suffering from PKU and perhaps be subjected unnecessarily to a rather trying and difficult therapeutic diet.

It should also be mentioned that PKU genes are rare in many ethnic groups. They are rare, for instance, in Ashkenazi Jews (Cohen *et al.*, 1961) and in American negroes (Katz and Menkes, 1964).

CHAPTER 25

THE GENETICS OF MALE HOMOSEXUALITY

Kallmann (1952) had been able to collect 37 male homosexuals who had monozygotic (MZ) co-twins and all of them turned out to be homosexuals as well. By contrast, in 26 same-sexed dizygotic (DZ) male twin pairs, the concordance for homosexuality was only 12 per cent. These findings suggested that male homosexuality was entirely genetic in origin. However, Kallmann (1960) soon realized that his results had been artificially distorted because it had been made difficult for him to find normal co-twins of male homosexuals. Today we still do not definitely know what the concordance rate for homosexuality is in male MZ twin pairs. Heston and Shields (1968) estimated that it lies between 40 and 60 per cent so that, if one partner of a male MZ twin pair is homosexual, the other partner is about just as likely to be homosexual as heterosexual. They felt certain that the concordance rate was much lower in DZ twin pairs. Unfortunately, they had to base their opinions on the investigations of only 5 MZ and 7 DZ pairs and these numbers are too small to allow reliable conclusions.

Since DZ twins are genetically comparable to non-twin siblings, it might be thought that investigations into the frequency of homosexuality in families could throw light on the genetic contribution to homosexuality. Yet this has not happened so far. West (1977, p. 77) explains: 'The secrecy that surrounds sexual habits, especially within the family circle, prevents the investigator obtaining reliable estimates of how many relatives of a known homosexual may be similarly inclined'.

However, if the sexual habits of siblings are hard to establish, the diagnosis of their sex certainly does not offer comparable difficulties. Such investigations were carried out originally by Lang and Jensch in Germany (cf. Lang, 1960) on almost 4,000 men known to the police for homosexual offences. The theoretical basis for these investigations turned out to be wrong, but its prediction that there would be more brothers than sisters among the siblings was confirmed, especially for the almost 2,500 homosexual men over 25 years of age. The male-female ratio among their siblings was $125 \cdot 2 : 100$ compared with a ratio of $106 \cdot 6 : 100$ among the siblings of nearly 1,300 heterosexual men. The difference was highly significant statistically ($P < 0 \cdot 001$). Not all subsequent investigators obtained similar results, but the numbers of homosexuals examined by them were not large enough to invalidate the above findings. For example, such experienced authors as Slater and Cowie (1971, p. 120) continue to hold the opinion that 'the Lang-Jensch data still have to be taken seriously'. Further research is obviously called for and future investigators may find it easier to obtain homosexual samples in the general population instead of having to rely on police records and hospital patients.

There are still other unusual findings in the families of male homosexuals (and apparently also of lesbians). Slater (1962) examined a consecutive series of 401 male homosexuals admitted to the Bethlem Royal and Maudsley Hospitals, London, during 1949–60 and established the ages of their mothers at the time of the patients' births. He took as his standard the mean maternal age of 28·5 years which had been derived by Penrose (1961) from the Registrar General returns for maternal ages at parturition in the general population of England and Wales in 1939. Since most of Slater's patients were born before 1939, this was an insecure standard. It was found that the mean maternal age at the birth of the homosexual patients was 31·3 years which was significantly higher than that in the general population. Slater thus put forward the hypothesis that some chromosomal anomaly associated with late maternal age may play a part in the causation of homosexuality.

Investigations by Tsuang (1966) seemed to indicate that late maternal ages might contribute not only to the occurrence of homosexuality but also to the occurrence of psychiatric diseases generally. He examined 501 male and 581 female adult patients discharged from the Maudsley Hospital, London, in 1961–62 with various psychiatric diagnoses. Using the same standard of maternal mean age as Slater, he found an apparently highly significant increase of maternal mean age at the birth of these patients to a value of 29·3. It thus seemed that Slater's hypothesis was not specific for homosexuality.

It turned out that the flaw in some of these conclusions was the standard of mean maternal age at parturition in the general population in 1939 which had been accepted as the norm. Abe and Moran (1969) examined 291 of Slater's male homosexual patients for whom the ages of both parents at the patients' birth were known. They, first of all, pointed to evidence that the mean maternal ages at parturition had consistently dropped from about 30 years at the beginning of this century to a figure below 29 years in the late 1930s. Using these figures, they arrived at a mean maternal age at parturition in the general population of 29·385 years. This was very near the value obtained by Tsuang in psychiatric patients and thus invalidated his conclusion.

Yet the mean maternal age at the birth of Slater's homosexual male patients was still significantly above 29·385. It was 31·692. But the figure was even higher for the patients' fathers; their mean age at the patients' birth was 34·940 compared with an estimated age of 31·785. On further investigation, it became clear that the high maternal age was only secondary to the shift in the paternal age. It thus seemed that the occurrence of homosexual tendencies was primarily related to the greater age of fathers.

But was this relation a genetic one or due to psychological influences? Moran (1972) appeared to favour the former possibility. West (1977), in his comprehensive survey of the problems of homosexuality, leaned towards the second possibility. He stated (p. 108): 'If elderly fathers are important [in the genesis of male homosexuality], it must be for some psychological reason, such as the inability of old men to inspire sons with an adequate image of masculinity'. Yet summing up all the available evidence, West concluded (p. 84): 'Hereditary factors may have considerably more importance than is generally acknowledged. . . . The final outcome as regards sexual orientation . . . depends upon the interaction between environmental circumstances and constitutional predisposition. . . . The hereditary factor may be of relatively less importance among homosexuals who are at ease with their gender role than among those whose erotic interests are linked with cross sex temperamental and personality characteristics'.

Since homosexuality is today increasingly tolerated as a variety of sexual inclinations, it does not often arouse therapeutic or medical concern, especially as there is no successful treatment for exclusive homosexuals of Kinsey grade five or six. Homosexuality is therefore today not generally counted among human diseases, though this attitude might change should some successful treatment for exclusive homosexuality be discovered tomorrow. In any case, homosexuality still features in the International Statistical Classification of Diseases under code number 302.0.

CHAPTER 26

THE GENETICS OF SCHIZOPHRENIA

In diseases which are due to highly damaging external noxae, such as severe physical traumas or virulent infections, genetic predispositions play no role. In all other diseases, both genetic factors and adjuvant circumstances have to be taken into account. In psychiatric diseases, those adjuvant circumstances are very often thought of in terms of adverse social influences. But this approach is too blinkered. The general gene milieu is certainly of great importance in this respect and so are physical conditions in the body and the environment. Whatever form the adjuvant circumstances take, they are bound to have their effect on the manifestations and development of adverse gene endowments. Even age is an adjuvant circumstance and has to be considered in estimating the life-time risk of the occurrence of a disease which is genetically determined to a greater or lesser extent.

The problem that has given rise to much debate in the literature on schizophrenia concerns the respective aetiological significance of genetic and other, especially environmental, factors. The significance of the genetic factor can be estimated, at least in theory, from the rate of schizophrenic illnesses in the relatives of schizophrenic patients. It should be significantly higher than the corresponding rate in the general population. Yet here we meet a number of snags.

First of all, how is the rate of schizophrenic illnesses in a general population or in the family of a schizophrenic patient to be assessed? Three indicators can be used for this purpose, though they are not equally helpful. One indicator bases itself on the occurrence of new illnesses in a particular time span, such as the number of first admissions of schizophrenics to psychiatric hospitals in, say, a year. This number, divided by the size of the population concerned, yields a rate that is technically known as 'incidence'. For example, the incidence of schizophrenia derived from first admissions to psychiatric hospitals in England and Wales in 1956 was 0·018%.

When we count not only the number of new schizophrenic patients but also the number of chronic schizophrenics during a particular time span, we obtain a rate known technically as 'prevalence'. It will obviously be greater than the incidence of schizophrenia. Jablensky and Sartorius (1975) reviewed the findings of 15 prevalence investigations of schizophrenia in 12 different countries and concluded that the one-year prevalence rates lie between 0·2% and 0·4%. Cultural differences thus did apparently not affect these prevalence rates to a great extent, though there were some variations due to different diagnostic inclinations.

The third indicator additionally takes into account the probability of future illnesses of a particular kind developing in a population during the lifetime of individuals. This yields a rate that is technically known as 'disease expectancy' or as 'lifetime morbidity risk'.

In considering the rate of schizophrenia in a general population or in the family of a schizophrenic patient, it is the third indicator of disease expectancy (or lifetime morbidity risk) which provides estimates of greatest usefulness. Unfortunately, research into the disease expectancy of schizophrenia in different populations have provided widely divergent results. Zerbin-Rüdin (1967) reviewed 20 investigations in 6 different European countries and found that there was a statistically significant variation between their findings. Disregarding these disagreements, she combined the results and arrived at disease expectancies of schizophrenia which ranged from 0·42% to 2·38% with a weighted mean disease expectancy of 1·17%. Slater and Cowie (1971) considered this mean rate 'unrealistic'. They suggested deleting a Swiss investigation which had yielded rather high values. In this way they obtained a mean disease expectancy of schizophrenia for the European general population of 0·85% which was close to the arbitrary figure of 0·8% that had been generally used in the past in genetic investigations of schizophrenia. In doing so, they obviously loaded the dice in favour of positive genetic findings. This runs counter to Sir Karl Popper's (1965) advice to scientists that 'every genuine test of a theory is [or should be] an attempt to falsify it, or to refute it'. In that spirit, it would seem preferable to accept 1·17% as the mean disease expectancy of schizophrenia in a European population, even though it is far from reliable. It certainly comes close to the lifetime risk of becoming schizophrenic in England and Wales by the age of 65 which Slater and Cowie (1971) calculated as being 1·1%. Even this figure can be suspected of being too low, since it is based only on patients who had been definitely diagnosed as schizophrenics; it thus omits to take note of many possible and probable schizophrenics. In the United States, where many psychiatrists diagnose schizophrenia more readily than their European colleagues do, the lifetime risk of this disease has been estimated to lie between 1% and 2% (Yolles and Kramer, 1969).

It must also be kept in mind that the disease expectancy of schizophrenia is not the same in different social classes. In the lowest social class it is about three times as high as in the two highest social classes. This had been noticed by Hollingshead and Redlich (1958) in New Haven and by Dunham (1965) in Detroit. It is also the case in Great Britain. It gave rise at one time to speculations that among the causes of schizophrenia may be the bad and solitary living conditions in the poorer areas of big towns (e.g. Faris and Dunham, 1939). However, it was eventually demonstrated, both in England and the United States, that the explanation lay in a tendency of schizophrenics to segregate from their families and to drift downwards in the social scale, a tendency that can show itself even before definite schizophrenic symptoms have made their appearance (e.g. Hare, 1956; Goldberg and Morrison, 1963; Turner and Wagenfeld, 1967).

In the first-degree relatives of schizophrenic patients the mean disease expectancies are much greater than in the general population, especially when not only definite, but also probable, diagnoses are taken into account. Zerbin-Rüdin (1967) reviewed about twenty-five relevant investigations and from her summaries the relevant rates have been calculated (Slater and Cowie, 1971; Gottesman and Shields, 1972; Shields, 1978). The mean expectancies of definite and probable schizophrenia in the sibs of schizophrenic patients is 10·2% and in their children 13·9% (if their spouses are healthy) or 46·3 % (if their spouses are schizophrenic as well). In their parents, the mean expectancy is relatively low, namely only 5·5%. This has been interpreted as an artefact, because schizophrenic patients, especially male patients, have a decreased probability of achieving parenthood. In the parents of schizophrenics, any predisposition towards the disease must therefore have been mild or delayed in its overt manifestation. Essen-Möller (1955) took this into account and calculated a correction of the disease expectancy in the parents of schizophrenics, based on the 'risk lives' of the parents. He obtained a corrected rate of 11%. This is gratifyingly close to the disease expectancies in the sibs and children of schizoprenic patients. The mean expectancies in second-degree relatives are 3·6% or less which agrees well with theoretical expectations.

Even stronger evidence for the role of genetic factors in the aetiology of schizophrenia has come from twin studies. Since monozygotic (MZ) twins have an identical gene endowment, they should have a significantly higher concordance rate for schizophrenia than same-sex dizygotic (DZ) twins who did not inherit the same gene set. One might expect in the same-sex DZ co-twin of a schizophrenic patient a mean disease expectancy approximating the value of 10·2% in other sibs which was mentioned above.

Gottesman and Shields (1972) reviewed the relevant literature and added their own carefully evaluated study of 55 schizophrenic twin pairs.

Twin researchers before 1960 had usually chosen their index cases from severe and chronic patients in psychiatric hospitals. For this reason and because of a probable bias in favour of positive genetic findings, early twin researchers came up with concordance rates of about 60% for MZ twins and about 15% for same-sex DZ twins. Rosenthal (1962) examined these results and arrived at the conclusion that the MZ concordance rate reported was 'misleadingly high'. Twin studies have since then been more carefully conducted and have included among their index cases patients with relatively mild forms of schizophrenia. The MZ concordance rate in mild schizophrenics tends to be lower than the analogous rate in severe schizophrenics. This may be one of the reasons (and there are obviously others) why recent investigators, especially those in Scandinavian countries, have reported lower MZ concordance rates. Kringlen (1967, 1968) in Norway and Fischer *et al.* (1969) in Denmark found a concordance rate of about 25% in MZ pairs with definite schizophrenia and only about 4–10% in same-sex DZ pairs with equally definite diagnoses. When the occurrence of probable schizophrenia in co-twins was also taken into account, the figures were raised to 38–48% in MZ twins and 10–19% in same-sex DZ twins.

The results obtained in Finland by Tienari (1963) caused some stir for a while, because he could not find any schizophrenics at all in the MZ co-twins of 16 patients in whom he had made the diagnosis of schizophrenia. In later reports (1968, 1971), however, he had to correct his figures so that they are now more in line with the results of other recent studies. Gottesman and Shields (1972), in their London-based research, pooled the diagnostic opinions of six experts and obtained from them consensus diagnoses for schizophrenia and probable schizophrenia. They arrived at a concordance rate of 50% in their 22 MZ pairs and 9% in their 33 same-sex DZ pairs. In one of his last contributions to this field of study, Shields (1978) remarked: 'If forced to make a best estimate of the average morbid risk for twins of schizophrenics, it would probably be wisest to rely on the recent studies [since 1960]. Rates of approximately 50% for MZ pairs and 17% for DZ pairs may not be far from the mark'. The 50% MZ concordance rate indicates that identical twins are as often discordant as concordant with regard to schizophrenia. The illness seems to derive in about equal parts from genetic endowment and environmental influences.

To clarify the contribution by environmental influences to the genesis of schizophrenia two avenues of research are available. One of these leads to the examination of the concordance rate for schizophrenia in MZ twins who had been separated from their parents at an early age and reared apart. Gottesman and Shields (1972) report on 17 such twin pairs with a schizophrenic concordance rate of 64·7%. Shields (1978) mentions '26 or 27' such twin pairs, though many of them had not been reported in detail or had been removed from their parents relatively late. In about two-thirds of them, both twins had schizophrenia or a schizophrenia-like illness. This suggests perhaps that unfavourable conditions of rearing may add their special part to making schizophrenic predispositions manifest.

The other line of research in this field concerns adoption studies. These have been largely conducted in Denmark by the US-Danish team of Rosenthal, Kety, Wender and Schulsinger, because the Danish social registry system facilitated the detection of adoptees and their families as well as the identification of psychiatric patients among them. Kety et al. (1975) examined the records of 5,483 persons who had been adopted in childhood by non-relatives. In 33 of these persons a consensus diagnosis of schizophrenia was made by three experts. From the remaining adoptees, they chose 33 matched controls who were psychiatrically healthy. They then interviewed the biological and adoptive relatives (parents, sibs and half-sibs) of these persons to establish how many of them were schizophrenics. They cast their diagnostic net unusually wide, because they postulated that a genetic predisposition towards schizophrenia is likely to manifest itself in a wide spectrum of psychiatric disabilities. However, we shall here only consider their diagnoses of a relatively narrow spectrum disorder consisting of borderline or more severe schizophrenia. Even then one may expect some positive diagnoses among relatives that could be supposed to be free from any schizophrenic taint, namely the biological relatives of the healthy adoptees and the adoptive relatives of the healthy and schizophrenic adoptees. There were 339 such relatives and 17 of them were diagnosed as having a schizophrenic spectrum disorder of the relatively narrow kind—a prevalence rate of 5%. By contrast, in the 170 biological relatives of the schizophrenic adoptees, there were 28 with such a diagnosis—a prevalence rate of 16·5%. This was a statistically significant difference (P < 0·01). Yet the unusual diagnostic approach of this study and of others by the same US-Danish team makes it impossible to compare their findings with other investigators in this field.

Adoption studies may also examine what happens to the children of schizophrenic mothers who were unable to rear them. Heston (1966) examined 47 persons who had been adopted as children because their mothers had been chronic schizophrenic patients in Oregon State Psychiatric Hospitals. He found that in adulthood (mean age 35·8 years) there were 5 schizophrenics among them— a prevalence rate of 11% which corresponded to a disease expectancy of 16·6%. There were no schizophrenics in a control group.

Heredity thus undoubtedly plays a significant part in the genesis of many of the diseases which we at present subsume under the diagnosis of schizophrenia. There is indeed already a good deal of inconclusive debate about the genetic models that would best fit the observations made in the studies on schizophrenic families and twins (cf. Slater and Cowie, 1971; Gottesman and Shields, 1972; Shields, 1978).

But genetic predispositions are not sufficient causes of schizophrenia, since they need adjuvant circumstances to be transformed into overt illnesses. Nor are they necessary causes of schizophrenia, because there are schizophrenic and schizophrenia-like illnesses which need no special genetic underpinning, but are due to organic or toxic conditions that interfere with normal brain functions, e.g. head injuries (Achté et al., 1969), epilepsy (Slater et al., 1963), amphetamine intoxication (Connell, 1958), and other lesions (cf. Davison and Bagley, 1969; Lishman, 1978).

There have also been assertions that social conditions by themselves are responsible for schizophrenia (e.g. Bateson et al., 1956; Lidz et al., 1957; Wynne et al., 1958; Laing and Esterson, 1964). Yet these assertions have not stood the test of scientific scrutiny (Leff, 1978).

Of greater practical importance have been studies designed to elucidate some of the social influences which can precipitate a schizophrenic illness in predisposed persons. Brown and Birley (1968) and Birley and Brown (1970) found that in the three weeks before the onset or relapse of their schizophrenic illness about 60 per cent of the patients had experienced abrupt changes in their social environment or life situation for which they bore no responsibility (e.g. change of residence, changes in their jobs, changes in their families through birth, marriage or death, changes in their relationship with a partner of the opposite sex). Brown, Birley and Wing (1972) examined the quality of the emotional relationship between a schizophrenic patient and the relative with whom he lives. They found that an emotionally overcharged relationship in which criticism or anxious overprotection were openly expressed was significantly associated with a high relapse rate. Vaughn and Leff (1976) replicated this study and confirmed its findings. They also observed that the injurious effect of an emotionally overcharged relationship could be mitigated, if the patient could avoid too much face-to-face contact with the relative.

CHAPTER 27

THE GENETICS OF MANIC-DEPRESSIVE ILLNESSES (AFFECTIVE ILLNESSES)

The disease expectancy of affective illnesses is not known with any degree of certainty. There are many reasons for this. One of them is that the readiness to diagnose an affective illness has steadily increased in recent years. This may have been largely due to the availability of adequate anti-depressant therapies and to the steadily growing realization that many depressions manifest themselves under the guise of symptoms which are somatic, phobic or obsessional rather than obviously depressive. Kral (1958) was one of the first in modern times to draw attention to these 'masked' depressions. Since there is a general tendency for affective illnesses to become more severe, and therefore more diagnosable, with age, one would expect to obtain a frequent history of past anxiety-dominated illnesses in patients whose liability to depressive episodes is first recognized, when they are past middle age—and often not even then. Post (1965), in a section on 'masked depressions', for instance, pointed out: 'There are probably many elderly people with long-standing neurotic complaints, where underlying depressions fail to be recognized'. It is therefore not surprising to find that estimates of the rate of affective illnesses among psychiatric patients vary widely. They vary, first of all, in different cultures. In Eastern and Southern Africa, for example, few psychiatric patients were diagnosed as depressive or manic-depressive, e.g. 1·6% in Kenya (Carothers, 1947) and 3·8% in South Africa (Laubscher, 1938). In West Africa, on the other hand, the percentage of affective disorders among psychiatric patients was higher, e.g. 22–23% in Ghana (Tooth, 1950; Weinberg, 1965) and 17% in Nigeria (Leighton et al., 1963). The Nigerian psychiatrist Lambo (1965) remarked that low rates of depressions in Africans are more apparent than real, because cultural factors 'damp down depression and enhance or exaggerate excitement'.

Yet even within similar cultural environments, the diagnosis of affective illnesses in psychiatric patients shows great divergencies. It had been known for some time, for instance, that psychiatrists in the United States and in England differed widely in their diagnostic habits in that the former preferred the diagnosis of schizophrenia in their patients and the latter the diagnosis of an affective disorder.

Kramer (1961) showed that, for both sexes, manic-depressive diagnoses in first admissions to mental hospitals in England and Wales in 1956 was nine times larger than in first admissions to public and private mental hospitals in the United States in 1957 (36 versus 4 per 100,000 of the general population, i.e. 0·036% versus 0·004%). To examine the significance of this difference a combined American-British research team with fairly uniform diagnostic habits was set up (the 'US/UK Diagnostic Project') under the general guidance of the American psychologist, J. Zubin, with one branch headed by J. E. Cooper (Institute of Psychiatry, London) and the other by B. J. Gurland (New York State Department of Mental Hygiene). They began by studying patients from nine New York and nine London mental hospitals. The diagnoses made by the psychiatrists in the respective hospitals in New York and London were compared with those made by the two research teams (Kendell, 1971; Cooper et al., 1972). The diagnosis of an affective illness was made by the New York hospital psychiatrists in 6·8% of their patients and by the London hospital psychiatrists in 39·1% of theirs, a highly significant difference (P <0·01). The corresponding figures for the two research teams were 32·3% in New York and 43·7% in London, a difference which was still significant, though less so (P <0·05). It turned out that the difference between the two research teams was largely due to a more frequent diagnosis of depressive neuroses in London than in New York. This may possibly reflect a greater readiness in London to admit patients with mild depressions to mental hospitals.

There are also diagnostic differences between psychiatrists in England, France and Germany as far as affective illnesses are concerned, though not with regard to schizophrenia (Kendell et al., 1974). English psychiatrists are most disposed to diagnose affective illnesses among their patients (23%), German psychiatrists less so (14%) and French psychiatrists least of all (5%). The difference between English and German psychiatrists is significant at the 0·02 level, the other differences at the 0·001 level.

In addition to these diagnostic variations in different countries, there has been a steady increase in the diagnosis of affective illness in the last few decades. In England and Wales, first admissions with this diagnosis increased by about 80% for males and about 90% for females between 1952 and 1960. The increase was particularly marked for young patients between 15 and 25. It has continued at a reduced rate after 1960. Slater and Cowie (1971) calculated from the 1960 figures of first admissions the lifetime risk of admission to a psychiatric hospital with an affective illness during a life-span of 75 years to be 2·4% for males and 3·9% for females. These figures rose by 1966 to 3·5% and 5·8% respectively. They may still be too low as they only take patients into account whose illness had led to a hospital admission. Helgason (1971) found slightly higher lifetime disease expectancies in Iceland, when he included mild depressions. His figures were 5·2% for men and 8·3% for women (6·8% for both sexes) and they were similar to those in other Scandinavian countries.

There is no doubt that the lifetime disease expectancy for affective illnesses in the general population is higher than that for schizophrenia.

The role of genetic factors in the aetiology of affective illnesses may again be examined with the help of family and twin studies. Zerbin-Rüdin (1967) examined 25 family studies by 11 authors into the incidence of affective illness in the first-degree relatives (parents, sibs and children) of patients with such an illness. All these studies were conducted before 1960. Slater and Cowie (1971) calculated lifetime expectancies from their results. They were between about 8% and 12% for a definite affective psychosis. When probable affective illnesses and suicides were added, they rose to between 12% and 16%. They were certainly above the diagnosed rates in the general population before 1960.

It should be noted that the parents of patients with an affective illness did not have a reduced lifetime expectancy for this illness as is the case with the parents of schizophrenic patients. The reason is that the occurrence of an affective illness does not lower the likelihood of achieving parenthood, whereas the occurrence of a schizophrenic illness does.

Following the studies and views of Stenstedt (1952), Leonhard et al. (1962), Angst (1966), Perris (1966), Angst and Perris (1968), Winokur et al. (1969) and others, it has become a frequent practice to divide affective illnesses into bipolar and unipolar ones. There is unfortunately little agreement about the criteria that should be applied in the differential diagnosis. On the whole, it seems that a bipolar illness is diagnosed, when a hypomanic or manic episode has occurred, even in the absence of any depressive periods at any time. Since definitely manic symptoms are of relatively rare occurrence, bipolar (i.e. truly manic-depressive) illnesses are obviously less frequent than unipolar ones. The assumption has been made that different genetic models should be applied to the groups of bipolar and unipolar illnesses. Yet it is also possible that the two groups of illnesses are distinguished only by a more pronounced upswing of mood in bipolar disorders (Gershon et al., 1975).

Several authors have examined the morbidity risks in first-degree relatives of patients with unipolar and bipolar illnesses. Kay (1978) has presented a survey of their findings. It appears that for unipolar depressives the risk of an affective illness (which is also usually unipolar) in first-degree relatives lies between 11% and 16% (i.e. it is similar to the range of risks calculated on the basis of earlier studies). For bipolar manic-depressives (or recurrent manics) the risk of an affective illness (which is more often unipolar than bipolar) in first-degree relatives tends to be somewhat higher. When personal interviews with the family members were conducted and the diagnostic net cast wide, risks as high as 35% (Winokur et al., 1969, 1971) and even 39% (Mendlewicz and Rainer, 1974) have been reported. But these high figures are exceptional. The usual lifetime expectancy risks for the first-degree relatives of bipolar patients is found to be around 20% (Angst, 1966; Perris, 1966; James and Chapman, 1975).

When one parent of a unipolar depressed patient had an affective illness, the morbidity risk in the patient's sibs increased to 26%; and when both parents had affective illnesses, the risk rose to 43% (Winokur and Clayton, 1967). For bipolar patients, Winokur et al., (1969) found that the already high morbidity risk in sibs was not further raised by an affective illness in one or both parents.

Age also is a factor in determining the morbidity risks in relatives. Late onset of an affective illness (whether unipolar or bipolar) in a patient is associated with a lowered morbidity risk in first-degree relatives. For example, Hopkinson and Ley (1969) found that onset of an affective illness after the age of 40 was associated with a morbidity risk in first-degree relatives of 12·5% (as given by Slater and Cowie, 1971), but onset before the age of 40 with a morbidity risk of 28·9%—a highly significant difference. A similar lowering of the morbidity risk in first-degree relatives in late onset affective illness has been noticed by other authors (e.g. Winokur et al., 1971; Cadoret, 1976).

Twin studies have yielded fairly widely divergent results. Slater and Cowie (1971) reviewed the results of seven relevant investigations. The reported concordance rates in MZ twins varied from 33% to 96% and in same-sexed DZ twins from 0% to 39%. Slater and Cowie were bold enough to summate these figures which were obviously hardly comparable. They obtained concordance rates of about 72% in MZ twins and 19% in same-sex DZ twins. They added ruefully: 'This can be regarded as a plausible estimate, but it cannot be justified logically'.

Price (1968) was able to collect the case histories of 12 MZ twin pairs who had been reared apart from an early age and of whom one at least had an affective illness. He regarded 8 of them as concordant (67%).

It has recently been established that affective illnesses are associated with a biochemical pathology which may be largely due to genetic predispositions. Ashcroft and Sharman (1960) and Coppen *et al.* (1965) have drawn attention to the fact that the metabolism of certain monoamines, especially of noradrenaline (norepinephrine) and dopamine, is disturbed in manic-depressive patients. As a result fewer of these amines are available in the brain. Antidepressant drugs apparently owe their success to their ability to raise the level of these amines in relevant parts of the brain. It is interesting that the same amines, and particularly dopamine, are active in the 'pleasure centres' of the brain—the 'brain reward system' as it has come to be called (Olds, 1977; Routtenberg, 1978).

In depressive patients, there is also an increase of about 50% of the body's 'residual sodium' which is made up for the most part of intracellular sodium (Coppen and Shaw, 1963). In manic patients, this increase is twice as large (Coppen *et al.*, 1966; Shaw, 1966). On recovery, the intracellular sodium returns to normal values. These findings apply, of course, to the body as a whole, but there is no reason to assume that the brain is exempt from them. If there is too much sodium in nerve cells, this would interfere with their functions through a lowering of the normal electric potential across their membranes. The effectiveness of lithium treatment and prophylaxis in some patients with affective disorders may derive from its capacity to replace and thus to reduce intracellular sodium. (For a review of the biochemical pathology of affective illnesses see Coppen, 1967; Gibbons, 1968; Schildkraut, 1969).

Genetic influences never work in isolation. Adjuvant and precipitating circumstances also have their role to play. It is therefore not surprising that affective illnesses may be causally related to various organic diseases and toxic factors, e.g. cerebral tumours (Minski, 1933; Rieke, 1975), neurosyphilis (Dewhurst, 1969), multiple sclerosis (Surridge, 1969; Kahaná *et al.*, 1971), subarachnoid haemorrhage (Storey, 1972), as yet undiagnosed malignant tumours in various parts of the body (Fras *et al.*, 1967; Whitlock, 1978), after virus infections (Rimon and Halonen, 1969; Lycke *et al.*, 1974), during medication with hypotensive drugs (Bulpitt and Dollery, 1973), and so on.

Much attention has been paid to social influences which may provoke or aggravate an affective illness in predisposed persons. Ever since Freud's paper on Mourning and Melancholia (1917), attempts have been made to examine the relationship between the loss of a loved object and the onset of a depressive illness. Parkes (1964) found confirmatory evidence for Freud's views on the origin of depression. His research disclosed that depressive illnesses developed in widows and widowers within six months of the death of the spouse with a frequency that was six times greater than expected. Similar observations were made by Clayton and her co-workers (Clayton et al., 1972; Bornstein et al., 1973; Clayton, 1975). They mentioned as aggravating circumstances the absence of children living nearby and the lack of financial and religious support.

Bereavement has also been found to be associated with increased mortality. Young et al. (1963), reported an increment of 40% in the mortality rates of widowers in the first six months after bereavement and this applied particularly to younger people below the age of thirty-four. They considered several possible explanations, but concluded that 'the "desolation effect" of being widowed may be at least a good part of the explanation'. Rees and Lutkins (1967) examined the mortality rate after the death of a close relative in a small Welsh market-town. Their results showed that the mortality rate was 4·76% within the first year of bereavement compared with a rate of only 0·68% in a control group—a highly significant difference ($P = 0.001$). The rate was significantly higher in widowers than widows. 19·6% of 51 widowers and 8·5% of 105 widows died in the first year of bereavement ($P = 0.05$). Indeed 13·7% of the widowers died within the first six months and only 5·9% in the second six months—again a significant difference ($P = 0.05$).

The association between emotionally significant life events and depressions have been systematically studied in London by Brown and his colleagues (1973a, b; 1978a) and in New Haven by Paykel (1974, 1978) and his colleagues (1969). Although there have been methodological differences between these two research teams, their results have been similar in many respects. They found that threatening life events or 'exit events' (loss of partners through death or separation) can provoke depressive reactions and that distressing life situations (e.g. domestic disturbances, difficulties at work, lack of close ties with relatives or friends, no current employment, three or more children under fourteen at home, lower social class) may increase the vulnerability of persons so that they are more liable to become depressed. Brown's team has been studying women in a London Borough of whom only some were patients; the others were 'cases' with much milder complaints. Taking both patients and 'cases' together, Brown et al. (1975), found among them an annual incidence of 10% of psychiatric disturbances (mostly depressions) and an annual prevalence of 16%. These are unusually high rates and thus suggest the possibility of an excessive readiness to diagnose psychiatric disturbances. Tennant and Bebbington (1978) have examined this possibility and come to the conclusion that some of Brown's 'cases' were women with distress reactions rather than a genuine psychiatric morbidity. This interpretation has been rejected by Brown and Harris (1978b). In a general review of the literature on the links between life events and psychiatric illness, Andrews and Tennant (1978) point out that the evidence shows that less than 10% of depressive illnesses are provoked by life events. They can thus be of only limited clinical or preventive importance. Paykel (1978) seems to agree with that conclusion. He stresses that threatening life events are 'very often not followed by psychiatric illness. . . . There may be a good deal of additional emotional distress which is not clearly within the range of psychiatric abnormality'.

CHAPTER 28

PSEUDO-HALLUCINATIONS

Hare (1973) reported an embarrassing experience of his. He acted as an examiner in a post-graduate examination of doctors aspiring to become specialists in psychiatry. Among the obligatory questions the doctors had to answer was one on pseudo-hallucinations. He was baffled, because he did not know what the correct answer to this question was. So he set out to find enlightenment in the psychiatric literature. To his amazement he found that the leading English textbooks did not mention pseudo-hallucinations at all or only in passing, though without any attempt to define or describe them. In American textbooks, the word 'pseudo-hallucination' did not appear anywhere.

On widening his searches he learned that the term had been coined by the German psychiatrist, Kandinsky (1885), and had gained currency, because it was discussed at some length by the influential German philosopher-psychiatrist, Karl Jaspers, in his book *Allgemeine Psychopathologie* (1948, orig. 1913). There it was mentioned that one of the characteristics of pseudo-hallucinations was the lack of '*Leibhaftigkeit*' (p. 60). Hoenig and Hamilton, in their translation of Jaspers' book (1962) rendered this term as 'concrete reality' (p. 70). Fish (1967, p. 19) suggested that a better rendering would be 'substantiality'. However, this also seems to me to miss the exact sense intended by Jaspers. A better and nearer translation is perhaps 'corporeality'. Let us then quote—and paraphrase—how Fish presented Jaspers' views: 'Jaspers claimed that while true hallucinations are corporeal and appear in objective space, pseudohallucinations lack corporeality and appear in subjective space'.

Fish mentioned that there had been much discussion in the past about the concept of pseudo-hallucinations. In particular, he remarked: 'Some authors have added to the confusion by calling hallucinations which are not considered to be real by the patient "pseudohallucinations" '. When Hamilton (1974) edited a revised edition of Fish's book, he deleted this remark. Indeed he altered, without acknowledgment, the opinion held by Fish in that he inserted into Fish's description of pseudo-hallucinations the clause 'known to be not real perceptions' (p. 19).

When Hare (1973) examined Jaspers' views on pseudo-hallucinations, he found them inconsistent and perplexing. In the end he came to the conclusion that the hallmark of pseudo-hallucinations was that they were accompanied by insight into their lack of an objective counterpart. He acknowledged that this view was in accord with the description of hallucinated patients given in the American textbook of psychiatry by Freedman and Caplan (1967, p. 567) who remarked, without mentioning the term 'pseudo-hallucination', that psychiatric patients can 'slip in and out of the hallucinatory state with intervals of insight and lucidity (hence Hughlings Jackson's term *mental diplopia*)'. (Italics in the original.) Hare was also in agreement with Sedman (1966a, b; 1967), a British author, who spoke explicitly of 'pseudo-hallucinations', examined them and decided that they were hallucinations which were 'recognized by the patient as not being veridical'.

Yet Hare did not feel comfortable about his conclusion that pseudo-hallucinations are distinguished from actual hallucinations, because they are accompanied by insight into their deceptive nature. He was discomfited by the fact that there are degrees of insight and that it may be partial and fluctuating. For this reason it is often not possible for the psychiatrist to be certain how much insight, if any, a hallucinated patient has into the deceptive nature of his experience. Therefore, Hare suggests in his final sentence 'the concept of pseudo-hallucination becomes largely superfluous'.

Should we accept this suggestion by Hare and drop the concept of pseudo-hallucinations altogether?

There are, however, reasons to think that the concept of pseudo-hallucinations is far from being superfluous, that it does in fact indicate a special class of psychological phenomena. Hare's ultimate doubt of the validity or usefulness of the concept may derive largely from his decision to restrict the terms 'hallucination' and 'pseudo-hallucination' to the designation of morbid phenomena exclusively. Their differential diagnosis is then a task for psychiatrists and involves an assessment of a patient's insight into the veridicality or deceptiveness of his hallucinated experiences. Since such an assessment is obviously highly subjective and unreliable, it follows that the clinical usefulness of a differential diagnosis between hallucinations and pseudo-hallucinations is open to doubt.

Yet such a clinical approach to the problem is far too narrow. The essential question is not whether the concept of pseudo-hallucinations is clinically useful. Fundamentally, the question is a phenomenological one and not restricted to the clinical milieu. There are hallucinations which are quite normal. Dreams are an obvious example. Indeed Hare mentions that American textbooks use the term 'hallucination' in its broad lay sense which covers phenomena like dreams. When dreams are experienced during sleep, they certainly are hallucinations, since they are wrongly accepted as veridical percepts. But there are occasional exceptions, when the dreamer is aware of dreaming and thus has insight into the unreality of his experience. Such a dream is a pseudo-hallucination. When a dream is remembered after awakening, the memory is of a perceptual experience that is recognized as non-veridical; it is therefore the memory of a pseudo-hallucination.

Hare rightly pointed out that pseudo-hallucinations are wrongly named. The prefix 'pseudo-' is not justified, because they are real hallucinations which happen to be accompanied by insight into their non-veridical nature. A better name might have been 'para-hallucinations'.

But linguistic niceties should not detract us from the recognition that the experience of pseudo-hallucinations (called by whatever name) can be distinguished by the person concerned from the experience of hallucinations, even if he may be sometimes uncertain and wavering in his differentiation.

We may thus conclude that pseudo-hallucinations deserve to be regarded as a special variety of hallucinations. They can be extero-cepted or interocepted phenomena and we shall consider some of them presently. Whether they are normal or morbid phenomena depends on whether they arouse therapeutic and/or medical concern.

Exteroceptive pseudo-hallucinations usually occur in the visual or auditory fields, though they may also be of an olfactory, gustatory, or tactile kind.

Remembered dreams have already been mentioned as a variety of pseudo-hallucinations of a mainly visual character. The same is true of hypnagogic and hypnopompic experiences. Other common visual pseudo-hallucinations are the after-images evoked by viewing brightly lit or highly coloured objects or surfaces.

Darkness can also produce visual pseudo-hallucinations, usually in the form of specks or clouds of coloured light. They have been called 'phosphenes' from the Greek word for 'light' and 'shining'. But darkness is not the only source of the appearance of phosphenes in the visual field. They can be artificially evoked by a blow on the head (seeing stars), by pressure exerted on the eyeballs, by low-voltage electric pulses applied to the temples or by electric stimulation of the visual cortex (Brindley and Lewin, 1968). Such phosphenes usually consist of scintillating points of coloured light arranged in the form of a lattice, chessboard, network or filigree, patterns which have been studied and depicted by Oster (1970). He also described a woman of excessive sensitivity to any pressure on her eyeballs so that rubbing her eyes inadvertently with a towel in the morning provoked such intense phosphenes that they interfered with her vision for hours afterwards.

Phosphenes initiated peripherally in the retina behave like afterimages in that they appear to move with the gaze. Phosphenes of more central origin can be of more complex figuration and do not move with the gaze, but just superimpose themselves on the visual field, wherever the gaze is directed.

Patients with a detached retina can see phosphenes in the form of light flashes or coloured clouds—an experience which has been called 'photopsia', though this term would be also applicable to the experience of seeing other kinds of phosphenes. The fortification spectra of migraine attacks are phosphenes of focal cortical origin (Richards, 1971). The experience of seeing these particular phosphenes has been distinguished by the name of 'teichopsia'—seeing walls of hexagonal towers.

Patients with acquired blindness may find a source of entertainment in the sight of phosphenes which may take the form of gorgeous views and dramatic happenings. Others may find these pseudo-hallucinations intolerable distressing, because there is no escape from them. Critchley (1965), for example, mentioned a woman of 60 whose blindness was due to cataracts. She saw a continuous rain of golden specks pouring down before her unseeing eyes and was driven so frantic that she submitted to two leucotomies.

Quite elaborate pseudo-hallucinations make their appearance in experiments of sensory deprivation, when persons are put into an environment in which visual stimuli are kept at an unpatterned uniformity (Bexton et al., 1954; Leff, 1968). Such environmental conditions also occur outside laboratories, for example during long drives on monotonous motorways, driving through fog or snowstorms, or when flying in the cloudless skies of high altitudes. McFarland and Moore (1957), for instance, reported that, among 50 American longhaul truck drivers, 30 had at some time seen a non-existent object or animal in their path which made them swerve automatically before they realized their mistake. Monotony combined with prolonged solitude can conjure up pseudo-hallucinations of a visual, auditory, olfactory or tactile kind in lonely explorers during a polar winter or in single-handed sailors in a transatlantic race (Bennett, 1973). The loneliness and sense of loss after the recent death of a spouse may similarly lead to pseudo-hallucinated glimpses of the missed spouse and to pseudo-hallucinated sounds of his or her voice, steps and movements.

Simple phosphene patterns may turn into elaborate scenes and sceneries in states of clouded consciousness and especially after taking hallucinogenic (psychotomimetic, psychedelic) drugs (cf. Klüver, 1966; Siegel, 1977).

Eidetic images (Allport, 1925; Haber, 1969) are not, strictly speaking, images, though their appearance can be brought about by an intentional act of recall. Yet they are not introspected phenomena on a mental stage like other recalled images; they are exterocepted visual pseudo-hallucinations which are seen in the black field of closed lids or, on opening the eyes, as pictures on a suitable surface.

Phantom limbs are also pseudo-hallucinations, though of an interocepted kind, giving rise to disturbing sensations of the posture of the missing limbs, of paraesthesiae in them, of feelings of heaviness, cold, cramp, or pain. They may move of their own accord or be moved at will, when the appropriate kinaesthetic pseudo-hallucinations are then felt.

In patients with paralyzed extremities, phantom limbs (or rather reduplicated limbs) can be experienced. When the position of the pseudo-hallucinated limbs is at variance with that of the paralyzed ones, a look at the latter may dispel the former. But this is not always the case and the discrepancy in position may cause distress. Brain (1956), for example, described a patient whose phantom legs were always experienced as extended in line with the trunk. When he was sat up in bed, the phantom legs were felt as passing through the mattress. Patients sometimes cannot tolerate such positional discrepancies and feel obliged to ask for their paralyzed limbs to be moved so that their positions coincide with those of the pseudo-hallucinated ones.

REFERENCES TO PART IV, RECENT DEVELOPMENTS

Abe, K. and Moran, P. A. P., 'Parental age and homosexuals'. *Brit. J. Psychiat.*, 1969, **115**, 313–317

Achté, K. A., Hillbom, E., and Aalberg, V., 'Psychoses following war brain injuries'. *Acta Psychiat. Scand.*, 1969, **45**, 1–18

Allport, G. W., 'Eidetic imagery'. *Brit. J. Psychol.*, 1925, **15**, 99–120

Andrews, G. and Tennant, C., 'Life event stress and psychiatric illness'. *Psychol. Med.*, 1978, **8**, 545–549

Angst, J., Zur Ätiologie und Nosologie Endogener Depressiver Psychosen— Berlin: Springer, 1966

Angst, J. and Perris, C., 'Zur Nosologie endogener Depressionen. Vergleich der Ergebnisse zweier Untersuchungen'. *Arch. Psychiat. Nervenkrankheiten*, 1968, **210**, 373–386

Ashcroft, G. W. and Sharman, D. F., '5-hydroxyindoles in human cerebrospinal fluid'. *Nature*, 1960, **186**, 1050–1051

Bateson, G., Jackson, D., Haley, J., and Weakland, J., 'Toward a theory of schizophrenia'. *Behav. Sci.*, 1956, **1**, 251–264

Bennett, G., 'Medical and psychological problems in the 1972 singlehanded transatlantic yacht race'. *Lancet*, 1973, **2**, 749–754

Bexton, W. H., Heron, W., and Scott, T. H., 'Effects of decreased variation in the sensory environment'. *Canad. J. Psychol.*, 1954, **8**, 70–76

Birley, J. L. T. and Brown, G. W., 'Crises and life changes preceding the onset or relapse of acute schizophrenia. Clinical aspects'. *Brit. J. Psychiat.*, 1970, **116**, 327–333

Bornstein, P. E., Clayton, P. J., Halikas, J. A., Maurice, W. L., and Robin, E., 'The depression of widowhood after thirteen months'. *Brit. J. Psychiat.*, 1973, **122**, 561–566

Brain, Sir Russell, 'The thirtieth Maudsley lecture: perception and imperception'. *J. Ment. Sci.*, 1956, **102**, 221–232

Brindley, G. S. and Lewin, W. S., 'The sensations produced by electrical stimulation of the visual cortex'. *J. Physiol.*, 1968, **196**, 479–493

Brown, G. W., Bhrolcháin, M. N., and Harris, T., 'Social class and psychiatric disturbance among women in an urban population'. *Sociology*, 1975, **9**, 225–254

Brown, G. W. and Birley, J. L. T., 'Crises and life changes and the onset of schizophrenia'. *J. Hlth. Soc. Behav.*, 1968, **9**, 203–214

Brown, G. W., Birley, J. L. T., and Wing, J. K., 'Influence of family life on the course of schizophrenic disorders: a replication'. *Brit. J. Psychiat.*, 1972, **121**, 241–258

Brown, G. W. and Harris, T., Social Origins of Depression. A Study of Psychiatric Disorder in Women—London: Tavistock, 1978a

Brown, G. W. and Harris, T., 'Social origins of depression: a reply'. *Psychol. Med.*, 1978b, **8**, 577–588

Brown, G. W., Harris, T., and Peto, J., 'Life events and psychiatric disorders. Part 2: Nature of causal link'. *Psychol. Med.*, 1973b, **3**, 159–176

Brown, G. W., Sklair, F., Harris, T. O., and Birley, J. L. T., 'Life events and psychiatric disorders. Part 1: Some methodological issues'. *Psychol. Med.*, 1973a, **3**, 74–87

REFERENCES TO PART IV, RECENT DEVELOPMENTS

Bulpitt, C. J. and Dollery, C. T., 'Side effects of hypotensive agents evaluated by a self-administered questionnaire'. *Brit. Med. J.*, 1973, **3**, 485–490

Cadoret, R. J., 'The genetics of affective disorder and genetic counselling'. *Soc. Biol.*, 1976, **23**, 116–122

Carothers, J. C., 'A study of mental derangement in Africans'. *J. Ment. Sci.*, 1947, **93**, 548–597

Clayton, P. J., 'The effect of living alone on bereavement symptoms'. *Am. J. Psychiat.*, 1975, **132**, 133–137

Clayton, P. J., Halikas, J. A., and Maurice, W. L., 'The depression of widowhood'. *Brit. J. Psychiat.*, 1972, **120**, 71–78

Cohen, B. E., Bodonyi, E., and Szeinberg, A., 'Phenylketonuria in Jews'. *Lancet*, 1961, **1**, 344–345

Connell, P. H., Amphetamine Psychosis—Maudsley Monograph No. 5. London: Chapman & Hall, 1958

Cooper, J. E., Kendell, R. E., Gurland, B. J., Sharpe, L., Copeland, J. R. M., and Simon, R., Psychiatric Diagnosis in New York and London—Maudsley Monograph No. 20. London: Oxford Univ. Press, 1972

Coppen, A., 'The biochemistry of affective disorders'. *Brit. J. Psychiat.*, 1967, **113**, 1237–1264

Coppen, A. and Shaw, D. M., 'Mineral metabolism in melancholia'. *Brit. Med. J.*, 1963, **2**, 1439–1444

Coppen, A., Shaw, D. M., Malleson, A., and Costain, R., 'Mineral metabolism in mania'. *Brit. Med. J.*, 1966, **1**, 71–75

Coppen, A., Shaw, D. M., Malleson, A., Eccleston, E., and Gundy, G., 'Tryptamine metabolism in depression'. *Brit. J. Psychiat.*, 1965, **111**, 993–998

Critchley, M., 'Acquired anomalies of colour perception of central origin'. *Brain*, 1965, **88**, 711–724

Davison, K. and Bagley, C. R., 'Schizophrenia-like psychoses associated with organic disorders of the central nervous system: A review of the literature'. In *Current Problems in Neuropsychiatry* (Ed. R. N. Herrington). *Brit. J. Psychiat.* Spec. Publ. No. 4.—Ashford, Kent: Headley Bros., 1969. Pp. 113–184

Dewhurst, K., 'The neurosyphilitic psychoses today: A survey of 91 cases'. *Brit. J. Psychiat.*, 1969, **115**, 31–38

Dunham, H. W., Community and Schizophrenia—Detroit: Wayne State Univ. Press, 1965

Essen-Möller, E., 'The calculation of morbid risk in parents of index cases as applied to a family sample of schizophrenics'. Acta Genetica et Statistica Medica (Basel), 1955, **5**, 334–342

Essen-Möller, E. and Hagnell, O., 'The frequency and risk of depression within a rural population in Scania'. *Acta. Psychiat. Scand.* Suppl. 162, **37**, 1961. Pp. 28–32

Faris, R. and Dunham, H., Mental Disorders in Urban Areas—Chicago: Univ. of Chicago Press, 1939

Fischer, M., Harvald, B., and Hauge, M., 'A Danish twin study of schizophrenia'. *Brit. J. Psychiat.*, 1969, **115**, 981–990

Fish, F., Clinical Psychopathology. Signs and Symptoms in Psychiatry—Bristol: Wright, 1967. (See also Hamilton, M.)

Fras, I., Litin, E. M., and Pearson, J. S., 'Comparison of psychiatric symptoms in carcinoma of the pancreas with those in some other intra-abdominal neoplasms'. *Am. J. Psychiat.*, 1967, **123**, 1553–1562

Freud, S., Mourning and Melancholia (1917)—Republished in *Standard*

REFERENCES TO PART IV, RECENT DEVELOPMENTS

Edition of the Complete Psychological Works of Sigmund Freud—London: Hogarth Press, 1957, **14,** 239

Gershon, E. S., Baron, M., and Leckman, J. F., 'Genetic models of the transmission of affective disorders'. *J. Psychiat. Research*, 1975, **12,** 301–317

Gibbons, J. L., 'Biochemistry of depressive illness'. In *Recent Developments in Affective Disorders*. (Eds. A. Coppen and A. Walk.) *Brit. J. Psychiat.* Spec. Publ. No. 2—Ashford, Kent: Headley Bros., 1968. Pp. 55–64

Goldberg, E. M. and Morrison, S. L., 'Schizophrenia and social class'. *Brit. J. Psychiat.*, 1963, **109,** 785–802

Gottesman, I. I. and Shields, J., Schizophrenia and Genetics—A Twin Study Vantage Point—New York and London: Academic Press, 1972

Haber, R. N., 'Eidetic images'. *Scient. Amer.*, 1969, **220,** 36–44

Hamilton, M. (ed.), Fish's Clinical Psychopathology. Signs and Symptoms in Psychiatry. (Revised Reprint.) Bristol: Wright, 1974

Hare, E. H., 'Family setting and the urban distribution of schizophrenia'. *J. Ment. Sci.*, 1956, **102,** 753–760

Hare, E. H., 'A short note on pseudo-hallucinations'. *Brit. J. Psychiat.*, 1973, **122,** 469–476

Helgason, T., 'Frequency of depressive states within geographically delimited population groups. 4. The frequency of depressive states in Iceland as compared with the other Scandinavian countries'. *Acta Psychiat. Scand.* Suppl. 162, **37,** 1961. Pp. 81–90

Heston, L. L., 'Psychiatric disorders in foster home reared children of schizophrenic mothers'. *Brit. J. Psychiat.*, 1966, **112,** 819–825

Hollingshead, A. and Redlich, R. C., Social Class and Mental Illness—New York: John Wiley, 1958

Hopkinson, G. and Ley, P., 'A genetic study of affective disorders'. *Brit. J. Psychiat.*, 1969, **115,** 917–922

Jablensky, A. and Sartorius, N., 'Culture and schizophrenia'. *Psychol. Med.*, 1975, **5,** 113–124

Jacobs, P. A., Brunton, M., Melville, M. E., Brittain, R. P., and McClemont, W. F., 'Aggressive behaviour, mental subnormality and XYY male'. *Nature* (Lond.), 1965, **208,** 1351–1352

James, N. McI. and Chapman, C. J., 'A genetic study of bipolar affective disorder'. *Brit. J. Psychiat.*, 1975, **126,** 449–456

Jaspers, K., Allgemeine Psychopathologie. Fifth Edition. Berlin and Heidelberg: Springer, 1948. (Orig. 1913)—General Psychopathology. Transl. J. Hoenig and M. W. Hamilton—Manchester Univ. Press, 1962

Kahaná, E., Leibowitz, U., and Alter, M., 'Cerebral multiple sclerosis'. *Neurology*, 1971, **21,** 1179–1185

Kallmann, F J., 'Comparative twin study on the genetic aspects of male homosexuality'. *J. Nerv. Ment. Dis.*, 1952, **115,** 283–298

Kallmann, F. J., Discussion of paper by Rainer *et al.* (q.v.), Psychosom. Med., 1960, **22,** 258–259

Kandinsky, V., Kritische und Klinische Betrachtungen im Gebiete der Sinnestäuschungen—Berlin: Friedlaender & Sohn, 1885

Katz, H. P. and Menkes, J. H., 'Phenylketonuria occurring in an American negro'. *J. Pediat.*, 1964, **65,** 71–74

Kay, D. W. K., 'Assessment of familial risks in the functional psychoses and their application in genetic counselling'. *Brit. J. Psychiat.*, 1978, **133,** 385–403

REFERENCES TO PART IV, RECENT DEVELOPMENTS

Kendell, R. E., 'Psychiatric diagnosis in Britain and the United States'. *Brit. J. Hosp. Med.*, 1971, **6**, 147–155

Kendell, R. E., 'The concept of disease and its implication for psychiatry'. *Brit. J. Psychiat.*, 1975, **127**, 305–315

Kendell, R. E., Pichot, P., and Cranach, M. v., 'Diagnostic criteria of English, French, and German psychiatrists'. *Psychol. Med.*, 1974, **4**, 187–195

Kety, S. S., Rosenthal, D., Wender, P. H., Schulsinger, F., and Jacobsen, B. In *Genetic Research in Psychiatry* (Eds. R. R. Fieve, D. Rosenthal, and H. Brill)—Baltimore and London: Johns Hopkins Univ. Press, 1975. Pp. 147–165

Klüver, H., Mescal and Mechanisms of Hallucinations—Univ. of Chicago Press, 1966

Kringlen, E., Heredity and Environment in the Functional Psychoses—London: Heinemann, 1967

Kringlen, E., 'An epidemiological-clinical twin study on schizophrenia'. In *The Transmission of Schizophrenia* (Eds. D. Rosenthal and S. S. Kety)—Oxford: Pergamon, 1968. Pp. 49–63

Laing, R. D. and Esterson, D., Sanity, Madness and the Family—London: Tavistock, 1964

Lambo, T. A., 'Neuropsychiatric observations in the western regions of Nigeria'. *Brit. Med. J.*, 1956, **2**, 1388–1394

Lang, T., 'Die Homosexualität' als genetisches Problem'. *Acta Genet. Med. (Roma)*, 1960, **9**, 370–381

Larson, C. A., 'An estimate of the frequency of phenylketonuria in South Sweden'. *Folia Hered. Path.* (Milano), 1954, **4**, 40–46

Laubscher, B. J. F., Sex, Custom and Psychopathology—London: Routledge, 1937

Leader Writer, 'What becomes of the XYY male?'. *Lancet*, 1974, **2**, 1297–1298

Leff, J. P., 'Perceptual phenomena and personality in sensory deprivation'. *Brit. J. Psychiat.*, 1968, **114**, 1499–1508

Leff, J., 'Social and psychological causes of the acute attack'. In *Schizophrenia: Towards a New Synthesis*. (Ed. J. K. Wing)—London: Academic Press and New York: Grune & Stratton, 1978. Pp. 139–165

Leighton, A. H., Lambo, T. A., Hughes, C. C., Leighton, D. C., Murphy, J. M., and Macklin, D. B., Psychiatric Disorder among the Yoruba—New York: Cornell Univ. Press, 1963

Leonhard, K., Korff, I., and Schulz, H., 'Die Temperamente in den Familien der monopolaren und bipolaren Psychosen'. *Psychiat. und Neurol.*, 1962, **143**, 416–434

Lidz, T., Cornelison, A. R., Fleck, S., and Terry, D., 'The intrafamilial environment of schizophrenic patients: II. Marital schism and marital skew'. *Am. J. Psychiat.*, 1957, **114**, 241–248

Lishman, W. A., Organic Psychiatry. Psychological Consequences of Cerebral Disorder—Oxford: Blackwell, 1978

Lycke, E., Norrby, R., and Roos, B-E., 'A serological study on mentally ill patients with particular reference to the prevalence of herpes virus infections'. *Brit. J. Psychiat.*, 1974, **124**, 273–279

McCready, R. A. and Hussey, M. G., 'Newborn phenylketonuria detection program in Massachusetts'. *Am. J. Pub. Hlth*, 1964, **54**, 2075–2081

McFarland, R. A. and Moore, R. D., 'Human factors in highway safety: A review and evaluation'. *New Engl. J. Med.*, 1957, **256**, 792–799

McHugh, P. R., 'The concept of disease in psychiatry'. In *Cecil-Loeb's*

Textbook of Medicine (Eds. P. B. Beeson and W. McDermott). 14th edition—Philadelphia, London, Toronto: W. B. Saunders, 1975. Pp. 562–563

Mendlewicz, J. and Rainer, J. D., 'Morbidity risk and genetic transmission in manic-depressive illness'. *Am. J. Hum. Genet.*, 1974, **26**, 692–701

Minski, L., 'The mental symptoms associated with 58 cases of cerebral tumour'. *J. Neurol. Psychopathol.*, 1933, **13**, 330–343

Moran, P. A. P., 'Familial effects in schizophrenia and homosexuality'. *Australia and New Zealand. J. Psychiat.*, 1972, **6**, 116–119

Nielsen, J. and Christensen, A.-L., 'Thirty-five males with double Y chromosome'. *Psychol. Med.*, 1974, **4**, 28–37

Olds, J., Drives and Reinforcements: Behavioral Studies of Hypothalamic Functions—New York: Raven Press, 1977

Oster, G., 'Phosphenes'. *Scient. American*, 1970, **222**, 83–87

Parkes, C. M., 'Recent bereavement as a cause of mental illness'. *Brit. J. Psychiat.*, 1964, **110**, 198–204

Partington, M. W., 'Observations on phenylketonuria in Ontario'. *Canad. Med. Assoc. J.*, 1964, **90**, 1312–1315

Paykel, E. S., 'Recent life events and clinical depression'. In *Life Stress and Psychiatric Illness* (Eds. E. K. Gunderson and R. H. Rahe). Springfield, Ill.: Charles C. Thomas, 1974. Pp. 134–163

Paykel, E. S., 'Contribution of life events to causation of psychiatric illness'. *Psychol. Med.*, 1978, **8**, 245–253

Paykel, E. S., Myers, J. K., Dienelt, M. N., Klerman, G. L., Lindenthal, J. J., and Popper, M. P., 'Life events and depression: A controlled study'. *Arch. Gen. Psychiat.*, 1969, **21**, 753–760

Penrose, L. S., 'Parental age and non-disjunction'. In *Human Chromosome Abnormalities* (Ed. W. M. Davidson and D. R. Smith)—London: Staples Press, 1961

Perris, C. (Ed.), 'A study of bipolar (manic-depressive) and unipolar depressive psychoses'. *Acta Psychiat. Scand.*, Suppl. 194, 1966

Pitcher, D. R., 'The XYY syndrome'. *Brit. J. Hosp. Med.*, 1971, **5**, 379–393

Popper, Sir Karl, Conjectures and Refutations. The Growth of Scientific Knowledge—London: Routledge & Kegan Paul, 1965

Price, J., 'The genetics of depressive behaviour'. In *Recent Developments in Affective Disorders. A Symposium* (Eds. A. Coppen and A. Walk). *Brit. J. Psychiat. Spec. Publ. No. 2.* Ashley, Kent: Headley Bros., 1968, Pp. 37–54

Price, W. H., Unpublished reference by Leader Writer, *Lancet*, 1974, **2**, 1297

Price, W. H., Strong, J. A., Whetmore, P. B., and McClemont, W. F., 'Criminal patients with XYY sex-chromosome complement'. *Lancet*, 1966, **1**, 565–566

Rainer, J. D., Mesnikoff, A., Kolb, L. C., and Carr, A., 'Homosexuality and heterosexuality in identical twins'. *Psychosom. Med.*, 1960, **22**, 251–258

Rees, W. D. and Lutkins, S. G., 'Mortality and bereavement'. *Brit. Med. J.*, 1967, **4**, 13–16

Richards, W., 'The fortification illusions of migraines'. *Scient. Amer.*, 1971, **224**, 89–95

Rieke, J., 'Über depressive Psychosen im Verlaufe von Hirntumorerkrankungen'. *Nervenarzt*, 1975, **46**, 152–159

Rimon, R. and Halonen, P., 'Herpes simplex virus infection and depressive illness'. *Dis. Nerv. Syst.*, 1969, **30**, 338–340

Rosenthal, D., 'Problems of sampling and diagnosis in the major twin studies of schizophrenia'. *J. Psychiat. Res.*, 1962, **1**, 116–134

REFERENCES TO PART IV, RECENT DEVELOPMENTS

Routtenberg, A., 'The reward system of the brain'. *Scient. Amer.*, 1978, **239**, 122–131

Scadding, J. G., 'Diagnosis: The clinician and the computer'. *Lancet*, 1967, **2**, 877–882

Schildkraut, J. J., 'Neuropsychopharmacology and the affective disorders'. *New Engl. J. Med.*, 1969, **281**, 197–201; 248–255; 302–308

Sedman, G., 'A comparative study of pseudohallucinations, imagery and true hallucinations'. *Brit. J. Psychiat.*, 1966a, **112**, 9–17

Sedman, G., 'Inner voices: phenomenological and clinical aspects'. *Brit. J. Psychiat.*, 1966b, **112**, 485–490

Sedman, G., 'Experimental and phenomenological approaches to the problem of hallucinations in organic psychosyndromes'. *Brit. J. Psychiat.*, 1967, **113**, 1115–1121

Shaw, D. M., 'Mineral metabolism, mania and melancholia'. *Brit. Med. J.*, 1966, **2**, 262–267

Shields, J., 'Genetics'. In *Schizophrenia. Towards a New Synthesis* (Ed. J. K. Wing)—London: Academic Press and New York: Grune & Stratton, 1978. Pp. 53–87

Siegel, R. K., 'Hallucinations'. *Scient. Amer.*, 1977, **237**, 132–140

Slater, E., 'Birth order and maternal age of homsexuals'. *Lancet*, 1962, **1**, 69–71

Slater, E., Beard, A. W., and Glithero, E., 'The schizophrenia-like psychoses of epilepsy'. *Brit. J. Psychiat.*, 1963, **109**, 95–150

Slater, E. and Cowie, V., The Genetics of Mental Disorders—London: Oxford Univ. Press, 1971

Stenstedt, Å., 'A study in manic-depressive psychosis: Clinical, social and genetic investigations'. *Acta Psychiat. Scand.*, Suppl. 79, 1952

Stephenson, J. B. P. and McBean, M. S., 'Diagnosis of phenylketonuria (phenylalanine hydroxylase deficiency, temporary and permanent)'. *Brit. Med. J.*, 1967, **3**, 579–581

Storey, P. B., 'Emotional disturbances before and after sub-arachnoid haemorrhage'. In *Physiology, Emotion and Psychosomatic Illness* (Eds. R. Porter and J. Knight). Ciba Foundation Symposium No. 8 (new series)—Amsterdam: Associated Scientific Publishers, 1972. Pp. 337–343

Surridge, D., 'An investigation into some psychiatric aspects of multiple sclerosis', *Brit. J. Psychiat.*, 1969, **115**, 749–764

Taylor, F. Kräupl, 'A logical analysis of the medico-psychological concept of disease'. *Psychol. Med.*, 1971, **1**, 356–364 and 1972, **2**, 7–16

Taylor, F. Kräupl, 'The medical concept of the disease concept'. *Brit. J. Psychiat.*, 1976, **128**, 588–594

Taylor, F. Kräupl, The Concepts of Illness, Disease and Morbus—Cambridge Univ. Press, 1979

Taylor, M. and Abrams, R., 'A genetic study of early and late onset affective disorders'. *Arch. Gen. Psychiat.*, 1973, **28**, 656–658

Tennant, C. and Bebbington, P., 'The social causation of depression: A critique of the work of Brown and his colleagues'. *Psychol. Med.*, 1978, **8**, 565–575

Tienari, P., 'Psychiatric illnesses in identical twins'. *Acta Psychiat. Scand.*, Suppl. 171, 1963

Tienari, P., 'Schizophrenia in monozygotic male twins'. In *The Transmission of Schizophrenia* (Eds. D. Rosenthal and S. S. Kety)—Oxford: Pergamon, 1968. Pp. 27–36

Tienari, P., 'Schizophrenia and monozygotic twins'. In *Psychiatrica Fennica*

REFERENCES TO PART IV, RECENT DEVELOPMENTS

(Ed. K. A. Achté). Helsinki: Helsinki Univ. Central Hosp., 1971. Pp. 97–104. (quoted from Gottesman and Shields, q.v.)

Tooth, G., Studies in Mental Illness on the Gold Coast—London: H.M.S.O., 1950

Tsuang, M-T., 'Birth order and maternal age of psychiatric in-patients'. *Brit. J. Psychiat.*, 1966, **112**, 1131–1141

Turner, R. J. and Wagenfeld, M. O., 'Occupational mobility and schizophrenia: An assessment of the social causation and social selection hypotheses'. *Am. Sociol. Rev.*, 1967, **32**, 104–113

Vaughn, C. E. and Leff, J. P., 'The influence of family and social factors on the course of psychiatric illness. A comparison of schizophrenic and depressed neurotic patients'. *Brit. J. Psychiat.*, 1976, **129**, 125–137

Weinberg, S. K., 'Cultural aspects of manic-depression in West Africa'. *J. Hlth. Hum. Beh.*, 1965, **6**, 247–253

Whitlock, F. A., 'Suicide, cancer and depression'. *Brit. J. Psychiat.*, 1978, **132**, 269–274

Winokur, G., Cadoret, R., Dorzab, J., and Baker, M., 'Depressive disease'. *Arch. Gen. Psychiat.*, 1971, **24**, 135–144

Winokur, G. and Clayton, P., 'Family history studies. I. Two types of affective disorders separated according to genetic and clinical factors'. In *Recent Advances in Biological Psychiatry*. Vol. 9 (Ed. J. Wortis)—New York: Plenum Press, 1967. Pp. 35–50

Winokur, G., Clayton, P. J., and Reich, T., Manic Depressive Illness—Saint Louis: C. V. Mosby Comp., 1969

Wynne, L. C., Ryckoff, I., Day, J., and Hirsch, S., 'Pseudo-mutuality in the family relations of schizophrenics'. *Psychiatry*, **21**, 205–220

Yolles, S. F, and Kramer, M., 'Vital statistics'. In *The Schizophrenic Syndrome* (Eds. L. Bellak and L. Loeb)—New York: Grune & Stratton, 1969. Pp. 66–113

Young, M., Benjamin, B., and Wallis, C., 'The mortality of widowers'. *Lancet*, 1963, **2**, 454–456

Zerbin-Rüdin, E., 'Endogene Psychosen'. In *Humangenetik, ein kurzes Handbuch* (Ed. P. E. Becker), Vol. V/2—Stuttgart: Thieme, 1967. Pp. 446–577

REFERENCES (CHAPTERS 1–21)

1. Abercrombie, M. L. J., 'The observer and his errors'. *J. psychosom. Res.*, 1964, **8**, 169
2. Abraham, H. C., 'Therapeutic and psychological approach to cases of unconsummated marriage'. *Brit. med. J.*, 1956, **1**, 837
3. Ackerknecht, E. H., *A Short History of Medicine* New York: Ronald Press. 1955
4. Ackerknecht, E. H., 'Contributions of Gall and the phrenologists to knowledge of brain functions'. In *The History and Philosophy of Knowledge of the Brain and its Functions* (ed. Poynter) Oxford: Blackwell. 1958
5. Ackner, B., 'Depersonalization'. *J. ment. Sci.*, 1954, **100**, 838
6. Akeleitis, A. J. E., 'Psychiatric aspects of myxoedema'. *J. nerv. ment. Dis.*, 1936, **83**, 22
7. Alexander, M. C., 'Lilliputian hallucinations'. *J. ment. Sci.*, 1926, **72**, 187
8. Allison, R. S., *The Senile Brain. A Clinical Study* London: Edward Arnold. 1962
9. Allport, F. H., *Social Psychology* Boston: Houghton Mifflin. 1924
10. Allport, G. W., *Personality. A Psychological Interpretation* London: Constable. 1938
11. *Amer. J. Psychiat.*, Historical Note: 'The word psychiatry'. 1950/51, **107**, 868
12. Anderson, E. W., 'A study of the sexual life in psychoses associated with childbirth'. *J. ment. Sci.*, 1933, **79**, 137
13. Anderson, E. W., 'An experimental approach to the problem of simulation in mental disorder'. *Proc. roy. Soc. Med.*, 1956, **49**, 513
14. Annell, A.-L., 'School problems in children of average and superior intelligence. A preliminary report'. *J. ment. Sci.*, 1949, **95**, 901
15. Anthony, E. J., 'An experimental approach to the psychopathology of childhood: encopresis'. *Brit. J. med. Psychol.*, 1957, **30**, 146
16. Ardis, J. A. and McKellar, P., 'Hypnagogic imagery and mescalin'. *J. ment. Sci.*, 1956, **102**, 22
17. Asher, R., 'Myxoedematous madness'. *Brit. med. J.*, 1949, **2**, 555
18. Asher, R., 'Munchausen syndrome'. *Lancet*, 1951, **1**, 339
19. Babinski, J., 'Contribution à l'étude des troubles mentaux dans l'hémiplégie organique cérébrale (anosognosie)'. *Rev. Neurol.*, 1914, **27**, 845
20. Backman, E. L., *Religious Dances in the Christian Church and in Popular Medicine* London: Allen and Unwin. 1952
21. Baker, J. P. and Farley, J. D., 'Toxic psychosis following atropine eye-drops'. *Brit. med. J.*, 1958, **2**, 1390
22. Barber, Th. X., 'Experimental evidence for a theory of hypnotic behavior: II. Experimental controls in hypnotic age-regression'. *Int. J. clin. exp. Hypnos.*, 1961, **9**, 181
23. Barker, J. C., 'The syndrome of hospital addiction (Munchausen syndrome)'. *J. ment. Sci.*, 1962, **108**, 167
24. Barron, F., Jarvik, M. E., and Bunnell, St. Jr., 'The hallucinogenic drugs'. *Scient. Amer.*, 1964, **210**, 29

25. Bartlett, F. C., *Remembering. A Study of Experimental and Social Psychology* Cambridge University Press. 1954
26. Bay, E., 'Über den Begriff der Agnosie'. *Nervenarzt*, 1951, **22**, 179
27. Bay, E., Lauenstein, O., and Cibis, P., 'Ein Beitrag zur Frage der Seelenblindheit'. *Psychiat. Neurol. med. Psychol.*, 1949, **1**, 73
28. Beach, F. A. and Jaynes, J., 'Effects of early experience upon the behaviour of animals'. *Psychol. Bull.*, 1954, **51**, 239
29. Beard, A. W., 'The schizophrenia-like psychoses of epilepsy. II. Physical aspects'. *Brit. J. Psychiat.*, 1963, **109**, 113
30. Beard, G. M., 'Experiments with the "Jumpers" or "Jumping Frenchmen" of Maine'. *J. nerv. ment. Dis.*, 1880, **7**, 487
31. Beecher, H. K., 'The powerful placebo'. *J. Amer. med. Ass.*, 1955, **159**, 1602
32. Bekény, G. and Péter, A., 'Über Polyopie und Palinopsie'. *Psychiat. et Neurol.*, 1961, **142**, 154
33. Belbin, E., 'The influence of interpolated recall upon recognition'. *Quart. J. exp. Psychol.*, 1950, **2**, 163
34. Bell, E. T., *Mathematics, Queen and Servant of Science* London: G. Bell. 1952
35. Bell, J., 'Huntington's chorea', in *Treasury of Human Inheritance* (ed. R. A. Fisher) Cambridge University Press. 1934
36. Benjamin, H., 'Transvestism and trans-sexualism'. *Int. J. Sexol.*, 1953, **7**, 12
37. Bennett, D. H., 'The body concept'. *J. ment. Sci.*, 1960, **106**, 56
38. Benton, A. L. and Joynt, R. J., 'Early descriptions of aphasia'. *A.M.A. Arch. Neurol.*, 1960, **3**, 205
39. Bercel, N. A., Travis, L. E., Olinger, L. B., and Dreikurs, E., 'Model psychoses induced by LSD-25 in normals. I. Psychophysiological investigation with special reference to the mechanism of the paranoid reaction'. *Arch. Neurol. Psychiat.*, 1956, **75**, 588
40. Berg, I., 'Change of assigned sex at puberty'. *Lancet*, 1963, **2**, 1216
41. Beringer, K., *Der Mescalinrausch. Seine Geschichte und Erscheinungsweise* Berlin: Springer. 1927
42. Berrington, W. P., Liddell, D. W., and Foulds, G. A., 'A re-evaluation of the fugue'. *J. ment. Sci.*, 1956, **102**, 280
43. Best, H. L. and Michaels, R. M., 'Living out "future" experience under hypnosis'. *Science*, 1954, **120**, 1077
44. Bexton, W. H., Heron, W., and Scott, T. H., 'Effects of decreased variation in the sensory environment'. *Canad. J. Psychol.*, 1954, **8**, 70
45. Bickel, H., Gerrard, J., and Hickmans, E. M., 'Influence of phenylalanine intake on phenylketonuria'. *Lancet*, 1953, **2**, 812
46. Bickford, J. A. R. and Ellison, R. M., 'The high incidence of Huntington's chorea in the Duchy of Cornwall'. *J. ment. Sci.*, 1953, **99**, 291
47. Bivin, G. D. and Klinger, M. P., *Pseudocyesis* Bloomington, Ind.: Principia Press. 1937
48. Black, St., Humphrey, J. H., and Niven, J. S. F., 'Inhibition of Mantoux reaction by direct suggestion under hypnosis'. *Brit. med. J.*, 1963, **1**, 1649
49. Blackham, H. J., *Six Existentialist Thinkers* New York: Harper. 1959
50. Bleuler, E., *Dementia Praecox or the Group of Schizophrenias* (1911). Transl. J. Zinkin. New York: Int. Univ. Press. 1950
51. Bliss, E. L. and Branch, C. H. H., *Anorexia Nervosa. Its History, Psychology and Biology* New York: Hoeber. 1961

52. Blomfield, J. M. and Douglas, J. W. B., 'Bedwetting. Prevalence among children aged 4 to 7 years'. *Lancet*, 1956, **1**, 850
53. Bockner, S., 'Gilles de la Tourette's disease'. *J. ment. Sci.*, 1959, **105**, 1078
54. Boole, G., *An Investigation of the Laws of Thought* (1854) Reprinted, New York: Dover
55. Bowlby, J., *Maternal Care and Mental Health*. Geneva: *W.H.O. Monograph No.* **2**. 1951. Republished in abridged form as *Child Care and the Growth of Love*. Penguin Books. 1953
56. Bowlby, J., Ainsworth, M., Boston, M., and Rosenbluth, D., 'The effect of mother-child separation; a follow-up study'. *Brit. J. med. Psychol.*, 1956, **29**, 211
57. Brain, W. R., 'Sleep: normal and pathological'. *Brit. med. J.*, 1939, **2**, 51
58. Brain, Sir Russell, The Thirtieth Maudsley Lecture: 'Perception and imperception'. *J. ment. Sci.*, 1956, **102**, 221
59. Brain, Sir Russell, *Speech Disorders. Aphasia, Apraxia and Agnosia* London: Butterworths. 1961
60. Brain, Lord, 'Psychosomatic medicine and the brain-mind relationship'. *Lancet*, 1964, **2**, 325
61. Brazier, M. A. B., 'The evolution of concepts relating to the electrical activity of the nervous system. 1600 to 1800'. in *The History and Philosophy of Knowledge of the Brain and its Functions* (ed. Poynter) Oxford: Blackwell. 1958
62. Brentano, F. C., *Psychologie vom Empirischen Standpunkte* Leipzig: Duncker & Humblot. 1874
63. Breuer, J. and Freud, S., *Studies in Hysteria* (1895) Trans. Brill. New York: *Nerv. Ment. Dis. Monogr.* Series No. 61. 1950
64. *Brit. med. J.*, Leader on the 'Schizophrenic syndrome in childhood'. 1961, **2**, 945
65. Bromberg, W., *The Mind of Man. A History of Psychotherapy and Psychoanalysis* New York: Harper. 1959
66. Brown, G. W., Carstairs, G. M., and Topping, G., 'Post-hospital adjustment of chronic mental patients'. *Lancet*, 1958, **2**, 685
67. Brown, W. M. G., Harnden, D. G., Jacobs, P. A., Maclean, N., and Mantle, D. J., *Abnormalities of the Sex Chromosome Complement in Man*. London: HMSO Medical Research Council Special Report Series No. 305. 1964
68. Bruner, J. S. and Goodman, C. C., 'Value and need as organizing factors in perception'. *J. abnorm. soc. Psychol.*, 1947, **42**, 33
69. Brussel, J. A. and Hitch, K. S., 'Military malingerer'. *Mil. Surgeon*, 1943, **93**, 33
70. Burt, C., *The Factors of the Mind* London Univ. Press. 1940
71. Burt, C., The Twenty-sixth Maudsley Lecture: 'The assessment of personality'. *J. ment. Sci.*, 1954, **100**, 1
72. Byrd, R. E., *Alone* New York: Putnam. 1938
73. Cairns, D., 'Phenomenology' in *History of Philosophical Systems* (ed. V. Ferm) Paterson, N.J.: Littlefield, Adams. 1961
74. Cameron, A. J., 'Heroin addicts in a casualty department'. *Brit. med. J.*, 1964, **1**, 594
75. Cantril, H., *The Invasion from Mars* Princeton Univ. Press. 1940
76. Carstairs, G. M., 'Social factors in the outcome of mental illness'. *Proc. roy. Soc. Med.*, 1959, **52**, 279

77. Carter, C. O., *Human Heredity* Penguin Books. 1962
78. Cattel, R. B., *Personality* New York: McGraw-Hill. 1950
79. Chapman, J. and McGhie, A., 'Echopraxia in schizophrenia'. *Brit. J. Psychiat.*, 1964, **110**, 365
80. Chapman, L. F. and Wolff, H. G., 'Disease of the neopallium and impairment of the highest integrative functions'. *Med. Clin. N. Amer.*, 1958 (May), 677
81. Cherry, C., *On Human Communications* New York: Science Editions. 1961
82. Clarke, E. and Melnick, S. C., 'The Munchausen syndrome or the problem of hospital hobos'. *Amer. J. Med.*, 1958, **25**, 6
83. Close, H. G., 'Two apparently normal triple-X females'. *Lancet*, 1963, **2**, 1358
84. Lord Cohen, 'Epilepsy as a social problem'. *Brit. med. J.*, 1958, **1**, 672
85. Cohen, E. A., *Human Behaviour in the Concentration Camp* London: Cape. 1954
86. Cole, J. O. and Katz, M. M., 'The psychotomimetic drugs: an overview'. *J. Amer. med. Ass.*, 1964, **187**, 758
87. Comte, A., *System of Positive Polity or Treatise on Sociology* Paris: Carilian-Goeury and V. Dalmont. 1851/54
88. Connell, P. H., *Amphetamine Psychosis*. Maudsley Monographs. No. 5. London: Chapman and Hall. 1958
89. Coplestone, F., *Contemporary Philosophy. Studies of Logical Positivism and Existentialism* London: Burns and Oates. 1956
90. Coppen, A. and Kessel, N., 'Menstruation and personality'. *Brit. J. Psychiat.*, 1963, **109**, 711
91. Corning, W. C. and John, E. R., 'Effect of ribonuclease on retention of conditioned response in regenerated planarians'. *Science*, 1961, **134**, 1363
92. Courtauld, A., Obituary notice in *The Times* of 5th March, 1959
●93. Cowie, V., 'Phenylpyruvic oligophrenia'. *J. ment. Sci.*, 1951, **97**, 505
94. Creak, M., 'Childhood psychosis. A review of 100 cases'. *Brit. J. Psychiat.*, 1963, **109**, 84
95. Creak, M. *et al.*, 'Schizophrenic syndrome in childhood. Progress report (April, 1961) of a working party'. *Brit. med. J.*, 1961, **2**, 889
96. Crick, F. H. C., 'The genetic code'. *Scient. Amer.*, 1962, **207**, 66
97. Critchley, M., 'Huntington's chorea and East Anglia'. *J. State Med.*, 1934, **42**, 575
98. Critchley, M., 'The body image in neurology'. *Lancet*, 1950, **1**, 335
99. Critchley, M., 'Types of visual perseveration: "palinopsia" and "illusory visual spread"'. *Brain*, 1951, **74**, 267
100. Critchley, M., *The Parietal Lobes* London: Arnold. 1953
101. Critchley, M., 'Personification of paralysed limbs in hemiplegics'. *Brit. med. J.*, 1955, **2**, 284
102. Critchley, M., 'Medical aspects of boxing, particularly from a neurological standpoint'. *Brit. med. J.*, 1957, **1**, 357
103. Critchley, M., 'Dr. Samuel Johnson's aphasia'. *Med. Hist.*, 1962, **6**, 27
104. Critchley, M., 'The neurology of psychotic speech'. *Brit. J. Psychiat.*, 1964, **110**, 353
105. Critchley, M., 'Psychiatric symptoms and parietal disease: differential diagnosis'. *Proc. roy. Soc. Med.*, 1964, **57**, 422

REFERENCES (CHAPTERS 1-21)

106. Critchley, M., *Developmental Dyslexia* London: Heinemann. 1964
107. Dalton, K., 'Effect of menstruation on schoolgirls' weekly work'. *Brit. med. J.*, 1960, **1**, 326
108. Dalton, K., 'Schoolgirls' behaviour and menstruation'. *Brit. med. J.*, 1960, **2**, 1647
109. Dalton, K., 'Menstruation and crime'. *Brit. med. J.*, 1961, **2**, 1752
110. Daniels, L. E., 'Narcolepsy'. *Medicine*, 1934, **13**, 1
111. Davies, D. L., 'Psychiatric illness in those engaged to be married'. *Brit. J. prev. soc. Med.*, 1956, **10**, 123
112. Davis, K., 'Final note on a case of extreme isolation'. *Amer. J. Sociol.*, 1947, **52**, 432
113. Dekker, E. and Groen, J., 'Reproducible psychogenic attacks of asthma. A laboratory study'. *J. Psychosom. Res.*, 1956, **1**, 58
114. Dennis, W., 'The significance of feral man'. *Amer. J. Psychol.*, 1941, **54**, 425
115. Dewhurst, C. J. and Gordon, R. R., 'Change of sex'. *Lancet*, 1963, **2**, 1213
116. Dewhurst, K. and Pearson, J., 'Visual hallucinations of the self in organic diseases'. *J. Neurol. Neurosurg. Psychiat.*, 1955, **18**, 53
117. Dewhurst, W. G. and Eilenberg, M. D., 'Folie à trois. Case report'. *J. ment. Sci.*, 1961, **107**, 486
118. Dominion, J., Serafetinides, E. A., and Dewhurst, M., 'A follow-up study of late-onset epilepsy. Psychiatric and social findings'. *Brit. med. J.*, 1963, **1**, 431
119. Donath, J., 'Zur Kenntnis des Anancasmus. (Psychische Zwangs-zustände)'. *Arch. Psychiat. Nervenk.*, 1897, **29**, 211
120. Dostoevski, F. M., *The House of the Dead* (1862)
121. Doswald, D. C. and Kreibich, D. K., 'Zur Frage der posthypnotischen Hautphänomene'. *Mh. prakt. Derm.*, 1906, **43**, 634
122. Drew, G. C., Colquhoun, W. P., and Long, H. A., 'Effect of small doses of alcohol on a skill resembling driving'. *Brit. med. J.*, 1958, **2**, 993
123. Dunham, H. W., 'Social psychiatry'. *Amer. sociol. Rev.*, 1948, **13**, 183
124. Dunlap, H. F. and Moersch, F. P., 'Psychic manifestations associated with hyperthyroidism'. *Amer. J. Psychiat.*, 1935, **91**, 1215
125. Durkheim, E., *Le Suicide* Paris (1897) *Suicide. A Study in Sociology* Trans. Spaulding and Simpson. London: Routledge and Kegan Paul. 1952
126. Eaton, J. W. and Weil, R. J., *Culture and Mental Disorders. A Comparative Study of the Hutterites and Other Populations* Free Press of Glencoe. 1955
127. Edwards, G., 'Alcoholism as a public health problem in the U.S.A.'. *Lancet*, 1962, **1**, 960
128. Eilenberg, M. D., 'Psychiatric illness and pernicious anaemia: a clinical re-evaluation'. *J. ment. Sci.*, 1960, **106**, 1539
129. Ellis, W. G., 'Latah. A mental malady of the Malays'. *J. ment. Sci.*, 1897, **43**, 32
130. Eysenck, H. J., 'The logical basis of factor analysis'. *Amer. Psychol.*, 1953, **8**, 105
131. Eysenck, H. J., *Structure of Human Personality*. 2nd ed. London: Methuen. 1959
132. Eysenck, H. J., 'Classification and the problem of diagnosis', in *Handbook of Abnormal Psychology* (ed. Eysenck) London: Pitman. 1960
133. Eysenck, H. J. and Prell, D., 'The inheritance of neuroticism: an experimental study'. *J. ment. Sci.*, 1951, **97**, 441

134. Eysenck, S. B. G., 'Neurosis and psychosis: an experimental analysis'. *J. ment. Sci.*, 1956, **102**, 517
135. Faber, K., *Nosography. The Evolution of Clinical Medicine in Modern Times* 2nd ed. New York: Hoeber. 1930
136. Faris, R. E. L., 'Ecological factors in human behavior', in *Personality and Behavior Disorders* (ed. J. McV. Hunt). New York: Ronald Press. 1944
137. Festinger, L., *A Theory of Cognitive Dissonance* New York: Row, Peterson. 1957
138. Festinger, L., Riecken, H. W., Jr., and Schachter, S., *When Prophecy Fails* Univ. Minneapolis Press. 1956
139. Fölling. A., 'Über Ausscheidung von Phenylbrenztraubensäure in den Harn als Stoffwechselanomalie in Verbindung mit Imbezillität'. *Z. physiol Chem.*, 1934, **227**, 169
140. Ford, C. E., Jones, K. W., Polani, P. E., Almeida, J. C. de, and Briggs, J. H., 'A sex-chromosome anomaly in a case of gonadal dysgenesis (Turner's syndrome)'. *Lancet*, 1959, **1**, 711
141. Ford, C. S. and Beach, F. A., *Patterns of Sexual Behavior* London: Eyre and Spottiswoode. 1952
142. Foundeur, M., Fixsen, C., Triebel, W. A., and White, M. A., 'Post-partum mental illness; a controlled study'. *Arch. Neurol. Psychiat.*, 1957, **77**, 503
143. Frank, R. T., 'The hormonal cause of premenstrual tension'. *Arch. Neurol. Psychiat.*, 1931, **26**, 1053
144. Franklin, A. W. (ed.), *Word Blindness or Specific Developmental Dyslexia* London: Pitman. 1962
145. Freedman, D. G., King, J. A., and Elliott, O., 'Critical period in the social development of dogs'. *Science*, 1961, **133**, 1016
146. Freud, S., 'Über den Ursprung des N. Acusticus'. *Monatsschr. f. Ohrenheilkunde*, 1886, **20**, 245 and 277
147. Freud, S., *Zur Auffassung der Aphasien.* (1891) *On Aphasia* Trans. E. Stengel. London: Imago. 1953

References 148–165 are taken from: Freud, S., *Standard Edition of the Complete Psychological Works of Sigmund Freud* London: Hogarth Press
148. 'On the grounds for detaching a particular syndrome from neurasthenia under the description "anxiety neurosis"' (1895) 1962, **3**, 87
149. 'A reply to criticisms of my paper on anxiety neurosis' (1895) 1962, **3**, 119
150. 'Character and anal eroticism' (1908) 1959, **9**, 167
151. 'The psycho-analytic view of psychogenic disturbances of vision' (1910) 1957, **11**, 209
152. 'Psycho-analytic notes upon an autobiographical account of a case of paranoia (dementia paranoides)' (1911) 1958, **12**, 1
153. 'The dynamics of the transference' (1912) 1958, **12**, 97
154. 'On beginning the treatment. (Further recommendations on the technique of psycho-analysis. I)' (1913) 1958, **12**, 121
155. 'Some character-types met with in psycho-analytic work' (1915) 1957, **14**, 309
156. 'On transformations of instinct as exemplified in anal erotism' (1917) 1955, **17**, 125
157. 'Mourning and melancholia' (1917) 1957, **14**, 239

158. 'The psychogenesis of a case of homosexuality in a woman' (1920) 1955, **18**, 145
159. 'Psycho-analysis' (1923) 1955, **18**, 235
160. 'An autobiographical study' (1925) 1959, **20**, 7
161. 'Psychoanalysis' (1926) 1959, **20**, 259
162. 'Inhibitions, Symptoms and Anxiety' (1926) 1959, **20**, 77
163. 'Libidinal Types' (1931) 1961, **21**, 215
164. 'Why war?' Letter to Einstein in 'Thoughts on Civilization, War and Death' (1932) 1957, **14**, 273
165. 'New introductory lectures on psycho-analysis' (1933) 1964, **22**, 3
    [end of references from Freud: *Standard Edition*]

166. Freud, S., *Leonardo da Vinci and a Memory of his Childhood* (1910) Trans. Tyson, Introduction by Farrell. London: Pelican Books. 1963
167. Freud, S., *Introductory Lectures on Psycho-analysis. A Course of Twenty-Eight Lectures delivered at the University of Vienna* (1916–1917) Trans. Riviere. 2nd ed. London: Allen and Unwin. 1929
168. Freud, S., *The Origins of Psycho-Analysis. Letters to Wilhelm Fliess, Drafts and Notes* (1887–1902) London: Imago. 1954
169. Frisch, K. v., 'Dialects in the language of the bees'. *Scient. Amer.*, 1962, **207**, 79
170. Fritsch, G. and Hitzig, E., 'Über die elektrische Erregbarkeit des Grosshirns'. *Arch. Anat. Physiol. wiss. Med.*, 1870, **37**, 300
171. Gairdner, D., 'The fate of the foreskin. A study of circumcision'. *Brit. med. J.*, 1949, **2**, 1433
172. Galton, F., 'The history of twins as a criterion of the relative powers of nature and nurture'. *Fraser's Magazine*, 1875, **12**, 566
173. Galton, F., 'Psychometric experiments'. *Brain*, 1879/80, **2**, 149
174. Galton, F., *Inquiries into Human Faculty and its Development* London: Macmillan. 1883
175. Galton, F., 'Measurement of character'. *Fortnightly Rev.*, 1884, **36**, 179
176. Galton, F., 'Regression towards mediocrity'. *J. Anthropol. Inst.*, 1886, **15**, 246
177. Galton, F., 'Co-relations and their measurement, chiefly from anthropometric data'. *Proc. roy. Soc.*, 1888/89, **45**, 135
178. Ganser, S. J., 'Über einen eigenartigen Dämmerzustand'. *Arch. f. Psychiat. Nervenk.*, 1898, **30**, 633
179. Ganser, S. J., 'Zur Lehre vom hysterischen Dämmerzustande'. *Arch. f. Psychiat. Nervenk.*, 1904, **38**, 34
180. Gardner, M., *Fads and Fallacies in the Name of Science* New York: Dover. 1957
181. Garwood, K., 'Superstition and half-belief'. *New Society*, 1963, **1**, 13
182. Gerard, D. L. and Houston, L. G., 'Family setting and the social ecology of schizophrenia'. *Psychiat. Quart.*, 1953, **27**, 90
183. Ghabrial, F. and Girgis, S. M., 'Reorientation of sex: report of two cases'. *Int. J. Fertil.*, 1962, **7**, 249
184. Gibbens, T. C. N., Pond, D. A., and Stafford-Clark, D., 'A follow-up study of criminal psychopaths'. *J. ment. Sci.*, 1959, **105**, 108
185. Giel, R., Knox, R. S., and Carstairs, G. M., 'A five-year follow-up of 100 neurotic out-patients'. *Brit. med. J.*, 1964, **2**, 160
186. Glithero, E. and Slater, E., 'The schizophrenia-like psychoses of epilepsy. IV. Follow-up record and outcome'. *Brit. J. Psychiat.*, 1963, **109**, 134

187. Gödel, K., 'Über formal unentscheidbare Sätze der Principia Mathematica und verwandter Systeme'. Monatsh. f. Mathem. u. Physik, 1931, **38**, 173—*On Formally Undecidable Propositions of Principia Mathematica and Related Systems* Trans. B. Meltzer with Introduction by R. B. Braithwaite. Edinburgh: Oliver and Boyd. 1962

188. Goldin, S., 'Lilliputian hallucinations. Eight illustrative case histories'. *J. ment. Sci.*, 1955, **101**, 569

189. Goldin, S. and MacDonald, J. A., 'The Ganser state'. *J. ment. Sci.*, 1955, **101**, 267

190. Goldman, F., 'Breastfeeding and character formation. II. The etiology of oral character in psychoanalytic theory'. *J. Personality*, 1950, **19**, 189

191. Goldstein, K., *Aftereffects of Brain Injuries in War* London: Heinemann. 1942

192. Goldstein, K. and Gelb, A., 'Psychologische Analysen hirnpathologischer Fälle auf Grund von Untersuchungen Hirnverletzter'. *Z. ges. Neurol. Psychiat.*, 1918, **41**, 1

193. Gooddy, W., 'Directional features of reading and writing'. *Proc. roy. Soc. Med.*, 1963, **56**, 206

194. Gooddy, W. and Reinhold, M. 'Congenital dyslexia and asymmetry of cerebral function'. *Brain*, 1961, **84**, 231

195. Goode, G. B., 'Sleep paralysis'. *Arch. Neurol.*, 1962, **6**, 228

196. Gowers, W. R., *A Manual of Diseases of the Nervous System* London: Churchill. 1888

197. Graves, R., *The Greek Myths* Penguin Books. 1955

198. Green, T. C., 'The incidence of drug addiction in Great Britain and its prevention'. *Proc. roy. Soc. Med.*, 1960, **53**, 921

199. Greenberg, H. P., 'Crime and *folie à deux*: review and case history'. *J. ment. Sci.*, 1956, **102**, 772

200. Greene, R., 'Mental performance in chronic anoxia'. *Brit. med. J.*, 1957, **1**, 1028

201. Greene, R. and Dalton, K., 'The premenstrual syndrome'. *Brit. med. J.*, 1953, **1**, 1007

202. Gregory, R. L., 'Human perception'. *Brit. med. Bull.*, 1964, **20**, 21

203. Grünthal, E. and Störring, G. E., 'Über das Verhalten bei umschriebener, völliger Merkunfähigkeit'. *Mschr. Psychiat. Neurol.*, 1930, **74**, 254

204. Grünthal, E. and Störring, G., 'Völliger isolierter Verlust der Merkfähigkeit. Organische CO-Schädigung oder hysterische Verdrängung? (Entgegnung zu Schellers Darlegung in dieser Z.,) 1950, **21**, 49.' *Nervenarzt*, 1950, **21**, 522 (See also Scheller, H., 'Bemerkungen zu der vorstehenden Entgegnung'.) *Nervenarzt*, 1950, **21**, 524

205. Grünthal, E. and Störring, G. E., 'Abschliessende Stellungnahme zu der vorstehenden Arbeit von H. Völkel und R. Stolze über den Fall B'. *Mschr. Psychiat. Neurol.*, 1956, **132**, 309

206. Gurney, E. and Myers, F. W. H., 'Visible apparitions'. *Nineteenth Century*, 1884, **16**, 68

207. Haggard, E. A., Brekstad, A., and Skard, A. G., 'On the reliability of the anamnestic interview'. *J. abnorm. soc. Psychol.*, 1960, **61**, 311

208. Halbwachs, M., *Les Causes du Suicide* Paris: Alcan. 1930

209. Hald, J. and Jacobson, E., 'A drug sensitizing the organism to ethyl alcohol'. *Lancet*, 1948, **2**, 1001

210. Hallgren, B., *Specific Dyslexis ('Congenital Wordblindness')* Acta Psychtai., *(Kbh.) Suppl.* 65, 1950
211. Halverson, H. M., 'Genital and sphincter behavior of the male infant'. *J. gen. Psychol.*, 1940, **56**, 95
212. Hamilton, J. A., *Post-partum psychiatric problems* Saint Louis: Mosby. 1962
213. Hamilton, Sir William, *Lectures on Metaphysics and Logic* (ed. Mansel and Veitch). Edinburgh: Blackwood. 1877
213a. Hammond, W. A., 'Miryachit: a newly described disease of the nervous system and its analogues'. *Brit. med. J.*, 1884, **1**, 758
214. Hampson, J. L., 'Determinants of psychosexual orientation (gender role) in humans'. *Canad. psychiat. Ass. J.*, 1963, **8**, 24
215. Hare, E. H., 'The ecology of mental disease'. *J. ment. Sci.*, 1952, **98**, 579
216. Hare, E. H., 'Mental illness and social conditions in Bristol'. *J. ment. Sci.*, 1956, **102**, 349
217. Hare, E. H., 'Family setting and the urban distribution of schizophrenia'. *J. ment. Sci.*, 1956, **102**, 753
218. Hare, E. H., 'The origin and spread of dementia paralytica'. *J. ment. Sci.*, 1959, **105**, 594
219. Hare, E. H., 'Masturbatory insanity: the history of an idea'. *J. ment. Sci.*, 1962, **108**, 1
220. Harlow, H. F. and Harlow, M. K., 'Social deprivation in monkeys'. *Scient. Amer.*, 1962, **207**, 137
221. Harris, H., *The Group Approach to Leadership-Testing* London: Routledge and Kegan Paul. 1949
222. Hartmann, E. v., *Philosophy of the Unconscious* Transl. Coupland. London: Kegan Paul, Trench, Trübner. 1931
223. Hartshorne, H. and May, M. A., *Studies in Deceit* London: Macmillan, 1928
224. Hawkings, J. R., Jones, K. S., Sim, M., and Tibbets, R. W., 'Deliberate disability'. *Brit. med. J.*, 1956, **1**, 361
225. Hearnshaw, L. S., *A Short History of British Psychology. 1840–1940.* London: Methuen. 1964
226. Heaton-Ward, W. A., 'Psychopathic disorder'. *Lancet*, 1963, **1**, 121
227. Hécaen, H. et Ajuriaguerra, J. de, 'L'apraxie de l'habillage; ses rapports avec la planotopokinésie et les troubles de la somatognosie'. *Encéphale*, 1942–45, **35**, 113
228. Hecker, J. F. C., *Die Tanzwuth, eine Volkskrankheit im Mittelalter.* Berlin: Enslin. 1832.—*The Dancing Manias* Trans. Babington. Philadelphia: Haswell. 1837
229. Heidegger, M., *Sein und Zeit* Halle: Niemeyer. 1927
230. Henderson, D. K. and Gillespie, R. D., *A Textbook of Psychiatry* 5th ed. London: Oxford University Press. 1940
231. Hermelin, B. and O'Connor, N., 'Reading ability of severely subnormal children'. *J. ment. Defic. Res.* 1960, **4**, 144
232. Heron, W., Doane, B. K., and Scott, T. H., 'Visual disturbances after prolonged perceptual isolation'. *Canad. J. Psychol.*, 1956, **10**, 13
233. Hess, E. H., 'Ethology. An approach toward the complete analysis of behavior' in *New Directions in Psychology* New York: Holt, Rinehart and Winston. 1962. Ch. 3
234. Hildebrandt, H., 'Über Krampf des Levator ani beim coitus'. *Arch. f. Gyn.* 1872, **3**, 221
235. Hill, D., 'The psychiatry of the epileptic'. *Proc. roy. Soc. Med.*, 1963, **56**, 714

236. Hippocrates, 'The sacred disease' in *The Medical Works of Hippocrates* Trans. Chadwick and Mann. Oxford: Blackwell. 1950
237. Hirschfeld, M., *Die Transvestiten, eine Untersuchung über den erotischen Verkleidungstrieb mit umfangreichem, casuistischem und historischem Material* Berlin: Pulvermacher. 1910
238. Hoenig, J., Anderson, E. W., Kenna, J. C., and Blunden, R., 'Clinical and pathological aspects of the mnestic syndrome'. *J. ment. Sci.*, 1962, **108,** 541
239. Hoffer, W., 'Diaries of adolescent schizophrenics (hebephrenics)'. *Psychoanal. Study of the Child*, 1946, **2,** 293
240. Holzel, A., Komrower, G. M., and Schwarz, V., 'Galactosemia'. *Amer. J. Med.*, 1957, **22,** 703
241. Howard, P., Leathart, G. L., Dornhorst, A. C., and Sharpey-Shafer, E. P., 'The mess trick and fainting lark'. *Brit. med. J.*, 1951, **2,** 382
242. Howells, J. G. and Layng, J., 'Separation experiences and mental health'. *Lancet*, 1955, **2,** 285
243. Hunter, R. and MacAlpine, I., *Three Hundred Years of Psychiatry. 1535–1860*. London: Oxford Univ. Press. 1963
244. Hurwitz, J. and Furth, J. J., 'Messenger RNA'. *Scient. Amer.*, 1962, **206,** 41
245. Husserl, E., *Ideen zu einer Reinen Phänomenologie und Phänomenologischen Philosophie*. Halle. (1913) *Ideas: General Introduction to Pure Phenomenology* Trans. W. R. B. Gibson. London: Allen and Unwin. 1931
246. Hydén, H., 'Biochemical changes in glial cells and nerve cells at varying activity'. in *Biochemistry of the Central Nervous System* (ed. Brücke) London: Pergamon Press. 1959
247. Hydén, H., 'Satellite cells in the nervous system'. *Scient. Amer.*, 1961, **205,** 62
248. Ingram, T. T. S., 'The Association of speech retardation and educational difficulties'. *Proc. roy. Soc. Med.*, 1963, **56,** 199
249. Isbell, H., 'The pharmacology of opiates and similar addiction-producing drugs'. *Proc. roy. Soc. Med.*, 1960, **53,** 925
250. Isbell, H., Fraser, H. F., Wikler, A., Belleville, R. E., and Eisenman, A. J., 'An experimental study of the etiology of "rum fits" and delirium tremens'. *Quart. J. Stud. Alcohol*, 1955, **16,** 1
251. Jacobs, P., Baikie, A. G., Brown, W. M. C., MacGregor, T. N., Maclean, N., and Harnden, D. G., 'Evidence for the existence of the human "super female" '. *Lancet*, 1959, **2,** 423
252. Jacobs, P. A. and Strong, J. A., 'A case of human intersexuality having a possible XXY sex-determining mechanism'. *Nature*, 1959, **183,** 302
253. Jacobsen, E., 'Biochemical methods in treatment of alcoholism, with special reference to antabuse'. *Proc. roy. Soc. Med.*, 1950, **43,** 519
254. Jacobsen, E. and Martensen-Larsen, O., 'Treatment of alcoholism with tetraethylthiuram disulfide (antabuse)'. *J. Amer. med. Ass.*, 1949, **139,** 918
256. Jaspers, K., *Reason and Existenz* Trans. W. Earle. London: Routledge and Kegan Paul. 1956
257. Jaspers, K., *General Psychopathology* Trans. J. Hoenig and M. W. Hamilton. Manchester University Press. 1963
258. Jellinek, E. H., 'Fits, faints, coma and dementia in myxoedema'. *Lancet*, 1962, **2,** 1010

259. Jellinek, M., *The Disease Concept of Alcoholism* New Haven, Conn.: Hillhouse, 1960
260. Johnson, D. M., 'The "phantom anaesthetist" of Mattoon: a field study of mass hysteria'. *J. abnorm. soc. Psychol.*, 1945, **40**, 175
261. Jolliffe, N., Bowman, K. M., Rosenblum, L. A., and Fein, H. D., 'Nicotinic acid deficiency encephalopathy'. *J. Amer. med. Ass.*, 1940, **114**, 307
262. Jones, E., *Sigmund Freud. Life and Work* London: Hogarth Press. 1953
263. Jones, H. E., 'Environmental influences on mental Development' in *Manual of Child Psychology* (ed. L. Carmichael) London. Chapman and Hall. 1946
264. Jones, K., *Lunacy, Law and Conscience. 1744–1845* London: Routledge and Kegan Paul. 1955
265. Juda, A., 'Neue psychiatrisch-genealogische Untersuchungen an Hilfsschulzwillingen und ihren Familien: I. Die Zwillingsprobanden und ihre Partner'. *Z. ges. Neurol. Psychiat.*, 1939, **166**, 265
266. Jung, C. G., 'On the psychology and pathology of so-called occult phenomena' (1902) in *Collected Works* London: Routledge and Kegan Paul. 1957, **1**, 3
267. Jung, C. G., 'On simulated insanity' (1903) in *Collected Works* London: Routledge and Kegan Paul. 1957, **1**, 159
268. Jung, C. G., 'Cryptomnesia' (1905) in *Collected Works* London: Routledge and Kegan Paul. 1957, **1**, 95
269. Jung, C. G., *Psychological Types* (1921). London: Routledge and Kegan Paul. 1923
270. Jung, R., 'Über eine Nachuntersuchung des Falles Schn. von Goldstein und Gelb'. *Psychiat. Neurol. med. Psychol.*, 1949, **1**, 353
271. Kahn, E., 'The Emil Kraepelin memorial lecture' in *Epidemiology of Mental Disorder* (ed. B. Pasamanick) Washington: Amer. Ass. Advancement of Science. Publication No. 60. 1959
272. Kalinowsky, L. B., 'Problems of war neuroses in the light of experience in other countries'. *Amer. J. Psychiat.*, 1950, **107**, 340
273. Kallmann, F. J., 'Comparative twin studies on the genetic aspects of male homosexuality'. *J. nerv. ment. Dis.*, 1952, **115**, 283
274. Kallmann, F. J., *Heredity in Health and Mental Disorder*. London: Chapman and Hall. 1953
275. Kalmus, H., *Tune Deafness and its Inheritance* Lund: Hereditas. Suppl. 605. 1949
276. Kant, I., *Anthropologie in Pragmatoscher Hinsicht* (1798) (ed. Starke) 1831
277. Kaufmann, W., *Existentialism from Dostoevsky to Sartre*. New York: Meridian Books. 1956
278. Kay, D. W. K. and Leigh, D., 'The natural history, treatment and prognosis of anorexia nervosa, based on a study of 38 patients'. *J. ment. Sci.*, 1954, **100**, 411
279. Kay, D. W. K., and Roth, M., 'Physical accompaniments of mental disorder in old age'. *Lancet*, 1955, **2**, 740
280. Kay, D. W. K., Roth, M., and Hopkins, B., 'Affective disorders arising in the senium. I. Their association with organic cerebral degeneration'. *J. ment. Sci.*, 1955, **101**, 302
281. Kidd, C. B., Knox., R. S., and Mantle, D. J., 'A psychiatric investigation of triple-X chromosome females'. *Brit. J. Psychiat.*, 1963, **109**, 90

282. Kiloh, L. G. and Brandon, S., 'Habituation and addiction to amphetamines'. *Brit. med. J.*, 1962, **2**, 40
283. Kinsey, A. C., Pomeroy, W. B., and Martin, C. F., *Sexual Behavior in the Human Male* Philadelphia: Saunders. 1948
284. Kinsey, A. C., Pomeroy, W. B., Martin, C. E., and Gebhard, P. H., *Sexual Behavior in the Human Female* Philadelphia: Saunders. 1953
285. Kleinsorge, H. and Klumbies, G., *Technik der Hypnose für Ärzte.* Jena: Fischer. 1961
290. Klinefelter, H. F., Reifenstein, E. C., and Albright, F., 'Syndrome characterized by gynecomastia, aspermatogenesis without a-leydigism, and increased excretion of follicle-stimulating hormone'. *J. clin. Endocrinol.*, 1942, **2**, 615
291. Klintworth, G. K., 'A pair of male monozygotic twins discordant for homosexuality'. *J. nerv. ment. Dis.*, 1962, **135**, 113
292. Kluckhohn, C., 'Culture and behavior' in *Handbook of Social Psychology* (ed. Gardner Lindzey) Cambridge, Mass.: Addison-Wesley. 1954, **2**, 921
293. Klüver, H., *Mescal: The 'Divine' Plant and its Psychological Effects* London: Kegan Paul, Trench, Trübner. 1928
294. Kohler, I., 'Experiments with goggles'. *Scient. Amer.*, 1962, **206**, 62
295. Kolb, L., *Drug Addiction* Springfield, Ill.: Thomas. 1962
296. Kolb, L. C., Rainer, J. D., Mesnikoff, A., and Carr, A., 'Divergent sexual development in identical twins'. *Proc. 3rd World Congr. Psychiat.*, 1961, **1**, 530
297. Konorski, J., 'Trends in the development of physiology of the brain'. *J. ment. Sci.*, 1958, **104**, 1100
298. Kraepelin, E., *Compendium der Psychiatrie* Leipzig. 1883
299. Krafft-Ebing, R. v., *Ein Lehrbuch der Gerichtlichen Psychopathologie mit Berücksichtigung der Gesetzgebung von Oesterreich, Deutschland und Frankreich* Stuttgart: Enke. 1875
300. Kral, V. A., 'Psychiatric observations under severe chronic stress'. *Amer. J. Psychiat.*, 1952, **108**, 185
301. Kral, V. A., 'Masked depression in middle-aged men'. *Canad. med. Ass. J.*, 1958, **79**, 1
302. Krasner, L., 'Studies of the conditioning of verbal behavior'. *Psychol. Bull.*, 1958, **55**, 148
303. Krasner, L., 'A technique of investigating the relationship between behavior cues of examiner and verbal behavior of patient'. *J. cons. Psychol.*, 1958, **22**, 364
304. Kretschmer, E., *Körperbau und Charakter* 20th ed. Berlin: Springer. 1951
305. Kuhn, H., 'Existentialism' in *History of Philosophical Systems* (ed. V. Ferm) Paterson, N.J.: Littlefield, Adams. 1961
306. Kulenkampf, C. and Bauer, A., 'Herzphobie und Herzinfarkt. Zur Anthropologie von Angst und Schmerz'. *Nervenarzt*, 1962, **33**, 289
307. *Lancet*, Leading article on 'Pop "pot"'. 1963, **2**, 989
308. Landers, J. J., 'Observations on foreign-body swallowing in prisons'. *J. Ment. Sci.*, 1949, **95**, 897
309. Laplace, P. S., 'A philosophical essay on probabilities' in *The Structure of Scientific Thought* (ed. Madden) London: Routledge and Kegan Paul. 1960

310. Larssen, T., Sjögren, T., and Jacobson, G., 'Senile dementia. A clinical, sociomedical and genetic study'. *Acta psychiat. scand.*, 1963, **39**, Suppl. 167
311. Lasagna, L., 'Psychological effects of medication. Some explored and unexplored psychological variables in therapeutics'. *Proc. roy. Soc. Med.*, 1962, **55**, 773
312. Lawley, D. N. and Maxwell, A. E., *Factor Analysis as a Statistical Method* London. Butterworths. 1963
313. Lee, S. (ed.), 'Mary Tudor' in *Dictionary of National Biography* London: Smith, Elder. 1893
314. Leigh, D., *The Historical Development of British Psychiatry. Vol. I. 18th and 19th Centuries* London: Pergamon. 1961
315. Lejeune, J., Gautier, M., et Turpin, R., 'Étude des chromosomes somatiques de neuf enfants mongoliens'. *C. rend. Acad. Sc. Paris.*, 1959, **248**, 1721
316. Leroy, R., 'The syndrome of Lilliputian hallucinations'. *J. nerv. ment. Dis.*, 1922, **56**, 325
317. Lewis, A. 'Melancholia: prognostic study and case material'. *J. ment. Sci.*, 1936, **82**, 488
318. Lewis, A., 'J. C. Reil's concepts of brain functions' in *The History and Philosophy of Knowledge of the Brain and its Functions* (ed. Poynter) Oxford: Blackwell. 1958
319. Lewis, A., 'Amnesic syndromes. The psychopathological aspect'. *Proc. roy. Soc. Med.*, 1961, **54**, 955
320. Lewis, A. and Fleminger, J. J., 'The psychiatric risk from corticotrophin and cortisone'. *Lancet*, 1954, **1**, 383
321. Lewis, H., *Deprived Children* London: Oxford University Press. 1954
322. Lewis, H. E., Harries, J. M., Lewis, D. H., and Monchaux, C. de, 'Voluntary solitude. Studies of men in a singlehanded transatlantic sailing race'. *Lancet*, 1964, **1**, 1431
323. Lhermitte, J., 'Visual hallucinations of the self'. *Brit. med. J.*, 1951, **1**, 431
324. Liddell, E. G. T., *The Discovery of Reflexes* Oxford: Clarendon Press. 1960
325. Lifton, R. J., '"Thought reform" of Western civilians in Chinese communist prisons'. *Psychiatry*, 1956, **19**, 173
326. Lilly, J. C., 'Mental effects of reduction of ordinary levels of physical stimuli on intact healthy persons'. *Psychiat. Res. Rep. Amer. Psychiat. Ass.*, 1956, **5**, 1
327. Linnaeus, C., *Genera Morborum* Uppsala. 1763
328. Lorenz, K. Z., 'Der Kumpan in der Umwelt des Vogels'. *J. Ornithol.*, 1935, **83**, 137 and 289
329. Lorenz, K. Z., 'Über die Bildung des Instinktbegriffes'. *Naturwiss.*, 1937, 289, 307, and 324
330. Lorenz, K. Z., 'The comparative method in studying innate behaviour patterns'. *Symposia Soc. exp. Biol.*, 1950, **4**, 221
331. Lorenz, K. Z., 'The evolution of behavior'. *Scient. Amer.*, 1958, **199**, 67
332. Lukianowicz, N., 'Autoscopic phenomena'. *Arch. Neurol. Psychiat.*, 1958, **80**, 199
333. Lundquist, G., 'A comparative study of pathogenesis, course, and prognosis with delirium tremens'. *Acta. Psychiat. (Kbh)*, 1961, **36**, 443
334. Luria, A. R., 'Memory and the structure of mental processes. (A

psychological study of a case of an exceptional memory)'. *Problems of Psychology*, Pergamon Press. 1960, No. 1 and 2, 81 and *The Mind of a Mnemonist*. London: Jonathan Cape, 1969

335. Lyon, R. Ll., 'Huntington's chorea in the Moray Firth area'. *Brit. med. J.*, 1962, **1**, 1301
336. McConnell, J. V., Jacobson, A. L., and Kimble, D. P., 'The effects of regeneration upon retention of a conditioned response in the planarian'. *J. comp. physiol. Psychol.*, 1959, **52**, 1
337. Mackay, C., *Extraordinary Popular Delusions and the Madness of Crowds* London: Richard Bentley (1841) Reprinted, London: Harrap. 1956
338. McKellar, P., *Imagination and Thinking. A Psychological Analysis* London: Cohen and West. 1957
339. Maclay, W. C. and Guttmann, E., 'Mescalin hallucinations in artists'. *Arch. Neurol. Psychiat.*, 1941, **45**, 130
340. Madden, E. H. (ed.), *The Structure of Scientific Thought. An Introduction to Philosophy of Science* London: Routledge and Kegan Paul. 1960
341. Magoun, H. W., *The Waking Brain* Springfield: Thomas. 1958
342. Malan, M., 'Zur Erblichkeit der Orientierungsfähigkeit im Raum'. *Z. morphol. Anthropol.*, 1940, **39**, 1
343. Malleson, J., 'Vaginism: management and psychogenesis'. *Brit. med. J.*, 1942, **2**, 213
344. Margerison, J. H., 'The psychiatry of the epileptic'. *Proc. roy. Soc. Med.*, 1963, **56**, 715
345. Margetts, E. L., 'The concept of the unconscious in the history of medical psychology'. *Psychiat. Quart.*, 1953, **27**, 115
346. Martin, J. P., Hurwitz, L. J., and Finlayson, M. H., 'The negative symptoms of basal gangliar disease. A survey of 130 postencephalitic cases'. *Lancet*, 1962, **2**, 1 and 62
347. Mayer-Gross, W., 'Retrograde amnesia'. *Lancet*, 1943, **2**, 603
348. Mayer-Gross, W., 'Experimental psychoses and other mental abnormalities produced by drugs'. *Brit. med. J.*, 1951, **2**, 317
349. Mayer-Gross, W., 'The diagnosis of depression'. *Brit. med. J.*, 1954, **2**, 948
350. Mayer-Gross, W., Slater, E., and Roth, M., *Clinical Psychiatry* 2nd ed. London: Cassell. 1960
351. Menninger, W. C., *Psychiatry in a Troubled World* New York: Macmillan. 1948
352. Merton, R. K., *Social Theory and Social Structure* Free Press of Glencoe, 1949
353. Meyer, A., The Thirty-fourth Maudsley Lecture: 'Emergent patterns of the pathology of mental disease'. *J. ment. Sci.*, 1960, **106**, 785
354. Meynert, Th., *Psychiatrie. Klinik der Erkrankungen des Vorderhirns* Vienna: Braumüller. 1884
355. Meynert, Th., *Klinische Vorlesungen über Psychiatrie auf Wissenschaftlichen Grundlagen für Studirende und Ärzte, Juristen und Psychologen* Vienna: Braumüller. 1890
356. Miller, J. F. W., Court, S. D. M., Walton, W. S., and Knox, E. G., *Growing Up in Newcastle-upon-Tyne* London: Oxford University Press. 1960
357. Miller, G. A., *Language and Communication* New York: McGraw-Hill. 1951
358. Miller, G. A., 'The psycholinguists. On the new scientists of language'. *Encounter*, 1964, **23**, 29

359. Miller, H., 'Accident neurosis'. *Brit. med. J.*, 1961, **1**, 919 and 992
360. Miller, H., 'The long-term prognosis of severe head injury'. *Lancet*, 1965, **1**, 225
361. Minski, L. and Guttmann, E., 'Huntington's chorea: a study of thirty-four families'. *J. ment. Sci.*, 1938, **84**, 21
362. Moncrieff, A., 'Further experiences in the treatment of phenylketonuria'. *Brit. med. J.*, 1961, **1**. 763
363. Moncrieff, A. A., *et al.*, 'Treatment of phenylketonuria. Report to the Medical Research Council of the conference on phenylketonuria'. *Brit. med. J.*, 1963, **1**, 1691
364. Money, J. (ed.), *Reading Disability. Progress and Research Needs in Dyslexia* Baltimore: Johns Hopkins Press. 1962
365. Money, J., Hampson, J. G., and Hampson, J. L., 'Hermaphroditism: recommendations concerning assignment of sex, change of sex, and psychological management'. *Johns Hopkins Hosp. Bull.*, 1955, **97**, 284
366. Money, J., Hampson, J. G., and Hampson, J. L., 'An examination of some basic sexual concepts: The evidence of human hermaphroditism'. *Johns Hopkins Hosp. Bull.*, 1955, **97**, 301
367. Money, J., Hampson, J. G., and Hampson, J. L., 'Sexual incongruities and psychopathology: The evidence of human hermaphroditism'. *Johns Hopkins Hosp. Bull.*, 1956, **98**, 43
368. Moody, R. L., 'Bodily changes during abreaction'. *Lancet*, 1946, **2**, 934
369. Moore, N. P., 'A study of pathological drunkenness'. *J. ment. Sci.*, 1942, **88**, 570
370. Morgan, W. P., 'A case of congenital word blindness'. *Brit. med. J.*, 1896, **2**, 1378
371. Morley, M., Court, D., Miller, H., and Garside, R. F., 'Delayed speech and developmental aphasia'. *Brit. med. J.*, 1955, **2**, 463
372. Morton, J. H., Additon, H., Addison, R. G., Hunt, L., and Sullivan, J. J., 'Clinical study of premenstrual tension'. *Amer. J. obst. Gynecol.*, 1953, **65**, 1182
373. Morton, L. T., 'Daniel McNaughton's signature'. *Brit. med., J.*, 1956, **1**, 107
374. Moruzzi, G. and Magoun, H. W., 'Brain stem reticular formation and activation of the EEG'. *Electroenceph. clin. Neurophysiol.*, 1949, **1**, 455
375. Munn, A. M., *Free-Will and Determinism* London: MacGibbon and Kee. 1960
376. Nagel, E. and Newman, J. R., *Gödel's Proof* London: Routledge and Kegan Paul. 1959
377. Neumann, J. v., *Mathematical Foundation of Quantum Mechanics* Princeton Univ. Press. 1955
378. Nirenberg, M. W., 'The genetic code'. *Scient. Amer.*, 1963, **208**, 80
379. Nurcombe, B., 'Children who set fires'. *Med. J. Australia*, 1964, **1**, 579
380. Oswald, I., 'Sudden bodily jerks on falling asleep'. *Brain*, 1959, **82**, 92
381. Oswald, I., *Sleeping and Waking. Physiology and Psychology* Amsterdam: Elsevier. 1962
382. Pai, M. N., 'The nature and treatment of "writer's cramp"'. *J. ment. Sci.*, 1947, **93**, 68
383. Palmai, G., 'Psychological observations on an isolated group in Antarctica'. *Brit. J. Psychiat.*, 1963, **109**, 364

384. Parker, N., 'Homosexuality in twins: a report on three discordant pairs'. *Brit. J. Psychiat.*, 1964, **110**, 489
385. Parkes, C. M., 'Recent bereavement as a cause of mental illness'. *Brit. J. Psychiat.*, 1964, **110**, 198
386. Parnell, R. W., *An Introduction to Practical and Applied Somatometry* London: Arnold. 1958
387. Partridge, M., 'Drug addiction'. *Proc. roy. Soc. Med.*, 1960, **53**, 919
838. Pauling, L., Itano, A., Singer, S. I., and Wells, I. C., 'Sickle cell anaemia, a molecular disease'. *Science*, 1949, **110**, 543
389. Pavlov, I. P., 'Experimental psychology and psychopathology in animals' (1903), *Selected Works* Moscow: Foreign Languages Publ. House. 1955, 151
390. Pavlov, I. P., *Conditioned Reflexes. An Investigation of the Physiological Activity of the Cerebral Cortex* Oxford Univ. Press (1927) Republished, New York: Dover. 1960
391. Penfield W., The Twenty-ninth Maudsley Lecture: 'The role of the temporal cortex in certain psychical phenomena'. *J. ment. Sci.*, 1955, **101**, 451.
392. Penfield, W., 'Centrencephalic integrating system'. *Brain*, 1958, **81**, 231
393. Penfield, W. and Erickson, T. C., *Epilepsy and Cerebral Localisation* London: Baillière, Tindall and Cox. 1941
394. Penrose, L. S., 'Maternal age in familial mongolism'. *J. ment. Sci.*, 1951, **97**, 738
395. Penrose, L. S., *On the Objective Study of Crowd Behaviour* London: H. K. Lewis. 1952
396. Penrose, L. S., 'Paternal age in mongolism'. *Lancet*, 1962, **1**, 1101
397. Penrose, L. S., *The Biology of Mental Defect* 3rd ed. London: Sidgwick and Jackson. 1963
398. Pick, A., 'Clinical studies'. *Brain*, 1903, **26**, 242
399. Piercy, M., 'The effects of cerebral lesions on intellectual functions: a review of current research trends'. *Brit. J. Psychiat.*, 1964, **110**, 310
400. Piercy, M., Hécaen, H., and Ajuriaguerra, J. de, 'Constructional apraxia associated with unilateral cerebral lesions—left- and right-sided cases compared'. *Brain*, 1960, **83**, 225
401. Pinneaux, S. R., 'The infantile disorders of hospitalism and anaclitic depression'. *Psychol. Bull.*, 1955, **52**, 429
402. Pleydell, M. J., 'Huntington's chorea in Northamptonshire'. *Brit. med. J.*, 1954, **2**, 1121
403. Pollitt, J. D., 'Natural history studies in mental illness. A discussion based on a pilot study of obsessional states'. *J. ment. Sci.*, 1960, **106**, 93
404. Pond, D. A., 'Narcolepsy: a brief critical review and study of eight cases'. *J. ment. Sci.*, 1952, **98**, 595
405. Pond, D. A., 'The psychiatry of the epileptic'. *Proc. roy. Soc. Med.*, 1963, **56**, 710
406. Pond, D. A., Bidwell, B. H., and Stein, L., 'A survey of epilepsy in fourteen general practices. I. Demographic and medical data'. *Psychiat. Neurol. Neurochir*, 1960, **63**, 217
407. Popper, K. R., *The Poverty of Historicism* London: Routledge and Kegan Paul. 1961
408. Post, F., 'Senile confusion'. *Brit. med. J.*, 1955, **2**, 315

REFERENCES (CHAPTERS I-2I)

409. Post, F., *The Significance of Affective Symptoms in Old Age. A Follow-up Study of One Hundred Patients* Maudsley Monographs. No. 10. London: Oxford Univ. Press. 1962

410. Prentice, W. C. H., 'After-effects in perception'. *Scient. Amer.*, 1962, **206,** 44

411. Prichard, J. C., *A Treatise on Insanity and Other Disorders Affecting the Mind* London: Sherwood, Gilbert, and Piper. 1835

412. Rainer, J. D., 'Homosexuality and heterosexuality in identical twins'. *Psychosom. Med.*, 1960, **22,** 251

413. Randell, J. B., 'Transvestism and trans-sexualism. A study of 50 cases'. *Brit. med. J.*, 1959, **2,** 1448

414. Rank, O., 'Schopenhauer über den Wahnsinn'. *Ztrlblatt. f. Psychoanalyse*, 1910, **1,** 69

415. Reed, T. E. and Neel, J. V., 'Huntington's chorea in Michigan. 2. Selection and mutation'. *Amer. Hum. Genet.*, 1959, **11,** 107

416. Reeves, J. W., *Body and Mind in Western Thought* Penguin Books. 1958

417. Rees, L., 'The premenstrual tension syndrome and its treatment'. *Brit. med. J.*, 1953, **1,** 1014

418. Rees, L., 'Constitutional factors and abnormal behaviour' in *Handbook of Abnormal Psychology* (ed. Eysenck) London: Pitman. 1960

419. Reil, J. C., *Rhapsodien über die Anwendung der Psychischen Curmethode auf Geisteszerrüttungen* Halle: Curt. 1803

420. Reinhold, M., 'The effect of laterality on reading and writing'. *Proc. roy. Soc. Med.*, 1963, **56,** 203

421. Révész, G., *Psychology and Art of the Blind* London: Longmans, Green. 1950

422. Rey, J. H. and Coppen, A. J., 'Distribution of androgyny in mental patients'. *Brit. med. J.*, 1959, **2,** 1445

423. Rhine, J. B., *The Reach of the Mind* London: Faber and Faber. 1948

424. Rhine, J. B., *New Frontiers of the Mind* Penguin Books. 1950

425. Riese, W., 'Descartes's ideas of brain function' in *The History and Philosophy of Knowledge of the Brain and its Functions* (ed. Poynter) Oxford: Blackwell. 1958

426. Roberts, J. A. Fraser, 'Observations on a representative group of children of school age, with an account of some family and social characteristics of the brightest, the average and the dullest'. *Proc. Amer. Ass. ment. Defic.*, 1939, **44,** 79

427. Roberts, J. A. Fraser, *An Introduction to Medical Genetics* 3rd ed. London: Oxford Univ. Press. 1963

428. Rolleston, J. D., 'Penis captivus: a historical note'. *Janus*, 1935, **39,** 196

429. Rosanoff, A. J., Handy, L. M., and Plesset, I. R., *The Etiology of Child Behavior Difficulties, Juvenile Delinquency and Adult Criminality, with Special Reference to their Occurrence in Twins* Psychiat. Monogr. No. 1. Sacramento: Dept. of Institutions. 1941

430. Roth, M., 'The natural history of mental disorder in old age'. *J. ment. Sci.*, 1955, **101,** 281

431. Rothschild, D., 'Pathologic changes in senile psychoses and their psychobiologic significance'. *Amer. J. Psychiat.*, 1937, **93,** 757

432. Sack, W. T., 'Psyche und Haut' in *Handbuch der Haut und Geschlechtskrankheiten* (ed. Jadassohn) Berlin: Springer. 1933

433. Sainsbury, P., *Suicide in London* Maudsley Monographs. No. 1. London: Chapman and Hall. 1955

434. Salfield, D. J., 'Observations on elective mutism in children'. *J. ment. Sci.*, 1950, **96**, 1024
435. Sargant, W., 'Chemical tranquillizers'. *Brit. med. J.*, 1956, **1**, 939
436. Sargant, W., *Battle for the Mind. A Physiology of Conversion and Brainwashing* London: Heinemann. 1957
437. Sauvages, F. B. de, *Pathologia Methodica, seu de Cognosendis Morbis* 3rd ed. Leyden: 1759
438. Schanck, R. L., *A Study of a Community and its Groups and Institutions Conceived of as Behaviors of Individuals*. Psychol. Monogr., 1932, **43**, No. 195
439. Schein, E. H., 'The Chinese indoctrination program for prisoners of war. A study of attempted "brainwashing" '. *Psychiatry*, 1956, **19**, 149
440. Scheller, H., 'Völliger isolierter Verlust der Merkfähigkeit.— Organische CO-Schädigung oder hysterische Verdrängung? (Nachuntersuchung des Falles Br. von Grünthal und Störring)'. *Nervenarzt*, 1950, **21**, 49
441. Scheller, H., 'Ein Sekunden-Gedächtnis? Kritische Betrachtungen und neue Ermittlungen zum Falle Br. v. Grünthal und Störring'. *Nervenarzt*, 1956, **27**, 216
442. Schilder, P., *The Image and Appearance of the Human Body* New York: Internat. Univ. Press. 1935
443. Schopenhauer, A., *The World as Will and Idea* Trans. Haldane and Kemp. London: Trübner. 1883
444. Seager, C. P., 'A controlled study of post-partum mental illness'. *J. ment. Sci.*, 1960, **106**, 214
445. Sears, R. R., *Survey of Objective Studies of Psychoanalytic Concepts* New York: Soc. Sci. Res. Counc., 1951
446. Senden, M. v., *Raum- und Gestaltungsauffassung bei operierten Blindgeborenen vor und nach der Operation* Leipzig: Barth. 1942.—*Space and Sight. The Perception of Space and Shape in the Congenitally Blind Before and After Operation* Trans. Heath. London: Methuen. 1960
447. Serafetinides, E. A. and Dominion, J., 'A follow-up study of late-onset epilepsy'. *Brit. med. J.*, 1963, **1**, 428
448. Shannon, C. E., 'Prediction and Entropy of Printed English' *Bell. Syst. tech. J.*, 1951, **30**, 50
449. Sheldon, J. H., 'On the natural history of falls in old age'. *Brit. med. J.*, 1960, **2**, 1685
450. Sheldon W. H., Stevens, S. S., and Tucker, W. B. *The Varieties of Human Physique* London: Harper. 1940
451. Shepherd, M., 'Morbid jealousy: some clinical and social aspects of a psychiatric symptom'. *J. ment. Sci.*, 1961, **107**, 687
452. Shepherd, M. and Gruenberg, M. M., 'The age of neuroses'. *Milbank Mem. Fd. Quart.*, 1957, **35**, 258
453. Sherif, M., *The Psychology of Social Norms* New York: Harper. 1936
454. Sherrington, Sir Charles, *The Endeavour of Jean Fernel* Cambridge Univ. Press. 1946
455. Sherrington, Sir Charles, *Man on his Nature* Penguin Books. 1955
456. Shields, J., *Monozygotic Twins Brought Up Apart and Brought Up Together. An Investigation into the Genetic and Environmental Causes of Variation in Personality* London: Oxford Univ. Press. 1962
457. Shields, J. and Slater, E., 'Heredity and psychological abnormality' in *Handbook of Abnormal Psychology* (ed. Eysenck) London: Pitman. 1960

REFERENCES (CHAPTERS 1-21)

458. Sim, M. and Sussman, I., 'Alzheimer disease: its natural history and differential diagnosis'. *J. nerv. ment. Dis.*, 1962, **135**, 489

459. Simoneit, M., *Wehrpsychologie: ein Abriss ihrer Probleme und Politischen Folgerungen* Berlin: Bernard and Graefe. 1933

460. Simpson, L. and McKellar, P., 'Types of synaesthesia'. *J. ment. Sci.*, 1955, **101**, 141

461. Sinclair-Gieben, A. H. C., 'Evaluation of treatment of warts by hypnosis'. *Lancet*, 1959, **2**, 480

462. Slater, E., 'The M'Naghten rules and modern concepts of responsibility'. *Brit. med. J.*, 1954, **2**, 713

463. Slater, E., 'Birth order and maternal age of homosexuals'. *Lancet*, 1962, **1**, 69

464. Slater, E. and Beard, A. W., 'The schizophrenia-like psychoses of epilepsy. I. Psychiatric aspects'. *Brit. J. Psychiat.*, 1963, **109**, 95

465. Slater, E. and Beard, A. W., 'The schizophrenia-like psychoses of epilepsy. V. Discussion and conclusion'. *Brit. J. Psychiat.*, 1963, **109**, 143

466. Slater, E. and Glithero, E., 'The schizophrenia-like psychoses of epilepsy. III. Genetical aspects'. *Brit. J. Psychiat.*, 1963, **109**, 130

467. Smythies, J. R., 'A logical and cultural analysis of hallucinatory sense-experience'. *J. ment. Sci.*, 1956, **102**, 336

468. Snyder, L. H., 'The inheritance of taste deficiency in man'. *Ohio J. Sci.*, 1932, **32**, 436

469. Quoted from Spearman, C., *Psychology Down the Ages* London: Macmillan. 1937

470. Spitz, R. A., 'Hospitalism. An inquiry into the genesis of psychiatric conditions in early childhood'. *Psychoanal. Study Child.* New York: Internat. Univ. Press, 1945, **1**, 53

471. Spitz, R. A., 'Hospitalism. A follow-up report'. *Psychoanal. Study Child.* New York: Internat. Univ. Press, 1946, **2**, 113

472. Spitz, R. A. *Die Entstehung der Ersten Objektbeziehungen. Direkte Beobachtungen an Säuglingen während des Ersten Lebensjahres* Stuttgart: Klett. 1957

473. Spitz, R. A. and Wolf, K. M., 'Anaclitic depression. An enquiry into the genesis of psychiatric conditions in early childhood. II'. *Psychoanal. Study Child.* New York: Internat. Univ. Press, 1946, **2**, 313

474. Stalnaker, J. M. and Riddles, E. E., 'The effect of hypnosis on long delayed recall'. *J. gen. Psychol.*, 1932, **6**, 429

475. Starkey, M. L., *The Devil in Massachusetts. A Modern Enquiry into the Salem Witch Trials* London: Robert Hale. 1952

476. Stengel, E., 'On the aetiology of fugue states'. *J. ment. Sci.*, 1941, **87**, 572

477. Stengel, E., 'Further studies on pathological wandering. (Fugues with the impulse to wander)'. *J. ment. Sci.*, 1943, **89**, 224

478. Stengel, E., 'A clinical and psychological study of echo-reactions'. *J. ment. Sci.*, 1947, **93**, 598

479. Stengel, E., 'The syndrome of visual alexia with colour agnosia'. *J. ment. Sci.*, 1948, **94**, 46

480. Stengel, E., 'Some clinical observations on the psychodynamic relationship between depression and obsessive-compulsive symptoms'. *J. ment. Sci.*, 1948, **94**, 650

481. Stengel, E., 'A comparative study of psychiatric classifications'. *Proc. roy. Soc. Med.*, 1960, **53**, 123

482. Stengel, E., 'The complexity of motivations to suicidal attempts'. *J. ment. Sci.*, 1960, **106**, 1388
483. Stengel, E., *Suicide and Attempted Suicide* Penguin Books. 1964
484. Stengel, E. and Cook, N. G., *Attempted Suicide*. Maudsley Monographs. No. 4. London: Chapman and Hall. 1958
485. Stern, W., 'The psychology of testimony'. *J. abnorm. soc. Psychol.*, 1939, **34**, 3
486. Stoll, W. A., 'Lysergsäure-Diäthylamid, ein Phantastikum aus der Mutterkorngruppe'. *Schweiz. Arch. Neurol. Psychiat.*, 1947, **60**, 279
487. Stratton, G. M., 'Vision without inversion of the retinal image'. *Psychol. Rev.*, 1897, **4**, 341 and 463
488. Strauss, B. S., *An Outline of Chemical Genetics* Philadelphia: Saunders. 1960
489. Sydenstricker, V. P., 'Neurological complications of malnutrition; psychic manifestations of nicotinic acid deficiency'. *Proc. roy. Soc. Med.*, 1943, **36**, 169
490. Symonds, Ch., 'Concussion and its sequelae'. *Lancet*, 1962, **1**, 1
491. Talland, G. A., 'The psychopathology of the amnesic syndrome' in *Topical Problems in Psychiatry and Neurology* (ed. Grünthal) Basel: Karger. 1964, **1**, 443
492. Tavel, M. E., 'A new look at an old syndrome: delirium tremens'. *Arch. intern. Med.*, 1962, **109**, 129
493. Taylor, F. Kräupl, 'Collective emotions and mental epidemics'. London: *New Scientist*. 1956, No. 4, 40
494. Taylor, F. Kräupl, *The Analysis of Therapeutic Groups* Maudsley Monographs. No. 8. London: Oxford Univ. Press. 1961
495. Taylor, F. Kräupl and Hunter, R. C. A., 'Observation of a hysterical epidemic in a hospital ward'. *Psychiat. Quart.*, 1958, **32**, 821
496. Terman, L. and Oden, M. H., *Twenty-Five Years' Follow-Up of a Superior Group* Standard Univ. Press. 1947
497. Tetlow, C., 'Psychoses of childbearing'. *J. ment. Sci.*, 1955, **101**, 629
498. Thompson, W. R., 'The inheritance and development of intelligence' in *Genetics and the Inheritance of Integrated Neurological and Psychiatric Patterns* (ed. Hooker and Hare) Research Publications of the Assoc. for Research in Nerv. and Ment. Dis. London: Baillière, Tindall and Cox. 1954, **33**, Chapter 13
499. Thorpe, W. H., *Learning and Instinct in Animals* London: Methuen. 1956
500. Thurstone, L. L., *The Vectors of the Mind* Univ. Chicago Press. 1935
501. Thurstone, L. L., *Multiple Factor Analysis* Univ. Chicago Press. 1947
502. Tibbetts, R. W. and Hawkings, J. R., 'The placebo response'. *J. ment. Sci.*, 1956, **102**, 60
503. *The Times*, Leader on 'Drug addiction in Britain' 16th April, 1958
504. Tinbergen, N., *The Study of Instinct* Oxford: Clarendon Press. 1951
505. Tischner, R., *Franz Anton Mesmer. Leben, Werk und Wirkungen*. Münchn. Beitr. Geschichte und Literatur d. Naturwiss, und Medizin. H. 9/10. 1928
506. Tizard, B. and Margerison, J. H., 'Psychological functions during wave-spike discharge'. *Brit. J. soc. clin. Psychol.*, 1963, **3**, 6
507. Torup, E., 'A follow-up study of children with tics'. *Acta Paediat.* (Uppsala), 1962, **51**, 261

508. Tramer, M., 'Elektiver Mutismus bei Kindern'. *Z. Kinderpsychiat.*, 1934, **1**, 30
509. Trethowan, W. H., 'An experimental approach to the problem of simulation in mental disorder. II. Experimental data'. *Proc. roy. Soc. Med.*, 1956, **49**, 515
510. Trouton, D. S., 'Placebos and their psychological effects'. *J. ment. Sci.*, 1957, **103**, 344
511. Trouton, D. S., 'Psychopharmacology'. *Science News*, Penguin Books. 1958, No. 47, 31
512. True, R. M., 'Experimental control in hypnotic age regression states'. *Science*, 1949, **110**, 583
513. Tuke, D. H., 'Artificial insanity, chiefly in relation to mental pathology'. *J. ment. Sci.*, 1866, **11**, 56 and 174
514. Turner, H. H., 'A syndrome of infantilism, congenital webbed neck and cubitus valgus'. *Endocrinology*, 1938, **23**, 566
515. Underwood, F. W. and Honigmann, I. A., 'A comparison of socialization and personality in two simple societies'. *Amer. Anthropol.*, 1947, **49**, 557
516. Vallance, A., *Very Private Enterprise* London: Thames and Hudson. 1955
517. Vernon, P. E., *Personality Assessment. A Critical Survey* London: Methuen. 1964
518. Victor, M. and Yakovlev, P. I., 'S. S. Korsakoff's psychic disorder in conjunction with peripheral neuritis. A translation of Korsakoff's original article with brief comments on the author and his contribution to clinical medicine'. *Neurology*, 1955, **5**, 394
519. Völkel, H. and Stolze, R., 'Nachuntersuchung und Versuch einer epikritischen Deutung des Falles B. von E. Grünthal und G. E. Störring'. *Mschr. Psychiat. Neurol.*, 1956, **132**, 291
520. Walker, C. H. M. and Languth, P. R., 'Developmental speech anomalies in apparently normal children'. *Brit. med. J.*, 1956, **2**, 1455
521. Walshe, F. M. R., 'Some reflections upon the opening phase of the physiology of the cerebral cortex, 1850–1900' in *The History and Philosophy of Knowledge of the Brain and its Functions* (ed. Poynter) Oxford: Blackwell. 1958.
522. Walton, J. N., Ellis, E., and Court, S. D. M., 'Clumsy children: Development apraxia and agnosia'. *Brain*, 1962, **85**, 603
523. Wardener, H. E. de and Lennox, B., 'Cerebral beri-beri (Wernicke's encephalopathy)'. *Lancet*, 1947, **1**, 11
524. Watson, J. D. and Crick, F. H. C., 'Genetical implications of deoxyribose nucleic acid'. *Nature*, 1953, **171**, 964
525. Watts, C. A. H., 'The incidence and prognosis of endogenous depression'. *Brit. med. J.*, 1956, **1**, 1392
526. Watts, C. A. H., 'The mild endogenous depression'. *Brit. med. J.*, 1957, **1**, 4
527. Weinstein, E. A. and Kahn, R. L., 'The syndrome of anosognosia'. *Arch. Neurol. Psychiat.*, 1950, **64**, 772
528. Weitzenhoffer, A. M., *Hypnotism. An Objective Study in Suggestibility* London: Chapman and Hall. 1953
529. Welford, A. R., 'On changes of performance with age'. *Lancet*, 1962, **1**, 335
530. Wenner, A. M., 'Sound communication in honeybees'. *Scientific Amer.*, 1964, **210**, 116

531. Wernicke, C., *Der Aphasische Symptomenkomplex. Eine Psychologische Studie auf Anatomischer Basis* Breslau: Cohn and Weigert. 1874
532. Wernicke, C., *Lehrbuch der Gehirnkrankheiten für Ärzte und Studirende* Kassel: Fischer. 1881
533. West, D. J., *Psychical Research Today* London: Duckworth. 1954
534. West, D. J., *Homosexuality* London: Duckworth. 1955
535. West, D. J., 'Parental figures in the genesis of male homosexuality'. *Internat. J. soc. Psychiat.*, 1959, **5**, 85
536. Whyte, L. L., *The Unconscious Before Freud* London: Tavistock. 1962.
537. Wiener, N., *Cybernetics or Control and Communication in the Animal and the Machine* New York: Wiley. 1948
538. Williams, D., 'The psychiatry of the epileptic'. *Proc. roy. Soc. Med.*, 1963, **56**, 707
539. Williams, D. and Wilson, T. G., 'The diagnosis of the major and minor syndromes of basilar insufficiency'. *Brain*, 1962, **85**, 741
540. Wilson, S. A. K., *Modern Problems in Neurology* London: Arnold, 1928
541. Wolberg, L. R., *Medical Hypnosis* New York: Grune and Stratton, 1948
542. Wolff, S., '*Folie à trois*: a clinical study'. *J. ment. Sci.*, 1957, **103**, 355
543. Wolstenholme, G. E. W. and Millar, E. C. P. (ed.), *Ciba Foundation Symposium on Extrasensory Perception* London: Churchill. 1956
544. Woltman, H. W., 'The mental changes associated with pernicious anaemia'. *Amer. J. Psychiat.*, 1924, **3**, 435
545. Woolf, L. I., Griffiths, R., and Moncreiff, A., 'Treatment of phenylketonuria with a diet low in phenylalanine'. *Brit. med. J.*, 1955, **1**, 57
546. Wootton, B., *Social Science and Social Pathology* London: Allen and Unwin. 1959
547. Yandell, D. W., 'Epidemic convulsions'. *Brain*, 1881, **4**, 339
548. Yap, P. M., 'The latah reaction: its pathodynamics and nosological position'. *J. ment. Sci.*, 1952, **98**, 515
549. Yap, P. M., 'Suicide in Hong Kong'. *J. ment. Sci.*, 1958, **104**, 266
550. Zangwill, O. L., 'On a peculiarity of recognition in 3 cases of Korsakow's psychosis'. *J. Brit. Psychol.*, 1941, **31**, 230
551. Zangwill, O. L.. 'Neurological studies and human behaviour'. *Brit. med. Bull.*, 1964, **20**, 43
552. Zausmer, D. M., 'Treatment of tics in childhood; review and follow-up study'. *Arch. Dis. Childh.*, 1954, **29**, 261
553. Zingg, R. M., 'Feral man and extreme cases of isolation'. *Amer. J. Psychol.*, 1940, **53**, 487
554. Zubek, J. P., 'Effects of prolonged sensory and perceptual deprivation'. *Brit. med. Bull.*, 1964, **20**, 38

NAME INDEX

Abe, K., 285
Abercrombie, M.L.J., 95
Abraham, H. C., 196
Achté, K.A., 292
Ackerknecht, E. H., 12, 112
Ackner, B., 102
Akeleitis, A. J. E., 72
Alexander, M. C., 106
Allison, R. S., 120, 121, 213
Allport, F. H., 157
Allport, G. W., 12, 147, 305
Anderson, E. W., 72, 212, 253
Andrews, G., 300
Angst, J., 296
Anthony, E. J., 220
Ardis, J. A., 70
Aristotle, 25
Ashcroft, G. W., 298
Asher, R., 72, 276

Babinski, J., 65, 271
Backman, E. L., 237
Baker, J. P., 73
Barber, Th. X., 244
Barker, J. C., 276
Barron, F., 71
Bartlett, F. C., 206
Bateson, G., 292
Bay, E., 96, 257
Beach F. A., 187
Beard, A. W., 229
Beard, G. M., 234
Beecher, H. K., 43
Bekény, G., 101
Belbin, E., 207
Bell, E. T., 110
Bell, J., 54
Benjamin, H., 188
Bennett, D. H., 101
Bennett, G., 304
Benton, A. L., 200
Bercel, N. A., 70
Berg, I., 186
Beringer, K., 70
Berrington, W. P., 262
Bexton, W. H., 94, 304
Bickel, H., 56, 71

Bickford, J. A. R., 54
Birley, J. L. T., 292
Bivin, G. D., 275
Black, St., 274
Blackham, H. J., 34
Bleuler, E., 122, 123
Blomfield, J. M., 219
Bockner, S., 196
Boole, G., 110
Bornstein, P. E., 299
Bottomley, Horatio, 267
Bouillaud, J. B., 15
Bowlby, J., 86
Braid, J., 240
Brain, Sir Russell, 15, 35, 96, 105,
    121, 198, 199, 218, 305
Braithwaite, R. B., 111
Bramwell, Lord, 177
Brazier, M. A. B., 11
Brentano, F., 29
Brindley, G. S., 303
Broca, P., 15
Bromberg, W., 11
Brown, G. W., 87, 292, 299, 300
Brown, W. M. G., 49, 50
Bruner, J. S., 102
Brussel, J, A., 253
Bulpitt, C. J., 298
Burt, C., 38
Burton, Robert, 247
Byrd, R. E., 84

Cadoret, R. J., 297
Cairns, D., 29
Cameron, A. J., 74
Cantril, H., 246
Carothers, J. C., 294
Carrol, Lewis, 69, 123
Carstairs, G. M., 87
Carter, C. O., 56
Chapman, J., 193
Charcot, J.-M., 242, 270
Cherry, C., 26
Chiarugi, V., 247
Clarke, E., 276
Clayton, P. J., 299
Close, H. G., 50

Cohen, B. E., 283
Cohen, E., 88
Cohen, Lord, 227
Cole, J. O., 86
Comte, A., 29
Connell, P. H., 74, 292
Cooper, J. E., 295
Coplestone, F., 34
Coppen, A., 72, 298
Corning, W. C., 202
Courtauld, A., 84
Cowie, V., 55
Creak, M., 121, 197, 199
Crick, F. H. C., 52
Critchley, M., 54, 67, 97, 99, 101, 123, 200, 304
Cullen, W., 11

Dalton, K., 72
Daniels, L. E., 195, 221
Darwin, Charles, 15
Davis, K., 85
Davison, K., 292
Dax, M., 15
Dekker, E., 252
Dennis, W., 85
Descartes, R., 8f, 233
Dewhurst, C. J., 186
Dewhurst, K., 106, 298
Dewhurst, W. G., 129
Dominion, J., 227
Donath, J., 163
Dostoevski, F. M., 87, 88
Doswald, D. C., 274
Drew, G. C., 69
Du Bois-Reymond, E. F., 11
Dunham, H. W., 87, 289
Dunlap, H. F., 72
Durkheim, E., 84, 142

Edwards, G., 75
Eilenberg, M. D., 71, 129
Einstein, A, 111, 198
Ellis, Havelock, 70
Ellis, W. G., 235
Essen-Möller, E., 289
Eysenck, H. J., 38, 39, 148, 241

Faber, K., 6
Faris, R., 289
Faris, R. E. L., 87
Fechner, G. T., 29

Fernel, J., 7
Festinger, L., 113
Fischer, M., 290
Fish, F., 301
Fölling, A., 55
Ford, C. E., 49
Ford, C. S., 187
Fouchy, de, 200
Foundeur, M., 72
Frank, R. T., 72
Franklin, A. W., 98
Fras, I., 298
Freedman, D. G., 183
Freud, S., 13, 16, 19, 29, 93, 96, 182, 184, 206, 207, 248, 298
Fritsch, G., 16

Gairdner, D., 118
Galen, 112, 247
Gall, F. J., 12f, 147
Galton, F., 58, 60, 62, 105
Galvani, L., 11
Ganser, S. J., 240, 264
Gardner, M., 167
Garwood, K., 119
Gerard, D. L., 87
Gershon, E. S., 296
Ghabrial, F., 186
Gibbens, T. C. N., 175
Gibbons, J. L., 298
Glithero, E., 229
Gödel, K., 111
Goldberg, E. M., 289
Goldin, S., 106
Goldstein, K., 66, 225, 257
Gooddy, W., 98
Goode, G. B., 221
Gottesman, I. I., 289, 290, 291, 292
Gowers, W. R., 66
Green, T. C., 74
Greenberg, H. P., 129
Greene, R., 68, 72
Gregory, R. L., 100
Grünthal, E., 258, 259
Gurland, B. J., 295
Gurney, E., 208

Haber, R. N., 305
Haggard, E. A., 208
Halbwachs, M., 84, 142
Hald, J., 72
Hallgren, B., 63, 98

Halverson, H. M., 182
Hamilton, J. A., 72
Hamilton, M., 301
Hammond, W. A., 235
Hampson, J. L., 186
Hare, E. H., 87, 116, 289, 301f
Harlow, H. F., 85
Hauser, Kaspar, 85
Hawkings, J. R., 276
Heaton-Ward, W. A., 175
Hécaen, H., 198
Hecker, J. F. C., 237
Heidegger, M., 34
Helgason, T., 296
Henderson, D. K., 256
Hermelin, B., 98
Heron, W., 94
Hess, E. H., 95, 183
Heston, L. L., 292
Hildebrandt, H., 196
Hill, D., 227
Hippocrates, 12
Hirschfeld, M., 188
Hoenig, J., 212
Hoffer, W., 123
Hollingshead, A., 289
Holzel, A., 71
Hopkinson, G., 297
Hornby, Sir Edmund, 208
Howard, B., 269
Howells, J. G., 86
Hunter, R., 70
Hurwitz, J., 52
Husserl, E., 29, 34
Huxley, Aldous, 70
Hydén, H., 202

Ingram, T. T. S., 98
Isbell, H., 74, 75
Itard, J. M. G., 85

Jablensky, A., 287
Jackson, Hughlings, 96
Jacobs, P. A., 49, 50, 281
Jacobsen, E., 72
James, N.McI., 297
Jaspers, Karl, 31, 32, 34, 93, 144, 301
Jellinek, E. H., 72
Jellinek, M., 75
Jesus, 114
Johnson, D. M., 246

Johnson, Samuel, 200
Jolliffe, N., 71
Jones, K., 176
Juda, A., 62
Jung, C. G., 206, 253
Jung, R., 257

Kahaná, E., 298
Kahn, E., 37
Kalinowsky, L. B., 255, 256
Kallmann, F. J., 62, 185, 187, 284
Kalmus, H., 63
Kandinsky, V., 301
Kant, I., 11
Katz, H. P., 283
Kaufmann, W., 34
Kay, D. W. K., 121, 297
Kendell, R. E., 279, 295
Kety, S. S., 291
Kidd, C. B., 50
Kierkegaard, S., 34
Kiloh, L. G., 74
Kinsey, A. C., 116, 185, 219
Kleinsorge, H., 244
Klinefelter, H. F., 49
Klintworth, G. K., 62, 185
Klüver, H., 70, 305
Koch, R., 41
Kolb, L., 73
Kolb, L. C., 62, 185
Kohler, I., 101
Konorski, J., 83
Korsakoff, S. S., 213
Kraepelin, E., 14, 37f, 122
Krafft-Ebing, R. v., 14
Kral, V. A., 142, 158
Kreuger, Ivar, 267
Kringlen, E., 290
Kuhn, H., 34
Kulenkampf, C., 83

Laing, R. D., 292
Lambo, T. A., 294
Landers, J. J., 276
Lang, T., 284
Laplace, P. S., 17
Larson, C. A., 283
Larssen, T., 121
Lasagna, L., 43
Laubscher, B. J. F., 294
Lawley, D. N., 38
Lee, S., 275

337

Leff, J. P., 292, 304
Leigh, D., 70, 179
Leighton, A. H., 294
Lejeune, J., 50
Leonhard, K., 296
Leroy, R., 106
Lewis, A., 14, 73, 149, 154, 212
Lewis, H., 86
Lewis, H. E., 84
Lhermitte, J., 106
Liddell, E. G. T., 11
Lidz, T., 292
Lifton, R. J., 127
Lilly, J. C., 94
Linnaeus, C. v., 37, 84, 85
Lishman, W. A., 292
Lorenz, K. Z., 95, 183
Lukianowicz, N., 106
Lundquist, G., 75
Luria, A. R., 209
Lycke, E., 298
Lyon, R. Ll., 54

Mach, E., 29
McConnell, J. V., 202
McCready, R. A., 283
McFarland, R. A., 304
McHugh, P. R., 279
MacKay, C., 237
McKellar, P., 105
Maclay, W. C., 70
McNaughton, D., 176f
Madden, E. H., 111
Magoun, H. W., 216
Malleson, J., 196
Margerison, J. H., 227
Martin, J. P., 198
Mary Tudor, 275
Maudsley, H., 147
Mayer-Gross, W., 70, 72, 142
Mendlewicz, J., 297
Menninger, W. C., 253, 255
Merton, R. K., 114
Mesmer, F. A., 239f
Meyer, A., 12
Meynert, T., 16, 19
Miller, J. F. W., 219
Miller, G. A., 26
Miller, H., 256
Minski, L., 54, 298
Moncrieff, A., 56
Money, J., 98, 186

Moody, R. L., 274
Moore, N. P., 72
Moran, P. A. P., 285
Morgagni, G. B., 7
Morgan, W. P., 98
Morley, M., 198
Morton, J. H., 72
Morton, L. T., 176
Moruzzi, G., 23
Munn, A. M., 17, 18

Nagel, E., 111
Neumann, J. v., 17
Neumann, Theresa, of Konnersreuth,
  275
Newton, I., 144, 234
Nielsen, J., 281
Nietzsche, F., 206
Nirenberg, M. W., 52

Olds, J., 298
Oster, G., 304
Oswald, I., 216, 218, 220

Pai, M. N., 196
Palmai, G., 88
Parker, N., 62, 185
Parkes, C. M., 145, 299
Partington, M. W., 283
Partridge, M., 74
Pasteur, L., 41, 240
Pauling, L., 55
Pavlov, I. P., 81f, 112
Paykel, E. S., 299, 300
Penfield, W., 23, 227
Penrose, L. S., 50, 51, 52, 59, 115,
  285
Perris, C., 296
Pick, A., 214
Piercy, M., 198
Pinel, P., 85
Pinneaux, S. R., 86
Pio, Padre, 275
Pitcher, D. R., 281
Plato, 187, 247
Pleydell, M. J., 54
Pond, D. A., 195, 221, 227
Popper, Sir Karl, 114, 288
Post, F., 121, 294
Prentice, W. C. H., 100
Prichard, J. C., 179
Price, J., 297

Price, W. H., 281, 282
Puységur, Marquis de, 240

Rainer, J. D., 62, 185
Randell, J. B., 188
Reed, T. E., 54
Rees, L., 72
Rees, W. D., 299
Reeves, J. W., 8
Reil, J. Ch., 14, 247
Reinhold, M., 98
Révész, G., 96
Rhine, J. B., 167
Richards, W., 304
Rieke, J., 298
Riese, W., 8
Rimon, R., 298
Roberts, J. A. Fraser, 56, 59
Rollestone, J. D., 196
Rosenthal, D., 290, 291
Roth, M., 121
Rothschild, D., 121
Routtenberg, A., 298
Russell, Bertrand, 110

Sack, W. T., 274
Sainsbury, P., 84, 142
St. Francis of Assisi, 275
Salfield, D. J., 199
Sargant, W., 73. 144, 237, 238
Sauvages, F. B. de, 36f
Scadding, J. G., 279
Schank, R. L., 157
Schein, E. H., 127
Scheller, H., 259
Schilder, P., 101
Schildkraut, J. J., 298
Schulsinger, F., 291
Seager, C. P., 72
Sedman, G., 302
Senden, M. v., 96
Serafetinidis, E. A., 227
Shannon, C. E., 26
Shaw, D. M., 298
Sheldon, J. H., 195
Shepherd, M., 131
Shereshevski, S. V., 210
Sherif, M., 102
Sherrington, C. S., 7, 21
Shields, J., 61f, 63, 290, 292
Siegel, R. K., 305
Sim, M., 121

Simpson, L., 94
Sinclair-Gieben, A. H. C., 241
Slater, E., 63, 177, 229, 285, 286, 288, 289, 292, 295, 296, 297
Smythies, J. R., 104
Spearman, C., 25
Spitz, R. A., 86
Spurzheim, J. G., 13
Stalnaker, J. M., 243
Starkey, M. L., 246
Stengel, E., 35, 97, 142, 149, 154, 193, 262
Stenstedt, Å., 296
Stephenson, J. B. P., 283
Stern, W., 207
Stoll, W. A., 70
Storey, P. B., 298
Stratton, G. M., 101
Strauss, B. S., 54, 56
Surridge, D., 298
Sydenham, Th., 6
Sydenstricker, V. P., 71
Symonds, Ch., 67

Talland, G. A., 212
Tavel, M. E., 75
Taylor, F. Kräupl, 126, 237, 246, 279f
Tennant, C., 300
Terman, L., 95
Tetlow, C., 72
Thompson, W. R., 59
Thorpe, W. H., 95
Thurstone, L. L., 38
Tibbetts, R. W., 43
Tienari, P., 290
Tinbergen, N., 95
Tischner, R., 239
Tizard, B., 228
Tooth, G., 294
Torup, E., 196
Tramer, M., 199
Trethowan, W. H., 253
Trouton, D. S., 43
True, R. M., 244
Tsuang, M-T., 285, 286
Tuke, D. H., 241
Turner, H. H., 49
Turner, R. J., 289

Vallance, A., 267
Vaughn, C. E., 293

339

Vesalius, A., 112
Victor, M., 212
Völkel, H., 259

Walker, C. H. M., 198
Walshe, F. M. R., 15
Walton, J. N., 197
Wardener, H. E., 76
Watson, J. D., 52
Watts, C. A. H., 142
Weinberg, S. K., 294
Weinstein, E. A., 65
Weitzenhoffer, A, M., 241
Welford, A. R., 120
Wender, P. H., 291
Wesley, John, 238
West, D. J., 167, 186
Whitlock, F. A., 298
Wiener, N., 22
Williams, D., 195, 227
Wilson, S. A. K., 195, 221

Winokur, G., 296, 297
Wolberg, L. R., 241, 274
Wolff, S., 129
Wolstenholme, G. E. W., 167
Woltman, H. W., 71
Woolf, L. I., 56
Wootton, Barbara, 177, 178
Wundt, W., 29
Wynne, L. C., 292

Yandell, D. W., 238
Yap, P. M., 142
Yolles, S. F., 288
Young, M., 299

Zangwill, O. L., 214
Zausmer, D. M., 196
Zerbin-Rüdin, E., 288, 296
Zingg, R. M., 85
Zubek, J. P., 94
Zubin, J., 295

SUBJECT INDEX

Abasia, 198
Abnormality
  by individual standards (norms), 4,
    279
  by population standards (norms), 4,
    279
  morbid, 3
Absent-mindedness
  and habitual mannerisms, 234
  complete, 236
  partial, 233f
Accident neurosis, 256
Achromatopsia, 99
Act-phenomena, 28, 30
  of exteroception, 28
  of interoception, 28
  of introspection, 28
Addiction, 73f
  alcohol, 75
  amphetamine, 74
  barbiturates, 74
  cocaine, 74
  heroin, 74
  morphine, 74
Adolescent behaviour problems, 197
Aetiology, 40f
  endogenous, 42
  exogenous, 42
  generally pathogenic, 44
  genetic, 46, 47f
  idiosyncratically pathogenic, 44
  perceived, 43, 77f
  physiogenic, 43, 64f
  precipitating, 45
  predisposing, 45
  prospective analysis of, 40
  psychogenic, 43, 77f
  retrospective analysis of, 40
  unperceived, 43, 64f
Affect
  feelings of perplexity, 136
  incongruity of, 136
  poverty of, 136
  psychopathology of, 136, 151f, 173f
Affective illnesses, 37
  and intracellular sodium, 298
  and monoamine metabolism, 298

and recent bereavement, 299
and senile dementia, 121
and significant life events, 299f
bipolar, 296
biochemical pathology of, 298
family studies of, 296f
diagnostic variations of, 294, 295
genetics of, 294f, 296f
in different cultures, 294
lifetime morbidity risk of, 295f
recent increase in their diagnosis,
  294, 295
symptomatic, 298
twin studies of, 297
unipolar, 296
After images, 104, 303
Aggression, abnormal, 174, 180
Agnosia, 96f
  auditory, 99
  colour, 99
  hysterical, 296
  spatial, 97, 198
  tactile, 97
  visual, 97, 257
Agoraphobia, 159
Agraphia, 200
Akathisia, 196
Akinesis, 191
Alcohol abuse, 75, 173
  and cultural differences, 75
Alcohol intoxication, 69
  acute, 69, 222
  and bout drinkers, (dipsomaniacs),
    75
  and delirium tremens, 75
  and hallucinosis, 76
  and hypomelancholia, 143
  and Korsakoff syndrome, 76, 20
  and memory blackouts, 75
  and peripheral polyneuritis, 76
  and possibility of wrong diagnosis,
    69, 70
Alcoholism, 75, 174
Alertness, 215
Alienists, 38
Alleles, 53
Alloaesthesia, 99

341

Alloerotic objects, 184
Allport, F. H.
  and pluralistic ignorance, 157
Alzheimer disease, 121
Amnesia
  and hysterical fugues, 262
  for recent events, 213
  organic, 212
  post-concussional, 212
  post-hypnotic, 242
  post-trance, 262
  post-traumatic,
  retrograde, 212, 262, 263
  retrogressive, 213
Amnesic syndrome, 65, 212, 225
Amphetamine addiction, 74
  and paranoid states, 75
Anaesthesia
  hysterical, 269, 270
  phallic, 271
  vaginal, 271
Anankastic symptoms, 163
Angina pectoris
  contrasted with cardiac phobia, 83
Animal magnetism, 239
Anomie, 84
  and suicide, 84
Anosognosia, 65, 271
Anoxia, 68, 69
  in mountaineers, 68
Antabuse (disulfiram), 72
Anxiety-dominated neuroses, 151f
Anxiety neurosis, 155f
  and hysterical symptoms, 251
Anxiety, neurotic
  after depressions, 154
  after functional psychoses, 154
  after organic psychoses, 154
  and pluralistic isolation, 158
Anxiety state, reactive, 79
Aphasia
  developmental, 198
  jargon, 99
  motor, 199
  nominal, 121
  sensory, 99
Apparitions, 106
Apraxia, 197, 264
  and abasia, 198
  and clumsy children, 197
  and social neuroses, 197
  constructional, 198

developmental, 197
dressing, 99, 198
facial, 198
ideational, or ideo-motor, 198
organic, 197
trunk, 198
Aprosody, 200
Aristotle
  and consciousness, 25
Artificial insanity, 241
Astereognosis, 97
Asthma, bronchial, 252
Atropine, idiosyncrasy, 72
Attention
  centre of, 233
  fringe of, 233
Attentiveness, 215
Autism, 199
Auto-erotism, 182, 183
Autokinetic illusion, 102
Automatic
  obedience, 193, 234, 235
  writing, 235
Automatism, 66
  and absent-mindedness, 233
  and delirium, 223
  and senile dementia, 121
  occupational, 223
Autonomic functions
  hysterical disorders of, 274f
Autoregulation
  and cybernetics, 22
  and feedback devices, 22
  and redundant information, 26
Autoscopy, 106
Autosuggestibility, 250, 253, 254
Autosuggestion, 242
  and hysteria, 249f
  and psychosomatic symptoms, 252
Axioms, 110

Babinski, J.
  and anosognosia, 271
Baldness, premature, 57
Barbiturate addiction, 74
Battle fatigue, 255
Beach, F. A.
  and homosexuality, 187
Beard, G. M.
  and the 'Jumpers' religious sect, 234
Bedrooms
  and sexual secrecy, 182

Beliefs (*see also* Convictions)
  absolute, 115
  ambivalent, 111, 116, 151, 155
  and psychosocial changes, 114
  and self-fulfilling prophecies, 114
  and therapeutic fashions, 115
  collective, 111f, 146
  hypochondriacal, 250, 251, 253f
  individual, 113
  intensification after cognitive
    dissonance, 113f
  magic, 166
  self-falsifying, 114
  self-indulgent, 259f
  self-verifying, 114, 146, 149
Beliefs, collective, 111f
  causing cultural friction, 113
  false, 125
  in psychiatry, 146f
Belle indifférence, 248, 272
Bereavement
  and affective illness, 299
  and increased mortality rates, 299
  and pseudo-hallucinations, 304
Bestialism, 188
Bibliomania, 163
Bleuler, E.
  and dissociation of ideas, 123
Blindness, 304
  and acquired vision, 96
Body image disorders, 101, 103, 127
  and hypochondriacal delusions,
    134
Body sway test, 241
Bondage, emotional, 273
Boole, G.
  and Boolean algebra, 110
  and symbolic, logic, 110
Bouillaud, J. B.
  and motor speech centre, 15
Boxers
  and punch-drunkenness, 67
Bradykinesis, 193
Braid, J.
  and hypnosis, 240
Brain
  mechanistic view of, 78
Brain reward system,
Brain washing, 127
Bramwell, Lord
  and the M'Naghten rules, 177
Breath-holding attacks, 269

Brentano, Franz
  and act-psychology, 29
Broca, P.
  and motor speech centre, 15
Buggery, 189
Burton, Robert
  and love melancholy, 247
Byrd, R. E., Admiral
  and social isolation, 84

Cardiac phobia
  contrasted with angina pectoris, 83
Carpopedal spasms, 191, 269
  and hyperventilation, 191, 269
Carroll, Lewis
  and the mad hatter, 69
Catalepsy, 192
Cataplexy, 195, 222
Catastrophic reaction, 65, 225
Catatonia, 191
  and automatic obedience, 193
  and echo reactions, 193
  and *flexibilitas cerea*, 192
  and hyperkinesis, 192
  and negativism, 192
  and reiterated stereotyped activities,
    192
  and *Schnauzkrampf*, 192
Causal explanation, 33
Causes
  adjuvant, 40
  contributory, 40
  endogenous, 42
  exogenous, 42
  generally pathogenic, 44
  idiosyncratically pathogenic, 44
  perceived, 43
  physiogenic, 43
  precipitating, 45
  predisposing, 45
  psychogenic, 43
  salient, 40
  specific, 40
  unperceived, 43
Centrencephalic integrating system,
  15, 23
Cerebral arteriosclerosis, 144
Chance influences, 40
Charcot, J.-M.
  and hypnosis, 242
  and hysteria, 242
  and hysterical stigmata, 270

Chiarugi, V.
  and pathogenic sexual frustration,
    247
Childbirth
  and personality changes, 72
  and sexual frigidity, 72
Chorea
  Huntington, 54, 121
  rheumatic, 6, 196
  Sydenham's, 6
Choreomaniacs, 237
Chromosomal sex
  and gender role, 186
Chromosomes, 47
  autosomal (or autosomes), 48
  complement of, 47
  diploid number of, 47
  haploid number of, 47
  homologous pairs, 48
  monosomy of, 49
  non-disjunction of, 48
  sex chromosomes 48f
  translocation of, 51
  trisomy of, 49, 281
Circumcision, 117f
Circumstantial speech
  in mentally subnormal people, 124
  in normal aphasia, 125
  in paranoid patients, 124
  in schizophrenics, 124
Class, logical, 109
  and its defining properties, 109
Claustrophobia, 159
Clumsy children, 197
Cocaine addiction
  and delirious states, 74
Cognitive dissonance, 113
Cogwheel rigidity, 193
Cohen, E.
  and lack of privacy, 88
Colour blindness or weakness, 56, 99
Coma, 67, 224
Compensation neurosis, 256f
  and Mr. Schn., 257
  and Mr. Br., 258f
Compulsions, 163
  counterphobic, 172
Compulsive
  checking, 170
  doing-and-undoing, 170
  indecision, 169f
  ruminations, 169

to-and-fro activities, 170
  washing, 170
Compulsive rituals, 168f
  and hopeful half-beliefs, 168
  and their concealment, 170f
  and their time-wasting effect, 170
  in schizophrenics, 192
  mental variety, 169
  motor variety, 169, 170
Comte, A.
  and sociology, 29
Concepts
  descriptive, 109
  explanatory, 109, 144
  perceptual, 109
Concern
  medical, 280
  therapeutic, 3, 280
Concussion, 67, 69, 212
Conditioned reflexes, 82
  paradoxical and ultraparadoxical
    reactions, 82
Conditioning, instrumental, 112
Confabulation,
  and pathological lying (*pseudologia
    fantastica*), 266
  hysterical, 266
  in children, 266
Confidence tricksters, 260, 267
  and Ivar Kreuger, 267
  and Horatio Bottomley, 267
Confusional state, organic, 65, 66, 97,
    212, 224f
Conscience, 164
Conscious experiences, 24f
  and Aristotle, 25
  as existential experiences, 25, 215
  their cognitive, affective and conative
    varieties, 25
Consciousness, 15, 24, 215f
  altered, 215, 236f
  and existential act-phenomena, 215
  and existential object-phenomena,
    215
  and sensorium, 215
  clear, 215
  degrees of lucidity, 215
  hysterical disorders of, 261f
  psychopathology of, 215f
Consciousness (Sensorium), altered
  obfuscation, 65, 121, 211, 212, 215,
    222f, 229, 262, 272

Consciousness—*cont.*
  sleep, 215
  trance, 215, 236f
Consciousness, clouded, 65
  and hallucinogenic (psychotomimetic) drugs, 70
  and hypoglycaemia, 70
  and hysterical fugues, 262
Consciousness, seat of,
  and cerebral cortex, 15
  and Darwin, 15
  Hippocrates' view of, 12
  19th century views of, 15
Content phenomena, 28
Conversion hysteria, 248
Convictions, (*see also* Beliefs)
  absolute, 115, 125
  ambivalent, 115, 116, 151, 155
  and heresies, 115
  and social solidarity, 115
  collective, 111f, 146
  false, 125
  hypochondriacal, 250, 251, 253f
  individual, 113
  self-falsifying, 114
  self-fulfilling, 114
  self-indulgent, 259f
  self-verifying, 114, 146, 149
Conviction, self-verifying
  and hypnosis, 245, 249
  and hysterical symptoms, 249
Coronary thrombosis, 83
Correlational calculus, 58
Cortisone idiosyncrasy, 73
Counterphobic compulsions, 172
Courtauld, A.
  and social isolation, 84
Cranioscopy, 13
Crime, 175f
Cryptomnesia, 206f
  and post-hypnotic suggestions, 243
  and unconscious plagiarism, 206
  partial, 213
Cullen, W.
  and *vis nervosa*, 11
Cunnilingus, 189
Cybernetics, 22

Dance epidemics, 237
Danger situations
  and hysterical symptoms, 252

and hysterical trance states, 251
and *stigmata diaboli*, 252
and unreality feelings, 251
Darwin, Ch.
  and seat of consciousness, 15
Da-sein, 87
David, Kingsley
  and a socially isolated child, 85
Dax, M.
  and motor speech centre, 15
Deafness
  high-tone, 99
  hysterical, 269
  through loud noise, 78
  tune, 63
Déjà vu illusion, 102, 227
Delinquency, juvenile, 63
Delirium, 66, 223
  and automatisms, 223
  hysterical, 261
  subacute, 224
  tremens, 75, 195, 223
Delusional,
  atmosphere, 103
  hallucinations, 105
  illusions of body image, 103
  illusions of reference, 103
  mood, 103
Delusions, 102, 125f, 158
  as absolute, idiosyncratic, ego-involved, incorrigible and often preoccupying convictions, 125f
  depressive, 133, 145f
  erotic, 130, 132, 137
  grandiose, 133, 137
  hypochondriacal, 134
  induced, 129
  isolated, 129
  litigious, 130, 132, 137
  of guilt and unworthiness, 133
  of jealousy, 130, 131, 137
  of nihilism, 134
  of persecution, 130, 136, 137
  of reference, 130f
  paranoid, 130f
  self-verifying, 128f, 132
  shared, 129
  systematized, 129
Dementia, 120f
  praecox, 122
  presenile, 121
  senile, 121

Demonological theories, 162
  and obsessions, 162
  and possessions, 162
Depersonalisation feelings, 102, 228
  hysterical, 251
Depression, 124, 133, 134, 148, 262, 294f
  (*see also* affective illnesses)
  agitated, 191
  after reserpine, 73
  and delusions, 133
  and hypochondriacal delusions, 134
  and panic attacks, 143, 154
  and psychoanalytic theories, 148
  and stupor, 191
  endogenous, 144f
  hyperkinetic, 191
  masked, 294
  neurotic, 38, 141, 146
  organic, 144
  psychotic, 145f, 171
  reactive, 141, 143
  retarded, 191
Derealization, 228
  hysterical, 251
Dermatitis artefacta, 274, 275, 276
Dervishes, dancing, 237
Descartes, R.
  and body-mind dichotomy, 8, 11, 233
Determinism, universal
  and free will, 17
  and quantum mechanics, 17
Diabetes mellitus, 71
Diplopia, 101
Dipsomania, 73, 163
  and self-indulgence, 173
Disability pensions, 256
Disadvantage, biological, 279
Disease
  aetiology of, 40f
  and its pathology, 7
  as clinical entity, 5f, 36, 279
  as pathological entity, 8
  autonomous, 89
  concept of, 3f
  clinical syndrome of, 6
  definition of, 5, 279f
  endogenous, 45, 88
  existential, 88
  expectancy of, 288

  genetic, 53
  hereditary, 53
  incidence of, 287
  lifetime morbidity risk of, 288
  mental, 14
  molecular, 55
  natural history of, 6
  nervous, 14
  prevalence of, 287
  psychiatric, 10
  reactive, 45, 88
  sex-controlled (or sex-limited), 57
  sex-linked, 56
  Sydenham's view of, 6
Disease-rewarding situations, 254f
  and compensation neuroses, 256f
  and hypochondriacal desires, 254
  and hysterical symptoms, 255
  and malingering, 256f
  and war neuroses, 255
Disorientation
  in time, place and person, 65, 225
Disseminated sclerosis, 144, 195, 199, 298
Dissociation, 217
  of ideas, 123
Dissociative predisposition, 245
  and hysterical epidemics, 246
  and hysterical symptoms, 250
Disulfiram, 72
DNA (desoxyribonucleic acid), 52, 201, 202
Don Juanism, 189
Doppelgaenger, 106
Dostoevski, F. M.
  and lack of privacy, 87f
Down's syndrome, 50f
  and maternal age, 50
  and paternal age, 51
Dreams, 105, 303
  and REM (rapid eye movement) sleep, 216
  as pseudo-hallucinations, 303
  sexual, 219
Dreamy state, 228
Drug addiction, 73f
  and emotional dependance, 73
  and physical dependance, 73
  and withdrawal symptoms, 74
Drunkenness, pathological, 72
Du Bois-Reymond, E. F.
  and electric stimulation of nerves, 11

Durkheim, E.
  and *anomie*, 84
Dysarthria, 199, 223
Dyskinesis, 197f
Dyslalia, 199
Dyslexia, 63, 97f
  acquired, 97
  literal, 97
  specific developmental, 98
  verbal, 97
Dysmnesic syndrome, 65, 212, 225
  and compensation neurosis, 258
  and organic-confusional states, 225
  and senile dementia, 121

Eccentricities, 189
Echo reactions, 193
  echolalia, 193, 234, 235
  echopraxia, 193, 235
  manneristic, 234, 235
Ecology, 87
Education, 112
Ego, 16f
  infantile, 16
  primary, 16
  secondary, 16
Eidetic, images 105, 305
Einstein, A.
  and development aphasia, 198
  and mathematics, 111
Electricity, animal, 11
Electrocorticogram (ECG), 24
Electroencephalogram (EEG), 24, 216, 220, 227
Electronic brain, 26
Electrotherapy, 11
Ellis, Havelock
  and mescaline, 70
Emotional
  bondage, 273
  deviation, 173
  psychopathy, 173f
Emotions, hysterical disorders of, 272f
Encopresis, 220
Endopathology, 7, 40
Energy, nervous, 11
Engrams, 30
Enuresis, 219
Epidemics
  dance, 237
  hysterical, 245, 246

mental, 115
Epilepsy, 38, 62, 124, 144, 227f
  and organic-confusional states, 227
  and schizophrenia-like psychoses, 229, 292
  Jacksonian, 227
  myoclonic, 227
  psychomotor, 229
  temporal lobe, 229
Epileptic
  absence, 228
  aura, 228
  fuge, 229
  furor, 229
  major fit, 228, 261
  minor fit, 228
  prodromata, 228
  twilight state, 229
Epistemology, 28
Erotogenic zones, 182
Ethology, 95
  and instinct releasing mechanisms (IRMs), 183
Exhibitionism, 189
Existential experiences, 25, 215, 233
Existentialism, 33f
  and existential illness, 88
  Da-sein, 88
  So-sein, 88
Exteroception, 28, 93f
Extrapunitive, 164
Extrasensory psi-phenomena, 167
Extraversion, 39

Factor analysis, 12, 38f
Faculties
  and factor analysis, 12
  Gall's view of, 12
Fashions, therapeutic, 115
Feedback devices, 22
Fellatio, 189
Feral children, 84f
  Kaspar Hauser, 85
  the wild boy of Aveyron, 85
  the wild girl of the Champagne, 85
Fernel, Jean
  and pathology, 7
Festination, 194
Festinger, L.
  and cognitive dissonance, 113
Fetishism, 188

Flexibilitas cerea, 192
Flight of ideas, 124
Folie à deux (trois, etc.), 129
Folie de doute, 166
Ford, C.S.
  and homosexuality, 187
Forgetting
  and confabulation, 213
  mnestic decay, 205
  mnestic inaccessibility, 205
  through retroactive inhibition, 211
Fortification spectra, 106, 304
Fortuitous influences, 40
Fouchy de
  and motor aphasia, 200
Four letter-words, 118
Free will, 17f
Freud, S.
  and agnosia, 96
  and Brentano, 29
  and ideally typical mind, 93
  and infantile sexual reactions, 182, 184
  and melancholia, 298
  and Meynert, 16
  and origin of eighth nerve, 13
  and point-to-point projection of periphery on cortex, 19
  and private religion of obsessive-compulsive patients, 167
  and sexual aetiology of hysteria, 248
  and unconscious plagiarism, 206, 207
Frigidity, 72
  hysterical, 271
Fugue, epileptic, 262f
Fugue, hysterical, 262f
  and memory loss of personal identity, 263f
  and retrograde amnesia, 262f

Galactosaemia, 71
Galen
  and his anatomical errors, 112
  and hysteria, 247
Gall, F. J.
  and cerebral localization, 13
  and factor analysis, 12
  and personality, 147
  and phrenology, 13
  his brain-anatomical achievements, 13

Galton, F.
  and "regression towards mediocrity", 58
  and twin studies, 60
Galvani, L.
  and animal electricity, 11
Gamblers
  and magic half-beliefs, 167
Ganser syndrome, 264f
Gender role, 186
  and chromosomal sex, 186
  and trans-sexualism, 188
Genes, 47f
  abnormalities of, 52f
  alleles, of, 53
  and DNA, 52
  and mutation, 53
  dominant, 53
  locus of, 47
  major, 52
  minor, 53
  multifactorial, 53
  pathogenic, 54f
  recessive, 54
  sex-controlled, 57
  sex-limited, 57
  specific, 52
General paralysis of the insane (G.P.I.), 133, 144, 145, 199
Genetic-constitutional factors, 153
Genital
  emotions, 182
  reactions, 182
Genius, 189f
Geriatric patients, 213
Gerontophilia, 188
Gilles de la Tourette syndrome, 196, 199
Globus hystericus, 161, 247
Gödel, K.
  and the incompleteness of mathematics, 111
Goldstein, K
  and catastrophic reaction, 65, 225
Gospel according to St. John, 166
Grand mal, 228
Grave's disease, 72
Green blindness and weakness, 56
Grief reaction, 145, 299
Grimacing, 107

Haemoglobin, 54

Haemophilia, 56f
  and Queen Victoria, 57
Half-beliefs, 115f, 155
  magic, 166, 167, 168
  obsessional, 166
  perpetuated by superstitious fears, 116
Hallgren, B.
  and dominant gene in specific dyslexia, 63
Hallucinations, 66, 104f, 301f
  auditory, 106
  delusional, 105
  dream, 216
  extracampine, 106
  functional, 104
  gustatory, 107
  hysterical, 272
  induced, 107
  Lilliputian, 106
  motor, 107
  negative, 107, 269
  normal, 105f
  olfactory, 107
  pathological, 106
  proprioceptive, 108
  tactile, 107
  visual, 106
Hallucinogenic drugs, 70, 101, 305
Halverson, H. M.
  and infantile genital reactions, 182
Hangover
  after alcohol excess, 68, 75
  after cerebral anoxia, 68
Harlow, H. F.
  and experiments on social isolation, 85f
Hashish, 70, 175
Hatters' shakes, 68
Hauser, Kaspar, 85
Heidegger, M.
  and existentialism, 34
Hereditary disease, 53f
Hermaphrodites
  true, 186
  pseudo-, 186
Heteropsychic experiences, 30f
  and psychogenetic intuitive understanding, 31
  and static intuitive understanding, 31
Heterosuggestibility

  and body-sway test, 241
  in hypnosis, 241
  in post-hypnotic state, 241
Heterosuggestion, 239
Heterozygosity, 53
Hippocrates
  and the seat of consciousness, 12
Histrionic
  as opposed to hysterical, 248
  behaviour, 248
  personality, 248, 254, 272
  submissiveness, 273
Homicide, 145, 177
  motiveless, 174, 220, 228
Homicide Act (1957), 177
Homosexuality, 62, 174, 175, 185f
  and ancient Greece, 187
  and special family constellations, 185
  and twin research, 185
Homosexuality, male
  age of their fathers, 286
  age of their mothers, 285f
  concordance in twins, 185, 284
  family frequency, 284
  genetics of, 284f
  preponderance of male sibs, 284
Homozygosity, 55
Hornby, Sir Edmund
  and paramnesia, 208
Humoral theories of insanity, 70
Huntington's chorea, 54, 121
Husserl, E.
  and phenomenology, 29
Huxley, Aldous
  and mescaline, 70
Hyperkinesis, 191, 195f
  and akathisia, 196
  and mental subnormality, 196, 197
  and restless legs, 196
  catatonic, 192
Hypermnesia, 209f
  and 'idiot savant', 210
  and mnemonists, 209f
  specific, 210
Hyperpnoea, 191
  hysterical, 268
Hypersomnia, 221
  idiopathic, 221
  symptomatic, 221
Hyperthymic conditions, 140
Hyperventilation, 191

Hyperventilation—*cont.*
  and carpopedal spasms, 191
  hysterical, 268
Hypnagogic
  hallucinations, 218, 303
  state, 105, 217
Hypnopompic
  hallucinations, 218, 303
  state, 105, 217
Hypnosis, 240f
  and age regression, 244
Hypochondriacal
  convictions, 249, 250, 251, 253f
  delusions, 134, 250
  phobias, 160, 251
Hypochondriacal desires
  and disease-rewarding situations,
    254
Hypochondriacal symptoms
  and hypomelancholia, 143
  as compared with malingered
    symptoms, 253f
  non-psychotic, 134, 253
  psychotic, 134
Hypochondriasis, 253
Hypoglycaemia, 70
Hypokinesis, 191, 193, 195f
Hypomanic symptoms, 138f, 154
  and self-indulgence, 173
Hypomelancholia, 141f, 154
  and alcohol abuse, 143
  and hypochondriacal symptoms, 143
  and illicit love affairs, 143
  and panic attacks, 143
  and urge to confess, 142
Hypothymic conditions, 140
Hysteria, 242, 247f, 253f
  and dermatitis artefacta, 274f
  and disorders of autonomic functions,
    274f
  and disorders of consciousness, 261f
  and disorders of emotions, 272f
  and disorders of memory, 263f
  and disorders of motility, 267f
  and disorders of perception, 269f
  and emotional bondage, 273
  and hypochondriasis, 254
  and malingering, 254, 256f
  and Munchausen syndrome, 276
  arctic, 235
  artificial, 242
  descriptive psychopathology of, 261f

disease of, 249, 253f
due to self-verifying hypochondriacal
    convictions, 249, 253f
dynamic psychopathology of, 247f
symptoms of, 249f
Hysterical
  abasia, 268
  agnosia, 269, 270
  ambiguity of term 'hysterical', 248
  amenorrhoea, 275
  anaesthesia, 269f
  analgesia, 269f
  aphonia, 267
  apnoea, 269
  astasia, 268
  ataxia, 270, 271
  blindness, 269f
  blisters, 274
  confabulations, 266
  deafness, 269f
  delirium, 261
  denial of organic symptoms, 271
  diplegia, 267
  dual personality, 264
  emotionality, 273
  epidemics, 246
  fainting, 269
  fits, 261
  fugue, 262f, 272
  gait disturbances, 268
  hallucinations, 271
  hemiplegia, 267
  hyperpnoea, 268f
  imperception, 269, 270
  infantilism, 265
  loss of personal identity, 263f, 272
  loss of postural sensations, 270
  loss of taste or smell, 269
  mutism, 268
  pain, 272
  paralyses, 267
  paramnesia, 260
  paraplegia, 267
  petechiae, 274
  phallic anaesthesia, 271
  pseudocyesis, 275
  pseudo-dementia, 264, 272
  puerilism, 265
  retention of urine, 275
  skin reactions, 274
  spite reactions, 274
  stigmata, 270

stigmata of Christ, 275
submissiveness, 273
tachypnoea, 268
trance, 261
tremors, 268
twilight states, 261
urticaria, 274
vaginal anaesthesia, 271
vomiting, 275
weals, 274

Ideally typical mind, 32, 93
Idioglossia, 99
Idiot savant, 210
Illness
  autonomous, 89
  endogenous, 45, 88
  existential, 88
  reactive, 45, 88
Illusions, 100f
  abnormal, 101
  delusional, 103
  normal, 100
  of familiarity, 102
  of unfamiliarity, 102
  of youthful appearance, 102
  pathological, 101
Images
  eidetic, 105, 305
  perseverated, 104
Imperception, 96
  hysterical, 269
Impersonal memories, 202, 203
  images, 203
  meanings, 203
  words, 203
Impotence, 161
Incidence of disease, 7, 287
Incongruity of affect, 136
Indifference, pathological, 65
Individual standard or norm, 4
Indoctrination, social, 112, 127
Induced insanity, 129
Infanticide Acts (1922 and 1938), 177
Infantile
  autism, 121, 197, 199
  auto-erotic reactions, 182
  hyperkinetic, syndrome, 197
  psychosis, 121, 197, 199
Inhibition, retroactive, 211
Innate releasing mechanisms (IRMs),
  183f, 189f

Insight, 144, 151
Insight psychology
  and ideally typical minds, 33
Insomnia, 222
Instinct releasers, sexual, 95, 183f
  allo-erotic, 183f
  bestialism, 188
  fetishism, 188
  gerontophilia, 188
  heterosexual, 184
  homosexual, 184
  necrophilia, 188
  paedophilia, 188
  pygmalionism, 188
  pyromania, 188
  transvestite clothing, 188
Insulin hypoglycaemia, 70
Intellect, 109f
  psychology of, 109f
  psychopathology of, 120f
Intellectual deficiency, 120
  acquired, 120f
  innate, 120
Intellectual deficiency, acquired
  dementia, 120f
  schizophrenia, 121f
Intelligence, 39, 58, 109f, 209, 211
Intelligence quotient (I.Q.), 58
International statistical classification of
  diseases (ICD), 37
Interneural pool, 21f
  and autoregulation, 21
Interneurones, 21
Interoception, 28, 93f
  and kinesthesis, 96
  and proprioception, 94
Intersex, 186
Intracranial pressure increase, 64f
Intrapunitive, 164
Introspection, 25, 28, 93
Introversion, 39
Intuitive insight (*see* Intuitive under-
  standing)
Intuitive understanding, 31f
  and causal explanation, 33
  and existentialism, 33f
  and ideally typical mind, 32
  and suicide, 32
  psychogenetic, 31
  static, 31
Irrationality, 126
  and cultural background, 126

Irresponsibility, serious, 180
Itard, J. M. G.
  and the wild boy of Aveyron, 85

Jackson, Hughlings
  and imperception, 96
Jamais vu illusion, 102
Jaspers, Karl
  and existentialism, 34
  and intuitive understanding, 144
  and pseudo-hallucinations, 301
  and 'Verstehende Psychologie', 31f, 93
Johnson, Samuel
  and motor aphasia, 200
Juda, A.
  and twin studies, 62
Jung, C. G.
  and malingering, 253
  and unconscious plagiarism, 206
Jumpers, 234

Kallman, F. J.
  and homosexual twins, 185, 284
  and twin studies, 62
Kant, I.
  and philosophers as expert psychiatric witnesses, 11
Kierkegaard, S.
  and existentialism, 34
Kinsey, A. C.
  and homosexuality, 185, 286
  and sexual dreams, 219
  and sexual practices, 116
Kleptomania, 163
  and self-indulgence, 173
Klinefelter syndrome, 49, 281
Koch, R.
  and pathogenic micro-organisms, 41
Korsakoff syndrome, 76, 20, 258
Kraepelin, E.
  and dementia praecox, 122
  and neuropathology, 14
  and psychiatric nosology, 37
Krafft-Ebing, R. v.
  and the term 'psychopathology', 14
Kral, V. A.
  and masked depression, 294
  and the disappearance of phobias in a German concentration camp, 158f

Lalling, 99
Language
  and redundancy of information, 26
Laplace, P. S.
  and universal determinism, 17
Latah, 235
Laughter, unintentional, 224
Lesbianism, 185
Limbic lobe, 205
Linnaeus, C. v.
  and clinical nosologies, 37
  and feral children, 84f
  and the wild girl of the Champagne, 85
Logical systems, 111
Logoclonia, 194
Logorrhoea, 99
Logos
  and scientific beliefs in natural laws, 166
  and the Gospel, 166
  and the Stoic school of philosophy, 166
Love-melancholy, 247
LSD (lysergic diethylamide), 70, 94, 101
Luria, A. R.
  and the mnemonist S. V. Shereshevski, 209f

M'Naghten rules, 176f, 179, 180
Macropsia, 101
Magic half-beliefs
  and fears, 116, 165f
  of gamblers, 167
  of obsessive-compulsive patients, 166f
Malingering, 253, 254, 263, 264, 270, 275, 276
  and hysteria, 254
Mania, 137f
  and flight of ideas, 124
  and grandiose delusions, 133
  and hyperkinesis, 191
  as self-indulgent obsession, 163
Mania à potu, 72
Manic-depressive illnesses, 294f
  (*see also* Affective illnesses)
  and hyperthymic conditions, 140
  and hypomanic symptoms, 138f
  and hypomelancholia, 141f
  and hypothymic conditions, 140

Manic-depressive—*cont.*
  and manic symptoms, 137f
  and physiochemical origins, 144, 298
  and psychotic depression, 145
Manic symptoms, psychotic, 137f
Mannerisms, 234
  automatic, 234
  cultural, 234, 235
  habitual, 234
  individual, 234
Mariguana, 70, 175
Marital disharmony, 72
Masochism, 189
Masturbation, 116f, 136, 147
  mutual, 189
Mathematics, 110, 111
Maudsley, H.
  and masturbation, 147
Mawlawis, 237
Medical concern, 280
Medicine-man, 237
Megalomania, 134
Meiosis, 47
Melancholia, 135, 145f, 171, 298
Memory, 201f
  (*see also* Reminiscence)
  after obfuscated experiences, 211f
  and limbic lobe, 205
  biological, 201
  consolidation of, 205
  decay of, 205
  falsified, 207
  hysterical disorders of, 263f
  impersonal, 202, 203
  inaccessibility of, 205
  long-term, 205
  mental, 201f
  non-mental, 201
  of dreams, 211, 303
  panoramic, 227
  personal, 202, 203
  racial, 201
  rote, 202
  schema, 30
  short-term, 205
  trace, 30, 201
  unit, 201
Memory objects, 204
  and subjective truth-value, 204, 207
  forgetting of, 205
Menopause, 72

Mental clouding (obfuscation), 65, 121, 215, 222f
Mental Deficiency Act (1913), 180
Mental diplopia, 302
Mental Health Act (1959), 180
Mental subnormality (deficiency), 38, 59, 124
  multifactorial, 59
  pathological, 59
  specific, 59
  subcultural, 59
Mercury encephalopathy, 68
  and hatter's shakes, 68
  and the mad hatter of Lewis Carrol, 69
Merton, R. K.
  and self-fulfilling prophecies, 114
Mescaline, 70, 94, 101
Mesmer, F. A.
  and animal magnetism, 239
  and therapeutic rapport, 239
  and trance induction, 239
Mesmerism, 240
Metamorphopsia, 101
Meynert, T.
  and function of individual cortical cells, 19
  and 'primary' (or 'infantile') and 'secondary' ego, 16
  and 'psycho'-sensory and 'psycho'-motor cortical areas, 16
Micrographia, 194
Micropsia, 101
Micro-sleep, 220
Migraine, 106, 304
Mind, ideally typical, 32, 33, 93, 144
Miryachit, 235
Misidentification, 100, 103, 104, 108
Mitosis, 47
Mnemonist, 209f
Mnestic
  consolidation, 205
  decay, 205
  inaccessibility, 205
  retention, 205f
  scanning, 204
  system, 205
Mnestic phenomena
  memory objects, 202
  remembering, 202
Mnestic processes
  and their putative nature, 201f

Modal frequency, 57
Molecular disease, 55
Mongolism (see Down's syndrome)
Moral
    defective, 180
    imbecility, 180
    insanity, 180
Morbid, 3
Morgagni, G. B.
    and pathological anatomy, 7
Morphine addiction, 74
Motility, hysterical disorders of, 267f
Multiple sclerosis, 144, 195, 199, 298
Munchausen syndrome, 276
Murder, 145, 177
    motiveless, 174, 220, 228
Mutations, 53f
Mutism, elective, 199
Mystical experience, 102
Myxoedema, 72

Narcolepsy, 195, 221
    and cataplexy, 195
    idiopathic, 221
    symptomatic, 221
Necrophilia, 188
Negativism, 192
Neologisms, 123
    in Lewis Carroll's Jabberwocky and
        The Hunting of the Snark, 124
    in schizophrenia, 123
Neumann, J. v.
    and quantum mechanics, 17
Neurology, 14f
Neurones, internuncial, 21
Neuropathology, 14
Neurosis, 11, 14, 38, 80, 82, 89, 151f,
        154, 155f, 158, 162f, 165f, 196, 251,
        155, 156
    accident, 256f
    anxiety, 155f, 251
    anxiety-dominated, 151f
    compensation, 256f
    Cullen's view of, 11
    experimental, 82
    obsessional, 165f
    obsessive-compulsive, 154, 162f
    occupational, 196
    social, 159, 197
    traumatic, 80, 89, 255, 256
    war, 255, 256
Neuroticism, 39

Newton, Sir Isaac
    and absent mindedness, 234
    and avoidance of excessive
        speculation, 144
    and empty interstellar space, 9
Nightmares, 218
Night nurses' paralysis, 221
Nocturnal jerks, 218
Normality
    actuarial, 4
    by individual standards (norms), 4
    by population standards (norms), 4
    ideal, 3
Nosography, 6
Nosology, 6
    aetiological, 41
    clinical, 36
    endopathological, 35
    psychiatric, 35f
Nymphomania, 139, 163
    and self-indulgence, 173

Obedience, automatic, 193, 234
Obfuscation, 65, 121, 211, 212, 215,
        222f
    and disorientation, 225
    and dysmnesia, 225
    and epilepsy, 227f
    and oneiroid manifestations, 222
    and organic-confusional states, 224
    and perseveration, 225
    and senile dementia, 121, 226
Object- (content-) phenomena, 28, 30
Objective symptoms, 36
Obsessional
    doubt, 166
    neurosis, 165f
    thoughts as magic charms, 167
Obsessional personalities, 164f
    and excessive social conformity, 164
    and extra-punitive reactions, 164
    and intra-punitive reactions, 164
Obsessions, 162, 194
    anxiety-dominated, 163
    self-indulgent, 163f
Obsessive-compulsive neurosis, 154,
        162f
    and fear of psychokinesis, 167
    and phobic attacks, 168
    as a private religion, 167
Oceanic feelings, 102
Oculogyric crises, 194, 196

Occupational
  cramps, 196
  neurosis, 196
Oedipal fears, 184
Oedipus
  complex, 184
  effect, 114
Oneiroid manifestations, 222
Opistotonus, 194, 196
Opium, 70
Organic-confusional states, 224
  and disorientation, 225
  and dysmnesia, 225
  and epilepsy, 227f
  and perseveration, 225
  and senility, 226
Orientation
  spatial, 63
  temporal, 214
Over-valued ideas, 162
  and preoccupation with them, 162

Paedophilia, 188
Palilalia, 194
Panic attacks
  in depressions, 143, 154
Paradoxical reaction, 82
Paragrammatism, 99
Para-hallucinations, 303
Paralysis
  agitans, 193f
  hysterical, 267
Paramnesia, 206f, 254, 266
  and reliability of testimony, 207f
  hysterical, 260
  reduplicative, 214
Paranoid delusions, 124, 128, 130f
  erotic, 132, 137
  grandiose, 133, 137
  litigious, 132, 137
  of jealousy, 131, 137
  of persecution, 130, 136, 137
  of reference, 130f
Paranoid schizophrenia, 130
  and emotional symptoms, 137
Paraphasia, 99
Parkinsonism, 193f, 199
  and bradykinesis, 193
  and cogwheel rigidity, 193
  and festination, 194
  and logoclonia, 194

  and micrographia, 194
  and oculogyric crises, 194
  and palilalia, 194
  and pill-rolling movements, 194
  post-encephalitic, 194
Passivity feelings, 123
Pasteur, L.
  and pathogenic micro-organisms, 41
Pathogenic predisposition, 45, 48
  and mutations, 53
  psychoneural, 78, 80
Pathogenic events
  aetiological significance of, 40f
  chance influences, 40f
  contributory (adjuvant) conditions, 40f
  general, 44
  idiosyncratic, 44, 78
  morbidity rate of, 40, 43f
  precipitating, 45
  predisposing, 45
  specific (salient) causes, 40f
  temporal origin of, 40, 45f
  topographical origin of, 40, 42f
Pathological experiences
  and psycho-pathogenic events, 77
Pathology, 7
  construed as endopathology, 7
Pathological
  disease entities, 8
  drunkenness, 72
  lying, 266
Pavlov, I. P.
  and conditioned reflexes, 82
  and experimental neuroses, 81f
  his psychiatric theories, 83
Pellagra, 71
Penfield, W.
  and the centrencephalic integrating centre, 23
Penis captivus, 196
Percept, 95
  allo-erotic, 183
  false, 103
  meaningful, 95
  schematic, 100f
  sensory, 95
Perception, 93f
  exteroception, 93
  hysterical disorders of, 269f
  interoception, 93
  introspection, 93

Perceptual derivation,
  and pseudo-hallucinations, 304
  and sensory hypersensitivity, 94
Pernicious anaemia, 71
Perplexity, 136
Perseverated images, 104, 105
Perseveration, pathological, 65, 97, 225
Personality, 42, 147f
  anankastic, 163
  depressive, 148
  disorders of, 60, 142
  dual, 264
  histrionic, 248, 254, 272
  obsessional (obsessive), 164f, 226
  schizothymic, 153
Persuasion, 112
Petit mal, 228
Phallic anaesthesia, hysterical, 271
Phantom anaesthetist, 246
Phantom limbs, 102, 108, 305
Phenomena
  act-phenomena (process-phenomena), 28
  object-phenomena (content-phenomena), 28
Phenomenology, 29f
  descriptive, 30
Phenylalanine hydroxylase, 283
Phenylketonuria (PKU), 55, 71, 283f
  heterozygous carriers, 283
  prevalence, 283
  wrong diagnosis, 283
Phobia, 155f, 159f, 168, 172
  and obsessive-compulsive neurosis, 168
  and pluralistic isolation, 158
  and superstition, 155
  as a pluralistic event, 158
  hypochondriacal, 160
  of particular objects and situations, 159
  sexual, 161
  social, 160, 268
  travel, 159
Phobophobia, 161
Phosphenes, 303f
Photopsia, 304
Phrenology, 13
Physiopathology, 8f
Pica, 72
Pick's disease, 121

Pill-rolling movements, 194
Pinel, P.
  and the wild boy of Aveyron, 85
Placebo, 43
Plagiarism, unconscious, 206, 235
Plato
  and homosexuality, 187
  and hysteria, 247
Pleasure centres, 298
Pluralistic,
  events, 158
  ignorance, 157
Polyopia, 101
Popper, Sir Karl
  and scientific theories, 288
  and the Oedipus effect, 114
Population standard or norm, 4
Possession, 162
Post-concussional symptoms, 67
  and hysterical trance states, 67
Post-hypnotic
  state, 241
  suggestion, 243
Poverty
  of affect (emotions), 136
  of thought, 122, 124
Predisposition, dissociative, 245
Predisposition, pathogenic, 45, 48, 53
  and mutations, 53
  psychoneural, 78, 80
  their assumed ubiquity in psychiatry, 80
Pregenital emotions, 182
Pregnancy
  and pica, 72
Premenstrual tension states, 72
Premonitions, 102
Prestige
  suggestibility, 112
  suggestions, 112
Prevalence of disease, 7, 287
Prichard, J. C.
  and emotional psychopathy, 179
  and 'moral insanity', 179
Primal scene, 184
Promiscuity, 189
Prophecies, self-fulfilling, 114
Propositions, universal, 109f
Prosopagnosia, 97
Pseudocyesis, 259f, 275
  and Mary Tudor, 275f

Pseudo-dementia
hysterical, 264
pseudo-, 265
Pseudo-hallucinations, 301f
and aquired blindness, 304
and dreams, 303
and eidetic images, 305
and hallucinogenic drugs, 305
and perceptual deprivation, 304
and phantom limbs, 305
and phosphenes, 303
and photopsia, 304
and social isolation, 304
and teichopsia, 304
exteroceptive, 303
interoceptive, 303, 305
Pseudologia fantastica, 266
Pseudo-pseudodementia, 265
Psi-phenomena, 167
Psyche, 8
Descartes' view of, 8f
Psychiatry, 10, 14
Psychoanalytic theories, 78, 148, 184
and anxiety-dominated neuroses, 152f
and depression, 148, 298
and instincts, 184
and Oedipal fears, 184
'Psychogenic'
its ambiguity, 77
Psychokinesis, 167
Psychological experiences
and anxiety-dominated neuroses, 151f
and psychogenic events, 77
and their presumed cortical localizations, 19, 20
Psychology
clinical, 147
of intellect, 109f
Psychoneural
autoregulation, 26
manifestations in behaviour, 24
manifestations in conscious experience, 24
manifestations in physiological part activities, 24
pool, 24f
processes, 21f, 25f
redundancy of information, 27
Psychopathogenic events, 77, 81f
and pathological experiences, 77

as idiosyncratic pathogenic events, 78
Psychopathology, 10, 14
descriptive, 39, 93
dynamic, 93, 233f
of effect, 136f, 151f, 173f
of consciousness, 215f
of hysteria, 247f
of hysterical symptoms, 261f
of intellect, 120f
of memory, 201f
of mobility, 191f
of perception, 93f
of trance states, 233f
phenomenological, 39
viewed as neuropathology, 14
Psychopathy, 38, 173f
aggressive, 174
antisocial, 190
sexual, 182f
Psychopathy, emotional, 173f
and concept of disease, 181
and crime, 175f
and self-indulgent actions, 173
and sex, 182f
and social norms, 173, 175
Psychosis, 14
artificial, 70
functional, 37, 136f
organic, 37
Psychosomatic diseases, 252
Psychoticism, 39
Psychotomimetic drugs, 70, 305
Puberty
and allo-erotic reactions, 183
Puerperal psychosis, 72
Punch-drunkenness, 67
Puységur, Marquis de
and artificial sleep, 240
Pygmalionism, 188
Pyromania, 163, 188

Quantum mechanics, 17

Rafa'is, 237
Rapport, 139
Reactivity, endogenous, 42
Reading disability
retarded, 98
specific, 98
Reasoning
deductive, 109

Reasoning—*cont.*
  inductive, 109
  inventive, 109
  irrational, 111
  rational, 109f
Recall, 204
Recidivism, 178
Recognition
  mental, 204
  perceptual, 204
Red blindness and weakness, 56
Redundancy of information, 26
  lack of in schizophrenic speech, 124
Reflex arc, 21, 81
Reflex responses
  after-discharges of, 21
  recruiting of, 21
Regression to the mean, 58
Reil, J. Ch.
  and pathogenic sexual frustration, 247f
  and 'psychiatry', 14
  and psychic methods of cure, 14
Remembering, 204
  mental recognition, 204
  perceptual recognition, 204
  recall, 204
Reminiscences,
  and anamnesis, 208
  and objective truth-value, 207
  and reliability of testimony, 207
  hallucinated, 227, 266
  unconscious, 243
Reserpine
  and depression, 73, 144
Responsibility, diminished, 177, 179, 281
Restless legs, 196
Reticular formation, 15, 23, 215, 221
Revivalist preachers, 237f
Rhine, J. B.
  and extrasensory psi-phenomena, 167
  and psychokinesis, 167
Ribosomes, 52
Right-left disorientation, 97, 98
RNA (ribonucleic acid), 52, 202
Roberts, J. A.
  and intelligence quotient, 59
Rock 'n roll dance, 237
Rote memories, 202f

Russell, Bertrand
  and mathematics, 110

Sadism, 189
Sargant, W.
  and religious trance induction, 238
Sauvages, F. B. de
  and clinical nosologies, 36
Schizoid symptoms, 153
Schizophrenia, 37, 62, 86, 104, 121f, 134, 136f, 153, 171, 193, 197, 199, 229, 141
  adolescent, 122, 136
  adoption studies of, 291
  and ambivalent movements, 193
  and barriers to communication, 124
  and circumstantial speech, 124
  and crowding of thoughts, 124
  and desire for social isolation, 87
  and diagnostic variations in different countries, 288, 294f
  and hypochondriacal delusions, 134
  and incoherent thought, 123
  and lack of redundancy in speech, 124
  and neologisms, 123
  and passivity feelings, 123
  and poverty of thought, 122
  and significant of life events, 292f
  and social class, 289
  and social drift, 289
  and thought blocking, 122
  catatonic, 191f
  childhood, 121, 197, 199
  disease expectancy of, 288
  genetics of, 287f
  incidence of, 287
  in families of schizophrenic patients, 287, 289
  lifetime morbidity risk of, 288
  paranoid, 124, 128, 130f, 136, 177
  prevalence of, 287f
  pseudoneurotic, 38
  simple, 122
  symptomatic, 229, 292
  twin studies of, 289f
Schizophrenia-like psychoses
  in epileptics, 229, 292
Schizophrenic
  apathy, 272
  feelings of perplexity, 136

SUBJECT INDEX

Schizophrenic—*cont.*
  giggle, 136
  handshake, 193
  incongruity of affect, 136
  increase of auto-erotic feelings, 136
  mannerisms, 192
  outbursts of temper, 136
  symptoms, 121f, 136
Schizothymic personality, 153
Schnauzkrampf, 192
Scoptophilia, 189
Scotomata, positive, 106, 269
Self-falsifying beliefs, 114f
Self-hypnosis, 244
Self-indulgence, 163, 173f
Self-indulgent convictions, 259f
  and confidence tricksters, 260
  and false pregnancies (pseudocyesis), 159f, 275
  and hysterical analgesia, 260
  and hysterical paramnesias, 260
Self-indulgent obsessions, 163
Self-mutilation, 223
Self-verifying beliefs, 114f
Semeiology, 93
Senescence, 120
Senile
  brain damage, 226
  dementia, 121
  drop attacks, 195
  organic-confusional states, 226
  pseudo-obsessional personalities, 226
  tremor, 195
Senility, 213
Sensation, 95
Sensorium (*see also* Consciousness), 215
  altered, 215
  degrees of lucidity, 215
Sensory anomalies, 94f
  after perceptual deprivation, 94
  hypersensitivity, 94f
  hyposensitivity, 95
  synaesthesia, 94
Sex act variations, 189
  buggery (sodomy), 189
  cunnilingus, 189
  fellatio, 189
  unusual positions, 189
Sexual anomalies, 182f, 187f
  bestialism, 188
  Don Juanism, 189
  exibitionism, 189

fetishism, 188
gerontophilia, 188
masochism, 189
necrophilia, 188
paedophilia, 188
pygmalionism, 188
pyromania, 188
sadism, 189
scoptophilia, 189
trans-sexualism, 188
transvestism, 188
voyeurism, 189
Sexual frigidity
  after childbirth, 72
Shaman, 237
Shellshock, 255f
Shields, J.
  and twin studies, 61, 63, 290, 292
Sickle cell anaemia, 55
Signs, clinical, 8, 279
Simultanagnosia, 97
Slater, E.
  and schizophrenia-like psychoses in epileptics, 229
  and twin studies, 63, 292, 297
Sleep, 24, 215f
  and EEG changes, 24, 216
  and hypersomnia, 221
  and insomnia, 222
  and narcolepsy, 221
  and nocternal jerks, 218f
  artificial, 240
  depth, 216
  hallucinosis, 218, 221
  masturbation, 219
  paralysis, 221
  partial, 217f, 236
  phobia, 222
  talking, 107, 219
  walking (somnambulism), 107, 220
Sleep, partial, 217f, 236
  and hypnagogic manifestations, 217
  and hypnopompic manifestations, 217
  and micro-sleep, 220
  and skill fatigue, 218
Social indoctrination
  and conditioning procedures, 112
  and education, 112
  and persuasion, 112
  and prestige suggestions, 112

Social isolation, 83f
  and feral children, 84f
  and loss of social cohesion (*anomie*),
    84
  and personality development, 86
  and pseudo-hallucinations, 304
  and psychiatric symptoms, 86
  desired by hermits, tramps, 87
  desired by schizophrenics, 87
  in solitary confinement, 83
  lack of, 87f
  of people in alien communities, 84
  of polar explorers, 84
Social phobias, 159
  and neurotic apraxia, 197
Sociology, 29
Sodomy, 189
Somnambulism, 66, 107, 220
  artificial, 240, 274
Somnolence, 211, 215
So-sein, 87
Space blindness, 97
Spasmodic movements, 196
Spasms, muscular
  facial, 196
  occupational, 196
  oculogyric crises, 194, 196
  opisthotonus, 196
  penis captivus, 196
  torticollis, 196
  vaginismus, 196
  writer's cramp, 196
Spatial orientation, 63
Speech centre, motor
  and Bouillaud, Broca and Dax, 15
Speech disturbance,
  aphasia, motor, 199
  aprosody, 200
  circumstantiality, 124
  developmental, 198
  dysarthria, 199
  dyslalia, 199
  elective mutism, 199
  incoherence, 123
  retardation, 124
  scanning, 199
  stammering, 199
Spiritualist medium, 237
Spurzheim, J. G.
  and phrenology, 13
Stage fright, 159
Stammering, 199

Stereognosis, 20
Stereotyped activities, 192, 197
Stern, W.
  and psychology of testimony, 207
Stigmata
  hysterical, 270
  diaboli, 252
  of Christ, 275
Stigmatists, 275
  Padre Pio, 275
  St. Francis of Assisi, 275
  Theresa Neumann of Konnersreuth,
    275
Stimuli
  and their spatial and temporal
    summation, 21
Stoic school of philosophy, 166
Stupor
  akinetic, 66n, 192
  cataleptic, 192
  catatonic, 192
  depressive, 191
  schizophrenic, 191
  unconscious, 66, 192, 224, 228
Subjective Symptoms, 36
Subnormality, mental, 38
  multifactorial, or subcultural, 59
  specific, or pathological, 59
Suggestibility, prestige, 112
Suggestion
  post-hypnotic, 243
  prestige, 112, 239
Suicide, 32, 73, 84, 142, 145, 223, 228
Superego, 164
Superstitions, 112, 116f, 155f
  and circumcision, 117
  and collective beliefs, 116
  and four letter-words, 118
  and hyperdermic injections, 117
  and masturbation, 116
  and taboos, 118
  self-recognized, 116f, 155f, 158
Sydenham, Th.
  and nosography, 6
Symptomatology, 93
Symptom
  anankastic, 163
  clinical, 3f, 279
  complex, 6, 279
  congenital, 53
  definition of, 5
  developmental, 53

SUBJECT INDEX

Symptom—*cont.*
  emotional, 77
  motivational, 77
  neuropsychiatric, 35
  objective, 36
  obsessive-compulsive, 162f
  phobic, 155f
  post-concussional, 67
  psychiatric, 35, 78
  psychogenic, 77
  psychosomatic, 35
  schizoid, 153
  sensory, 77
  subjective, 36
Synaesthesia, 94
  and hallucinogenic drugs, 94
Syndrome
  as symptom complex, 6, 279
  Klinefelter, 281
  XYY, 281f

Taboos, 118
Tachypnoea, 191
  and carpopedal spasms, 191
  hysterical, 268
Talk
  incoherence of, 123
  past the point, 264
Teichopsia, 106, 304
Terman, L.
  and intelligence quotient, 59
Testimony, 207
  its reliability, 207
Tetany, 191, 269
  and hyperventilation, 191, 269
Therapeutic
  concern, 3, 280
  rapport, 239
Thoughts
  autistic, 122
  blocking, 122
  circumstantial, 124
  crowding, of 124
  dereistic, 122
  hearing of, 107
  incoherence, of 123
  poverty of, 122
  retardation of, 124
Thymopathy, 173
Tics
  and Gilles de la Tourette syndrome,
    196

  motor, 163, 196
  vocal, 196
Torticollis, 194, 196
  spasmodic, 196
Traits, genetically determined, 57f
Tramps, 87
Trance, 215, 233f, 236f
  and cultural prestige, 237
  and dervishes, 237
  and prestige heterosuggestions, 239
  and revivalist preachers, 238
  and rock 'n roll dancers, 237
  and Voodoo dances, 237
  and war dances, 237
  collective, 237f
  hysterical, 67, 261
  induction of, 237
Trans-sexualism, 188
Transvestism, 188
Trauma
  physical, 64f
  psychogenic, 152
Traumatic neuroses, 255
Treatment
  fashions of, 115
  inspirational, 115
  moral, 14
  psychoanalytic, 115
  suggestive, 115
Tremor
  familial, 195
  intention, 195
  senile, 195
Trichotillomania, 163
Triple-X female, 50
Tuke, D. H.
  and artificial insanity, 241
Tune deafness, 63
Turner syndrome, 49
Twilight states
  hysterical, 261
  organic, 223, 236
Twins, 60f
  and concordance rate, 62
  dizygotic (or fraternal), 60, 185
  monozygotic (or identical), 60, 185

Ultraparadoxical reactions, 82
Unconscious
  experiences, 215
  plagiarism, 206, 235
  reminiscences, 243

Understanding, intuitive, 31, 124
Unreality feelings, 102
  in danger situations, 251
US/UK diagnostic project, 295

Vaginal anaesthesia, hysterical, 271
Vaginismus, 196
Vagrants, 87
'Verstehende Psychologie', 31
Vesalius, A.
  and Galen's Authority, 112
Vigilance, 215
Vis nervosa, 11
Vitamin deficiency, 71
  of vitamin B, 75
Voodoo dances, 237
Vorbeireden, 264
Voyeurism, 189

War neuroses
  and battle fatigue, 255f
  and shellshock, 255f
  and traumatic neurosis, 255f
Wernicke syndrome, 76
Wesley, John
  and trance induction, 238

Weiner, N.
  and cybernetics, 22
Wild boy of Aveyron, 85
Wild girl of the Champagne, 85
Witches, 147, 252
Wootton, Barbara
  and the concept of diminished
    responsibility, 177f
Word blindness, 63, 97
Word-deafness
  acquired, 99
  infantile, 99
World Health Organization, 2, 37
Writer's cramp, 196
Writing, automatic, 235

X chromosome, 48
XYY syndrome, 281f
  lifetime morbidity risk of, 282
  prevalence of, 281f

Y chromosome, 48
Yogi, 237

Zygote, 47